The Great War

and the

Golden Age of Hollywood Horror

66

The Great War and the Golden Age of Hollywood Horror

R. Bruce Crelin

Foreword by Sam Irvin

Midnight Marquee Press, Inc.
Baltimore, Maryland USA

All opinions expressed here are my own, and I am solely responsible for any errors, omissions, or other mistakes which might have made their way into the published version.

Illustrations are used for education purposes with no copyright claim.

Permission has been granted by James Curtis for reprinted material. I also thank him most heartily for his permission to quote freely from his biography, as well as from the pamphlet containing the letters which James Whale wrote from Hollywood in 1929.

To Allison, with Love,
for Putting up With Me

Cameraman and Ernest Thesiger create a bride for the Monster

Table of Contents

Acknowledgements

Eric McNaughton, a Facebook friend who I have had the pleasure of meeting in person; publisher of *We Belong Dead* magazine and its related book series, who made me a "published author" by printing several of my modest efforts in *70s Monster Memories* (Buzzy Krotik Productions 2015), *Unsung Horrors* (Buzzy Krotik Productions 2016), *"Monsters? We're British, Y'Know!": A Celebration of Peter Cushing* (Buzzy Krotik Productions 2017), *Son of Unsung Horrors* (Buzzy Krotik Productions 2018), *Into the Velvet Darkness: A Celebration of Vincent Price* (Buzzy Krotik Productions 2019), and *Spotlight on Horror: Classics of the Cinefantastique* (Buzzy Krotik Productions 2020), and gave me the inspiration and impetus to tackle a much bigger project. Indeed, this book was initially conceived as a concept for an article in *We Belong Dead* but got far too long for a magazine article and morphed into the volume which you now hold in your hands.

Bruce Hallenbeck (who I affectionately refer to as "The Other Bruce"), another Facebook friend I've met face-to-face; horror film expert, author of numerous genre books and articles, filmmaker, actor, and cryptozoologist; he was gracious enough to read an early draft of this book, and provide some much-needed advice and encouragement.

Troy Howarth, a Facebook friend who I have *not* yet had the pleasure of meeting in person; prolific author of a number of incredibly detailed and well-researched books on a wide range of genre topics, and deliverer of many audio commentaries on Blu-Ray discs, who also took the time to read an early draft and provide good words and encouragement.

Sam Irvin, another Facebook friend I have *not* yet met in person; film director, Co-Executive Producer of *Gods and Monsters*, and Rondo Award-winning author, who provided encouragement and pointed me in the direction of several valuable sources I used in putting this volume together, in addition to graciously agreeing to write the foreword.

Christopher Bram, author of *Father of Frankenstein*, who provided me with his thoughts and some good ideas, and a pamphlet containing three letters which James Whale had written from Hollywood in May and June 1929.

James Curtis, author of the definitive biography, *James Whale: a New World of Gods and Monsters*, who provided me with an enlargement of a portion of a group photograph of British officers, from the David Lewis Estate, which contains one of the few images of James Whale in uniform.

Finally, the late Paul Fussell, whose seminal book, *The Great War and Modern Memory*, gave me the inspiration for many of the ideas expressed in this book, as well as its title, and whose Rutgers College English course, "Literature and the Great War," broadened and deepened my understanding of the British experience in the trenches of Flanders and Picardy.

Foreword by Sam Irvin

Long before I directed such films as *Elvira's Haunted Hills*, co-executive produced *Gods and Monsters* and won Rondo Awards for my writing about horror movies, I was your typical monster kid growing up in the 1960s on a steady diet of classic Universal horror movies on Saturday afternoon's *Shock Theater* (televised on the local ABC affiliate), with heavy doses of *Famous Monsters of Filmland* magazines and building Aurora model kits of all the Universal Monsters.

From as early as I can remember, my very favorite movies were *Frankenstein* (1931) and *Bride of Frankenstein* (1935). I didn't know why at the time, but I somehow felt an intense identification with Boris Karloff's portrayal of Henry Frankenstein's so-called "Monster." But I never saw him that way. He may have been a freak of nature, but he was definitely not a monster. He was a victim of circumstances beyond his control, misunderstood by society. The true monster of the story was Frankenstein who callously abandoned his creature when his experiment did not go as well as he had hoped. And, of course, there was the insidious Dr. Pretorius who blackmails Frankenstein into collaborating on a female mate who rejects the "Monster" at first sight. How much humiliation can one innocent soul tolerate before blowing everyone—including himself—to kingdom come. Total annihilation. It was a tragedy to end all tragedies.

As a closeted gay teen, I was a freak of nature misunderstood by society. I was the monster—and my empathy for him was boundless. When I discovered that the director of these two films, James Whale, was also gay, everything suddenly made total sense to me. The two movies—but especially *Bride of Frankenstein*—were laden with gay subtext that had subliminally spoken to me as a naive kid in search of myself. As an informed adult, the subtext literally screamed out at me and grabbed me by the throat.

Boris Karloff in *Bride of Frankenstein*

I devoured biographies of James Whale by James Curtis and Mark Gatiss that helped me understand his unique point of view and what may have guided his interpretation of Mary Shelley's original *Frankenstein* novel (not to mention his other genre masterpieces *The Old Dark House* and *The Invisible Man*).

But there were more than just layers of gay subtext at work here. The horrors Whale witnessed as a soldier in the First World War clearly heightened his fascination for morbid subject matter. To what extent, one could only speculate as details of his service were sketchy at best.

When I read Christopher Bram's novel *Father of Frankenstein* (1995), a fictionalized account of Whale's retirement, with flashback interludes of his military service and his Hollywood years, I was struck by the richness of the material and how exploring the mind of this genius made an interesting case for how his own life had shaped his indelible art.

Sam Irvin on the *Bride of Frankenstein* set used in *Gods and Monsters*

I tried to option the book to write and direct a movie based on it—but Bill Condon had beat me to it by a couple of weeks. As fate would have it, I had met Bill through our mutual friend, actress Nancy Allen. One thing led to another and, fortuitously, I was able to join forces with Bill and co-executive produce the movie that became known as *Gods and Monsters* starring Sir Ian McKellen as James Whale—nominated for three Academy Awards including Best Actor (McKellen), and Best Supporting Actress (Lynn Redgrave). Deservedly and triumphantly, Bill won the Academy Award for Best Adapted Screenplay.

For flashback scenes, we recreated the laboratory set from *Bride of Frankenstein* and found the original Kenneth Strickfaden electrical equipment to authenticate the look as much as possible.

We also built a trench set and battlefield for the First World War flashbacks. Our budget was extremely limited, but our ingenious production designer Richard Sherman maximized every available dollar to create an impressionistic version of the sets from *Journey's End* (1930), Whale's own depiction of the First World War.

I remember when all of us were researching for *Gods and Monsters*, there was a ton of material to be found on Whale's *Frankenstein* films but scarcely anything on his military record and the details of his service. We wanted to know more but resources seemed out of reach or perhaps nonexistent. The need for these blanks to be filled-in was conspicuous.

Two decades later, I was delighted to learn that Bruce Crelin was writing the history book that we'd all been yearning to read: *The Great War and the Golden Age of Hollywood Horror*. This amazing study painstakingly uncovers all the elusive details of James Whale's service during the war—along with many other influential filmmakers of the day—and makes an extremely fascinating and thoroughly convincing case that so many of those classic, groundbreaking, genre-defining horror films of the early 1930s were, in fact, galvanized and shaped by the horrors of the First World War in a much stronger way than heretofore understood.

I know you will be as agog as I was absorbing every morsel of this page-turner. Cheers to Bruce for doing the meticulous grunt work of locating this treasure trove of material and making sense of it all.

Preface

The decade of the 1930s is generally regarded as the "Golden Age" of the American horror film, with Universal as the studio which set the trend. Indeed, the term "horror film" arose when, following the success of *Dracula* (1930),[1] Universal declared its intention to make "*another* horror film."[2] That "other" horror film was, of course, *Frankenstein* (1931). The decade would see a string of horror films from Universal, including *Murders in the Rue Morgue* (1931), *The Old Dark House* (1932), *The Mummy* (1932), *The Invisible Man* (1933), *The Black Cat* (1934), *Bride of Frankenstein* (1935), *Werewolf of London* (1935), *The Raven* (1935), *The Invisible Ray* (1935), *Dracula's Daughter* (1936), and *Son of Frankenstein* (1938). James Whale directed four of these films: *Frankenstein*, *The Old Dark House*, *The Invisible Man*, and *Bride of Frankenstein*, which are generally regarded by critics and fans alike as among the very best of these Golden Age Horrors. Whale, and other creative talents involved in these films, served with the British Army on the Western Front and saw combat in the First World War. The War influenced other Universal Horrors, as well.

This book will detail the War experiences of these individuals, and explore how those experiences, as well as the War itself, helped to shape Universal's Golden Age Horrors. In coming up with this idea, I am indebted to Paul Fussell's (1924-2012) seminal book, *The Great War and Modern Memory*,[3] which won the National Book Critics Circle Award for Criticism in 1975 and the National Book Award in the Arts and Letters category in 1976. Although covering other areas, Fussell's primary concern is the British Army on the Western Front. "This book is about the British experience on the Western Front from 1914 to 1918 and some of the literary means by which it has been remembered, conventionalized, and mythologized. It is also about the literary dimensions of the trench experience itself." As Fussell stated, his concern was with "what some future 'medievalist' may call The Matter of Flanders and Picardy."[4] The book is in print and very much available, and I cannot recommend it too highly.

Although many who had seen action in the War later published memoirs, all filtered in various degrees through the prisms of their own perspectives, a number of survivors of the War chose to express themselves in indirect, oblique terms. The following applies to J.B. Priestley, but this feeling was, of course, more widespread:

> There was an obvious reason behind Priestley's reluctance to address the Great War more directly, and one that he shared with many survivors of the conflict: the experiences that they had undergone were so scarring, so horrific, so traumatic, that many never wished to put themselves back into those dark places again, even in their imaginations.[5]

Siegfried Sassoon served in the trenches as an officer with the Royal Welch Fusiliers, was awarded the Military Cross and survived the War. In his poem, "Repression of War Experience," he writes of a veteran, at home in his study, who can still not escape the War:

> You're quiet and peaceful, sum-
>   mering safe at home;
> You'd never think there was a
>   bloody war on! . . .
> O yes, you would . . . why, you can
>   hear the guns.
> Hark! Thud, thud, thud,—quite
>   soft
> . . . they never cease –
> Those whispering guns—O Christ,
>   I want to go out
> And screech at them to stop—I'm
>   going crazy;
> I'm going stark, staring mad be-
>   cause of the guns.

This book will focus primarily upon three individuals who saw action with the British Army on the Western Front: James Whale, R.C. Sherriff, and J.B. Priestley, and who had considerable influence upon one or more of the Universal Golden Age Horrors. In doing my research, I was frankly surprised that nothing else on this subject

R.C. Sherriff in 1917

had been published or, if it had, was not readily available. For example, Whale's sexuality has been rather extensively explored (*see*, for example, *James Whale: A Biography* or *The Would-be Gentleman* by Mark Gatiss,[6] and the novel *Father of Frankenstein* by Christopher Bram,[7] upon which the film *Gods and Monsters* (1998) was based— Bram's book was re-titled *Gods and Monsters* as a tie-in with the film), and while his service in the War has been mentioned it has not, to the best of my knowledge, been analyzed in any sort of depth with reference to his work. After I completed my first draft, I became aware of a book by W. Scott Poole entitled *Wasteland: The Great War and the Origins of Modern Horror*, which was to be published on October 16, 2018.[8] Professor Poole's book, however, has a far different focus and scope than this modest volume. Professor Poole explores the effects which the Great War had upon the entire genre of horror. This book, however, has a much deeper, if narrower, focus; upon three men who served with the British Army in the trenches of the Great War, and how their War experiences affected a specific set of horror films in the 1930s. As far as I know, this impact has not yet been extensively explored. I hope this brief analysis is interesting and informative and will serve to inspire even more in-depth exploration of this subject.

1 For dating of the films, I have adopted the convention used by Jonathan Rigby, as set forth on page 7 of his book *American Gothic* (Signum Books 2017): "The years attached to films are, wherever possible, those of production, not necessarily release, meaning you'll find plenty of dates that differ from the standard ones given in other sources."

2 Gifford, Denis, *A Pictorial History of Horror Movies* 82 (Hamlyn 1973) (emphasis in original).

3 Fussell, Paul, *The Great War and Modern Memory* (Oxford University Press 1975).

4 Fussell, Preface x. Since this piece is primarily concerned with individuals who served with the infantry in the British Army on the Western Front, it will similarly be largely confined in scope. Of course, the War went forward on the Eastern Front, in Africa, and in Asia, as well as on the sea.

5 Hanson, Neil and Priestley, T. (eds.), *Priestley's Wars* Kindle ed., loc. 1813 (Great Northern Books 2008).

6 Gatiss, Mark, *James Whale: A Biography or The Would-be Gentleman* (Cassell 1995).

7 Bram, Christopher, *Father of Frankenstein* (E.P. Dutton 1995).

8 Poole, W. Scott, *Wasteland: The Great War and the Origins of Modern Horror* (Counterpoint 2018).

Chapter One
Background on the Great War—
Some History and Nomenclature

Preliminarily, as the Great War ended more than 100 years ago and many readers may therefore be unfamiliar with it, a brief capsule history of the War, and the conditions under which it was fought on the Western Front from the British perspective, is in order.[1] In June and July of 1914, the British expected a conflict in the near future. They did not, however, expect a conflagration which would engulf all the major European powers in a widespread war. Rather, they expected trouble in the northern part of Ireland, in Ulster, by Loyalists opposing a Home Rule Bill which would grant autonomy to Ireland. Ulster Loyalists had threatened armed rebellion, and the British Army garrison at the Curragh had mutinied, refusing to fire upon the Loyalist rebels. An Irish conflict eventually would come, not by Loyalists in Ulster but by Irish Republican rebels who, on Easter Monday, April 24, 1916, staged a widespread rising, taking over the General Post Office in Dublin, where Pádraig Pearse read out the Proclamation of the Republic. Known as the "Easter Rising," the rebellion was brutally suppressed by the British. Unlike the "Curragh Mutiny," British troops in Ireland showed no hesitation in firing upon the Republican rebels. The British reinforced the garrison in Dublin with troops from overseas (or, as the Irish rebel song says, "when Britannia's Huns with their long-range guns sailed in through the Foggy Dew"), and after six days of fighting the Republicans surrendered. Sixteen of the Rising's principal leaders were executed. Bullet marks can still be seen on the façade of the GPO.

WELSH FUSILIERS

Cigarette card featuring Royal Welch Fusiliers

What did happen in the summer of 1914 was a catastrophe which would engulf Europe, and a good part of the rest of the world, in a devastating war which would last for more than four years. Before discussing the War, however, a quick look at the organization of the British Army as it existed immediately prior to, and during, the War, is in order.

As for the structure of the British Army, the basic organizational component was the Regiment. Recruits were assigned to and processed through depots maintained by each Regiment. Each Regiment had its own history; some originated as far back as the

17th Century. For example, the Royal Welch Fusiliers, which numbered the war poets Robert Graves, Siegfried Sassoon, and David Jones among its members, was founded in 1689 as the 23rd Regiment of Foot, to take part in the war against the Jacobite King, James II. It received the title "The Welch Regiment of Fusiliers" in 1702, one of the first Regiments to be granted the title of "Fusilier" (from its new "fusil" muskets, an early type of flintlock which replaced the older matchlocks). Since its founding, the Regiment served in virtually every war in which Britain was engaged, including the Napoleonic Wars, where it saw action at the Battle of Waterloo, and in the American Revolutionary War, being the only British Regiment not to surrender its colors at Yorktown (the colors were wrapped around the body of an officer, under his clothes, who smuggled them out). It received its "Royal" designation in 1702, during the War of the Spanish Succession, where it saw action at Schellenberg and Blenheim. The Regiment ceased to exist as an independent entity on St. David's Day, March 1, 2006, when it was amalgamated with the Royal Regiment of Wales to form the Royal Welsh Regiment. The Royal Welch name continued as the First Battalion of the Royal Welsh Regiment until the First and Second Battalions were merged in 2014 to create the First Battalion, the Royal Welsh.

There were three primary components of infantry Regiments. The "Regular Army" Regiments were composed of battalions consisting of a small contingent of professional soldiers which had existed before the War. This was also known as the "Expeditionary Force," as it was intended to leave Britain to participate in overseas conflicts. "Territorials" were formed as additional battalions of Regular Army Regiments as a sort of "ready reserve," similar to the American National Guard, and intended for the "Home Defence" of Britain. They were not highly regarded by the High Command but were pressed into service in Belgium and France following heavy losses in the Regular Army and before the volunteers of the "New Army" could be brought into combat, generally giving good account of themselves. "New Army" Battalions (also known as "Kitchener's Army" or, disparagingly, as "Kitchener's Mob," as they were the brainchild of Lord Kitchener, then Secretary of State for War, who had called for 300,000 volunteers) were formed from volunteers who joined in 1914, also as additional battalions in existing Regiments. "Most of them would be expended on the Somme in 1916."[2] Due to the casualties suffered during the first two years of the War, and once conscription went into effect in 1916, these distinctions became less significant, as replacements were assigned to existing units.

A Regiment did not, however, go into combat as a single unit. It was divided into battalions, which became parts of brigades. The primary operational unit of infantry was a division, consisting of approximately 18,000 officers and men, commanded by a Major General [in American terms, a two-star general]. For most of the War, a British infantry division consisted of three infantry brigades, each under the command of a Brigadier [in American terms, a one-star general], as well as headquarters, artillery, and support units. An infantry brigade was

This WWI recruitment poster featuring Lord Kitchener was the most reproduced during the war.

composed of four battalions, each commanded by a Lieutenant Colonel. The pre-war strength of a battalion was 1,107 officers and Other Ranks (Privates and non-commissioned officers ("NCOs"—Corporals and Sergeants)), but by 1917 this number had dropped to as low as fewer than 500.

A battalion at full strength was composed of four infantry companies, each of 227 officers and Other Ranks, usually identified as "A" through "D," and sometimes "W" through "Z," and commanded by a Major or a Captain, and a machine gun section. Each company was divided into four platoons. A platoon was commanded by a Lieutenant or Second Lieutenant with a Platoon Sergeant as second-in-command. A typical infantry platoon consisted of one officer, two Sergeants, two or three Corporals, and 48 Privates. A platoon was further divided into four sections of 12 Privates each, commanded by a non-commissioned officer. The British soldier, and in particular the British Private, was known as a "Tommy." This term is said to stem from the 18th Century and the name "Tommy Atkins," used to identify the generic British soldier, in the same sense as "G.I. Joe" identified the generic American soldier. As Rudyard Kipling put it: "'For it's Tommy this, an' Tommy that, an' Chuck him out, the brute!' But it's 'Saviour of 'is country' when the guns begin to shoot."

At first, the "British Expeditionary Force" (B.E.F.) which went to France on August 15, 1914, consisted of only six infantry divisions and five cavalry brigades, divided into three Corps. I Corps, commanded by Lieutenant General [in American terms, a three-star general] Sir Douglas Haig, which consisted of the First and Second Divisions; II Corps, commanded by Lieutenant General

Sir James Grierson, which consisted of the Third and Fifth Divisions; and III Corps, commanded by Major General W.P. Pulteney, which consisted of the Fourth and Sixth Divisions. As the War progressed, the B.E.F. expanded rapidly. As the B.E.F. expanded, it was divided into Armies, commanded by a General [in American terms, a four-star general] and consisting of two or more Corps. The First Army, composed of the I, II, and Indian Corps, and the Second Army, composed of the III and IV Corps, were created in late December 1914. The Third Army was formed in July 1915, the Fourth in February 1916, and the Fifth in May 1916. The British Army deployed a total of 76 infantry divisions over the course of the War. A simple chart setting forth the typical, basic organization of the B.E.F. during the War may help to clarify things:

Organization:	Composed Of:
B.E.F. (commanded by a Field Marshall)	Two to Five Armies
Army (commanded by a General)	Two or more Corps
Corps (commanded by a Lieutenant General)	Two or more Divisions
Division (commanded by a Major General)	Three Brigades
Brigade (commanded by a Brigadier)	Four Battalions
Battalion (commanded by a Lt. Colonel)	Four Companies
Company (commanded by a Major or a Captain)	Four Platoons
Platoon (commanded by a Lieutenant or Second Lieutenant)	Four Sections
Section (commanded by a Sergeant or a Corporal)	One NCO, Twelve Privates

Of course, these organizations varied depending upon the phase of the War and the availability of manpower.

On June 28, 1914, a Serbian nationalist, Gavrilo Princip, shot and killed the presumptive heir to the throne of the Austro-Hungarian Empire, Archduke Franz Ferdinand, and his wife, the Duchess Sophie, as they rode in an open motorcar, touring the city of Sarajevo. (In "Goodbyeee," the sixth and final episode of the brilliant satirical television series *Blackadder Goes Forth* (1989), Private Baldrick (Tony Robinson) gives his understanding of how the War started: "I heard it started when a bloke called Archie Duke shot an ostrich 'cause he was hungry." This prompts Captain Blackadder (Rowan Atkinson) to point out: "I think you mean it started when the Archduke of Austro-Hungary got shot," to which Baldrick replies "No, there was definitely an ostrich involved, sir.") Germany issued what has been called a "blank check" to Austria-Hungary, assuring that Germany would back whatever decision it made with respect to Serbia if Russia should step in to defend its "Slavic brothers." With the German assurances in hand, and

The New York Times front page article June 29, 1914

after rejecting Serbia's reply to its ultimatum, Austria-Hungary declared war on Serbia on July 28 and bombarded Belgrade on the 29th. This prompted Russia to mobilize its army on the Austrian border, and on July 30 both Austria-Hungary and Russia ordered the mobilization of all their forces.

On July 31, Germany issued an ultimatum to Russia to cease its mobilization within 12 hours. The time expired with no response, and Germany ordered general mobilization and, ultimately, a declaration of war. General mobilization put the German General Staff's plans into action. The plan in the west, known as the "Schlieffen Plan," required an advance toward France through Luxembourg and neutral Belgium. German troops entered Luxembourg on August 1 and by August 2 the entire country had been occupied. Germany issued another ultimatum to France, demanding it stay neutral in the event of a war between Germany and Russia. France had mobilized its armies on August 1st.

Meanwhile, on July 28, the British fleet was ordered to sail to its war stations at Scapa Flow, on the north end of Scotland. On July 31, the British government dispatched two telegrams, one to Germany and one to France, seeking formal assurances that neither nation would violate Belgian neutrality. France replied it would not. Germany did not reply. On August 2, Germany issued an ultimatum to Belgium, stating it had "reliable information" that Belgium intended to aid France to cross Belgian territory in order to commence hostilities with Germany, but that if the Belgians permitted Germany free passage through Belgium in order to protect itself from "French aggression," then Germany would evacuate Belgian territory as quickly as possible and provide reparations to Belgium, to be exacted from France. Belgium rejected the ultimatum on August 3 and the German Army invaded Belgium on August 4. Britain declared war on Germany at 11:00 p.m. on August 4. The lines had been drawn: the primary belligerents were at war; Great Britain, France, and Russia; the "Triple Entente" or the "Allies," against Germany and Austria-Hungary; the "Central Powers."[3] Italy, a member of the "Triple Alliance" with Germany and Austria-Hungary, declared its neutrality at the beginning of the War. However, in the spring of 1915 Italy repudiated the Triple Alliance and entered the War on the Allied side, declaring war on Austria-Hungary on May 23. Declarations of war by Italy against the Ottoman Empire and Bulgaria came later in 1915, and against Germany in 1916.

Vast German armies swept through Belgium, advancing deep into France. Britain, acting both to support its guarantee of Belgian neutrality and in accordance with treaty obligations, sent the B.E.F. to the continent. On August 23, four divisions of the B.E.F., the entire British force engaged, were overwhelmed and forced to retreat from the town of Mons, in Belgium. This led to one of the first of many myths which would arise during the War, that of "The Angels of Mons," which had supposedly appeared in the skies over the battle and shielded the British retreat. This myth had its origin in a fictional story which did not mention angels at all.

> On September 29, 1914, Arthur Machen published in the *Evening News* an openly fictional romantic story, "The Bowmen," in which the ghosts of the English bowmen dead at Agincourt came to the assistance of their hard-pressed countrymen by discharging arrows which killed Germans without leaving visible wounds. Machen described these bowmen, who appeared between the two armies, as "a long line of shapes, with a shining about them." It was the *shining* that did it: within a week, Machen's fictional bowmen had been transformed into real angels, and what had been written as palpable fiction was soon credited as fact.[4]

The British executed an orderly tactical retreat, and two weeks later found themselves on the outskirts of Paris, fighting alongside the French to keep the Germans from capturing the city. In what was to be called the First Battle of the Marne ("[A]lthough *battles* is perhaps not the best word, having been visited upon these events by subsequent historiography in the interest of neatness and the assumption of something like a rational causality. To call these things *battles* is to imply an understandable continuity with earlier British history and to imply that the war makes sense in a traditional way."),[5] the French and the British stopped the German momentum and saved Paris (reinforcements being famously rushed to the front in Paris taxicabs). As the two sides sought to outflank each other to the north and west, they pushed the lines to the coast of the North Sea, to what would become, for more than three years, a fixed, entrenched line.

From the winter of 1914 until the spring of 1918 the trench system was fixed, moving here and there a few hundred yards, moving on great occasions as much as a few miles. . . . From the North Sea coast of Belgium the line wandered southward, bulging out to contain Ypres [Pronounced "Eeeep;" in British Army slang it was "Wipers."], then dropping down to protect Béthune, Arras, and Albert. It continued south in front of Montdidier, Compiègne, Soissons, Reims, Verdun, St. Mihiel, and Nancy, and finally attached at its southernmost end to the Swiss border at Beurnevisin, in Alsace. The top forty miles—the part north of Ypres—was held by the Belgians; the next ninety miles, down to the river Ancre, were British; the French held the rest, to the south.[6]

There were three types of trenches: "firing trenches," "communications trenches," and "saps."

Firing trenches were where the troops lived and fought while at the front, usually arranged in three roughly parallel lines and ideally six to eight feet deep and four or five feet wide. The front-line trench faced the enemy positions across "no-man's land" (the area between opposing trench lines), which could be anywhere from 50 yards to one mile or so wide. From 50 to several hundred yards or so behind the front-line trench was the support trench, with the reserve line trench some 50 to several hundred yards or so behind the support line. The idea was that this would provide a defense in depth in case of attack. If the front-line trench was overrun or captured, the support and reserve lines provided extra layers of defense, or a place from which a counterattack could be mounted.

These trenches were not dug straight—they "zig zagged" or were cut into square bays which, viewed from above, looked like crenellations on a castle. This was done to confine the blast of a shell which happened to fall into a trench to a small area, and to prevent the enemy from bringing "enfilade fire" (fire from the side) during a raid or an attack—if a trench were straight, an enemy could direct devastating fire down its entire length. A large sump was dug along the center at the bottom of the trench, to col-

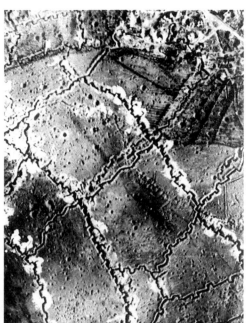

lect water (this was often a futile gesture, particularly in the wet ground of Flanders and Picardy, where the British trenches were dug in areas with high water tables and heavy rainfall), with wooden duckboards laid across to form a walking surface. The trench walls were supported with corrugated metal or bundles of rushes.

The front rim of the trench was generally built up with sandbags or earth into a parapet about a yard high, while a corresponding parados, somewhat less in height, was built up on the rear rim. Dugouts, for command posts or officers' quarters, were tunneled in from the sides of the trenches, as were smaller "funk holes," which could accommodate one or two men. The side of the trench facing the enemy had a "fire step," on which soldiers would stand at each morning and evening "stand to," or to shoot into no-man's land to repel attacks. The areas in front of the

Arial photograph of trenches at Beaumont Hamel, 1916. . Notice the 3 lines of firing trenches, running from the top & upper left to the bottom & lower right, and the communications trenches connecting them & heading to the rear.

trenches were protected by belts of barbed wire, "thickets of mock-organic rusty brown that helped give a look of eternal autumn to the front,"[7] placed and maintained by wiring parties who went out at night; showing one's head above the parapet in daylight invited almost certain death from a sniper's bullet.

Communications trenches ran roughly perpendicular to the firing trenches, connecting the front-line, support, and reserve lines together and to the rear area behind the trenches, allowing troops to move between the three lines and to and from the rear area without showing their heads above ground. These communications trenches could be more than a mile long, often ending in a village, and a pedestrian would be well below ground level before reaching the reserve trench. "Saps" were short, shallower trenches dug out from the front-line trench into no-man's land, toward the enemy trenches, to provide access to listening or forward observation posts or machine-gun positions.[8]

A "section" of the British line, usually about 300 yards wide, was occupied by a company (usually composed of 227 officers and "Other Ranks," abbreviated "OR"). Units would "rotate" in the trenches. After coming off a week or so period of "rest" in a rear area, a company would typically move up through the communications trenches to the front-line trench, to relieve another company which had been holding that section. After three days to a week or so in the front-line trench, the unit would be relieved and rotate to the support line, and then would similarly be relieved and rotate to the reserve line, before being again relieved and rotated back the rear area for another week or so of "rest." Of course, the pattern would vary. Even during the quietest times, some 7,000 officers and men were killed or wounded each day on the

British soldiers in the trenches during WWI

Western Front—the Staff called this "Wastage."[9]

"Model trenches" were built for public display in Kensington Gardens. They were neat, orderly, and tidy.

> The reality was different. The British trenches were wet, cold, smelly, and thoroughly squalid. Compared with the precise and thorough German works, they were decidedly amateur, reflecting a complacency about the British genius for improvisation. Since defense offered little opportunity for the display of pluck or swank, it was by implication derogated in the officers' *Field Service Pocket Book*. One reason the British trench system was so haphazard and ramshackle was that it had originally taken form in accord with the official injunction: "The choice of a [defensive] position and its preparation must be made with a view to economizing the power expended on defense in order that the power of offense may be increased." And it was considered really useless to build solid fortifications anyway: "An occasional shell may strike and penetrate the parapet, but in the case of shrapnel the damage to the parapet will be trifling, while in the case of a shell filled with high explosive, the effect will be no worse on a thin parapet than on a thick one. It is, therefore, useless to spend time and labor on making a thick parapet simply to keep out shell." The repeatedly revived hopes for a general breakout and pursuit were another reason why the British trenches were so shabby.[10]

The trenches were also infested with rats, lice, and other vermin.

British and German troops celebrating a Christmas truce in 1914.

A strange event occurred at Christmas, 1914, principally on the British sector. It was not universal across the entire line, but in many places British and German troops left their trenches and fraternized with their opposite numbers in no-man's land. This became known as the Christmas Truce of 1914.[11] The soldiers traded souvenirs, food, and tobacco. Many Germans spoke English, as many had lived in Britain before the War—there had been many German waiters and barbers working in London, for example. Impromptu football matches were arranged. The High Command, however, was *not* pleased with this development. If the soldiers began to view each other as human beings, they would hesitate to kill the enemy. Fraternization was banned and those defying the ban would be punished, perhaps shot. No such Christmas truce occurred again during the War.

The commander of the B.E.F. at the time was Field Marshal [in American terms, a five-star general] Sir John French. The British High Command's overall strategy was to press the offensive in an effort to break through the German lines into the enemy's rear, thereby breaching the static trench line and leading to a war of maneuver in which the Germans would be driven from France and Belgium and decisively defeated. The British High Command envisioned horse cavalry streaming through the broken German line and racing into Germany. Cavalry reserves were in place behind the lines for nearly every British offensive; they would never go into action. Some of these offensives were designed to coordinate with attacks advanced by the French Army in the southern part of the line, or to relieve pressure upon the massive siege going forward at the French fortress of Verdun, which lasted from February through December 1916. The

French (and the Germans) had suffered massive casualties during the German assault on Verdun, with the French suffering some 162,000 killed and 215,000 wounded, and the Germans suffering 143,000 killed and 194,000 wounded. Verdun weakened the morale of the French Army, and its morale was broken by a disastrous offensive on the River Aisne in April 1917. In early May, a mutiny began when the French 2nd Division refused to follow its officers' orders, and by the end of the month the mutiny had spread through most of the French Army. This is an oversimplification, of course, as it is far beyond the scope of this work to provide a detailed analysis of the strategy and tactics employed by the British Army.

In March 1915, the British mounted their first offensive, on a narrow front of 1,000 yards at Neuve Chapelle. Although the British made some early gains, the attack was ultimately unsuccessful due to a lack of reserves to exploit the initial breakthrough, as well as vigorous German counterattacks. In April 1915, the Germans attacked the British line at Ypres, in an action which came to be known as the "Second Battle of Ypres," using chlorine gas as a weapon. The British had no effective protection against gas at that time and suffered many casualties. The attack was unsuccessful. The British tried again in May at Festubert, with a similar assault. Again, initial success could not be exploited, and this attack failed, as well.

The "lesson" which the British High Command learned from these offensives was that they were unsuccessful because they were launched on too narrow a front and with insufficient numbers of attacking troops. Their solution, which was tried again and again, was to make the offensives bigger, on wider fronts, with greater numbers of troops, and with more intense artillery bombardments prior to the infantry rising from their trenches and walking across no-man's land to attack.

The first of these "bigger" assaults was the Battle of Loos. It was to be co-ordinated with a French offensive in the Champagne region. These joint British and French offensives were intended to draw German attention away from the Eastern Front, in order to relieve pressure upon the bedraggled Russian Army. In late September 1915 six divisions were to go forward on a six-and-a-half-mile front, which would theoretically address the deficiencies of the earlier offensives and achieve the desired breakthrough. A massive artillery barrage would precede the attack, serving both to kill large numbers of the enemy and to cut the wire in front of the German trenches, to clear an easy path for the attacking British infantry.

This time, too, the British were to use chlorine gas themselves; euphemistically referred to as "the accessory," it was to be discharged from cylinders, where it was supposed to blow across no-man's land into the German trenches. Robert Graves, poet, novelist, literary critic, and curmudgeon, who would later produce a considerable body of literary work, including *I, Claudius, Claudius the God, Sergeant Lamb of the Ninth,* and *The White Goddess,* served as an officer in the Royal

Welch Fusiliers, and took part in the Battle of Loos. It did not bode well that the gas-companies who would discharge the "accessory" were described by Captain Thomas, a character Graves called "The Actor," as "Chemistry-dons from London University, a few straight from school, one or two N.C.O.s of the old-soldier type, trained together for three weeks and then given a job as responsible as this. Of course they'll bungle it. How could they do anything else?"[12] Graves described the attack in his memoirs, *Goodbye to All That*, as a "Bloody balls-up: "[13]

> It seems that at half-past four an R.E. [Royal Engineers] captain commanding the gas-company in the front line phoned through to divisional headquarters: "Dead calm. Impossible discharge accessory." The answer he got was: "Accessory to be discharged at all costs." Thomas had not over-estimated the gas-company's efficiency. The spanners for unscrewing the cocks of the cylinders proved, with two or three exceptions, to be misfits. The gas-men rushed about shouting for the loan of an adjustable spanner. They managed to discharge one or two cylinders; the gas went whistling out, formed a thick cloud a few yards off in No Man's Land, and then gradually spread back into our trenches. The Germans, who had been expecting gas, immediately put on their gas-helmets: semi-rigid ones, better than ours. Bundles of oily cotton waste were strewn along the German parapet and set alight as a barrier to the gas. Then their batteries opened on our lines. The confusion in the front trench must have been horrible; direct hits broke several of the gas-cylinders, the trench filled with gas, the gas-company stampeded.[14]

Again, the British attained initial success, but were stopped once more, primarily by massed machine-gun fire. The British artillery barrage, which had largely been shrapnel rather than high explosive, failed to cut the German barbed wire. Although the British had numerical superiority, the German machine guns were devasting.[15] Graves again:

> One of "C" [Company] officers told me later what happened. It had been agreed to advance by platoon rushes with supporting fire. When his platoon had gone about twenty yards, he signalled them to lie down and open covering fire. The din was tremendous. He saw the platoon on his left flopping down too, so he whistled the advance again. Nobody seemed to hear. He jumped up from his shell-hole, waved, and signalled "Forward!"
> Nobody stirred.

He shouted: "You bloody cowards, are you leaving me to go on alone?"

His platoon-sergeant, groaning with a broken shoulder, gasped: "Not cowards, sir. Willing enough. But they're all f---ing dead." The Pope's Nose [a German strong point] machine gun, traversing, had caught them as they rose to the whistle.[16]

"So appalled were the Germans at the effect of their machine guns that they called the battle the 'Field of Corpses at Loos' (Der Leichenfeld von Loos)." After five attempts to break through the German lines, the attack was called off.[17] Of the nearly 10,000 British soldiers who took part in the unsuccessful attack, some 8,250 were killed or wounded. The dead included Rudyard Kipling's son, John, whose body was never recovered.[18]

On December 19, 1915, Sir Douglas Haig, now a full General (Haig would be promoted to Field Marshal in January 1917) who had been in command of the B.E.F.'s I Corps, replaced Field Marshall Sir John French as commander of the B.E.F. Haig was a Scotsman, born in Edinburgh on June 19, 1861. His family owned the famous Haig & Haig whisky distillery. He was a cavalry officer who certainly looked the part of a bold commander; tall and handsome, with a square jaw, military moustache, and always immaculately attired in superbly tailored uniforms. Unfortunately, his chief attributes were stubbornness and a complete lack of imagination. His advice to the War Council in mid-1915 was that "The machine gun is a much over-rated weapon and two per battalion is more than sufficient."[19]

Haig's plan for 1916 was to stage an even bigger attack in conjunction with the French, on a wider front and with more men, preceded by an even longer and more intensive artillery barrage. The place chosen for the assault, astride the River Somme, was not selected based on any

The horrific gas attack at the 1915 Battle of Loos

military advantage offered to the attackers by the terrain, but simply by reason that it was where the British and French lines met. The attack would take place at the south end of the British lines and the north end of the French, coordinated with a French assault. It would have been difficult to have selected a worse site for conducting offensive operations.

In this sector of the front, the Germans occupied a number of ridges above the Franco-British positions. German soldiers could easily look down on their enemies' lines and observe troop movements and other preparations, while the British and French remained blind to German activity. Perhaps more seriously, attacking troops would have to advance uphill to reach the defending Germans.[20]

Had the British High Command taken the time to have studied the battles of the American Civil War, they would have realized the futility of attacking uphill towards a well-defended position. The Union Army attempted such an attack upon the Confederates, lodged behind a stone wall atop Marye's Heights, at the Battle of Fredericksburg on December 11, 1862, and the Confederates did the same against the Union on Cemetery Ridge, similarly lodged behind a stone wall, at the Battle of Gettysburg on July 3, 1863. Both attacking armies were slaughtered. In these battles, the defenders were equipped with muzzle-loading single-shot muskets which could, at best, fire three rounds per minute. The machine guns used by the Germans could fire some 200 times faster; from 500-600 rounds per minute.

General Haig, himself, recognized the strength of the German positions in early 1916:

> The enemy's position to be attacked was of a very formidable character, situated on a high, undulating tract of ground, which rises to more than 500 feet above sea-level, and forms the watershed between the Somme on the one side and the rivers of south-western Belgium on the other.
>
> . . . .
>
> During nearly two years' preparation he had spared no pains to render these defences impregnable. The first and second systems each consisted of several lines of deep trenches, well provided with bomb-proof shelters and with numerous communication trenches connecting them. . . . [E]ach system was protected by wire entanglements, many of them in two belts forty yards broad, built of iron stakes interlaced with barbed wire, often almost as thick as a man's finger.
>
> The numerous woods and villages in and between these systems of defence had been turned into veritable fortresses. . . .
>
> The existing cellars were supplemented by elaborate dugouts, sometimes in two storeys, and these were connected up by passages as much as thirty feet below the surface of the ground.
>
> . . . .

These various systems of defence, with fortified localities and other supporting points between them, were cunningly sited to afford each other mutual assistance and to admit of the utmost possible development of enfilade and flanking fire by machine guns and artillery. . . .

Behind his second system of trenches, in addition to woods, villages and other strong-points prepared for defence, the enemy had several other lines already completed. . . .

. . . .

On portions of the front opposing first-line trenches were more widely separated from each other; while in the valleys to the north were many hidden gun positions from which the enemy could develop flanking fire on our troops as they advance across the open. [21]

In short, the British and the French could not have chosen a worse place to mount an attack if they had tried.

As the factories at home produced war matériel, Haig and his staff spent months devising the plans for the "Big Push." Troops trained behind the lines to prepare for the assault.

Training for the planned Anglo-French offensive on the Somme was continuous. On April 25 Siegfried Sassoon was among the recipients of a lecture by a Major on the bayonet. He later recalled the Major's phrases:

If you don't kill him, he'll kill you.

Stick him between the eyes, in the throat, in the chest, or round the thighs.

If he's on the run, there's only one place; get your bayonet into his kidneys; it'll go in as easy as butter.

Kill them, kill them; there's only one good Boche and that's a dead un! Quickness, anger, strength, good fury, accuracy of aim. Don't waste good steel. Six inches are enough— what's the use of a foot of steel sticking out of a man's neck? Three inches will do him, and when he coughs, go find another. [22]

Preparations for the coming Big Push went forward on the home front, as well. Factories churned out millions of rounds of artillery shells, which would be needed for the massive bombardment which would precede the attack. With

TWO HUNDRED KILLED BY ZEPPELIN RAID LAST NIGHT

FIRE FOLLOWS EXPLOSION OF BOMB DROPPED FROM AIRSHIP, CAUSING EXPLOSION IN MUNITIONS PLANT IN KENT—TWO HUNDRED EMPLOYEES OF THE PLANT ARE KILLED—MUCH DAMAGE IS REPORTED TO HAVE BEEN DONE AT YARMOUTH—MOST DISASTROUS OF THE· RAIDS WHICH HAVE BEEN MADE UPON THE ENGLISH COAST—ADMIRALTY IS SECRETIVE.

LONDON, April 4.—The minister of war munitions today announced that two hundred persons were killed, following an explosion of powder in a munitions plant in Kent.

The explosion was caused by fire, which broke out in the factory early this morning, and it is reported that the fire was caused by a bomb hurled from a German airship.

It is believed that the airships concerned were the same which raided the eastern coast of Scotland last night, and that the raid was continued south along the coast. It is also reported that considerable damage was done at Yarmouth by the same raiders.

The government is using every endeavor to suppress the damage done by the raiders, but the newspapers make the statement that the latest raid of the German air fleet was the most destructive of any previous made.

LONDON, April 4.—Ten persons were killed and eleven injured last night when German Zeppelins raided the east coast of Scotland and rained bombs down upon the shipyards and munition depots of Edinburgh and Leith.

The raid occurred during the darkest hours of the night, and six of the giant aircraft were engaged. The docks at Edinburgh and Leith, and important shipyards on the Tyne were the objects of the German raid, and a number of bombs were dropped at these points.

Just what damage was done at these points is being concealed, but it is admitted that considerable property was destroyed.

The continued raids by the Zeppelins has raised an intense hatred of the Germans throughout the country, and it is feared by the authorities that the people may be incited to take revenge on the German prisoners of war and interned subjects of Germany in the prison camps. Guards have been doubled about the camps, and all persons are forbidden to approach them.

As we shall see in a later chapter, a Zeppelin raid will play a key role in the first film James Whale would direct for Universal.

most of the able-bodied male population in the military, much of this effort in Britain fell to women. By April 1916, some 200,000 women were employed in war industries. When dealing with such volatile materials there were, of course, accidents. "On April 2, [1916] an accidental explosion at a munitions factory at Faversham in Kent, killed 106 workers, many of them women."[23]

The plan was that a five-day artillery barrage would precede the attack. Bad weather forced a two-day postponement of the attack, so the artillery had two more days of firing. Over the seven days, British artillery fired an estimated 1,627,824 shells into the German defenses.[24] Even with the massive number of guns firing, however, the 22,000-yard (about 12.5 mile) front of the attack meant that the artillery was too spread out to truly saturate the German lines. Through manufacturing errors and poor quality control, a significant percentage of these shells failed to explode. As had been the case at Loos, many of the shells were shrapnel rather than high explosive and failed to cut the substantial tangles of German barbed wire. The barrage inflicted little damage upon the German defenders, who simply decamped with their machine guns into their deep, well-constructed, concrete-reinforced dugouts, and waited out the bombardment.

The barrage lifted from the German front lines to their rear areas, and at 7: 28 a.m. on the first of July 1916, the officers blew their whistles and some 100,000 British infantrymen in 11 divisions of the Fourth Army, on a front 12 and a half miles wide, climbed from their trenches to make their way across no-man's land to attack the German trench line. They were supported by two divisions of the Third Army's diversionary attack on Gommecourt to the north. When the barrage shifted from the German front to their rear areas, the German front-line troops emerged from their dugouts, fitted their machine guns, and awaited the arrival of the oncoming British infantry. The German machine guns opened up, and the German artillery, largely unscathed by the British bombardment, laid down its own barrage on the British lines. The British suffered the greatest defeat at the heavily fortified areas to the north and south of the river Aisne, at the villages of Serre, Beaumont Hamel, Thiepval, Ovillers, La Boisselle, and Fricourt.[25] The communications trenches leading back from the British front lines were choked with wounded moving toward the rear, so the troops coming forward to reinforce the attack had to leave the safety of the trenches and advance from the rear overland. By the end of the day, July 1, 1916, the British had suffered nearly 60,000 casualties, with nearly 20,000 of those dead.

Despite these horrendous losses, the British continued to press the attack. One innovation did appear for the first time during the Somme campaign. Seeking a way to crush German wire and protect attacking infantry, Winston Churchill conceived the idea of armored "landships." This would evolve into a tracked vehicle designed to cross no-man's land, crush barbed wire entanglements, and drive over trenches. When these weapons were first being manufactured, a cover story was made up that their steel hulls were "water tanks" for storage at the front. The name "tank" stuck and tracked armored vehicles have been so called since then. The first British tanks did not look like the modern vehicles. Viewed from the side, they resembled large, rounded parallelograms with treads running all the way

Winston Churchill's landship

around their outside edge. Guns were carried in sponsons which protruded from the vehicles' sides. The first model to see action, the Mark I, was built in two versions. The "male" version, intended to drive the enemy from its trenches by longer range fire, carried two 40 caliber 6-pounder guns and four Hotchkiss machine guns, while the "female" version, intended for use against infantry in the open, carried four Vickers .303 and one Hotchkiss machine guns. On September 13, 1916, the British tanks saw action for the first time, during what came to be known as the Battle of Flers-Courcelette. Although they caused panic among the Germans, too few of them were engaged to make any practical impact upon the outcome of the battle. They were lightly armored, enough to repel rifle and machine gun fire, but not enough to resist artillery. As they were slow and often became stuck, they made excellent targets for enemy artillery. Nevertheless, the British improved the design and continued to use the tanks throughout the War. The French developed their own tanks, as well. Their Renault light tank was the first to display what would become the common configuration for the tank: a treaded chassis topped by a rotating turret containing a gun. The Germans were slow to develop their own tank, and their model, the A7V, was large and unwieldy, basically a large metal box, and only about 20 were built, appearing on the field only during the last year of the War. In the interwar years, of course, the Germans would refine their hardware and their tactics, with their tanks leading the "Blitzkrieg" at the beginning of the Second World War.

Fighting continued on the Somme front until November 18, 1916. The British and the French did not achieve a breakthrough, although they did manage to push the German lines back some six miles on a 16-mile-wide front. Total British and Commonwealth (including Canada, Australia, New Zealand, South Africa, and Newfoundland) casualties over the course of the battle were approximately 420,000, with nearly 95,000 of those having been killed or missing.

Despite the heavy losses, the British High Command saw the Somme as a modest victory. The Germans had also incurred heavy casualties, estimated at between 465,000 to 600,000 total casualties, with some 165,000 of those having

Mark V tank

been killed and some 38,000 taken prisoner. The German line had not broken, but it had been pushed back in both the British sector in the north and the French sector in the south. Again, the lesson learned was to try an even bigger attack in 1917. This time, the High Command was to pick a time and a place that would make conditions even worse than they had been on the Somme.

The 1917 attack would come in Belgium, in Flanders, on the northernmost end of the British line. It would be launched from the trenches in the bulge toward the German lines, known as a "salient," around the town of Ypres. This salient was a particularly brutal place for the British to defend, as the bulge made most of the British line around Ypres vulnerable to artillery fire from the sides and the rear as well as the front. The opposing German lines were on much higher ground, allowing the Germans to observe almost the entirety of the British positions, while the British could see almost nothing of the German defenses without using aircraft to observe the enemy. As well, in the best of times, this area of the line experienced heavy rains and a high water table. When the British trenches weren't intolerably damp, they were filled with water. The surrounding area, including no-man's land, was often a sea of glutinous mud. Paul Fussell's succinct description of the battle and its prelude is far better than any description I could offer:

British soldiers in the trenches during the Battle of the Somme

> On January 1, 1917 Haig was elevated to the rank of Field Marshal, and on March 17, 1917, Bapaume—one of the main first-day objectives of the Somme jump-off nine months before—was finally captured.

The Germans had announced unrestricted submarine warfare. It was only a matter of time before the United States would enter the war. However, Allied planners knew it would be some time before American troops would arrive in France in any numbers.

> On April 9 the British again tried the old tactic of head-on assault, this time near Arras in an area embracing the infamous

Wounded soldiers are carried to safety during Operation Michael

Vimy Ridge. . . . The attack, pressed for five days, gained 7000 yards at the cost of 160,000 killed and wounded. The same old thing. But on June 7 there was something new, something finally exploiting the tactic of surprise. Near Messines, south of Ypres, British miners had been tunneling for a year under the German front lines, and by early June they had dug twenty-one horizontal mineshafts stuffed with a million pounds of high explosive a hundred feet below crucial points in the German defense system. At 3:10 in the morning these mines were set off all at once.

Nineteen of the mines went off. They were said to have been so powerful that the shock was felt in London. One of the mines which failed to detonate went off in the middle of a farmer's field in July 1955. Luckily, no one was injured. The other undetonated mine is still sitting there.[26]

The attack at Messines had been masterminded by General Sir Herbert Plumer. Fussell called him "a sort of intellectual's hero" of the British military. He lacked the military bearing of Haig – Plumer was short and plump, with white hair. However, he had the imagination which Haig lacked.[27] The Germans were completely surprised by the mines, and Vimy Ridge was captured with a cost of 16,000 casualties, remarkably low for a major British attack.

If Messines showed what imagination and surprise could do, the attack toward Passchendaele, on the northern side of the Ypres Salient, indicated once more the folly of reiterated abortive assaulting. . . . This time the artillery was relied on to prepare the ground for the attack, and with a vengeance: over 10 days four million shells were fired. The result was highly ironic, even in this war where irony was a staple. The bombardment churned up the ground; rain fell and turned the dirt to mud. In the mud the British assaulted until the attack finally attenuated three-and-a-half months later. Price: 370,000 British dead and wounded and sick and frozen to death. Thousands literally drowned in the mud. It was a reprise of the Somme, but worse. [28]

As it had on the Somme in 1916, the Passchendaele attack would wind down in November:

> After weeks of frustration, the attack finally (and literally) bogged down in early November. Lieutenant General Sir Launcelot Kiggell, of the Staff, "paid his first visit to the fighting zone":

>> As his staff car lurched through the swampland and neared the battleground he became more and more agitated. Finally he burst into tears and muttered, "Good God, did we really send men to fight in that?"
>> The man beside him, who had been through the campaign, replied tonelessly: "It's worse further on up."[29]

The trench lines on the Western Front remained essentially static until the great German spring offensive of 1918, dubbed "Operation Michael." Following the Bolshevik revolution in 1917 and the subsequent armistice between Russia and Germany, the Germans were able to shift large numbers of troops from the Eastern to the Western Front. At 4:30 in the morning on March 21, 1918 the Germans mounted a massive assault against the British lines in the Somme sector, on a 40-mile-wide front. The Germans achieved a breakthrough, advancing 40 miles into the British rear. The British lost 150,000 men on the first day, with 90,000 of those having been taken prisoner, and total British casualties rose to 300,000 over the next six days. The advance petered out due to its own success, with the German troops stopping to loot and drink wine.[30]

The United States, which had declared war on Germany in April 1917, had some two million soldiers in France by the summer of 1918. The Allies, aided by

the presence of fresh American troops (the British and the Germans were weakened by the attrition of nearly four years of war), counterattacked in August 1918, breaking through the German lines and leading to a war of maneuver. Hostilities would end with the Armistice at 11: 00 a.m. on November 11, 1918 ("the eleventh hour of the eleventh day of the eleventh month"—allowing the killing to go on between the agreement to end the fighting and the coming of this "symbolic" date and time—some commanders were ordering attacks right up until the final minute before the Armistice took effect).

> And speaking of the last act, there is one unforgettable vignette which if true is fine, and which if apocryphal is even better. It is Herbert Essame's memory of the German machine gunner signaling the closing of a long run on November 11, 1918: "On the Fourth Army front, at two minutes to eleven, a machine gun, about 200 yards from the leading British troops, fired off a complete belt without a pause. A single machine-gunner was then seen to stand up beside his weapon, take off his helmet, bow, and turning about walk slowly to the rear."[31]

The War with Germany would not end formally until the Treaty of Versailles was signed on June 28, 1919,[32] exactly five years after the assassination of the Archduke and his wife. Chief aspects of the War were trench warfare, the dominance of the defensive over the offensive, the machine gun (which tipped the balance in a significant way to the defense), the use of poison gas as a weapon, aerial combat, the introduction of the tank, and heavy use of artillery. British and Empire casualties in the War amounted to more than 1,115,000 dead and nearly 2,100,000 wounded.

1 For anyone interested in learning more about the War, there are thousands of books available, some covering the entire War and some covering individual topics in great detail. For a good, general overview of the entire War in a single volume, I would recommend Gilbert, Martin, *The First World War: A Complete History* (Henry Holt 1994).

MEMBER OF THE ASSOCIATED PRESS

THE KOKOMO DAILY TRIBUNE

PAID CIRCULATION FRIDAY...8,461

VOL. XXXVI—NO. 254   FOUR O'CLOCK EDITION   KOKOMO, IND., SATURDAY, JUNE 28, 1919.   TWELVE PAGES   PRICE—TWO CENTS.

TREATY ENDING WORLD WAR HAS BEEN SIGNED

PRESIDENT APPEALS TO AMERICA TO RATIFY PEACE PACT PROMPTLY

SIGNING OF PEACE TREATY BY GERMANY AND ALLIES FORMALLY ENDS WORLD WAR

German Delegates Placed Signature at 3:13 O'clock in Presence of Great Gathering— Allied Delegates Followed—China Refused to Sign and Remained Away—All Ceremonies Completed at 3:49 O'clock—Premier Clemenceau Presided.

IMPRESSIVE SCENE AT EPOCH MAKING EVENT

Versailles, June 28.—The world war was formally ended to-day by the signing of the peace treaty with Germany. The epochal meeting in the hall of mirrors began at 3:10 o'clock and the German delegation, the first to sign, affixed their signatures at 3:13 o'clock. They were followed by the

Germany Signs.
By Edmund Vance Cooke

She signs it with the pen, who thought to sign it with the sword;
Blood of her veins and golden gains she freely, vainly poured,
And prestige she that coveted and honor she had stored,
Yet day by day her shame and guilt grow like a Jonah's gourd,
Till now she signs it with a pen, who hoped to use the sword.

So ever when a pride-mad prince shall pledge a blood-red day!
So ever when wolf-men shall lead sheep-minded men astray!
So ever, when a tribe would crush its brother tribes to clay!
So even to us should we forsake our ancient, lawful way
Or dare to raise the cankered sword the Prussian casts away!

PRESIDENT SENDS MESSAGE URGING AMERICAN PEOPLE ACCEPT THE PEACE TREATY

Wants No Change or Reservations As to Document or League Covenant—"Furnishes Charter For New Order of Affairs in World" —Expresses Strong Faith in Instrument— Starts Home Tonight—Interest Now Centers In Senate Action.

PEACE NOT FULLY MADE UNTIL RATIFICATION

Washington, June 28.—President Wilson in an address to the American people on the occasion of the signing of the peace treaty, made a plea for the acceptance of the treaty and the covenant of the league of nations, without change or reservation. His message, given out here by Secretary Tumulty said:

2 Fussell, 10.

3 This synopsis of the start of the War is largely based upon Tuchman, Barbara, *The Guns of August* (The Easton Press 1987). First published in 1963, it was awarded the Pulitzer Prize for General Non-Fiction that year. Although now somewhat dated and largely confined to events which occurred between June 28 and August 31, 1914, it remains a good, readable source on the origins of the War. More recent books on the origins of the War, which cover broader scopes, are Clark, Christopher, *The Sleepwalkers: How Europe Went to War in 1914* (HarperCollins 2013) and MacMillan, Margaret, *The War That Ended Peace: The Road to 1914* (Random House 2013).

4 Fussell, 116 (emphasis in original).

5 Fussell, 8-9 (emphasis in original).

6 Fussell, 36.

7 Fussell, 42.

8 *See generally* Fussell, 41-2.

9 Fussell, 41.

10 Fussell, 43-4.

11 *See* Weintraub, Stanley, *Silent Night: The Story of the World War I Christmas Truce* (The Free Press 2001) for a full account of this event.

12 Graves, Robert, *Goodbye to All That* 133 (Folio Society 1981).

13 Graves, 136.

14 Graves, 137.

15 Gilbert, Martin, *The First World War: A Complete History* 197-201 (Henry Holt 1994).

16 Graves, 140.

17 Gilbert, 199.

18 Gilbert, 200-01.

19 Gilbert, 199.

20 Foley, Robert T. and McCartney, Helen (eds.), *The Somme: An Eyewitness History* 2 (Folio Society 2006).

21 Foley and McCartney, 2-5 (quoting Boraston, J.H. (ed.), *Sir Douglas Haig's Despatches, December 1915-April 1919* 21-3 (J.M. Dent and Sons 1919)).

22 Gilbert, 239.

23 Gilbert, 238.

24 Foley and McCartney, 10.

25 Foley and McCartney, 11.

26 This was the case when Paul Fussell wrote his book in 1975 and remains so today, some 45 years later. To the British Tommy, the town of Ploegsteert was knows an "Plugstreet." Messines was

Lochnagar Mine Crater at La Boisselle

not, however, the first or only time the British made use of mining under the German lines. For example, at 7: 28 a.m. on the morning of July 1, 1916, 10 mines were exploded under the German lines at the beginning of the Battle of the Somme. The Lochnagar Mine Crater at La Boisselle has been preserved as a memorial. Today, there is grass growing in the crater and it looks quite pastoral. My wife and I visited the crater as part of a tour of the Somme battlefield in May 2008. A similar maneuver was attempted in the American Civil War. In June 1864, the Union Army had laid siege to the town of Petersburg, Virginia. The attackers and defenders had both entrenched, their lines previewing what would happen on the Western Front in the Great War some 50 years later. Soldiers from the 48th Pennsylvania Volunteer Infantry, a unit from the Schuylkill County anthracite coal region, had dug a mineshaft under a strong point in the Confederate lines, cleared out a large chamber, packed it with 320 20-pound kegs of black powder, and sealed it off. Two brigades of African American soldiers, who were led by white officers in segregated units, known as "United States Colored Troops (U.S.C.T.)," were selected to make the initial attack after the mine had been detonated, and were trained intensively for two weeks, practicing how to fan around the crater, get to the Confederate rear, and open a larger breach in the line to allow additional waves of attacking troops through. This training stressed that the men *were not* to venture down into the crater. The day before the attack, which would become known as the "Battle of the Crater," an order came down specifying that the initial attack would not be made by the trained U.S.C.T. soldiers, but instead by brigades of white troops. On July 30, at 4: 44 a.m., the mine was detonated, blowing a crater 60 feet across, 200 feet wide, and from 10 to 30 feet deep. The attacking white soldiers did what they were *not* supposed to do—they ventured down into the crater. As more and more Union soldiers packed into the confined space, the Confederates recovered and began shooting down at the men trapped at the bottom of the crater. The attack, which likely would have been a huge success had the initial plans been followed, turned into a fiasco. There are conflicting theories about the reason for this last-minute switch. One is that the switch was prompted by racism on the part of the Union High Command, and the belief that the African American troops were incapable of successfully completing the mission. The alternate view is that the Union High Command feared being accused of deliberately and callously sacrificing the U.S.C.T. soldiers in the event the attack proved unsuccessful, resulting in the slaughter of the attackers.

27 Anyone interested in learning more about General Plumer should read *Plumer: The Soldiers' General*, by Geoffrey Powell (Pen & Sword Books Ltd. 1990). His standard biography, *Plumer of Messines*, by General Sir Charles Harington (John Murray 1935), was reprinted by Pickle Partners Publishing in 2017 and is available as an e-book. The 1935 hardcover is out of print but is readily available online from used book sites such as AbeBooks.com.

28 Fussell, 14-16.

29 Fussell, 84 (quoting Gibbs, *Philip*, *Now it Can be Told* 245 (New York 1920)).

30 Fussell, 16-18.

31 Fussell, 196 (quoting Essame, Herbert, *The Battle for Europe, 1918* 206 (Batsford 1972)).

32 Although signed by President Woodrow Wilson, the Treaty was never ratified by the United States Senate, and hence a technical state of war still existed between the Central Powers and the United States until the enactment of the Knox-Porter Resolution on July 2, 1921, which formally ended hostilities between the United States and the Central Powers. The United States subsequently entered into peace treaties with Austria (August 24, 1921), Germany (August 25, 1921), and Hungary (August 29, 1921).

Chapter Two
"Oh, Give them Irony and Give them Pity."
—Ernest Hemingway, *The Sun Also Rises*[1]

Although Hemingway's novel, *The Sun Also Rises*, is not a work about the War, Hemingway did serve as an ambulance driver in Italy in June 1918, for some two months, before being wounded in the legs and continuing to render aid to Italian soldiers despite his injuries. He spent six months in hospital as a result of his wounds and was awarded the Italian Silver Medal of Bravery. His novel, *A Farewell to Arms*, is based upon his wartime experiences. The novel's hero, Frederic Henry, is an American medic serving in the Italian Army. He is wounded and falls in love with Catherine Barkley, an English nurse. This quotation from *The Sun Also Rises*, however, captures two of the key elements of how the British experience on the Western Front was remembered: irony and pity.

Ernest Hemingway, 1918

Irony:

> Irony is the attendant of hope, and the fuel of hope is innocence. One reason the Great War was more ironic than any other is that its beginning was more innocent. "Never such innocence again," observes Philip Larkin, who has found himself curiously drawn to regard with a wondering tenderness not the merely victimized creatures of the nearby Second World War, but the innocents of the remote Great War, those sweet, generous people who pressed forward and all but solicited their own destruction.[2]

Perhaps remembrance had tinged the summer of 1914 with glories which had never really existed, but the contrast between that bright summer and the bleakness of the War which would come at its end made a stark dividing line.

> Although some memories of the benign last summer before the war can be discounted as standard romantic retrospection

turned even rosier by egregious contrast with what followed, all agree that the prewar summer was the most idyllic for many years. It was warm and sunny, eminently pastoral. One lolled outside on a folding canvas chaise, or swam, or walked in the countryside. One read outdoors, went on picnics, had tea served from a white wicker table under the trees. You could leave your books on the table all night without fear of rain. Siegfried Sassoon was busy fox hunting and playing serious county cricket. Robert Graves went climbing in the Welsh mountains. Edmund Blunden took country walks near Oxford, read Classics and English, and refined his pastoral diction. Wilfred Owen was teaching English to the boys of a French family living near Bordeaux. David Jones was studying illustration at Camberwell Art School. And for those like [Lytton] Strachey who preferred the pleasures of the West End, there were splendid evening parties, as well as a superb season for concerts, theater, and the Russian ballet.

For the modern imagination that last summer has assumed the status of a permanent symbol for anything innocently but irrevocably lost. Transferred meanings of "our summer of 1914" retain the irony of the original, for the change from felicity to despair, pastoral to anti-pastoral, is melodramatically unexpected.[3]

Thus, the extreme divergence between the idyllic summer of 1914 and the horrors which would come with the War set the stage for the many ironies which would follow.

The world of 1914 was also essentially a static world, with set ideas and expectations from the past which were assumed would endure forever:

Furthermore, the Great War was perhaps the last to be conceived as taking place within a seamless, purposeful "history" involving a coherent stream of time running from past through present to future. The shrewd recruiting poster depicting a worried father of the future being asked by his children, "Daddy, what did *you* do in the Great War?" assumes a future whose moral and social pressures are identical with those of the past. Today, when each day's experience seems notably *ad hoc*, no such appeal would shame even the most stupid to the recruiting office. But the Great War took place in what was, compared with ours, a static world, where the values appeared stable and where the meanings of abstractions seemed permanent and reliable. Everyone knew what Glory was, what Honor meant. It was not until eleven years after the war that Hemingway could declare in *A Farewell to Arms* that "abstract words such as glory, honor, courage, or hallow were obscene beside the concrete names of villages, the numbers of roads, the names of rivers, the numbers of regiments and the dates." In the summer of 1914 no one would have understood what on earth he was talking about.[4]

The War would serve to forever uproot these concepts.

Situational irony is rooted, of course, in the discrepancy between expectations and actuality. The more these elements diverge, the greater the irony. This applies to expectations of how the War would progress at the time it began against what would actually occur. There had not been a widespread war in Europe among its major powers since the Franco-Prussian War in 1870-71, which saw France defeated, its loss of Alsace-Lorraine, and the unification of the various German states into a single nation. Britain had not known a major war for nearly a century, since the defeat of Napoleon at Waterloo in 1815. "There had been no war between the Great Powers since 1871. No man in the prime of his life knew what war was like. All imagined that it would be an affair of great marches and great battles, quickly decided. It would be over by Christmas."[5]

Daddy, what did YOU do in the Great War?

When the War first broke out, many in Britain foresaw a swift victory. The prevailing belief was that the War would be over, as A.J.P. Taylor wrote, "by Christmas." This was the view in Germany, as well. Kaiser Wilhelm II told troops departing for the front in August 1914 "You will be home before the leaves have fallen from the trees."[6] Secretary of State for War, Lord Kitchener, at an August 7, 1914 meeting of the War Council, "shocked his colleagues by suggesting that the war might prove to be a long one."[7]

Fussell relates an obituary from the London *Times* of August 9, 1914, in which one Arthur Sydney Evelyn Annesley, a 49-year old ex-Captain in the Rifle Brigade, is said to have committed suicide by flinging himself under a heavy van due to worry "that he was not going to be accepted for service."[8] Many were like ex-Captain Annesley, eager to sign up to fight. Many felt the War would be over before they had their chance to seek glory. This attitude is exemplified by the poet Rupert Brooke, who enlisted in the British Army in August 1914. His letters home during the autumn and winter of 1914-15 relate how he found "It's all great fun."[9] In his horribly naïve poem, "Peace," Brooke gave thanks to God for being born at a time he was given the chance to go to war: "Now, God be thanked Who has matched us with His hour." The War would purify those who volunteered to serve:

> To turn, as swimmers into cleanness leaping,
> Glad from a world grown old and cold and weary,
> Leave the sick hearts that honour could not move,
> And half-men, and their dirty songs and dreary,
> And all the little emptiness of love!

Instead of "leaping" into "cleanness," the "swimmers" who went to War would see filthy, fetid trenches, rotting corpses, the blood and mud of the Somme and Passchendaele. "If the war had actually been written by [Thomas] Hardy it could scarcely offer a bolder irony than that by which Brooke's 'swimmers' of 1914 metamorphose into the mud-flounderers of the Somme and Passchendaele sinking beneath the surface."[10] Brooke, himself, would die an ironic death on February 28, 1915 aboard a French hospital ship in the Aegean Sea, of sepsis caused by an infected mosquito bite, while on his way to participate in the disastrous landings at Gallipoli.

This enthusiasm and desire to go to war would be reflected in other poems, as well, such as Charles Sorley's "All the Hills and Vales Along," telling of soldiers singing as they march off to war: "And the singers are the chaps, Who are going to die perhaps: "

> On marching men, on
> To the gates of death with song.
> Sow your gladness for earth's reaping,
> So you may be glad, though sleeping.
> Strew your gladness on earth's bed,
> So be merry, so be dead.

Robert Nichols was commissioned a Second Lieutenant in the Royal Field Artillery. As Robert Graves wrote, he "served only three weeks in France, with the gunners, and got involved in no show; but, being highly strung, he got invalided out of the army and went on to lecture on British war-poets in America for the Ministry of Information. He read Siegfried's poems and mine, and started a legend of Siegfried, himself, and me as the new Three Musketeers, though the three of us had never once been together in the same room."[11] In his poem, "The Day's March," Nichols speaks of "the wind of death" which "Throws a clean flame." Thomas Hardy, otherwise a master of irony (for example, in "Ah, Are you Digging on My Grave?," the voice of a buried woman asks the question, and finds it is her beloved dog—however, the dog was merely digging to bury a bone, unaware his late mistress was buried beneath) would write, in "Men Who March Away (Song of the Soldiers; September 5, 1914): "

> In our heart of hearts believing
> 　Victory crowns the just,
> 　And that braggarts must
> 　Surely bite the dust,
> Press we to the field ungrieving,
> In our heart of hearts believing
> 　Victory crowns the just.

The prevailing view at the outset of the War was to liken it to a sporting event; all good, clean fun.

> In nothing, however, is the initial British innocence so conspicu-
> ous as in the universal commitment to the sporting spirit. Before
> the war, says Osbert Sitwell:
>
> > [W]e were still in the trough of peace that had
> > lasted a hundred years between two great con-
> > flicts. In it, such wars as arose were not general,
> > but only a brief armed version of the Olympic
> > Games. You won a round; the enemy won the
> > next. There was no more talk of extermina-
> > tion, or of Fights to a Finish, than would occur
> > in a boxing match.[12]

As Paul Fussell further points out, the classic equation between war and sport— cricket, in this case—had been established by Sir Henry Newbolt in his poem "Vitaï Lampada," a public-school favorite since 1898:

> There's a breathless hush in the close tonight–
> 　Ten to make and the match to win –
> A bumping pitch and a blinding light,
> 　An hour to play and the last man in.
> And it's not for the sake of a ribboned coat,
> 　Or the selfish hope of a season's fame,
> But his Captain's hand on his shoulder smote–
> 　"Play up! play up! and play the game!"
> [The cricketer then finds himself as an officer leading troops in a
> colonial war. As his men are dying around him, he exhorts them
> in the same way as his cricket captain had previously done.]

The author of these lines was a lifetime friend of Douglas Haig.[13]
Lord Norcliffe, in his propaganda booklet entitled *Lord Northcliffe's War Book*, extolled the virtues of football [this is, of course, the sport known as "soccer" in the U.S.] as being even better than cricket at fostering the superiority of the British soldier over that of the German:

> Our soldiers are individual. They embark on little individual enterprises. The German . . . is not so clever at these devices. He was never taught them before the war, and his whole training from childhood upwards has been to obey, and to obey in numbers.

The reason is simple:

> He has not played individual games. Football, which develops individuality, has only been introduced into Germany in comparatively recent times.[14]

The mania for football and the desire to show sporting flair at the front would lead to the practice of kicking a football towards the German lines while attacking. While this may have served as a morale booster, it was singularly dangerous for the kicker. One Captain W.P. Nevill, a company commander in the 8th East Surrey Regiment, purchased four footballs while on leave, distributing one to each company in his battalion before the attack on the Somme. He offered a prize to the first platoon which kicked its ball up to the German front

Soccer match team receiving trophy in 1918 during The Great War.

line. Making a splendid kick to start the advance of his own company, Captain Nevill was killed instantly. "Two of the footballs are preserved today in English museums."[15]

> The innocent army fully attained the knowledge of good and evil at the Somme on July 1, 1916. That moment, one of the most interesting in the whole long history of human disillusion, can stand as the type of all the ironic actions of the war. . . . Haig wrote his wife just before the attack: "I feel that every step in my plan had been taken with the Divine help"? "The wire has never been so well cut," he confided to his diary, "nor the artillery preparation so thorough." [reference omitted]. . . . Thirteen years after that day Henry Williamson recalled it vividly:

>> I see men arising and walking forward; and I go forward with them, in a glassy delirium wherein some seem to pause, with bowed heads, and sink carefully to their knees, and roll slowly over, and lie still. Others roll and roll, and scream and grip my legs in uttermost fear, and I have to struggle to break away, while the dust and earth on my tunic changes from grey to red.
>>   And I go on with aching feet, up and down across ground like a huge ruined honeycomb, and my wave melts away, and the second wave comes up, and also melts away, and then the third wave merges into the ruins of the first and second, and after a while the fourth wave blunders into the remnants of the others, and we begin to run forward to catch up with the barrage, gasping and sweating, in bunches, anyhow, every bit of the months of drill and rehearsal forgotten, for who could have imagined that the "Big Push" was going to be this?"
>> [reference omitted]

> What assisted Williamson's recall is precisely the ironic pattern which subsequent vision has laid over the events. [16]

Of course, even if kicking footballs into no-man's land had given a brief boost to the attacking troops' morale, raising their hopes of victory, those hopes were dashed as soon as the German machine guns began cutting down the attacking British soldiers. The irony was that the Somme attack, intended to break through the German lines and win the War, resulted in massive casualties on July 1, with some 20,000 killed or missing and 40,000 wounded. The cavalry deployed behind the lines to exploit the breakthrough would never go into action. "Thus, Private E.T. Radband: 'My strongest recollection: all those grand-looking cavalrymen, ready mounted to follow the breakthrough. What a hope!'"[17] The battle would grind on for more than four months, gaining several dozen square miles of territory while having no appreciable effect upon the outcome of the War. This territory would be paid for with a total of 420,000 British and Commonwealth casualties, with nearly 95,000 of those having been killed or missing.

> Another private, Gunner Charles Bricknall, recalling the war many years later, likewise behaves as if his understanding of the irony attending events is what enables him to recall them. He was in an artillery battery being relieved by a new unit fresh from England:

> > There was a long road leading to the front line which the Germans occasionally shelled, and the shells used to drop plonk in the middle of it. This new unit assembled right by the wood ready to go into action in the night.

> What rises to the surface of Bricknall's memory is the hopes and illusions of the newcomers:

> > They was all spick and span, buttons polished and all the rest of it.

> He tries to help:

> > We spoke to a few of the chaps before going up and told them about the Germans shelling the road, but of course they was not in charge, so up they went and the result was they all got blown up.

> Contemplating this ironic issue, Bricknall is moved to an almost Dickensian reiterative rhetoric:

> > Ho, what a disaster! We had to go shooting lame horses, putting the dead to the side of the

road, what a disaster, which could have been avoided if only the officers had gone into action the hard way [i.e., overland, avoiding the road]. That was something I shall never forget." [reference omitted]

It is the *if only* rather than the slaughter that helps Bricknall "never forget" this. A slaughter by itself is too commonplace for notice. When it makes an ironic point it becomes memorable.[18]

The major British assaults mostly all had ironic outcomes. The assault at Loos in September 1915 was, as stated previously, aptly described by Robert Graves as a "Bloody balls-up." The British High Command put great store in the planned use of chlorine gas, euphemistically referred to as "the accessory." The gas companies which were to discharge the "accessory," despite being poorly trained and organized and basically incompetent, got at least one thing right. The air was "dead calm" when the gas was to be discharged, meaning it would not blow towards the German lines (which were, in any event, well-prepared for an expected gas attack). The gas companies so advised the High Command, which ignored their advice and ordered the "accessory" discharged "at all costs." Of course, the gas settled back into the British trenches. The High Command's "brilliant" plan ended in disaster, as did the entire attack. The actuality fell far short of the expectations.

Not only would the Passchendaele attack come to a similar, ironic, end, but the British occupation of the Ypres Salient was itself highly ironic. The British line bulged out toward the German line to enclose the town of Ypres. The town itself had no strategic value to the Allies. Constant German shelling had reduced the town to rubble. Its most famous architectural casualty was the Cloth Hall, a massive building erected mostly during the 13th Century and completed early in the 14th, in 1304, which had served as a warehouse and marketplace for the Flanders cloth trade. As Edmund Blunden said, in his poem "Les Halles d'Ypre*s*:" "And the Cloth Hall crouches beside, disfigured with fire, The glory of Flan-

Robert Graves

Edmund Blunden

ders once." Destroyed by shelling, it was rebuilt after the War, between 1933 and 1967, and now houses the Flanders Fields Museum.

The British trenches in the Ypres Salient were low-lying and plagued with flooding and mud. The opposing German lines were on higher ground. This meant that not only were the Germans spared the worst of the flooding problems which plagued the British, they were also able to keep almost the entirety of the British trench lines, including not only the firing trenches but also the communications trenches connecting the front lines to the rear areas, under virtually constant observation.

The bulge in the British lines also meant that German artillery could fire into the British trenches, the town, and the rear areas, from three sides. Thus, not only did the town of Ypres have no strategic value to the Allies, the Salient itself was a huge tactical liability. This could have been easily solved by withdrawing from the Salient, straightening the British line to the rear of the town, selecting better ground for the trench lines in the process, and depriving the Germans of the ability to simply pound away at the British with artillery and cause significant casualties without the need to mount any major infantry offensives. This would have also served to shorten the British lines considerably, resulting in the need for fewer troops to man the trenches in Flanders. The British High Command, however, could not even contemplate such a wise strategic and tactical withdrawal, as the idea of giving up so many square miles of territory to the Germans was simply unthinkable.

Edmund Blunden was commissioned a Second Lieutenant in the Royal Sussex Regiment, and was posted to the Regiment's 11th Battalion, a Kitchener's Army unit, in May 1916. He would serve in that battalion until the end of the War and was awarded the Military Cross for "conspicuous gallantry in action" in January 1917. In his brilliant War memoir, *Undertones of War*, he related the following, terribly ironic, vignette. British miners had sunk a shaft in the trench and were tunneling under the German lines near Cambrin:

> Not far away from that shafthead, a young and cheerful lance-corporal of ours was making some tea as I passed one warm afternoon. I went along three firebays; one shell burst behind me; I saw its smoke faint out, and I thought all was as lucky as it should be. Soon a cry from that place recalled me; the

shell had burst all wrong. Its butting impression was black and stinking on the parados where three minutes ago the lance-corporal's mess-tin was bubbling over a little flame. For him, how could the gobbets of blackening flesh, the earth-wall sotted with blood, with flesh, the eye under the duckboard, the pulpy bone be the only answer? At this moment, while we looked with intense fear at so strange a horror, the lance-corporal's brother came round the traverse.[19]

While, at the beginning of the War the prevailing view was that it would be over quickly, as it wore on, this was replaced by the opinion it might never end.

But the likelihood that peace would ever come again was often in serious doubt during the war. One did not have to be a lunatic or a particularly despondent visionary to conceive quite seriously that the war would literally never end and would become a permanent condition of mankind. The stalemate and the attrition would go on indefinitely, becoming, like the telephone and the internal combustion engine, a part of the accepted atmosphere of the modern experience. Why indeed not, given the palpable irrationality of the new world? Why not, given the vociferous contempt with which peace plans were received by the patriotic majority on both sides?[20]

Edmund Blunden reflected this belief in his memoirs: "One of the first ideas that established themselves in my enquiring mind was the prevailing sense of the endlessness of the war. No one here appeared to conceive any end of it."[21]

Siegfried Sassoon wrote of a dream that still recurred at the time he wrote his memoirs, in which the War is still raging as late as 1936:

It varies in context and background, but always amounts to the same thing. The War is still going on and I have got to return to the front. I complain bitterly to myself because it hasn't stopped yet. I am worried because I can't find my active-service kit. I am worried because I have forgotten how to be an officer. I feel that I can't face it again, and sometimes I burst into tears and say "It's no good. I can't do it." But I know that I can't escape going back, and search frantically for my lost equipment.

Sometimes I actually find myself "out there" (though the background is always in England—the Germans have usually invaded half Kent). And, as in the first dream, I am vaguely gratified at "adding to my war experience". I take out a patrol and am quite keen about it.[22]

Paul Fussell reported, "One Divisional entertainment featured a sketch titled 'The Trenches, 1950.'" "The poet Ivor Gurney is one in whose mind such dreams finally filled all the space. He had fought with the Gloucester Regiment, and was wounded and gassed in 1917. He died in a mental hospital in 1937, where he had continued to write 'war poetry,' convinced that the war was still going on."[23]

The long stalemate on the Western Front would give rise to its own irony. The German Spring Offensive of 1918 achieved the decisive break through enemy lines which each side had striven in vain for more than three years to achieve. This presumptive portent of "victory" would lead not to victory, but to the defeat of the Central Powers some eight months later. Said Corporal J.H. Tansley: "One's revulsion to the ghastly horrors of war was submerged in the belief that this war was to end all wars and Utopia would arise. What an illusion!"[24] In the greatest final irony of the War, the harsh peace exacted from and enforced upon Germany under the Versailles Treaty would lead to the conditions which led to the rise of Adolf Hitler and the Nazi Party, and then to the Second World War. Some historians now argue that the terms were not so severe, and Germany was, in any event, never required to make all the reparations payments. Even if true, this would not have mattered—to the veterans of the German Army, the members of the Freikorps, and the Nazi Brownshirts of Hitler's Sturmabteilung, the perception was that Germany lost the War due to a "stab in the back," and had been humiliated by the Versailles Treaty—perception can, indeed, be more powerful than reality.

Pity:

Pity is another theme which runs through the recollection of the War experiences of those who saw action. The soldiers who fought at the front, Officers and Other Ranks alike, were thrust into situations entirely beyond their control, often by Staff Officers in the rear who had very little appreciation of the conditions which existed at the front. They were at the whim of not only German shells, bullets, and gas, and of the horrid conditions which existed in the trenches, but also of the plans laid out for them by the Staff. As Siegfried Sassoon wrote in his poem, "The General," the "cherry old card" who "did for" both Harry and Jack "by his plan of attack." Staff Officers were distinguished from line officers by their uniforms. The bands around the caps and the lapel tabs on the tunics of the Staff Officers were bright scarlet (called "The Red Badge of Funk" by the troops[25]—being utterly unsuited for camouflage and thus denoting the wearers as those whose places were far behind the front lines), while those of the line officers were khaki. "Red tabs connoted intellectual work performed at chairs and tables; khaki tabs, regardless of rank, connoted the work of command, cajolement, and negotiation of the sort performed by shop foremen. Anyone who had seen a factory in operation could sense what was implied by these tabs."[26]

The Staff was regarded as the enemy to the rear, perhaps even more dangerous to a line soldier's life than the Germans:

> In Sassoon's poems the opposition becomes the more extreme the more he allows his focus to linger on the Staff and its gross physical, moral, and imaginative remove from the world of the troops. "Base Details" is an example, with its utterly unbridgeable distinction between "the scarlet Majors at the base" and the "glum heroes" of the line sacrificed to their inept commands.[27]

"GHQ [General Headquarters] had heard of the trenches, yes, but as the West End hears of the East End—a nasty place where common people lived."[28] There is little wonder, then, that the plight of those soldiers in the line would inspire pity. This animosity would extend to the political leaders back in England, who had been responsible for starting, and continuing, the War. As G.K. Chesterton wrote in "Elegy in a Country Churchyard," mourning for "they that fought for England" who "have their graves afar: "

> And they that rule in England,
> In stately conclave met,
> Alas, alas for England
> They have no graves as yet.

The pity does not extend to the politicians or the Staff.

Wilfred Owen, commissioned a Second Lieutenant in the Manchester Regiment on June 4, 1916, was one of the most highly regarded of the War Poets.

> Up to now, for all his disappointment about missing the university and his frustrations over money, he had been a strikingly optimistic, cheerful young man, skilled in looking on the bright side and clever at rationalizing minor setbacks. But with his first experience of the trenches in the middle of January, 1917, everything changed. What he encountered at the front was worse than even a poet's imagination could have conceived. From then on, in the less than two years left to him, the emotions that dominated were horror, outrage, and pity: horror at what he saw at the front; outrage at the inability of the civilian world— especially the church—to understand what was going on; pity for the poor, dumb, helpless, good-looking boys victimized by it all.[29]

Owen "was in and out of the line half a dozen times during the first four months of 1917, but what finally broke him was an action in late April, when

Wilfred Owen

he had to remain in a badly shelled forward position for days looking at the scattered pieces of a fellow officer's body."[30] Despite being hospitalized for neurasthenia and then assigned to light duty in England, he insisted on returning to the front. "Having seen the suffering of the men, he had to be near them. As the voice of inarticulate boys, he had to testify on their behalf."[31] He would be awarded the Military Cross in October 1918. He was killed in action on November 4, 1918, only a week before the Armistice, at age 25, by enemy machine-gun fire while crossing the Sambre à l'Oise Canal in northern France. Speaking of a terrible irony, his parents would receive the telegram announcing his death as bells were ringing in Shrewsbury in celebration of the Armistice. In his introduction to the collection of his poems, first published posthumously in 1920[32], he wrote: "My subject is War, and the pity of War. The Poetry is in the pity—" This passage is inscribed upon the slate in Poet's Corner in Westminster Abbey, commemorating the War Poets of the Great War. In his poem, "Strange Meeting," he wrote of meeting a German soldier, after both their deaths:

"Strange friend," I said, "here is no cause to mourn."
"None," said that other, "save the undone years.
The hopelessness. Whatever hope is yours,
Was my life also. . . .
For of my glee might many men have laughed,
And of my weeping something had been left,
Which must die now. I mean the truth untold,
The pity of war, the pity war distilled.

Let us sleep now. . . .

Some simply became numb. In "Insensibility: "

And some cease feeling
Even themselves or for themselves.
Dullness best solves
The tease and doubt of shelling,
And Chance's strange arithmetic

Comes simpler than the reckoning of their shilling,
They keep no check on armies' decimation.

"Chance's strange arithmetic," which takes lives at a whim. The luck of the draw which fated a man to go over the top on the Somme or at Passchendaele, or the drop of a random shell which turned Blunden's "young and cheerful lance-corporal" heating a tin of tea into a pile of charred and mangled flesh in a trench near Cambrin. But this dullness destroys empathy and robs one of pity:

> But cursed are dullards whom no cannon stuns,
> That they should be as stones;
> Wretched are they, and mean
> With paucity that never was simplicity.
> By choice they made themselves immune
> To pity and whatever mourns in man
> Before the last sea and the hapless stars;
> Whatever mourns when many leave these shores;
> Whatever shares
> The eternal reciprocity of tears.

Owen would choose the empathy which breeds despair and, perhaps, madness, over the insensibility which deprives one of human feeing.

In early October, 1918, he writes his mother to explain why he has had to come to France again: "I came out in order to help these boys—directly by leading them as well as an officer can; indirectly, by watching their sufferings that I may speak of them as well as a pleader can." And then, sensing that "their sufferings" is too abstract to do the job, he indicates what he's really talking about: "Of whose blood lies yet crimson on my shoulder where his head was—and where so lately yours was—I must not now write." But he does write about it to a less shockable audience, Sassoon: "The boy by my side, shot through the head, lay on top of me, soaking my shoulder, for half an hour." *His head. My shoulder.* An improvement over *watching their sufferings.*[33]

Every British schoolboy studying Latin would learn this line from the *Odes* of Horace: "Dulce et decorum est pro patria mori," translated as "how sweet and proper it is to die for one's country." In his poem "Dulce Et Decorum Est," Owen would relate the experience of observing a gassed and dying soldier being transported in a cart as ripping all meaning from that phrase:

> If you could hear, at every jolt, the blood
> Come gargling from the froth-corrupted lungs,
> Obscene as cancer, bitter as the cud
> Of vile, incurable sores on innocent tongues,—
> My friend, you would not tell with such high zest
> To children ardent for some desperate glory,
> The old Lie: Dulce et decorum est
> Pro patria mori.

Isaac Rosenberg

"The pity, the pity war distilled" indeed.

Unable to secure employment, Isaac Rosenberg had enlisted in the British Army in October 1915. He was assigned to the 12th "Bantam" Battalion (units of men under the usual minimum height of five feet three inches) of the Sussex Regiment. Turning down an offer to apply for an officer's commission, he was promoted to Lance Corporal and transferred to the South Lancashire Regiment and then to the King's Own Royal Lancaster Regiment, arriving in France with this unit in June 1916. After having reported sick and reassigned, he would eventually be transferred to the 1st Battalion of the King's Own Royal Regiment and go back to the front. He was killed in action on April 1, 1918, during the German Spring Offensive, and buried in a mass grave. Paul Fussell rated Rosenberg's "Break of Day in the Trenches" as "the greatest poem of the war."[34] In "Dead Man's Dump," Rosenberg wrote:

> The wheels lurched over sprawled dead
> But pained them not, though their bones
>   crunched,
> Their shut mouths made no moan,

They lie there huddled, friend and foeman,
Man born of man, and born of woman,
And shells go crying over them
From night till night and now.

This is what remains of the soldiers he speaks of in "Break of Day in the Trenches: " "Strong eyes, fine limbs, haughty athletes" who are "Less chanced than [a rat] for life":

Bonds to the whims of murder,
Sprawled in the bowels of the earth,
The torn fields of France.

They end up as pitiable corpses, strewn into a dump where they are run over by carts.

Although the pity did not extend to the politicians back in England or the Staff behind the lines, as did Owen in "Strange Meeting," Siegfried Sassoon, in his poem "Glory of Women," makes clear the pity extends to German soldiers as well as British:

O German mother dreaming by the fire,
While you are knitting socks to send your son
His face is trodden deeper in the mud.

Sassoon also turns his wrath upon the civilians, comfortably at home. In "Suicide in the Trenches," he wrote of a pitiable "simple soldier boy Who grinned at life in empty joy" who "In winter trenches, cowed and glum, with crumps and lice and lack of rum," "put a bullet through his brain:"

You smug-faced crowds with kindling eye
Who cheer when soldier lads march by,
Sneak home and pray you'll never know
The hell where youth and laughter go.

In "Blighters," Sassoon writes of a music hall show, where "harlots shrill the chorus, drunk with din;"—"'We're sure the Kaiser loves our dear old Tanks!'"

I'd like to see a Tank come down the stalls,
Lurching to rag-time tunes, or "Home, sweet Home",
And there'd be no more jokes in Music-halls
To mock the riddled corpses round Bapaume.

There is no pity for the civilians back home, either.

R. Bruce Crelin

Priestley wrote of the songs of the War, distinguishing the false patriotism of the "home front" songs from the "sardonic" ones sung by the soldiers:

> The First War, unlike the Second, produced two distinct crops of songs: one for patriotic civilians . . .; the other, not composed and copyrighted by anybody, genuine folk song, for the sardonic front-line troops. Of these some were bawdy, like the famous "Mademoiselle from Armentières" and "The Ballad of Bollocky Bill the Sailor and the Fair Young Maiden"; some were lugubrious and homesick, without patriotic sentiment of any kind, like "I Want to go Home"; others were sharply concerned with military life from the standpoint of the disillusioned private. The best of these, with its rousing chorus of "I know where he is", asked in one lilting verse after another if you wanted the officer, the sergeant-major, the quartermaster-sergeant, and so-on, and then told what these nuisances were up to. The last verse and chorus, however, changed the form and the mood, for here the battalion was the subject, and after "I know where it is" was repeated quietly there came the final reply:

> It's hanging on the old barbed wire.
> I've seen 'em, I've seen 'em,
> Hanging on the old barbed wire.

> And to this day [1962, when his book was published] I cannot listen to it unmoved. There is a flash of pure genius, entirely English, in that "old", for it means that even that devilish enemy, that deathtrap, the wire, has somehow been accepted, recognised and acknowledged almost with affection, by the deep rueful charity of this verse. I have looked through whole anthologies that said less to me.[35]

1 Hemingway, Ernest, *The Sun Also Rises* 116 (The Easton Press 1990).
2 Fussell, 18-19.
3 Fussell, 23-4.
4 Fussell, 21 (quoting Hemingway, Ernest, *A Farewell to Arms* 191 (New York 1929)).
5 Taylor, A.J.P., *The First World War* 22 (Perigee Books 1980).
6 Tuchman, 119.
7 Gilbert, 37.
8 Fussell, 19.
9 Fussell, 25 (quoting Keynes, Geoffrey (ed.), *Letters of Rupert Brooke* 625 (New York 1968)).
10 Fussell, 301.
11 Graves, 255.
12 Fussell, 25 (quoting Sitwell, Osbert, *Great Morning!* 199 (Boston 1947)).
13 Fussell, 25-6.
14 Fussell, 26 (quoting Harmsworth, Alfred, 1st Viscount Northcliffe, *Lord Northcliffe's War Book* 86 (A.L. Burt Company 1917)).

15 Fussell, 27.
16 Fussell, 29-30.
17 Fussell, 32.
18 Fussell, 30-1 (emphasis in original).
19 Blunden, Edmund, *Undertones of War* 45-6 (Folio Society 1989).
20 Fussell, 71.
21 Blunden, 17.
22 Sassoon, Siegfried, *Sherston's Progress* 52 (Folio Society 1993).
23 Fussell, 73-4.
24 Fussell, 32.
25 Fussell, 83.
26 Fussell, 83.
27 Fussell, 82-3.
28 Gibbs, Philip, *Now It Can Be Told* 245 (New York 1920).
29 Fussell, 289.
30 Fussell, 289.
31 Fussell, 290.
32 Owen, Wilfred, *Poems* (Chatto & Windus, 1920).
33 Fussell, 296 (emphasis in original) (quoting Owen, William Harold, and Bell, John, eds., *Wilfred Owen: Collected Letters* 580-1 (Oxford University Press 1967)).
34 Fussell, 250.
35 Priestley, J.B., *Margin Released: A Writer's Reminiscences and Reflections* Kindle Ed. loc. 1505-1515 (W. Heinemann 1962).

Chapter Three
A Brief History of
Universal Pictures and its Horror Films
From *Dracula* to *The Creature Walks Among Us*

Carl Laemmle was a diminutive German immigrant who bought up a string of cinemas in Chicago around the turn of the 20th Century. Bucking the Edison Patents Company, which monopolized film distribution at that time, he established his own production company, named Independent Motion Picture Company, or "IMP," in order to supply films to his cinemas. In 1912 he merged IMP, and several other independent film production outfits, into the Universal Film Manufacturing Company. In 1915, he opened Universal City, a huge studio built on the 230-acre Taylor Ranch in Los Angeles,[1] having paid $165,000 [about $4.2 million in 2019 dollars, adjusted for inflation][2] for the land.[3]

> Monday, March 15, 1915, was the gala opening day of Universal City, California. Ten thousand stars, starlets, dignitaries, reporters, extras and curiosity seekers thronged at the gates, beholding actress Laura Oakley presenting the $285 [about $7,200 in 2019 dollars, adjusted for inflation] gold key to the city to the founder, Carl Laemmle. His none-too-inspiring acceptance speech became a part of his legend and lore: "I hope I didn't make a mistake in coming out here."
>
> Laemmle opened the gates, the band played, the crowd marched in singing the "Star-Spangled Banner," cowboys galloped through the streets firing their sixshooters, a buckaroo blew up the dam of a mountain reservoir (flooding some outbuildings) and the day climaxed with a rodeo and a grand ball. Universal City—to be trumpeted by studio publicists as "an eternal monument to the vison of Carl Laemmle, pioneer picture producer",—was open for business.[4]

Laemmle named his son, Carl Jr., as head of production at Universal in 1929 as a 21st birthday present, and he would become the driving force in the front office behind Universal's Golden Age Horrors, acting as producer. Carl Sr. was not, apparently, overly fond of horror films.[5]

Universal's major star in the silent era was Lon Chaney, "The Man of 1,000 Faces." He was known for creating horrific make-up effects for such films released on the heels of the end of the First World War as *The Hunchback of Notre Dame* (1923) and *The Phantom of the Opera* (1924). Denis Gifford asked, "what was his world appeal at a time when genuine grotesques, the victims of war, begged at every street corner?"[6] Perhaps seeing contrived disfigurements on the screen was a sort of catharsis; a means of processing and dealing with emotions evoked by the genuine article.

Before the dawn of the "horror film," Universal's "prestige" picture was *All Quiet on the Western Front* (1930), based upon the novel of the same name by Erich Maria Remarque. (Carl Sr. had asked R.C. Sherriff to write the screenplay. Sherriff declined the offer.)[7] The film, directed by Lewis Milestone, tells the story of Paul Baumer (Lew Ayres), a student in Germany who, caught up with patriotic fervor on

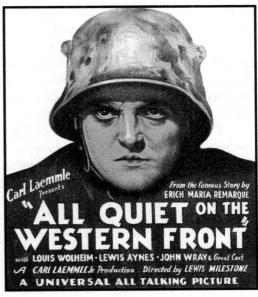

the home front, enlists in the army, only to find the horrors of war on the Western Front, disillusionment and, finally, death. The film was immensely popular and well-received and was nominated for Academy Awards for Outstanding Production (a/k/a Best Picture), Best Director, Best Writing, and Best Cinematography, winning the Awards for Outstanding Production and Best Director.

Although Remarque's novel has been hailed as a "realistic" portrayal of the horrors of the First World War, in contrasting the British "theatrical" mode of expressing war experiences with that of the German, Paul Fussell pointed out that *All Quiet* has more in common with Gothic fiction than any objective recording of facts:

> Instead of reaching toward the cool metaphor of stage plays, Remarque, in *All Quiet* . . . invoke[s] overheated figures of nightmares and call[s] upon the whole frenzied machinery of Gothic romance. Chapter 4 of *All Quiet* enacts a mad and quite un-British Gothic fantasia as a group of badly disorganized German troops is shelled in a civilian cemetery. Graves are torn asunder, coffins are hurled in the air, old cadavers are flung out—and the narrator and his chums preserve themselves by crawling into the coffins and covering themselves with the stinking cerements. This will remind us less of *Hamlet* than of, say, *The Monk*.[8]

This scene is depicted in the film, as well, although not as graphically as described by Remarque in the book. Thus, even a "prestige" film from Universal, dealing with serious themes from the Great War, manages to sneak in some elements of Gothic horror. *All Quiet on the Western Front* would also have another, more concrete, influence on Universal's horror films, from the Golden Age through the 1940s. The outside sets constructed as Paul's German hometown for *All Quiet* were used in *Frankenstein*, and virtually every subsequent Universal horror film through the mid-1940s, as the various quaint villages in Universal's non-specific Mittel-European milieu (even standing in for Wales in *The Wolf Man*).

The four films directed by James Whale, *Frankenstein*, *The Old Dark House*, *The Invisible Man*, and *Bride of Frankenstein*, will be discussed later on, in connection with an analysis of the War experiences of Whale, R.C. Sherriff, and J.B. Priestley, and how those experiences influenced these films. The discussions of the following films, and later on, of the four films directed by James Whale, contain spoilers and give away plot points. As these films are all at least six decades old, and anyone interested in this book has most likely already seen them all, I cannot imagine I am giving anything away. However, for those of you who don't want to be "spoiled," as Edward Van Sloan said in the prologue added to *Frankenstein* after it was previewed: "Well, we've warned you!" All the major Universal Horrors, from the silents through the 1950s, are available on Blu-Ray and are all stunningly rendered.

Regarding the rest of the Universal Golden Age Horror Films, as previously stated, Universal's first foray into what would later become known as "horror films" was *Dracula* (1930). The film was not, however, based directly upon the eponymous novel by Bram Stoker, but rather upon a stage play written by Hamilton Deane and later adapted by John Balderston. Universal acquired the film rights to these two plays, as well as to Stoker's book and a play commissioned by Stoker's widow, Florence, written by Charles Morrell (which David J. Skal refers to as "that ghastly vanity production of Mrs. Stoker's, the Morrell thing. . . ").[9] The film draws most of its content from the Deane and Balderston plays and bears only a passing resemblance to the novel.

In the film, Renfield (Dwight Frye) travels to Transylvania to assist Count Dracula (Bela Lugosi) with his purchase of real estate in England. Renfield tells an innkeeper (Michael Visaroff) that he must continue to the Borgo Pass that night to meet Count Dracula. The innkeeper warns him that it is Walpurgis Night—the night of evil: "No. You mustn't go there. We people of the mountains believe in the castle there are vampires. Dracula and his wives—they take the form of wolves and bats. They leave their coffins at night and they feed on the blood of the living." Despite this warning and after receiving a crucifix on a chain from the innkeeper's wife (Barbara Bozoky: "For your mother's sake"), Renfield continues on to the Borgo Pass, where he is met at midnight by Count Dracula's mysterious coach. Dracula enslaves Renfield and promises him lives—flies, spiders, and rats—and Renfield accompanies Dracula on a ship to England. Dracula gains entry to a box at the theater where he meets Dr. Seward (Herbert Bunston), his daughter, Mina (Helen Chandler), and Mina's friend,

Lucy Weston (Frances Dade). The grounds of the estate Dracula has purchased, Carfax Abbey ("It reminds me of the broken battlements of my own castle in Transylvania"), adjoin the grounds of Dr. Seward's sanitarium. After turning Lucy into a vampire, Dracula sets his sights on Mina. Mina's health begins to decline mysteriously. Dr. Seward cannot diagnose her malady, so he sends for Dr. Van Helsing (Edward Van Sloan), physician and occult expert. Van Helsing soon determines that Mina has been the victim of a vampire ("The strength of the vampire is that people will not believe in him.") and identifies Dracula as the vampire. Van Helsing and Dr. Seward, along with Mina's fiancé, Jonathan Harker (David Manners), trace Dracula to his lair. Dracula kills Renfield before he must return to his coffin, where he is staked (tastefully off camera) by Van Helsing, freeing Mina from Dracula's influence.

Dracula was directed by Tod Browning, who has been criticized as having produced a rather flat and listless production. Apart from the sequence at the beginning of the film, where the camera glides through the catacombs beneath Castle Dracula, revealing the coffins of Dracula's three vampire brides and Dracula as well (and a few misplaced opossums), the camera remains static for most of the rest of the picture, which has the character of a filmed stage play, hearkening back to the earlier tableaux of George Méliès. (This dynamic early sequence is said to have been due to the efforts of the film's cinematographer, Karl Freund, rather than of Browning's.) Still, the film contains several atmospheric scenes. Renfield arrives at Castle Dracula, where he enters a huge decaying hall (populated by a few misplaced armadillos) and is met by Dracula descending a high, broad staircase. As the wolves howl outside, Dracula says "Listen to them—children of the night. What music they make." As Renfield follows Dracula up the stairs, he paws his way through vast spiderwebs, curiously undisturbed by Dracula's passage. "The spider spinning its web for the unwary fly. The blood is the life—Mr. Renfield." Dracula offers Renfield wine: "This is very old wine." When Renfield asks the Count if he will join him in a drink, Dracula replies: "I never drink—wine." Renfield's insane laughter as he looks up from the hold of the derelict ship which has arrived at Whitby Harbor still can raise the hairs on the back of one's neck. Frye's performance was, and remains, one of the high points of the film. Edward Van Sloan makes a stolid and determined Van Helsing, even if his performance now appears a bit stiff to modern eyes. Lugosi's performance as Dracula, while now regarded as clichéd, was powerful and set an image of a vampire far different from that presented in Stoker's novel. A Spanish language version of the film, *Drácula* (1930), was shot simultaneously with the English language version, at night, using the same sets. George Melford directed Carlos Villarias as Drácula and Lupita Tovar as Eva. The Spanish version is longer than the English one and is regarded as being more visually dynamic.

Murders in the Rue Morgue (1931), set in 1845 Paris, was a project given to director Robert Florey after *Frankenstein* had been assigned to James Whale. Florey, who had lost out on his bid to direct *Frankenstein*, would direct this (very) loose adaptation of Edgar Allan Poe's short story. Lugosi, who had either been passed over for, or rejected, the role of the Monster in *Frankenstein* (whichever version you choose to believe) would play the mad Dr. Mirakle, with a curly wig and a large unibrow. Mirakle, like Caligari in *The Cabinet of Dr. Caligari* (1919) before him, has a sideshow at a carnival. Where Caligari had Cesare, the somnambulist (Conrad Veidt), Mirakle has Erik (Charles Gemora), an intelligent ape.

Gemora wears a gorilla costume, while several close-ups of Erik are of an elderly, actual chimpanzee—there is no sign of the orangutan from Poe's story. Earnest young medical student Pierre Dupin (Leon Ames, credited as Leon Waycoff), his fiancée Camille L'Espanaye (Sidney Fox), his friend Paul (Bert Roach) and Paul's girlfriend Mignette (Edna Marion), visit Dr. Mirakle's show. Mirakle gives a lecture on evolution, which is his specialty, of sorts. Erik steals Camille's bonnet, which gives Mirakle the excuse to track her down to her home.

While not performing, Mirakle is kidnapping young women and injecting them with Erik's blood in order to create a mate for the ape. Not surprisingly, they all die, and end up dumped in the Seine. We see him kidnap a streetwalker (Arlene Francis), who meets the same fate, and her body is discovered in the river. Mirakle blames the deaths on the "rotten blood" which his victims had possessed—he believes he needs a woman with "pure" blood in order for his experiments to work. He decides Camille is such a "pure" woman. Meanwhile, Dupin has analyzed the blood of the victims and determined they all contain the same foreign substance. Camille has refused Mirakle's invitation to visit Erik, so he sends the ape to her apartment to kidnap her. Dupin hears screams coming from the apartment and rushes up to find the door locked. He breaks down the door to find that both Camille and her mother are missing. The police arrive and arrest Dupin for the crime. In the only parts of the film which closely follow Poe's story, several witnesses describe the women's screams and the voice of a man, but each witness says the man was speaking a lan-

guage which the witnesses themselves do not speak. The body of Camille's mother is found stuffed up the chimney in the fireplace (in Poe's story, it was Camille's body). The body is clutching a handful of ape hair. Dupin believes this points to Mirakle, and he leads the police to the doctor's lair. Erik kills Mirakle before he can inject the ape's blood into Camille, and escapes carrying Camille. After a chase across the rooftops, Dupin rescues Camille and shoots Erik dead. Carl Jr. disliked the film, and Florey's career at Universal would end shortly after the film's release.

The Mummy (1932) introduced another of the iconic Universal Monsters. In 1921, a British archeological expedition led by Sir Joseph Whemple (Arthur Byron) is in search of artifacts. Ancient Egypt was all the rage in 1932 when this film was made. In November 1922, one year after the fictional events which begin the film, Howard Carter and his sponsor, Lord Carnarvon, found an Egyptian tomb which had lain virtually untouched for some 3,000 years. This discovery capped a search that had lasted 31 years; a quest for a tomb which the searchers were not even sure actually existed. This would prove to be the tomb of the Pharaoh Tutankhamun, known as King Tut. The world followed the story closely as fabulous artifacts, many crafted from solid gold, were removed from the tomb. It took 10 years for all the items in the tomb to be removed and cataloged. There was also said to be a curse which would befall anyone who desecrated the tomb. This idea was bolstered when Lord Carnarvon suffered an infected mosquito bite and died on April 5, 1923, little more than three months after the tomb had been opened. All this meant that a film about the discovery of a cursed mummy was timely indeed in 1932.

The 1921 Whemple expedition discovers a previously unknown, intact tomb in the Egyptian desert. The tomb contains the mummy of Im-ho-tep (Karloff). Whemple's colleague, Dr. Muller (Edward Van Sloan, essentially reprising his *Dracula* role of Dr. Van Helsing), archeologist and occult expert, remarks that the viscera had not been removed from the body before it was entombed, suggesting the subject had been buried alive. There is also a small casket accompanying the mummy, inscribed with a curse. Muller warns the party not to open this casket. Overcome by curiosity, Whemple's young assistant, Ralph Norton (Bramwell Fletcher), opens the casket and removes a papyrus scroll. This is the sacred Scroll of Thoth, the key to life, "by which Isis raised Osiris from the dead." Norton begins to read the scroll. As he reads, Im-ho-tep opens his eyes and slowly begins to move. His hand reaches toward Norton and picks up the scroll. This causes Norton to lose his reason. Whemple and Muller return to the tomb to find the mummy and the scroll both missing, and Norton laughing insanely: "He went for a little walk! You should have seen his face!"

Ten years later, in 1931, Whemple and his son, Frank (David Manners), return to Egypt to mount another expedition. They are visited by an old Egyptian man named Ardath Bey (Karloff), who shows them an artifact he says he found in the desert, which he claims points to the location of the lost tomb of the Princess Ankh-es-en-amon. Following these directions, they discover the tomb. The Princess' mummy and artifacts are removed to the Cairo Museum and put on display. Dr. Muller quickly pegs Ardath Bey as the reanimated mummy of Im-ho-tep. In ancient Egypt, he had been a High Priest in love with the Princess Ankh-es-en-amon. When she died, he stole the Scroll of Thoth in an effort to bring her back to life but was discovered before he could complete his plan. As punishment for his sacrilege he was buried alive along with the sacred scroll, and now yearns to be reunited with his lost love. He seeks Helen Grosvenor (Zita Johann), who bears an uncanny resemblance to the Princess, as her reincarnation. He hypnotizes her and she meets him at the museum. The mummy plans to embalm her to make her into a living mummy like himself, so they can go through eternity together. She begs a statue of Isis for release—the statue's arm raises and emits a burst of light, destroying the Scroll of Thoth and causing the mummy to crumble into a pile of dust.

Universal's next effort was *The Black Cat* (1934). Of all of Universal's Golden Age horror films, this one most explicitly involves the War as a main plot element. Architect Hjalmar Poelzig (Boris Karloff) lives in a forbidding art-deco mansion on top of a mountain. The house resembles a fortress, with good rea-

Former POW Werdegast (Lugosi) gets his revenge on Poelzig (Karloff) in *The Black Cat*.

son: it is built upon the foundations of the destroyed Fort Marmaros. The house, unsurprisingly, also sits upon a vast cache of explosives, contained in the lower levels of the old fort. Poelzig had been an officer in the Austro-Hungarian Army, in command of the fort during the War. He betrayed the fort to the Russians, an event which led to the death, or capture, of its entire garrison. Dr. Vitus Werdegast (Bela Lugosi) was one of the Austro-Hungarian soldiers captured after Poelzig's betrayal. After meeting the mysterious Dr. Werdegast aboard a train, honeymooning American newlyweds, mystery writer Peter Alison (David Manners) and his wife, Joan (Jacqueline Wells), travel to their next destination by bus, accompanied by Werdegast. Driven half-mad by his long stint in a Soviet prisoner-of-war camp, Werdegast has come to pay a visit to Engineer Poelzig, seeking both the wife he left when he went off to war and revenge against Poelzig, the man who had betrayed him and all his comrades. As the bus makes its way through the rain, the driver regales his three passengers with tales of the War:

> This road was built by the Austrian Army. All of this country was one of the greatest battlefields of the War. Tens of thousands of men died here. The ravine down there was piled twelve deep with dead and wounded men. The little river below was swollen red, a raging torrent of blood. That high hill, yonder, where Engineer Poelzig now lives, was the site of Fort Marma-

R. Bruce Crelin

ros. He built his home on its very foundations. Marmaros—the greatest graveyard in the world!

Of course, the bus skids off the rain-slicked road and crashes. The driver is killed, and Dr. Werdegast and Mr. and Mrs. Alison are stranded. They end up at Poelzig's mansion, as his "guests." He is a Satan worshipper, and has plans for Joan Alison at his next Black Mass. Werdegast discovers his wife is dead, her body preserved and suspended in a vertical glass coffin, along with Poelzig's other "conquests." Poelzig's current mistress is Karen, Werdegast's daughter, who soon ends up dead at Poelzig's hand. Werdegast begins to exact his revenge upon Poelzig, by flaying the skin from the Engineer's living body, "Slowly, bit by bit." Peter sees Werdegast trying to assist his wife. Misinterpreting the doctor's actions, Peter shoots Werdegast. The mortally wounded doctor pulls the lever which will detonate the charges in the lower levels of the old fort. Mr. and Mrs. Alison escape the mansion in the nick of time, just before it is blown to bits in a spectacular explosion.

Their experiences in the War had clearly affected both the film's principals in a negative way. As Poelzig says: "Did we not both die here in Marmaros 15 years ago? Are we any the less victims of the War than those whose bodies were torn asunder? Are we not both the living dead?" Curiously, however, the men involved in creating *The Black Cat* had no personal experience of the War. The screenplay is credited to Peter Ruric, based upon a story by Ruric and Edgar G. Ulmer (the film's director), "suggested by the immortal Edgar Allan Poe classic." The film, of course, has nothing whatsoever to do with Poe's short story, "The Black Cat," but its atmosphere is imbued with the bizarre sensibilities displayed in Poe's work. The only remote connection to the Poe story is that Werdegast suffers from ailurophobia ("an intense and all-consuming horror of cats"), and the occasional appearance of a black cat in Poelzig's house produces hysteria in Werdegast. Ruric, born as George Carrol Sims in Des Moines, Iowa in 1902, also wrote pulp fiction under the pen name Paul Cain. He did not serve in the First World War and was 17 years old when the War ended. Similarly, Ulmer, born in what is now the Czech Republic in 1904, was only 14 years old in 1918 and did not serve in the War. The War did provide a powerful backdrop for the film, although neither the director nor screenwriter were personally involved.

Indeed, the only notable participant in *The Black Cat* with personal experience in the War was Bela Lugosi. He served as an infantryman in the Austro-Hungarian Army from 1914-1916. According to his son, Lugosi "volunteered for service when patriotism called," and, having been wounded, was decorated with the Austro-Hungarian equivalent of the American Purple Heart.[10]

> Lugosi had served as an infantry captain and for a time in the imperial army's elite ski patrol corps on the eastern front. He

suffered three wounds, though war neurosis apparently gave him his discharge and possibly saved his life. Reports as to what happened to him vary. There has been some unsympathetic speculation that he pretended mental instability. There's no evidence that he did not suffer like millions of others. Lugosi seldom spoke at all in specific terms about the Great War, but he did tell Anna Bakacs, an actress and a romantic interest in the 1920s, that he once burrowed underneath a large pile of corpses to save himself after the Russian army overran the Hapsburg trenches.[11]

It is impossible to know for certain, but it is very likely Lugosi relied upon his own experiences in the War in crafting the haunted character of Werdegast, whose psyche had been ravaged and torn by the War.

Werewolf of London (1935) would be Universal's first foray into the legend of the lycanthrope. (At least, the first Mittel-European version of the legend. In 1913, the Universal Film Manufacturing Company had released a silent film produced by the Bison Film Company entitled *The Werewolf.* This 18-minute silent film, now believed lost, was based upon Native American lore, and involved a Navaho woman who becomes a witch, and then teaches these skills

Bela Lugosi's military photo from his Austro-Hungarian Army service

to her daughter, who is able to transform herself into a wolf to seek vengeance against invading white settlers. One hundred years later, the daughter returns to kill again.) It introduces what would become the two main tropes of the werewolf "legend: " that a bite from a werewolf will turn a victim who survives into a werewolf, and that the full moon triggers the transformation from human to werewolf. Dr. Wilfred Glendon (Henry Hull) is a renowned botanist on an expedition in Tibet seeking the rare Mariphasa lupino lumino plant, whose flowers bloom only in moonlight. He finds a specimen but is attacked and bitten by a strange looking half-human beast. Back in England, he ignores his beautiful wife, Lisa (Valerie Hobson), and spends all his time in his greenhouse, using a special moonlight lamp to attempt to get the Mariphasa plant to bloom. Although he is neglecting his wife, he becomes jealous when her old beau, Paul Ames (Lester Matthews), shows up and starts spending time with her. Glendon also meets Dr. Yogami, of the University of Carpathia (Warner Oland, probably best known for playing the title character in a series of *Charlie Chan* pictures). Yogami tells Glendon they had met previously, but Glendon does not remember. Yogami is a werewolf, and it is he who had attacked Glendon in Tibet. Yogami was also seeking the Mariphasa plant (but he calls it the "Mariphasa lumina lupina"), as its flowers are a temporary antidote to what he calls "werewolfery." Comic relief is provided by Aunt Effie (Spring Byington), and by two old ladies in a pub, Mrs. Moncaster (Zeffie Tilbury) and Mrs. Whack (Ethel Griffies). These attempts largely fall flat–a representative example from Aunt Effie: she calls Yogami "Dr. Yokohama." Mrs. Moncaster and Mrs. Whack appear to be an attempt to intro-duce some James Whale-style eccentrics—their banter is annoying rather than amusing. Yogami steals the two blooming flowers from Glendon's plant, while the third bud stubbornly refuses to bloom. Yogami tells Glendon that "the were-wolf instinctively seeks to kill the thing it loves best." Glendon finally induces the third bud on the Mariphasa to bloom, but Yogami sneaks into Glendon's lab and uses the flower on himself. Glendon catches Yogami in the act, turns into a werewolf, and kills Yogami. Glendon enters the house looking for his wife, seek-ing "to kill the thing [he] loves best." Before he can kill Lisa, Paul arrives with Col. Sir Thomas Forsythe of Scotland Yard (Lawrence Grant) and a contingent of constables, who shoot Glendon, killing him—just regular lead bullets here; no need for silver bullets fired by the hand of one who loved him this time.

The Raven (1935) is another story "inspired" by the tales of Edgar Allan Poe, while having very little to actually do with those tales. Dr. Richard Vollin (Bela Lugosi) is a brilliant surgeon who no longer actively practices. He is also an avid, indeed obsessive, collector of everything having to do with Poe. He has a stuffed raven in his study, and even has a basement equipped with a number of the torture devices described in Poe's stories. Beautiful dancer Jean Thatcher (Irene Ware) is injured in an automobile accident. Vollin is the only doctor who can operate and save her. Jean's father, Judge Thatcher (Samuel S. Hinds), begs Vollin to operate. He refuses but relents when the other doctors tell him he is the only one with the skill to operate. When he sees how beautiful she is, he envisions her as his "lost Lenore." The operation cures her, and in gratitude she invites him to the theater to see her perform her new interpretive dance, "The Spirit of Poe." Not surprisingly, Vollin becomes obsessed with Jean (he's got an unusually obsessive personality, after all). He seeks a romantic relationship with her, but the Judge steps in to put a stop to it (and Jean is none too keen on the idea, either, being engaged to Jerry Halden (Lester Matthews)).

Meanwhile, escaped killer Edmond Bateman (Boris Karloff) arrives at Vol-lin's house. Bateman wants Vollin to change his face, thinking it might change his behavior: "Maybe if a man looks ugly, he does ugly things." Vollin operates, but not in the way Bateman intended. Vollin tampers with Bateman's seventh crani-

In _The Raven_, the tide has turned and it's Lugosi being tortured by Karloff.

al nerve, making him more hideously ugly than he could have ever imagined. He reveals Bateman's new face to him by placing him in a room lined with mirrors, which Bateman proceeds to smash. "Your monstrous ugliness breeds monstrous hatred. Good! I can use your hate." Vollin plans to use Bateman to exact his revenge upon Judge Thatcher and Jerry Halden and secures his cooperation by promising to restore his face after his revenge is complete. Trapping his intended victims in his house after inviting them for dinner, Vollin straps Judge Thatcher onto a slab beneath a slowly descending, razor-sharp pendulum blade, which will drop down and kill him in 15 minutes: "I like to torture!" Vollin will arrange a "wedding" by forcing Jean and Jerry into his Poe-inspired room with converging walls, which will crush them both to death. But upon hearing that Jean will also be crushed, Bateman turns on Vollin. Bateman rescues Jean, and having been shot, explodes the torture chamber's electrical control panel. Jerry escapes from the converging walls, the Judge is released from the slab in the nick of time, and Vollin, himself, dies screaming, crushed in his own torture device, as his stuffed raven falls symbolically to the ground.

Karloff and Lugosi would team up again in _The Invisible Ray_ (1935). Astronomer Janos Rukh (Boris Karloff), has discovered a device which allows him to use beams coming from the Andromeda Galaxy to look into the distant past. Using his device, he has tracked a meteor which crashed into Africa more than a billion years ago. His demonstration to two other scientists, Dr. Felix Benet (Bela

Lugosi) and Sir Francis Stevens (Walter Kingsford), convinces them to agree to accompany Rukh on an expedition to find the meteorite. They find the crater, but when Rukh descends down to the meteorite, he receives a dose of radiation from it: the meteorite is composed of a substance called "Radium X." Exposure to the element is fatal, but also renders the touch of one exposed fatal to anyone else. Benet develops an antidote to the element's fatal effects, but not a total cure, and Rukh must take periodic doses in order to remain alive. Benet takes a piece of the meteor back and is able to harness its powers to perform medical treatments, such as a cure for blindness. Rukh, who is pursuing similar research and has used Radium X to cure his mother's (Violet Kemble Cooper) blindness, believes Benet has stolen his work. He fakes his death and proceeds to murder the members of the expedition, using a ray he has developed from Radium X. Thinking Rukh is dead, his wife, Diana (Frances Drake) marries her lover, Ronald Drake (Frank Lawton), Stevens' nephew. Rukh manages to kill Stevens and his wife, Lady Arabella Stevens (Beulah Bondi), and Benet, but cannot bring himself to kill his wife. Rukh's mother, seeing what is going on, smashes the bottle of antidote Rukh is holding before he can drink it. Consumed by radiation, he begins to burst into flames, and jumps out the window, exploding into nothingness before he hits the ground.

The next Universal Gothic Horror was *Dracula's Daughter* (1936). It would be the last to be completed before the Laemmles lost control of the studio. A sequel to *Dracula*, the film begins just after *Dracula* left off. Dr. Von (as opposed to Van, as he was in *Dracula*) Helsing (Edward Van Sloan again) is arrested in Whitby by Sergeant Wilkes (E.E. Clive) and Constable Albert (Billy Bevan) for Dracula's "murder." He is sent on to Scotland Yard, in London, where he tells Sir Basil Humphrey (Gilbert Emery) that while he had destroyed Dracula, he could not have murdered him, as he was a vampire who had been dead for many centuries. Von Helsing consults his old star pupil, psychiatrist Dr. Jeffrey Garth (Otto Kruger). Countess Marya Zaleska from Transylvania (Gloria Holden) arrives at the Whitby jail, where Dracula's body is being held. Through hypnosis, she

and her servant, Sandor (Irving Pichel) abscond with Dracula's body, taking it to the woods and cremating it. The Countess believes that this action will cure her own vampirism by eliminating Dracula's influence over her. Of course, it does not, and the Countess is soon back on the prowl, seeking blood and using her ring to hypnotize her victims. The Countess meets Dr. Garth at a party and seeks his help to overcome her condition. Garth believes he can help her if her will is strong enough to resist her urges. Of course, the attempted cure does not work, and the Countess is soon victimizing young women. Realizing she cannot fight against her vampiric urges, she kidnaps Garth's secretary, Janet (Marguerite Churchill) in order to lure Garth to her castle in Transylvania. She arrives accompanied by her servant Sandor and pursued by Von Helsing and a contingent of policemen. Garth offers to substitute his life for that of Janet's—this fits in with the Countess' plans: she intended to turn Garth into a vampire to be her eternal companion. Sandor, seeing the Countess has broken her promise to give *him* eternal life, shoots an arrow through the Countess' heart. Von Helsing arrives with the police, who shoot Sandor dead. Sir Basil Humphrey comments on the Countess' beauty. Von Helsing replies: "She was beautiful when she died—a hundred years ago."

The advent of the Great Depression in 1929 precipitated many financial reversals. Despite the success of its films, Universal was in financial difficulties by the beginning of 1933, "in sufficiently dire straits to necessitate a studio shutdown, complete with laying-off of staff and suspension of contracts."[12] These difficulties would continue in 1935, in large part caused by the cost of James Whale's lavish production of *Show Boat*, set to begin shooting late in that year:

> Back on 1 November 1935, Carl Laemmle had sought to stave off financial ruin by arranging a loan from the Standard Capital Corporation of $750,000 [about $14 million in 2019 dollars, adjusted for inflation]. There was an ominous proviso, however—that, if the necessary $5.5 million [about $101 million adjusted for inflation] could be raised within 90 days, Standard Capital would take possession of the studio. When the money wasn't available by 1 February 1936, Laemmle made the suicidal gesture of granting Standard Capital an extension. The result was that, on 14 March, four days after the completion of *Dracula's Daughter*, the Laemmles lost control of the studio.[13]

The new management at Universal declared an unofficial moratorium on horror films. "To all intents and purposes, by the end of 1936 the horror genre was dead."[14]

However, in 1938, a desperate exhibitor in Los Angeles, looking for a novelty to attract business to his theater, screened a double bill of *Dracula* and *Franken-*

stein.[15] The double bill was a huge success and spread across the entire country, with tag lines like "WE DARE YOU TO SEE THEM TOGETHER; 'DRACULA' WITH BELA LUGOSI; 'FRANKENSTEIN' WITH BORIS KARLOFF."[16] The success of this re-release spurred the New Universal to go over the old ground again, with *Son of Frankenstein* (1938). The film "is sometimes considered part of a new cycle, but its production style, mood, and theme look back and not forward."[17] The film helped Universal earn a $1 million [about $18.4 million in 2019 dollars, adjusted for inflation] profit in 1939. "Indeed, the spread on the film published in 'Look' magazine on 28 February bore a title that was to prove prophetic: 'The Son of Frankenstein Starts a New Horror Cycle.'"[18] Although made under the auspices of the New Universal, it is generally regarded as the last of the Golden Age Universal Horrors.

Son of Frankenstein tells the story of Henry Frankenstein's son, Wolf (Basil Rathbone). He has inherited his father's grounds and estates near the village of Frankenstein (it had been Oldstadt in the first film). He leaves America and arrives by train with his wife, Elsa (Josephine Hutchinson) and their young son, Peter (Donnie Dunagan). They leave the station in a downpour and meet a cold reception from the Burgomaster (Lawrence Grant) and the villagers—the memories of the havoc wreaked by the Monster are still fresh, and they fear the son may carry on his father's work. Inspector Krogh of the local police (Lionel Atwill), with a wooden right arm, arrives to warn Wolf of the villagers' fears. Wolf doubts anyone in the area had ever even seen the Monster. Krogh tells him it was "the most vivid recollection of my life" when he was a small boy, about the age of Wolf's son. The Monster had been rampaging through the countryside, broke into the house, tossed Krogh's father aside, and tore the boy's right arm out "by the roots."

While exploring the ruins of his father's old laboratory, "that weird-looking structure across the ravine" which sits atop a boiling sulphur pit, Wolf runs into Ygor (Bela Lugosi), who had been squatting in the ruins. Ygor's head is on crooked and his cervical vertebrae protrude. He was hanged ("Because I stole bodies—they said"), pronounced dead, and his body thrown into the ruins ("they wouldn't bury me in Holy place—like churchyard"). He somehow managed to survive with a broken neck. He had been using the Monster (Karloff—the last time he would play the role in a Universal horror film (although he would occasionally don the makeup on special occasions, such as in the Halloween episode of the television program *Route 66* entitled "Lizard's Leg and Owlet's Wing," which aired on October 26, 1962)) to exact revenge upon the members of the jury who had sentenced him to death ("they died—dead! I died—live!"), but the Monster was struck by lightning while out "hunting," and now moves no more. He asks Frankenstein to revive the Monster ("Your father made him, Frankenstein, and he was your father, too!"), who is Ygor's friend ("He—does things for me."). Wolf restores the Monster's mobility, which is good enough for Ygor. Wolf wants to study the Monster, but Ygor says "you won't touch him again!" Ygor soon has the Monster out on the road, exacting revenge on the remaining jurymen.

Imaginative Peter has been hunting lions, tigers, and elephants on the estate. He also saw a giant in his bedroom. He says he made up the lions, tigers, and elephants, but the giant is real. Wolf realizes the Monster is loose in the castle. Wolf's butler, Benson (Edgar Norton) has disappeared. Ygor tells Wolf that Benson saw the Monster alive and ran away, but young Peter has Benson's watch—the giant gave it to him. Krogh searches the secret passage off Peter's room and finds Benson's body. Wolf confronts Ygor, who attacks him, and Wolf shoots him (apparently fatally) in self-defense. The Monster finds Ygor's body and carries his only friend into the crypt below the laboratory. The Monster, seeking revenge for Ygor, has taken Peter into the lab and it looks as though he is getting ready to toss the boy into the sulphur pit. Krogh confronts him, and the Monster pulls off Krogh's wooden arm. Wolf swings from a hanging chain, kicking the Monster into the boiling pit of sulphur. The film ends back at the train station, with Wolf giving the castle, grounds, and estate to the village of Frankenstein before he and his family depart to return to America.

Son of Frankenstein was a lavish production, "excelling *Bride* in expense and length."[19] The film's screenplay was under constant revision even as filming was going on. Director Rowland V. Lee allowed what was to be the very minor part of Ygor to be expanded greatly, resulting in what many believe to be Bela Lugosi's best screen performance. The film would also inspire what is probably the greatest comedy horror film ever made, *Young Frankenstein* (1974). Shot in black & white to capture the feel of the old Universal films, it was directed by comedy genius Mel Brooks. Brooks would co-author the screenplay with Gene Wilder, who starred, playing Frederick Frankenstein ("that's FRONK-inn-steen"), grandson of the famous mad scientist. The film is a loving tribute to the old Universal Horrors, and this is said to be due largely to Wilder's creative efforts. A highlight of the film is Kenneth Mars' portrayal of Inspector Kemp, clearly inspired by Lionel Atwill's Krogh. Not only does Kemp sport a wooden arm, he also wears an eye patch (with a monocle on top!). The film's basic plot structure is lifted from *Son*, although it also takes bits from *Frankenstein* and *Bride of Frankenstein*, stitching things together in much the same way as Frankenstein stitched together his Monster.

Following the success of *Son of Frankenstein*, the New Universal would start another cycle of horror films, which Denis Gifford referred to as "Not a Golden Age, perhaps a Silver Bullet Age, certainly a Universal Age."[20] The New Universal's follow-up to *Son of Frankenstein* was a sequel to *The Invisible Man*, *The Invisible Man Returns* (1939). The Invisible Man, of course, did not actually "return." A mere mortal, Jack Griffin had definitely died at the end of the first film. Universal had not yet reached the point where it would resurrect mere mortals who had died in a previous movie. Rather, this one takes place some four years after Jack Griffin's death, and involves his brother, Dr. Frank Griffin (John Sutton), who is employed by a colliery owned by Geoffrey Radcliffe (Vincent Price) and his brother, Michael. Frank has the formula for the invisibility drug which his brother had invented, now called "duocaine" instead of "monocaine" (twice as good, presumably!). As the film opens, Geoffrey is in prison, only hours away from execution for the murder of his brother, a murder he did not commit. Convinced the murder was committed by someone affiliated with the family business, Geoffrey persuades Griffin to administer the invisibility drug to him. Griffin warns Geoffrey that the drug eventually causes madness, but it is the only chance for Geoffrey to avoid execution and unmask the real murderer. Griffin visits Geoffrey in prison and injects him with the drug, allowing Geoffrey to escape under the gaze of the guards. Geoffrey suspects shady colliery employee, Willie Spears (Alan Napier, best known to American audiences for his role as Alfred, Bruce Wayne's loyal butler, in the 1960s *Batman* television series), suddenly promoted to foreman, of having had some role in his brother's murder. Geoffrey frightens Spears into telling him that Geoffrey's cousin, Richard Cobb (Cedric Hardwicke), had murdered Michael and framed Geoffrey in order to take over the family business. Geoffrey, as a disembodied voice, pursues Cobb onto an elevated tramway at the colliery, and Cobb falls to his death. Police Inspector Samson (Cecil Kellaway) has fired a shot which struck Geoffrey. He is taken to the hospital, but surgery cannot be performed on an invisible man. As the colliery employees line up to volunteer to donate blood, Dr. Griffin manages to perform a transfusion on Geoffrey, which renders him visible, allowing life-saving surgery to be performed.

As would be the case with the *Mummy* films, there would be more *Invisible Man* sequels, of varying quality. *The Invisible Woman* (1940) is played strictly for laughs and has no continuity with the first two films. The next film in the series, *Invisible Agent* (1942), returns to the original Invisible Man's family tree, and provides a boost to the Allied war effort, as well. Frank (Jon Hall), Jack Griffin's grandson, has changed his surname from Griffin to Raymond and opened a print shop, in order to distance himself from his grandfather's infamy. He still has his grandfather's formula. He considers it too dangerous to use, even when

WWII and Nazis were featured in *Invisible Agent*

Nazi agents try to steal it. However, the Japanese attack on Pearl Harbor steels Frank's resolve, and he makes the formula available to the U.S. Government, on condition he can make himself invisible in order to spy on the Nazis. He proceeds to dupe the Nazis, outwit Japanese agent Baron Ikito (Peter Lorre), romance a beautiful double agent, Maria Sorensen (Ilona Massey), and foil Hitler's secret plan against the U.S. The film has an interesting concept and is certainly the best of the final three *Invisible* films.

The final installment of the series, *The Invisible Man's Revenge* (1944), stars Jon Hall again, but as a different character, psychotic escaped murderer Robert Griffin (although sharing the surname, it is uncertain whether he is Jack's relative). He turns up at the home of Sir Jasper Herrick (Lester Matthews), his wife Lady Irene (Gale Sondergaard), and their daughter Julie (Evelyn Ankers), seeking revenge. He claims they abandoned him, injured, in the jungle, leaving him to die, before going off to discover diamond fields in which he was to have been a partner. He wants his share. They claim they thought he was dead when they left him, and the diamond fields had been lost through bad investments. This isn't true. Lady Irene drugs Griffin, and while he is unconscious, Irene and Jasper go through his pockets, steal the partnership agreement for the diamond fields, and throw the unconscious Griffin into a ditch, where he nearly drowns. Helped by Herbert Higgins (Leon Errol), a passing cockney cobbler, Griffin ends up in

R. Bruce Crelin

London where he meets eccentric scientist Dr. Peter Drury (John Carradine). Drury has discovered—guess what?—a formula for invisibility—which he has used to render his dog, Brutus, invisible. He experiments on Griffin, who uses his invisibility to return to the Herrick's home and force Jasper to sign over his entire estate to Griffin. Jasper also agrees that Griffin will marry Julie in the event he attains visibility again. Griffin then goes back to Drury's lab and forces a blood transfusion from Drury, which results in Griffin becoming visible and Drury dying—in order to reverse invisibility, the transfusion must take *all* of the donor's blood. Griffin then torches the laboratory, returning to the Herricks under the pseudonym Martin Field, but Brutus has followed him there. Herbert tries to blackmail Griffin/Field, and Griffin pays him £1,000 to go away, on condition he kills Brutus before he leaves. Beginning to turn invisible again, Griffin induces Julie's fiancé, Mark Foster (Alan Curtis), to accompany him into the cellar. Griffin knocks him out and begins another transfusion, just as Jasper, Herbert, and Chief Constable Sir William Travers (Leyland Hodgson), break into the cellar in time to save Mark's life, while the still-alive Brutus attacks and kills Griffin.

After *The Invisible Man Returns* would come a sequel to, of sorts—more in the nature of a "re-imagining" of—Karloff's *The Mummy*. *The Mummy's Hand* (1940) would abandon Karloff's Im-ho-tep and his lost love, the Princess Anck-es-en-amon, in favor of a new mummy, Kharis, and a new lost love, the Princess Ananka. The prevailing opinion was that Karloff's appearance in the bandages had been all too brief in *The Mummy*—in the next film, and all its subsequent sequels, the mummy would remain under wraps throughout. Instead of being brought to life via the reading of the Scroll of Thoth, this mummy would be revived with a brew made from the sacred Tana Leaves. A flashback, taken from the Karloff film, shows Kharis as a prince who had stolen the Tana Leaves in order to bring his beloved Princess Ananka back from the dead. Caught before he could complete his plan, he was sentenced to be buried alive, and "they cut out his tongue so the ears of the Gods would not be assailed by his unholy curses." A High Priest of the Cult of Karnak was assigned to keep Kharis alive by feeding him the juice brewed from three Tana Leaves once a night during the cycle of the full moon. Should unbelievers seek to desecrate Ananka's tomb, the juice of nine Tana Leaves would give him the power of movement and the ability to prevent or avenge the desecration.

Soon after a new High Priest, Andoheb (George Zucco) has been assigned and briefed on his duties, desecrators arrive in the form of archeologist Steve Banning (Dick Foran), his sidekick (and comic relief), Babe Jenson (Wallace Ford), their financial backer, magician Solvani (Cecil Kellaway), and his lovely daughter, Marta (Peggy Moran). Andoheb revives Kharis, but both the High Priest and the mummy take a shine to Marta. Andoheb kidnaps Marta, planning to inject himself and the woman with the Tana fluid, making them both immortal. Kharis intervenes and Banning and Jenson arrive on the scene just in time. Jenson shoots Andoheb. Kharis is about to take another swig of Tana fluid

Lon Chaney is the Mummy in the Universal sequels, above *The Mummy's Tomb*

when Marta tells Banning that Kharis must not be permitted to drink. Banning shoots the container from Kharis' hands, and as Kharis stoops to the floor to try to lick up the life-giving liquid, Banning overturns an oil lamp on the mummy, who goes up in flames. Kharis was played by Tom Tyler, who had been a star of cowboy films in the silent era. By this time, however, the once athletic Tyler was wracked by arthritis; Kharis' agonized, crippled walk was all too real.[21]

The Mummy's Hand would be followed, in quick succession, by three more sequels. As these sequels progressed, they became more and more formulaic, relying increasingly upon flashbacks and footage from previous *Mummy* films. *The Mummy's Tomb* (1942), running just a hair over one hour, begins with more flashbacks, this time from *The Mummy's Hand*, as an aged Steve Banning (Dick Foran again) relays what had happened 30 years before. The scene has shifted from Egypt to Mapleton, Massachusetts. A new High Priest of Karnak, Mehemet Bey (Turhan Bey), has been initiated by Andoheb (George Zucco again, still alive and kicking after 30 years—presumably the apparently fatal gunshot wounds he suffered at the end of the last movie were not). Bey has brought Kharis from Egypt with him. The film fails to explain how this was possible, Kharis having been incinerated at the end of the last installment. Taking a job as a cemetery caretaker, Bey brews up more Tana juice and Kharis is off killing infidels again, in the form of the members of the Banning expedition, their relatives and descendants. His first victim is Steve Banning, followed swiftly by Banning's sister, Jane (Mary Gordon). Hanson (Wallace Ford again) suspects the mummy is behind the deaths, and soon convinces Banning's son, Dr. John Banning (John Hubbard), before Hanson is himself dispatched by the mummy. Once again, both Kharis and the High Priest fall for a beautiful woman—this time it's Isobel Evans (Elyse Knox), Dr. Banning's fiancée, and once again the High Priest kidnaps the woman and brings her to his lair. The townspeople, bearing torches (if these scenes look familiar, it is because they were cuts taken from *Frankenstein*!),[22] converge on the hideout. The sheriff (Cliff Clark) shoots Bey while Kharis escapes with Isobel, carrying her, for some reason, back to the Banning house. John Banning confronts Kharis with a blazing torch, forcing him to drop Isobel but at the same time setting fire to the house. John and Isobel escape from the burning house, but the townsfolk keep the mummy inside by hurling flaming torches at him. Once again, Kharis is incinerated.

And once again, despite having been incinerated at the end of the last film, Kharis is back for more in *The Mummy's Ghost* (1944), said to take place two years after the events of *The Mummy's Tomb*. Once again, the film clocks in at just over an hour. Andoheb, with the help of more flashbacks, initiates a new High Priest, Yousef Bey (John Carradine). Andoheb tells Yousef that Kharis, despite having been incinerated a second time and with no one to feed him the juice of three Tana Leaves each month during the cycle of the full moon for the past two years in order to keep him alive, still lives. Yousef must go to Mapleton, Massachusetts and brew up *nine* Tana Leaves each night during the cycle of the full moon. The fumes will somehow revive Kharis and lure him to where the brew is located. Princess Ananka's mummy is in the Scripps Museum in Massachusetts. Yousef must travel to Massachusetts, revive Kharis, dispatch the rest of the unbelievers, and return Kharis and Ananka's mummy to Egypt. Professor Norman (Frank Reicher), at the college in Mapleton, gives a lecture on his theory of how the mummy had been kept alive with a brew made from leaves from the now-extinct Tana plant. Two of Professor Norman's students, Tom Hervey (Robert Lowery) and his girlfriend, Amina Mansori (Ramsay Ames), are intrigued by the Professor's theories. Amina, who is of Egyptian descent, had been studying ancient Egyptian history, and this has raised strange feelings in her mind. Of course, it turns out that Amina is the reincarnation of Princess Ananka. Ananka's mummy has disintegrated, and her soul has migrated to Amina's body. Once again, the High Priest falls for the woman, and Kharis strenuously objects. Yousef tries to feed Tana fluid to Amina—Kharis knocks the cup away and kills the High Priest. Kharis takes Amina, who has now transformed into Ananka, and carries her away. Her hair has turned completely white and she is aging rapidly. Pursued by a mob of villagers, Kharis carries his love deeper and deeper into a swamp, where they both sink blissfully into its depths.

The Mummy's Curse (1944), with a 62-minute running time, is the final installment of Universal's *Mummy* saga. It is set 15 years after its predecessor, despite having been released only some six months later. The film begins with a miracle of groundwater migration. The bodies of Kharis and Princess Ananka, last seen sinking into a swamp in Massachusetts at the end of *The Mummy's Ghost*, have now turned up in a Bayou in Louisiana, some 1,300 miles away (perhaps this setting is a holdover from the atmosphere of 1943's *Son of Dracula*). An engineering firm is attempting to drain the swamp, but the locals protest that the area is haunted by an ancient mummy and his bride. Dr. James Halsey (Dennis Moore) of the Scripps Museum, and his associate, Dr. Ilzor Zandab (Peter Coe), arrive to seek permission from the boss of the project, Pat Walsh (Addison Richards), to search for the lost mummies of Kharis and Princess Ananka. An unfortunate worker unearths Kharis and is promptly murdered for his troubles. The mummy has been spirited away to a deserted monastery by Ragheb (Martin Kosleck), who is secretly in cahoots with Zandab. Unbeknownst to everyone, Zandab is yet another High Priest seeking to revive Kharis. Ananka's mummy (Virginia Christine), partially uncovered by a bulldozer, arises from the ground. When she immerses herself in a pond, washing away the mud and debris with which she had been covered, she is revealed to be a beautiful young woman. Cajun Joe (Kurt Katch) finds Ananka wandering through the Bayou, muttering "Kharis," and takes her to Tante Berthe's (Ann Codee) honky-tonk. Berthe puts the woman to bed, only to be killed when Kharis bursts in, causing Ananka to flee into the night. Kharis abducts Ananka, who gets the Tana juice treatment from Zandab. Ragheb makes a play for Walsh's daughter, Betty (Kay Harding). This angers Zandab, who orders Ragheb to kill Betty. He kills Zandab instead. Halsey arrives, rescuing Betty, and Kharis pulls the building down on top of himself, Ananka, and Ragheb.

Universal's four *Mummy* sequels, churned out in more and more rapid succession from 1940 through 1944, are perhaps most notable for forming the framework of the plot structure for Hammer Films' *The Mummy* (1959), which borrows primarily from *The Mummy's Hand*. The Hammer film, a far superior effort, stars Peter Cushing as archeologist John Banning and Christopher Lee as Kharis. George Pastell plays the High Priest of Karnak, Mehemet Bey, who

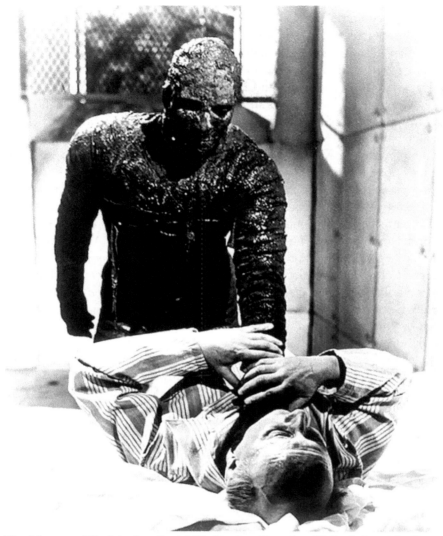

The Mummy (Christopher Lee) kills Stephen Banning (Felix Aylmer) in Hammer's
The Mummy.

brings Kharis to England to exact revenge upon the Banning party for dese-
crating Ananka's tomb, reviving him by reading the Scroll of Life (eschewing
the Tana Leaves of the Universal "sequels" and going back to the Karloff film).
Felix Aylmer plays father Stephen Banning, who has been confined to a mental
asylum since losing his reason at the dig in the desert when the mummy was discovered. Like Ralph Norton (Bramwell Fletcher) in Universal's *The Mummy*, he
revived Kharis by reading from a sacred scroll and was rendered insane observing the mummy's reawakening. He is killed by Kharis in a truly chilling scene,
where the mummy breaks into his isolation cell in the asylum. John Banning's
wife, Isobel, played by the gorgeous Yvonne Furneaux, is the image of Princess

Ananka and leads Kharis to his destruction in a swamp, echoing the ending of *The Mummy's Ghost*. The four Universal *Mummy* sequels are fun little films in their own rights, but film fans owe them a deep debt of gratitude for inspiring Hammer's masterpiece.

With *Son of Frankenstein* (1938), *Return of the Invisible Man* (1939), and *The Mummy's Hand* (1940), the New Universal has its first three horror films. "What the New Universal really needed was the New Karloff, the New Chaney. He was around; currently he was over at the Hal Roach studio, fighting a dinosaur"[23] in *One Million BC*. This new horror star would be Lon Chaney, Jr., son of the great Lon Chaney. Chaney did not want his son, Creighton Tull Chaney, to pursue an acting career, and at the time of Chaney's death young Creighton was on his way to a career in business. However, as Junior said, "the ham was there."[24] He embarked on a film career under the name Creighton Chaney, taking whatever roles came his way, including as extras, but his big break didn't come. "In 1937 he did change his name to Lon Chaney, Jr.—'They starved me into it'—but still the big break did not come."[25] In 1939 he replaced Broderick Crawford in the role of Lenny in the Los Angeles stage production of *Of Mice and Men*, giving a definitive performance. He was cast in the film version, starring alongside Burgess Meredith as George, and gave an equally impressive performance. Universal signed him to a five-year contract.

Chaney's first horror film for Universal would be *Man Made Monster* (1941). Based upon a treatment originally intended for Boris Karloff and Bela Lugosi, it was shelved as being too similar to *The Invisible Ray*.[26] With different actors, however, the New Universal decided to go forward with the project. Big Dan McCormick (Chaney) is the sole survivor of an accident in which a bus crashed into a high-tension tower. Having a natural resistance to electricity, he works in state fairs and carnival side-shows as "Dynamo Dan the Electrical Man," where he displays his abilities to withstand electric shocks. Dan is taken in by the kindly Dr. Lawrence (Samuel S. Hinds), an electro biologist who wishes to study Dan's resistance to electricity. Dan becomes infatuated with Lawrence's beautiful niece, June (Ann Nagel). Lawrence's colleague, mad scientist Dr. Rigas (Lionel Atwill), has a theory that infusing gradually more powerful electrical currents into human beings can increase their strength and lifespans, creating a race of powerful mindless beings whom Rigas can control. Dan's resistance to electricity makes him a perfect subject for Rigas' experiments. Rigas' treatments result in Dan's body being charged with electric current to the extent he begins to glow, and his touch kills. He is also under the complete control of Rigas. Without electricity, he becomes a listless hulk. Dr. Lawrence discovers Rigas' plans and tries to stop him. Rigas orders Dan to kill Lawrence, and Dan complies. Sentenced to die in the electric chair for Lawrence's murder, the massive jolt of electricity restores him to his glowing self, and he breaks free of the prison and goes off to exact his revenge upon Rigas. He kills Rigas and, donning an insulated rubber suit so his electrical charge will not dissipate, and he can touch June without killing her, he abducts June. His rubber suit tears when it is snagged on a barbed wire fence. Dan's life-giving electricity is discharged, and he dies. Barbed wire was, of course, ubiquitous on the Western Front in the Great War, but its appearance here would not seem to have any connection. It was originally developed in the middle part of the 19th Century and found its most widespread use as easily erected fencing to contain livestock. Dan's suit gets snagged on just such an agricultural fence, which provides a convenient device to both tear the rubber and provide a conductor for the electricity as it leaves his body.

Universal's next horror film would revisit, and revise, the lycanthropy theme first explored in *Werewolf of London*. This

would prove to be the defining role of Lon Chaney, Jr.'s career; what he would refer to as "my baby."[27] It would also see the "Jr." dropped from his name in the credits: from now on in the Universal Universe, he would be simply "Lon Chaney." In *The Wolf Man* (1941), Lawrence Stewart Talbot (Chaney), the second son of Sir John Talbot (Claude Rains), returns from America as heir to his ancestral home, Talbot Castle in Llanwelly, Wales, following the death of his elder brother. The relationship between father and his second son had been strained, but Sir John welcomes Larry home. After repairing his father's telescope, Larry focuses it upon the village and spies the beautiful Gwen Conliffe (Evelyn Ankers) through her bedroom window above her father's antique shop. Larry visits the shop and chats up Gwen, buying a cane topped with a silver wolf's head, inscribed with a five-pointed star in a circle, a pentagram. Gwen recites "even a man who is pure in heart and says his prayers by night may become a wolf when the wolfbane blooms and the autumn moon is bright." This bit of doggerel will be repeated several times in the film, and with some variation, in later sequels. Gypsies have arrived and set up camp near the village, with a carnival, and Larry invites Gwen to join him in a visit. Despite being engaged to local gamekeeper Frank

Andrews (Patric Knowles), she accepts. When Larry arrives that night to meet Gwen, she has brought along her friend, Jenny Williams (Fay Helm). The group visits a gypsy, Bela (Bela Lugosi), to have him tell their fortunes. When Bela looks at Jenny's palm, he sees the mark of the pentagram—a werewolf will see such a mark in the hand of his next victim—and quickly ends the fortune-telling session. While Larry and Gwen converse near a tree, they hear a blood-curdling scream. Larry runs to the scene and sees a wolf attacking Jenny. He beats the wolf with his silver-handled cane, killing it, but has been bitten on the chest in the process. The wolf has killed Jenny. Gwen finds the injured Larry and flags down an old gypsy woman, Maleva (Maria Ouspenskaya), who is passing by in a cart. Maleva brings Larry and Gwen to Talbot Castle and then quietly departs.

However, when Colonel Paul Montfort (Ralph Bellamy), the local police inspector, visits the scene of the attack, he finds not a dead wolf, but the body of Bela the Gypsy, with Larry's cane lying nearby. Larry insists he killed a wolf, and not a man, but it appears he has committed murder. When Larry opens his shirt to show Montfort the wound where the wolf had bitten him, there is nothing there. Maleva recites the following over Bela's body: "The way you walked was thorny, through no fault of your own. But as the rain enters the soil, the river enters the sea, so tears run to a predestined end. Your suffering is over, Bela, my son. Now you will find peace." Larry consults Maleva, who tells him Bela was a werewolf, and that anyone who is bitten by a werewolf and lives will become a werewolf themselves. Larry transforms into a half-man, half-wolf creature and roams the countryside committing murder, attaining human form again as the morning dawns. Larry sees the pentagram in Gwen's palm, returns to Talbot Castle and tells his father he killed Bela and will kill Gwen next. Sir John does not believe in werewolves and thinks Larry is suffering from a mental delusion. The villagers have banded together to hunt what they think is a wolf ravaging the countryside. Larry convinces his father to take the silver-handled cane with him when he joins in the hunt. As night falls, Sir John ties Larry to a chair and then leaves to meet the hunt. The moon rises, Larry transforms into a werewolf, breaks free from his bonds, and flees into the woods. He sees Gwen and begins to attack her. Hearing her screams, Sir John rushes in and beats the werewolf with the silver-handled cane. The dying werewolf transforms back into Larry, and Maleva recites her "The way you walk is thorny. . ." speech.

The Wolf Man contains much of what later came to be regarded as "authentic werewolf lore," assumed to have its origins in ancient Eastern European folk tales. This werewolf mythology was, in fact, created by the film's screenwriter, Curt Siodmak, borrowing some elements from *Werewolf of London* and adding some more of his own, and would come to be the accepted werewolf mythology for many years to come, both in Universal and other films. Chaney would go on to play Lawrence Talbot in three "proper" sequels and one Abbott & Costello film.

Universal's, and Chaney's, next horror film would be a sequel to *Son of Frankenstein*. *The Ghost of Frankenstein* (1941) takes place shortly after the events depicted in *Son*. Vengeful villagers form a mob and dynamite Frankenstein's castle in order to remove Frankenstein's "curse" from the town. Ygor (Lugosi again), who had apparently been shot to death by Wolf Frankenstein at the end of the last film, somehow manages to rise from amidst the rubble. It appears that hanging could not kill Ygor, and neither could bullets. Wandering through the catacombs beneath the ruined building, Ygor finds the Monster (Chaney). The boiling sulphur pit into which the Monster fell at the end of *Son* has now fully cooled and dried to crumbly dust. Ygor leads the Monster outside, telling him the sulphur had been good for him. As the pair walks through the forest, a violent thunderstorm breaks out. Ygor tries to get the Monster to seek shelter, but he walks out into a clearing, when lightning strikes the bolts on his neck. A lightning strike referred to in *Son of Frankenstein* caused the Monster to "move no more," but it has the opposite effect here. To Ygor's surprise, this restores the Monster's vigor: "The lightning. It is good for you! Your father was Frankenstein, but your mother was the lightning!" Ygor decides to take the Monster to Vasaria to see Frankenstein's second son, Ludwig (Cedric Hardwicke) to restore the Monster to full health. Ludwig is a "doctor of the mind," with two assistants: the kindly Dr. Kettering (Barton Yarborough) and the shady Dr. Bohmer (Lionel Atwill), who was formerly Frankenstein's teacher but now works under him due to some slight miscalculation he had once made. Their arrival in the town is a bit too high-profile, though. The Monster seeks to help a small girl recover a ball she has lost. His intentions are misinterpreted by the villagers. After a spot of mayhem, the Monster is overpowered and taken to court, where he is presumed to be an escaped lunatic. Dr. Ludwig Frankenstein is called in to examine the prisoner. He pretends not to recognize the Monster. This enrages the Monster, who breaks free and goes off with Ygor. Ygor and the Monster break into Ludwig's house. The Monster kills Dr. Kettering and grabs Ludwig's daughter, Elsa (Evelyn Ankers). Ludwig activates a knockout gas system he has installed to control unruly patients, and the Monster is subdued.

Ygor tells Ludwig to restore the Monster to full health. Ludwig, however, has decided to remedy the evil his father created by destroying the Monster. He changes his mind when his father's ghost appears to him in his laboratory, telling Ludwig not to destroy his life's work. The ghost says the Monster is evil "because unknowingly I gave it a criminal brain. With your knowledge of science, you can cure that." Ludwig resolves to replace the Monster's criminal brain with that of kindly Dr. Kettering. Dr. Bohmer is to assist with the operation, but Ygor secretly conspires with him. If Bohmer will see that Ygor's brain is taken from his own bullet-riddled, twisted, and crippled body and placed into the head of the Monster, Ygor will use his newfound strength to grant Bohmer all the wealth and power he could imagine. Bohmer switches brains, and the Monster awakes from the operation speaking in Ygor's voice: "I have the strength of a hundred men! I, Ygor, will live for ever!" Horrified, Ludwig exclaims "I've created a hundred times the Monster my father made!!" But Dr. Bohmer has made another of his "slight miscalculations:" Ygor's blood type does not match that of the Monster. This causes the Monster to go blind. "What good is a brain without eyes!" The Monster flings Bohmer into a generator, killing him. The lab bursts into flames, and the Monster is pinned under a fallen beam as fire consumes the structure.

Chaney, billed as "The New Master Character Creator,"[28] moved on to his next monster epic, *The Mummy's Tomb* (1942), already discussed above, and would play Kharis in the final two *Mummy* sequels, as well. After this would come the first of Universal's efforts of teaming its monsters, *Frankenstein Meets the Wolf Man* (1942). In an opening scene which rates as the best of the New Universal Horrors, and which would have worked just as well in the Golden Age, two grave robbers (Cyril Delevanty and Tom Stevenson) break into the Talbot family vault in the Llanwelly cemetery. It is now four years after Larry Talbot's death, and the two men have come seeking treasure which

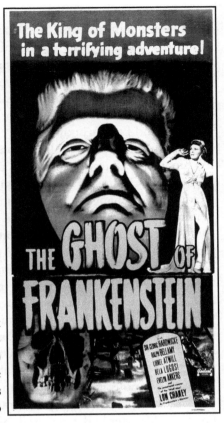

had supposedly been buried with Larry's body. When they remove the lid from the stone sarcophagus, they find Talbot's body, remarkably well-preserved, surrounded by bundles of wolfbane. As the light of the full moon shines through the windows of the crypt, a hairy hand reaches from the tomb and grabs one of the grave robbers by the wrist. [It is generally a very bad idea to seek treasure in coffins—a similar fate awaited Willie Loomis (John Karlen) when he opened vampire Barnabas Collins' (Jonathan Frid) sealed coffin in the Dan Curtis soap opera *Dark Shadows* and in the subsequent film version, *House of Dark Shadows* (1970). Willie wasn't killed, though, only enslaved by the vampire.] The other robber flees, leaving his companion to his fate. The Wolf Man ends up in the city of Cardiff, where he is found unconscious, as Talbot, with a severe head wound. Larry awakes in a hospital bed in Cardiff. Dr. Mannering (Patric Knowles) has operated on Larry, who has made a seemingly miraculous recovery from his serious injury. There is a full moon that night, Larry changes, escapes from the hospital room, and kills a policeman (Charles Irwin). Larry is found in his bed the next morning, the window in his hospital room wide open. Police Inspector Owen (Dennis Hoey, acting remarkably like Inspector Lestrade, the character he portrayed in several Basil Rathbone/Nigel Bruce *Sherlock Holmes* films) arrives in

Larry's room to investigate the murder of the constable. Larry tells Mannering and Owen about his curse, and that he is Larry Talbot from Llanwelly. Owen thinks Larry is crazy; the doctor thinks he is delusional due to his head injury. Owen calls the Llanwelly police station to check on Larry's story, and is told Lawrence Talbot had died four years earlier. Mannering and Owen travel to Llanwelly to investigate and see a photo of Larry which matches their man in the hospital. When the men visit the Talbot mausoleum, they find the sarcophagus open and Larry's body missing.

Meanwhile, Larry has been confined in a strait jacket at the hospital. The full moon rises, Larry changes, rips the strait jacket from his body with his teeth (astounding Owen and Mannering the next morning) and escapes through the window. After changing back to human form, Larry finds Maleva (Maria Ouspenskaya again). She offers to take Larry to Vasaria, to see the great Doctor Ludwig Frankenstein, who may be able to cure Larry's lycanthropy. After a long journey, they reach Vasaria, only to find that Dr. Frankenstein is dead, and his house is in ruins. Larry changes again, and as the Wolf Man falls into an icy cave below the house. He awakes in the morning as Larry, only to see Frankenstein's Monster (Bela Lugosi) encased in ice. Larry builds a fire and manages to free the Monster. He is able to communicate with the Monster and asks his help to find the records of Frankenstein's experiments, which Larry believes may contain secrets which could cure his condition. The Monster lurches about with outstretched arms, but Larry is unable to find the records. The reason for the Monster's curious gait was cut from the finished film. At the end of *The Ghost of Frankenstein*, after Ludwig had transplanted Ygor's brain into the Monster's head, the Monster had gone blind. Not only was this blindness supposed to have continued into the next film, but the Monster was also supposed to have continued speaking with Ygor's voice. However, preview audiences found the Monster speaking with Lugosi's voice to be absolutely hilarious, so all the Monster's lines were cut from the soundtrack (in some scenes, you can see Lugosi's mouth moving as though he was speaking, but no sound comes out), as were all the references to the Monster's blindness, making Lugosi's lurching about with his arms extended look particularly ridiculous.

In order to gain full access to the Frankenstein property, Talbot visits the local Burgomaster (Lionel Atwill), pretending to be interested in buying. The Mayor introduces Larry to Ludwig's daughter, Elsa Frankenstein (now a Baroness, played by Ilona Massey, rather than just plain Elsa, played by Evelyn Ankers). They agree to meet that evening at the village's "Festival of the New Wine." Dr. Mannering arrives, saying he has been following Larry and confronts him about the murders. In a rather grating performance, a villager (Adia Kuznetzoff) serenades the crowd with the "Song of the New Wine:" "For life is short and death is long, faro-la, faro-li! . . ." His song includes a jolly insult to the portly innkeeper, Vazec (Rex Evans), the host of the festivities—"He's barrel-bellied, dipper-lipped; For drinking wine, he's well-equipped; But where's his chest? It must have slipped! Faro, faro, faro-lo!" However, when he reaches Larry and Elsa and sings that he wishes them to "live eternally," Larry becomes enraged—he will "live eternally" under the curse of the werewolf, and that's the LAST thing he wants! The crowd's attention then shifts quickly from Larry's outburst to the Monster, who has arrived and goes on a rampage.

Larry and the Monster hop on a cart to make their escape, with the Monster rolling large wine casks off the back to deter pursuers. Larry, the Monster, Dr. Mannering, and Elsa all end up back at the castle. They find the Frankenstein records. Dr. Mannering has proposed using Frankenstein's apparatus to "drain their energy," thereby destroying the Monster and killing Larry, thus ending his suffering. Once he's got the Monster all hooked up, though, he changes his mind. Wanting to see Frankenstein's creation at full power, he restores the Monster's strength. Predictably, the Monster breaks free of his restraints and grabs Elsa. The full moon rises, conveniently, and Larry transforms into the Wolf Man. He attacks the Monster, who drops Elsa. The two monsters begin fighting, smashing the lab's furnishings, while Dr. Mannering and Elsa beat a hasty retreat. Meanwhile, a band of villagers, led by Vazec, has decided to remove the curse of the Frankensteins once and for all. They dynamite the dam lying above the castle, causing a torrent of water to break through the laboratory walls, washing both the Monster and the Wolf Man away.

Universal's next effort would be a "re-imagining" of its 1924 classic, *The Phantom of the Opera*. The new version, *Phantom of the Opera* (1943), would be filmed in glorious Technicolor. Rather than following the plot of the silent classic, its Phantom (Claude Rains) would get an elaborate backstory. Unlike Chaney's Erik, who was simply a disfigured madman, this Phantom would be a scorned musician. Violinist Erique Claudin has begun to lose feeling in his hand and is dismissed from the orchestra at the Paris Opera House. He is impoverished, as well, having spent his money on voice training for soprano Christine DuBois (Susanna Foster), with whom he has fallen in love. In desperation, he brings the manuscript of a concerto he has composed, his life's work, to a music publisher, Maurice Pleyel (Miles Mander), hoping to sell it. Pleyel brusquely dismisses Claudin. Hearing someone playing his composition in Pleyel's office (it is actually Franz Liszt (Fritz Lieber)), Claudin, erroneously, believes Pleyel has stolen his work. He breaks into Pleyel's office in a rage and murders him. Pleyel's assistant, Georgette (Renee Carson), throws a tray of acid in Claudin's face, horribly disfiguring him. He runs away in pain. Sought for the murder of the publisher, he hides in the sewers of Paris, making his way to the cellars of the Opera House, wearing a mask to hide his facial scarring. He secretly coaches Christine, while her dueling lovers, Anatole Garron (Nelson Eddy) and Raoul Daubert (Edgar Barrier) try to track him down.

The film was lavishly produced and was nominated for four Oscars: Best Cinematography, Color; Best Art Direction—Interior Decoration, Color; Best Sound Recording; and Best Music, Scoring of a Musical Picture, taking home

R. Bruce Crelin

the statuettes for Color Cinematography and Art Direction. The film looks marvelous, but it lacks the soul of the Lon Chaney silent version. An oft-voiced criticism, and one with which I tend to agree, is "too much opera—not enough Phantom!" Once again, it deserves a nod for inspiring a far superior version with a similar plot. As was the case with the Universal *Mummy* films, Universal's 1943 *Phantom* would inspire Hammer's *The Phantom of the Opera* (1962), starring Herbert Lom as musician Professor Petrie, who is disfigured by acid to become the Phantom, and Michael Gough as Lord Ambrose D'Arcy, the sleazy opera producer who steals Petrie's symphony and tries to have his wicked way with innocent young soprano Christine Charles (Heather Sears).

By the end of 1942, Lon Chaney had played three of Universal's "Big Five" monsters: Frankenstein's Monster, the Mummy, and the Wolf Man. He would add a fourth with Universal's next Gothic horror. *Son of Dracula* (1943) would see Chaney playing vampire Count Anthony Alucard. (Get it? In Hammer's *Dracula A.D. 1972* (1972), it would take Professor Lorrimer Van Helsing (Peter Cushing) a pad, a pencil, a pack of cigarettes, and half the night, to determine that "Alucard" is "Dracula" spelled backwards. He obviously wasn't a fan of the Universal Horrors.) Chaney does his best and is one of the first screen vampires to display great physical strength, but he is miscast as an undead Transylvanian Count. At least the film does not attempt to pass him off as Count Dracula himself. Occult expert (and Van Helsing stand-in) Professor Lazlo (J. Edward Bromberg) says Alucard is "probably a descendant of Count Dracula." Nevertheless, he appears too well-fed to be one of the undead, and too All-American to be a Transylvanian Count. He even exclaims "Put it out! Put it out, I tell ya!" as his coffin burns at the end of the picture. Still, the film contains a number of deft touches. Alucard's submerged coffin floats to the top of a pond in the Bayou and Alucard materializes on top from a wisp of smoke and rides his spooky boat into shore. The film also features Universal's first transformation of man into bat, done with the help of cartoon animation.

The film oozes atmosphere, as the Count shows up in the Bayous of Louisiana. He has come to escape the "dry and decadent" race of his homeland in favor of the "young and virile race" of America. Morose Kay Caldwell (Louise Albritton) has arranged a welcome party for the Count, whom she had met while traveling in Hungary. The train arrives with the Count's luggage, but without the Count. When he finally arrives at the house, Kay's father, Colonel Caldwell (George Irving), dies of a vampire-induced heart attack. Kay therefore inherits the family plantation, Dark Oaks. Kay breaks her engagement with life-long sweetheart Frank Stanley (Robert Paige), and becomes extremely chummy with the Count—the pair secretly marry. Meanwhile, Kay's sister, Claire (Evelyn Ankers), fearing her sister may be mentally ill, consults with family physician Dr. Harry Brewster (Frank Craven). Brewster calls his Hungarian friend, Professor Lazlo, to check Alucard's *bona fides*. The Professor soon determines that Alucard is a vampire. Frank confronts Alucard at Dark Oaks and shoots him. The bullet passes through Alucard without harming him, and hits Kay, apparently killing her. Brewster visits Dark Oaks and finds Kay in bed, still alive. But when Sheriff Dawes (Patrick Moriarity) visits the plantation the following day he finds Kay's dead body in a coffin. In jail following his arrest for Kay's murder, Frank receives a visit from Kay. Now a vampire, she tells Frank she still loves him, and only became involved with Alucard so she could become an immortal vampire. She offers to make Frank a vampire, and spend eternity with him, if he destroys Alucard. Frank escapes from jail, finds Alucard's coffin and destroys it by fire, so that the vampire cannot seek refuge there when the sun rises. He then goes to Dark Oaks and destroys Kay's body, as well.

Teaming two monsters in *Frankenstein Meets the Wolf Man* had been a hit at the box office. Why not, thought Universal, try an all-star extravaganza and throw in even more monsters. Boris Karloff would refer to Universal's next outing, *House of Frankenstein* (1944), as a "'monster clambake,' with everything thrown in—Frankenstein, Dracula, a hunchback and a 'man-beast' that howled in the night."[29] Mad scientist Dr. Gustav Niemann (Boris Karloff) is in prison for performing unnatural experiments. He regales his cellmate, the hunchback Daniel (J. Carrol Naish), with lectures on his work, in which he sought to transplant the brain of a human being into a dog. He draws elaborate notes and diagrams in chalk on the wall of the cell. He tells Daniel he can give him a new body to replace his deformed one. In an early scene, a turnkey (Charles Wagenheim) arrives to bring the prisoners their dinner—he had previously confiscated Niemann's chalk. As he nears the cell door, Niemann reaches out, grabs him by the throat and says, "give me my chalk!" The turnkey complies. A violent storm causes the wall of the cell to collapse. Niemann and Daniel take advantage of the fortuity and disappear into the dark of the night and the pouring rain. As they make their way through the woods, they come to a cart stuck in a muddy, rutted road. They help the owner get the cart moving again, and he offers them a ride. The owner of the cart is Professor Bruno Lampini (George Zucco), and the cart contains his traveling Chamber of Horrors, with its chief exhibit the coffin and skeleton of Count Dracula, with a stake through the space where his heart once was. (Again, this was a pretty impressive coup for Lampini. Universal's films were not strong on continuity; when last seen, Dracula's body was being cremated at the beginning of *Dracula's Daughter*. Lampini tells Niemann he found Dracula's staked skeleton at the vampire's castle in Transylvania—of course, at the end of *Dracula*, Van Helsing had staked the vampire at Carfax Abbey in Whitby which, in Universal's world, was apparently a suburb of London.)

In the first part of this episodic film, Niemann wants Lampini to travel on to Reigelberg so he can exact his revenge on those who had imprisoned him—revenge-seeking is a major plot element in many of the New Universal Horrors. Lampini refuses, and Niemann orders Daniel to kill him. Niemann takes Lampini's place, while Daniel poses as his assistant. They arrive in Reigelberg. Niemann removes the stake from Dracula's (John Carradine) skeleton, reviving him, but makes it quite clear he will destroy him again unless he obeys Niemann. Niemann uses Dracula to exact his revenge. Dracula, under the alias "Baron Latos," kills one of Niemann's enemies, Hussmann (Sig Ruman), the Burgomaster of Reigelberg, and seduces his daughter, Rita (Anne Gwynne). The villagers give chase, and Dracula absconds in a horse-drawn hearse, seeking to catch Lampini's caravan, which contains his coffin. Seeing the police in pursuit, Niemann unhitches the trailer from the wagon, causing it to crash, disgorging Dracula's coffin. Dracula cannot reach the coffin before the sun rises and becomes bleached bones in the sun.

The plot then moves to its second installment. Niemann and Daniel travel to the village of Frankenstein to seek Dr. Frankenstein's records in the ruins of the old castle (more continuity issues—would the records be in the ruins of Henry's and Wolf's old castle in Frankenstein, or in the ruins of Ludwig's old house in Vasaria?). On the way, they rescue a beautiful gypsy girl, Ilonka (Elena Verdugo), who was being mistreated. Daniel falls in love with the girl, but she recoils when she sees he is a hunchback. This causes Daniel to again implore Niemann to put his brain into a new body. At the castle, they discover both the Monster (Glenn Strange) and the Wolf Man (Chaney again), frozen in ice in the catacombs beneath the castle. Lon Chaney's performance as the Monster in *The Ghost of Frankenstein* was less than satisfactory and, besides, it would have been too difficult for him to play both the Monster and the Wolf Man in this film, and no one else could play his "baby," the Wolf Man. Bela Lugosi's performance in *Frankenstein Meets the Wolf Man* was even less satisfactory. The actor was aging, his health was not good, and he had difficulties moving while wearing the Monster's costume and make-up. Indeed, many of the Monster's more strenuous scenes in that film were played not by Lugosi, but rather by stunt men Gil Perkins or Eddie Parker.

The Wolf Man thaws out the Monster in _Frankenstein Meets the Wolf Man_

A new actor was needed to play the Monster, and Universal make-up specialist Jack P. Pierce found that Glenn Strange, who had appeared mostly as heavies in B-westerns (he would later play bad guy Butch Cavendish in four early episodes of _The Lone Ranger_ television series (1949-57), starring Clayton Moore and Jay Silverheels, and had a long-running part as Sam Noonan, the bartender at the Long Branch Saloon, in _Gunsmoke_ (1955-1975), in 239 episodes between 1961 and 1973), had a suitable facial contour. Boris coached his fellow cast member during the course of the production, as related by Strange:

> "Nobody ever helped anybody as much as Boris Karloff helped
> me. I never forgot that. I asked him for advice because I wanted
> to do this thing as near as he did. He would stay on the set and
> coach me on the walk and the movements and so forth."[30]

Strange actually gives a good account of himself as the Monster—several newspaper obituaries of Karloff carried a photograph of Glenn Strange as the Monster! Unfortunately, his roles as the Monster did not allow him to do very much, as he spent most of his time strapped to a gurney waiting to be revived.

After they are both thawed out, Larry Talbot agrees to help Niemann take the Monster back to his laboratory in Visaria (apparently a different place than Vasaria) in exchange for Niemann removing the werewolf curse from him. As

Niemann and Daniel tend to the Monster in the back of the wagon, Ilonka sits up front with Larry, who is driving, and falls in love with him. Along the way, Niemann kidnaps Ulman (Frank Reicher), his former lab assistant whose betrayal had sent Niemann to prison, and Strauss (Michael Mark), another of Niemann's enemies. Niemann plans to transplant Ulman's brain into the body of the Monster, and Strauss' brain into Talbot's body. This angers Daniel, who wants Niemann to put his brain into Talbot's body. Larry tells Ilonka his secret, and she knows a werewolf can only be killed by a silver bullet fired by the hand of one who loves him. Niemann revives the Monster, but once again, the full moon rises and the werewolf changes. The Wolf Man attacks Ilonka, who shoots and kills him with a silver bullet as she herself is dying. Daniel blames Niemann for the death of his beloved and attacks him. The Monster kills Daniel as the villagers arrive, bearing torches. The Monster picks up the injured Niemann and the villagers chase them into a nearby swamp, where, in an ending reminiscent of *The Mummy's Ghost*, they both sink into the quicksand.

The final installment in the New Universal's horror cycle would be another "monster clambake" (minus Karloff): *House of Dracula* (1945). This time, unlike

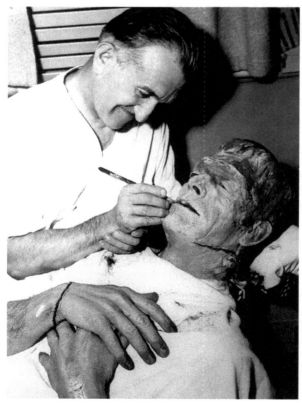

the episodic "Dracula part one, the Monster and the Wolf Man part two" structure of *House of Frankenstein*, all the monsters would be jumbled together (although the Count again finds himself being dispatched fairly early in the proceedings). Kindly Doctor Franz Edelmann (Onslow Stevens) has a clinic in Visaria. He has discovered a type of mold which will soften bone, allowing it to be re-shaped and re-formed. He intends to use it to reconfigure the spine of his hunchbacked assistant. The twist this time is that the hunchback is a woman; Edelmann's pretty nurse, Nina (Jane Adams). His biggest problem is that the mold is difficult to grow, making it

Jack Pierce creates the Monster in *House of Dracula*.

very time-consuming to obtain sufficient amounts for his

purposes. Count Dracula (John Carradine), again under the alias "Baron Latos," has come to Edelmann seeking a cure for his vampirism. Edelmann believes Dracula's vampirism is caused by a parasite in his blood, and that he can cure Dracula's condition with a series of blood transfusions.

Lawrence Talbot (Chaney again) also turns up at Edelmann's clinic, seeking a cure for his lycanthropy. The film fails to explain how he recovered from being killed at the end of the previous film with a silver bullet fired by the hand of one who loved him. Edelmann diagnoses Larry's condition as caused by pressure on his brain. Edelmann believes he can use his mold to soften and re-shape Talbot's skull, relieving the pressure and curing his lycanthropy. Due to the amount of time it takes to produce the mold, however, Edelmann will not be able to collect enough to perform the operation for another month. This will result in another cycle of the full moon, and another transformation for Larry. Despondent and not wanting to risk becoming a werewolf again, Larry attempts suicide by jumping off a cliff into the sea. Believing Larry may still be alive in one of the caves along the sea, Edelmann conducts a search, finding not only Larry, still very much alive, but also the Frankenstein Monster, clutching the skeleton of Dr. Niemann. Edelmann also discovers the cave presents the ideal conditions for growing his mold. Now that he can obtain large amounts of the mold much more quickly, he convinces Larry to return to his clinic for treatment. Edelmann will also have sufficient mold to re-shape Nina's spine.

Meanwhile, Dracula has an ulterior motive and may not really want to be cured. He has designs on Edelmann's other nurse, the gorgeous Miliza Morelle (Martha O'Driscoll). Dracula seeks to have her return with him to the land of the living dead. The perceptive Nina notices that Baron Latos casts no reflection in the mirror. She alerts Edelmann, who rushes out to save Miliza and induces Dracula to undergo another treatment. Edelmann is using himself to provide transfusions to Dracula. Dracula reverses the valves and Edelmann receives a dose of Dracula's tainted blood. Realizing what Dracula had done, Edelmann moves Dracula's coffin out into the sunlight, and Dracula becomes bleached bones in the sun once again. However, Edelmann notices himself gradually transforming into a vampire. He is normal by day, but at night the influence of Dracula's tainted blood asserts itself. Knowing he is changing, he quickly performs the operation on Talbot, which is a success—the full moon cycle comes, and for the first time since he had been bitten by Bela the Gypsy in *The Wolf Man*, Lawrence Talbot does not transform into a werewolf. Edelmann now seeks to perform his operation on Nina, but the influence of Dracula's blood now dominates him, and he is a far more vicious vampire than Dracula had been. He uses his equipment to revive the Monster. Nina tries to stop him, and Edelmann strangles her. Talbot shoots Edelmann, the Monster attacks Talbot and begins to wreck the laboratory. A fire breaks out and the Monster is trapped, as Larry and Miliza escape together into the night. Thus endeth the Universal Monster cycle which had begun in 1930.

R. Bruce Crelin

1945 would see another shake-up in the ownership of Universal. J. Arthur Rank, British entrepreneur and movie producer, arranged a four-way merger with his company, Universal, the independent film company International Pictures, and producer Kenneth Young, to form United World Pictures. This merger did not work out and was dissolved, resulting in the creation of Universal-International in mid-1946. Universal-International would revive the old Universal Monsters in comedies starring Abbott and Costello and would create one new monster of its own.

In *Abbott and Costello Meet Frankenstein* (1948), Chick Young (Bud Abbott) and Wilbur Grey (Lou Costello) would confront four of the old Universal Monsters. Chick and Wilbur are shipping clerks who receive two crates containing exhibits destined for McDougal's House of Horrors. The crates contain the bodies of the Frankenstein Monster (Glenn Strange) and Count Dracula (Bela Lugosi). The film is notable in that it would be Lugosi's second and final appearance as the Count; his only previous stint playing the part on film had been in *Dracula* (1930). Lawrence Talbot (Lon Chaney, Jr.) is on the trail of the two monsters, trying to destroy them. Despite having been cured of his lycanthropy in *House of Dracula*, Larry is back changing into a werewolf during the cycle of the full moon. The rather zany plot has Dracula and his sidekick, Dr. Sandra Mornay (Lenore Aubert), planning to put Wilbur's dim, docile, and compliant brain into the Monster, while a beautiful insurance investigator, Joan Raymond (Jane Randolph), tries to track down McDougal's missing exhibits. The film ends with Dracula and the Wolf Man plunging from a high balcony into the ocean, while the Monster is trapped on a burning pier. Chick and Wilbur escape in a boat, only to find their fellow passenger is the Invisible Man (the voice of Vincent Price). According to Gifford, Chaney disliked the film: "I used to enjoy horror films when there was thought and sympathy involved. Then they became comedies. Abbott and Costello ruined the horror field: they made buffoons out of the monsters."[31] However, looking back now after more than seven decades, *Abbott and Costello Meet Frankenstein* stands as a loving tribute and farewell to the old Universal Monsters. The pair would next meet the Invisible Man again in (what else?) *Abbott and Costello Meet the Invisible Man* (1952). In the duo's final film for Universal, *Abbott and Costello Meet the Mummy* (1955), Bud & Lou would mix it up with a mummy named Klaris (Eddie Parker), archeologist Dr. Gustav Zoomer (Kurt Katch), and evil High Priest Semu (Richard Deacon).

Universal-International would also introduce what is generally regarded as the last of the "classic" Universal Monsters. *Creature From the Black Lagoon* (1953) was shot in 3D. 3D had been a big fad in the early '50s, designed to lure audiences away from their newfangled television sets, which were becoming increasingly popular in the late 1940s and early 1950s. An archeologist, Dr. Carl Maia (Antonio Moreno), is searching for fossils in the jungles of the upper reaches of the Amazon, near the banks of one of the river's tributaries. He finds a fossil in a limestone deposit from the Devonian Period, which resembles a human forearm

Australian one-sheet for *Creature from the Black Lagoon*

bearing a webbed, clawed hand. Maia brings the fossil to the Instituto de Biologia Maritima to see if it can be identified. There he meets ichthyologist Dr. David Reed (Richard Carlson), his beautiful assistant (and fiancée) Kay Lawrence (Julia Adams), and Reed's boss, Dr. Mark Williams (Richard Denning). Believing the fossil might be some form of "missing link" between water and land animals and sensing the money and publicity which would come in the event such a creature was discovered, the overly ambitious Williams agrees to fund an expedition to fully excavate the area where the fossil was found. Maia, Williams, and Reed, along with their colleague, Dr. Edwin Thompson (Whit Bissell) and Kay Lawrence, soon find themselves on a chartered river steamer, the *Rita*, under the command of Captain Lucas (Nestor Paiva), heading towards Maia's camp.

When the party arrives at camp, they find that Luis (Rodd Redwing), one of his assistants whom Maia had left behind as a guard, has been killed; brutally mutilated, apparently by some animal. Lucas suggests that it was perhaps a jaguar (but the film has a couple of "teaser" shots of a webbed hand, looking exactly like the fossil but attached to something which is very much alive, reaching out of the water, perilously close to Kay's foot). Days of tedious digging in the limestone cliff fail to unearth any further fragments of the fossil. The party hypothesizes that part of the bank may have broken off and fallen into the river at some time in the ancient past, and that other parts of the fossil may lie in the river's bed. Lucas informs the scientists that this particular branch of the river ends in a lagoon, which the natives call the "Black Lagoon," due to the legend of a half-man, half-fish who lives there, and that anyone who goes there never returns alive. The scientists further theorize that the deposits from the bank may have gradually been washed down the river and into this lagoon. The party travels into the Black Lagoon aboard the *Rita*. David and Mark don their scuba gear and collect rock samples from the floor of the lagoon, which Carl identifies as matching the limestone deposits where the fossil was found. When Kay goes for a swim in the lagoon (wearing a white one-piece bathing suit—no one has ever looked better in a one-piece bathing suit than Julia Adams does in this film!), she is watched by a mysterious Creature, who swims below her. Sole credit for the marvelous Creature costume was taken by Universal-International's chief make-up man at the time, Bud Westmore. However, it has recently come out that the design of the costume was largely due to the efforts of one of Westmore's assistants, Millicent Patrick. Ricou Browning appeared as the Creature in the underwater scenes, while Ben Chapman wore the suit when the Creature was on dry land.

The expedition has put nets in the water to catch samples of the local fish for study. When the Creature follows Kay back toward the *Rita*, he becomes entangled in them. The people onboard catch glimpses of the Creature as he struggles in the netting, and the crew tries to winch them back aboard. When they finally come up, they are hopelessly shredded, and the Creature has escaped. David and Mark again don their scuba outfits, this time confronting the Gill-Man underwater. Mark wants to kill the Creature, fearing no one will believe it exists unless they bring back a body. David objects on the basis that the Creature would be more valuable to science alive. As this debate is going on, the Creature reaches up and grabs a crewman, Chico (Henry Escalante), dragging him overboard and killing him. Efforts to drug the Gill-Man by treating the water with a powder supplied by Lucas are only partially successful. Infatuated with Kay, the Gill-Man captures her and brings her ashore, killing Tomas (Perry Lopez), another crewman, before passing out from exposure to the drug. The party brings the Gill-Man back aboard the *Rita* and confines him in a caged tank. Of course, he escapes, grievously injuring Dr. Thompson in the process. David decides it is too risky to remain in the Black Lagoon and suggests leaving to return later with a better equipped expedition. Mark objects, but Lucas threatens him with a machete, and he backs down. However, the *Rita*'s departure is blocked by a tree which has been dragged across the opening of the lagoon. The Gill-Man prevents the party from clearing the blockage—he wants Kay to stay there. Mark and David go back into the water. Mark shoots the Gill-Man with a harpoon, but that doesn't stop the Creature from attacking, and killing, him. David goes back into the water with an air tank modified to shoot the drug mixture out under pressure and manages to subdue the Gill-Man long enough that the mouth of the lagoon can be cleared. However, just as the boat is beginning to get underway, the still groggy Gill-Man climbs on deck and grabs Kay. David follows to a cave on shore. Lucas and Maia manage to shoot the Gill-Man. David tells the men to stop firing as the Gill-Man staggers back into the water. He is last seen swimming in the lagoon, when his limbs suddenly stop moving and he sinks out of sight.

Creature From the Black Lagoon was successful enough to rate a sequel. *Revenge of the Creature* (1955) was also shot in 3D. The sequel was rushed in order to capitalize on the popularity of the first film and is a much weaker effort. One of its high points is the appearance of future superstar Clint Eastwood at the beginning of his film career, in a small role as a laboratory technician. This time, another expedition heads to the Black Lagoon. Lucas

Revenge of the Creature exhibitor handout

(Nestor Paiva again) has a new boat now, the *Rita II* (presumably his charter for the first expedition was quite lucrative). This expedition does not waste any time. As soon as they arrive, they drop dynamite into the lagoon, and the stunned Creature surfaces. The Gill-Man, in a coma, is taken to the Ocean Harbor ocean-arium in Florida. Ricou Browning again plays the Creature in the underwater action, while Tom Hennesy takes on the role for all the above-surface scenes. Ocean Harbor employee and shark wrangler Joe Hayes (John Bromfield) walks the Gill-Man around in a receiving tank, reviving him to such an extent he near-ly escapes. He is captured and chained to the bottom of a large aquarium tank containing an assortment of ocean fish. Ichthyology Professor Clete Ferguson (John Agar) and lovely graduate student Helen Dobson (Lori Nelson) undertake a program of study of the Gill-Man. Neither explains how the fresh-water Gill-Man is able to survive in a salt-water tank. Helen is the Gill-Man's love interest this time. Of course, the experiments go awry, Joe is killed, and the Gill-Man escapes from the oceanarium, overturns a car, and walks across the beach into the sea. The Gill-Man then spends his time stalking Helen, showing up outside her hotel room and killing her dog, Chris, who had gone outside to investigate. Clete and Helen, now an item, are enjoying an evening at a seaside night club when the Gill-Man bursts in, grabs Helen, and spirits her away. Search parties find Helen unconscious on the beach, where Clete manages to get her away, while the Creature is brought down in a hail of gunfire.

The Creature Walks Among Us **poster**

The next, and final, *Creature* film was not shot in 3D. The film has an interesting concept, an echo of James Whale's *Frankenstein*, which will be ex-plored later on. The monster is the sympathetic character, while one of the humans is the chief villain. *The Creature Walks Among Us* (1956) sees yet another expedition sent out to cap-ture the Gill-Man. This time, as the Creature (Ricou Browning again for the swimming scenes) climbs into one of the expedition's small motorboats, he is accidently doused with gasoline and set on fire. Badly burned, he is brought to Dr. William Barton's (Jeff Morrow) compound. The team treats the Creature's burns (the Creature, post-injuries, is played by Dan Me-gowan), but his gills have been de-stroyed by the fire. Barton discovers

the Creature has a set of small lungs, so he does a tracheostomy, allowing the Creature to breathe. Since his gills have been completely destroyed by the fire, he is no longer able to breathe underwater. As he heals, the doctors notice he has human-like skin under his scales and fingers where his webbed claws used to be. Dr. Thomas Morgan (Rex Reason) urges Barton to treat the Creature with kindness, but Barton, a quite unpleasant character, disagrees. In Barton's absence Morgan applies his theory of humane treatment, and this seems to work. The Creature becomes more docile. Indeed, he becomes a rather pitiful sight, appearing nearly human and dressed in a shapeless burlap smock. Meanwhile, Barton has become suspicious of what he believes to be an illicit relationship between his wife, Marcia (Leigh Snowden) and guide Jed Grant (Gregg Palmer). Jed mocks Barton and, while the Creature looks on, Barton kills Jed, dumping his body into the Creature's enclosure, in order that the Creature will be blamed for the killing. This enrages the Creature, who breaks free of his enclosure and pursues Barton into the house, throwing him from a second storey balcony. "Last seen the Gill-Man was heading out to sea, preserving sufficient natural instinct to steer clear of Abbott and Costello."[32]

These are, then, the major horror films of Universal, from the studio of the Laemmles, through the New Universal, and to Universal-International. There were, during this period, other Universal Horrors, mostly "B" pictures outside of the "canon" of the five (or six, counting the Gill-Man) major monsters, which are beyond the scope of this brief aside and synopsis. *Black Friday* (1940), *Horror Island* (1941), *The Black Cat* (1941), *The Night Monster* (1942), *Captive Wild Woman* (1942), *The Mad Ghoul* (1943), and others, are available on home video, many in six Blu-Ray sets recently released by Shout/Scream Factory, and worth a look.

R. Bruce Crelin

1 Gifford, 37.

2 Inflation calculations for historical U.S. dollars have been taken from the website *U.S. Inflation Calculator*, https://www.usinflationcalculator.com.

3 Riley, Philip J. (ed.), *MagicImage Filmbooks Presents Frankenstein* 11–Production Background by Gregory Wm. Mank (MagicImage Filmbooks 1989) (hereinafter "Mank, Production Background, *Frankenstein*").

4 Mank, Production Background, *Frankenstein* 11.

5 Carl Sr.'s niece, Carla, would appear in the opening scene of *Dracula* as the young woman traveling in the coach with Renfield. Ms. Laemmle lived until the age of 104, passing away in 2014.

6 Gifford, 60.

7 Curtis, James, *James Whale: A New World of Gods and Monsters* 74 (University of Minnesota Press 1998).

8 Fussell, 196.

9 Skal, David J., *Hollywood Gothic* 113 (W.W. Norton & Company 1990). Skal's book is a detailed and very enjoyable account of the convoluted story of *Dracula*, from Stoker's novel, through the stage plays, Universal's film, to other film and television treatments through 1990. I highly recommend it to anyone interested in the subject. Anyone wanting to learn more about Bram Stoker, the author of the novel, should definitely take a look at Skal's definitive biography, *Something in the Blood: The Untold Story of Bram Stoker, the Man Who Made Dracula* (Liveright Publishing Corp. 2016).

10 Osborn, Jennifer (ed.); Milano, Roy (photo captions), *Monsters: A Celebration of the Classics from Universal Studios* 38 (Del Ray Books, imprint of Random House, Inc. 2006), from an essay in the book written by Lugosi's son, Bela G. Lugosi. It has been said that lingering pain from his wounds led to the opiate addiction which would plague Lugosi in his later years.

11 Poole, loc. 4178-83.

12 Rigby, Jonathan, *American Gothic* 141 (Signum Books 2017).

13 Rigby, 171.

14 Rigby, 171.

15 Skal, David J., *The Monster Show: A Cultural History of Horror* 204 (W.W. Norton & Company 1993).

16 Skal, *The Monster Show* 202.

17 Skal, *The Monster Show* 206.

18 Rigby, 178.

19 Gifford, 124.

20 Gifford, 144.

21 Gifford, 135.

22 Gifford, 141.

23 Gifford, 131.

24 Gifford, 133.

25 Gifford, 133.

26 Gifford, 135.

27 Gifford, 136.

28 Gifford, 139.

29 Berg, Louis (May 12, 1946). "Farewell to Monsters" (PDF). *The Los Angeles Times* p. F12. Archived from the original (PDF) on September 20, 2009. Retrieved April 6, 2019.

30 Gifford, 143.

31 Gifford, 208.

32 Gifford, 177. While Denis Gifford is correct that the Creature would steer clear of Abbott & Costello on film, the Gill-Man did make an appearance with the duo on television, in a 1954 episode of *The Colgate Comedy Hour*. He also made a cameo appearance in an episode of *The Munsters*, "Love Comes to Mockingbird Heights," which aired in April 1965, as the Munsters' Uncle Gilbert.

Chapter Four
James Whale, Universal's Prime Director

As stated in the preface, four of the most significant films in Universal's Golden Age, *Frankenstein*, *The Old Dark House*, *The Invisible Man*, and *Bride of Frankenstein*, were directed by James Whale. "Had he made more than four films of this kind, he might well have established his own sub-genre (as did John Ford, Ernst Lubitsch, and Alfred Hitchcock) for he placed an indelible stylistic mark on his films that made them impossible to imitate."[1] As stated in Chapter Two, irony and pity were overriding motifs of the First World War and, in particular, of the way in which the British processed their memories of the War, and irony and pity would become chief elements in James Whale's horror films.

James Whale was born into a working-class family in "the unpromisingly bleak landscape of Dudley, Worcestershire,"[2] in the Black Country of the English Midlands, on July 22, 1889, the sixth of seven children. His father, William, was a blast furnaceman, and his mother, Sarah, a nurse.[3] He had to leave school as a teenager to work to help support his family. Too slight to work in the mines or the mills, he worked as a cobbler's assistant, raising money for himself by burning the soles of old shoes to save the nails to sell for scrap, and having a talent for art, he also earned money lettering signs for local businesses, and used his funds to attend night classes at the Dudley School of Arts and Crafts.[4]

Whale would spend most of his life attempting to distance himself from his working-class roots by assuming the identity of an upper-crust Englishman.

> Obviously talented, Whale was frustrated by the opportunities his low birth presented him with, as his friend Alan Napier recalled: "He had been a skinny, slightly undersized kid . . . . With his artistic talents and ambitions, he was a fish out of water. He had a dream." Whale began first to educate himself and then to alter his speech, eliminating the strong Black Country accent in favour of a clipped, upper-class tone. As gifted a mimic as he was, it took patience and time to effect the transformation. James Whale, the Dudley artisan, was disappearing. Whale's dream was to become an English gentleman.[5]

His efforts to transform himself were ultimately successful.

Many works mention or allude to Whale's War experience. It is a central theme, for example, underlying Christopher Bram's novel *Father of Frankenstein* and the film based upon it, *Gods and Monsters* (1998). The book, and the film, are fictionalized accounts of Whale's final days. The film shows James Whale (Ian McKellen), having his fictional gardener, Clayton Boone (Brendan Fraser), strip naked and don a World War I gas mask so that Whale can sketch him. However, I have not encountered any work which deals, in depth, with Whale's War expe-

The only photograph of James Whale in uniform which I have managed to come across. This is an enlarged section of a group photograph of British officers. James Whale appears near the center, his face partially obscured by the hat worn by the officer seated in front of him to his right, while the officer standing behind him to his left (evidently from a Scottish regiment, as he is wearing a Glengarry cap) has his right hand resting on Whale's left shoulder. This image was provided to me through the courtesy of James Whale's biographer, James Curtis. The full group photograph, from the David Lewis estate, is reproduced in Mr. Curtis' book, *James Whale: A New World of Gods and Monsters.*

riences and the influence which they may have had on his films.

When the War broke out in August 1914, James Whale was 25 years old. He was not at that time motivated to enlist, but when it became evident conscription would be instituted,[6] on October 7, 1915 he joined the Inns of Court Officer Training Corps at 10, Stone Buildings, Lincoln's Inn, London, WC as a Private, to seek a commission as an officer.[7] He is noted at the time to have been five feet, nine and a half inches tall, weighing 122 pounds.[8] He transferred to Bristol University as an officer cadet on February 26, 1916,[9] where "he was 'adopted' by a couple in Tyndall's Park who kept him in sweets and cigarettes and made sure he had a place to go on important holidays."[10] On January 21, 1916 he had applied for a commission as a Second Lieutenant, or Subaltern, in the 2/7th (Territorial) Battalion of the Worcestershire Regiment; his application was granted and he was transferred ("on probation") to the Regiment on July 21, 1916.[11]

Neither his service record,[12] nor the 2/7th War Diary (this is curious, as the War Diary is complete during the relevant period, and the arrivals of new officers were typically noted), reflects the date he actually joined the unit overseas, but it can be presumed it was within a week or so of his being transferred, as junior officers were in demand and the time to travel from England was relatively short. "Whale's commission was no mean feat for the son of a Dudley furnaceman, even allowing for the tremendously high casualty rate among junior officers on the Western Front. The life expectancy of a subaltern was three weeks."[13] Second Lieutenants were referred to as "Warts," as their rank insignia consisted of a single square diamond-shaped "pip" or "star." Originally worn on the sleeve of a flare-skirted officers' tunic, with a Sam Browne belt, riding breeches and boots, it was found this mode of dress made officers a more conspicuous target (the Germans were trained to try to shoot the officers first). It did not take long for officers to wear the same style tunics and trousers as the Other Ranks, with rank insignia moved to a less conspicuous place on the shoulders.[14] "By becoming a commissioned officer, Whale took a further step towards his goal of becoming an English gentleman. Furthermore, the war presented the chance to escape from Dudley and see something of the world, albeit under very trying circumstances."[15] "Very trying circumstances" is certainly an understatement.

At the time Whale was transferred to his unit on July 21, it was in the La Gorgue/Fauqussart/Lavantie/Neuvechapelle sector, north of Arras[16] and hence not involved in the bloody attack on the Somme. Even so, things were not easy when Second Lieutenant Whale arrived. The unit had gone into the trenches, relieving the 2/4th and 2/6th Gloucester Regiments on July 19 and 20. Entries in the 2/7th War Diary for the period when Second Lieutenant Whale joined the battalion are as follows:

July 19: Battening and standing to until we commenced relieving 2/4 and 2/6 GLOUCESTERS at—10 p.m. on left sector of FARQUASSART SECTION N14.1.N13.7

July 20: Completed relief of 2/4 & 2/6 GLOUCESTERS at 2.a.m. Repaired parapets, fetched in wounded and dead from NO MAN'S LAND and collected dead & salvage in trenches. ORK [Other Rank Killed] 1 Wounded 6. Notified from base adjutant evacuated sick to ENGLAND.

July 21: Brought in wounded man (2/4 GLOS[tr]) from NO MAN'S LAND during daylight; also wounded officer (LIEUT METCALFE 3/4 GLOS[tr]) and dead men after "stand-to" at night. Repaired parapet and collected salvage. O.R.W [Other Rank Wounded] 1

July 22: Trench routine. Battle H.Q. vacated and normal H.Q. occupied. 2 Batteries withdrawn from our immediate front. Re-wiring front—commences ORW 1 accidentally.

July 23: In addition to front already occupied today we relieved the 2/4th Battn O&B L I [Oxfordshire & Buckinghamshire Light Infantry] of the 184th Bgde with C & D Cos, our line being thus extended on left to Nad1.8. Trench routine and re-wiring the front—continues. Withdrew C Coy from DEAD END POST, being relieved by 2/8th Worcs. CAPT BUTCHER killed in action night of 23/7/16. ORW 2.

July 24: Trench routine. Re-wiring front—continued. 2/6 GLOUCESTERS sent party to retrieve their dead from NO MAN'S LAND & bury them. We supplied covering party. ORK 1 W 7.

July 25: Trench routine. Re-wiring front—continues. 2/6 GLOUCESTERS again sent party to retrieve their dead from NO MAN'S LAND & bury them, We supplying covering party. Thoroughly examined condition of wire on our front. 2nd LIEUT JOHNSTON died of wounds (received on the night of the 24/25th) in 1/2nd London [1/2nd (City of London) Battalion (Royal Fusiliers)] C.C.S. MERVILLE. O.R.W.1.

July 26: Relief by 2/4 GLOUCESTERS continued at 5 a.m. & completed by 9.30 a.m. DEADEND, HOUGOUMONT & PICANTIN POSTS taken over from 2/8th WORCESTERS & occupied by 1 platoon each. Also JOCK'S POSTS taken over at same time and occupied by 1 section.

July 27: Working parties—battening—A Coy relieved by 2/4 Glouc Rgmt & posts taken over on the 26th. B Coy took over WANGERIE, MASSELOT & ROADBEND POSTS in the afternoon from 2/4 Glouc. Regt. LIEUT HAWTRY G.H.C. & 2nd LIEUT HILL E.W. reported for duty. ORW.1 attached 183rd 183rd [sic] LTMB [Light Machine-Gun Battalion].

July 28: Working parties. Notified from base O.R.4 wounded sick to ENGLAND. 1 Serjt. transferred to A.S.C. 1 man sent to ENGLAND for evacuations

July 29: Working parties. Notified by DIV mining detachment—OR1 on the 2nd. C Coy relieved D Coy in above posts.

July 30: Working parties.

July 31: Working parties. D Coy relieved C Coy in above posts WANGERIE, MASSELOT & ROADBEND.

1.8.16: Relieved 2/8 WORC in R. section of FARQUAS-SART. Salvaged 1 Vickers Maxim 2 belts 2 boxes S.H.A. 10 rifles 1 Very pistol Bomb Bucket Equipment from NO MAN'S Land.

2.8.16: Trench routine. 1 O.R. wounded. 150 yds of front wired.

3.8.16: "450 RIFLE GRENADES fired with good results between 10 a.m. & 5 a.m. [so in original—probably should read "p.m."] 250 yds of front wired.

4.8.16: Shelled by enemy 5.9 [German artillery piece firing 5.9-inch diameter shells, known colloquially by the troops as "five-nines"] for 2 hours in afternoon. Casualties O.R. wounded 2. 100 yds of front wired.

[I would note that the two hours of shelling by German five-nines on the afternoon of August 4 most likely was in retaliation for the 450 rifle grenades fired by the 2/7th Worcesters on August 3. Regarding the less belligerent German units, there was often a "live and let live" attitude at the front—if you didn't bother them, they wouldn't bother you.]

5.8.16: Relieved by 2/8 WORC. in support at LAVANTIE. D Co in POSTS WANGERIE, MASSELOT & ROADBEND

The Great War and the Golden Age of Hollywood Horror

with 1 LEWIS GUN. Casualties wounded O.R. 2

6.8.16: Working parties. Battening. A Co in trenches at FARQUASSART. B Co in posts. 1 NCO killed. 2 OR wounded.

7.8.16: WORKING PARTIES. Battening. 1 NCO wounded. MAJOR WHITFIELD 1 HERTS T.F. [First Battalion, Hertfordshire Regiment, Territorial Forces] took over temporary command of Batt.

8.8.16: Working parties. Battening. C Co. in POSTS.

9.8.16: Relieved by 5 GLOS. Regt. At 9: 30 a.m. Moved to LE GRAND PACAUT vau L. GORGUE around 12: 15 p.m. 1 OR evacuate to ENGLAND.

10.8.16: Companies inspected by MAJOR WHITFIELD. Settling down in billets.[17]

So ended Second Lieutenant Whale's first tour in the trenches.

From August 9 until August 18, 1916 the battalion would be at "rest." This included company drill, firing on the range, practicing attacking, signaling aeroplanes, and route marches. Certainly not "restful," although at least casualties are noted as "NIL" throughout this period. On August 14, the Brigadier was present while the battalion practiced attacking. On the 15th the battalion participated in the Brigade horse show, with its members winning second prize in riding and driving, second prize in harnessing and hooking, and third prize in wrestling on horseback.[18] As an aside, although the 2/7th Battalion of the Worcesters was an infantry, and not a cavalry, unit, it still had a large contingent of horses. Horses were, after all, the main motive power for moving equipment and materiel around, pulling supply wagons, mobile kitchens, and artillery pieces. Indeed, even in the Second World War the Germans made considerable use of horses for transport work.

This period of "rest" was soon over. The battalion left on a route march from La Grand Pacaut to Croix Barbee at 2: 30 p.m. on the 17th. On the 18th they were back in the trenches:

18.8.16: Relieved 11th EAST LANCS in NEUVECHAPELLE section RT sector. Relief complete 12: 45 p.m. 2 2/8th Worcesters men joined from base. Casualties nil.

19.8.16: Trench routine casualties wounded O.R. 1.

20.8.16: Trench routine casualties wounded O.R. 2 when wiring.

21.8.16: Trench routine casualties wounded O.R. 2.[19]

On August 22, the battalion was relieved by 2/8th Worcesters and moved to the trenches in Croix Barbee, garrisoning posts at the St. Vaast, Angle, and Grotto Posts and A Company relieving the 2/8th Worcesters. One man was killed by shell fire on the 24th. On the 26th the battalion relieved the 2/5th Royal War-wicks in the Moated Grange sector, where they would remain until September 1. The entries for August 27 through the 31st all note "Trench routine," with eight Other Ranks wounded (one accidentally) on the 28th, three Other Ranks killed and one wounded on the 29th, one Other Rank wounded on the 30th and one Other Rank killed and two wounded on the 31st. The battalion was relieved by the 2/8th Worcesters on September 1 and another period of "rest" took place. This involved training, classes, church parade, a football match, and a relay race. On September 7, the 2/7th Worcesters were back in the trenches again, reliev-ing the 2/8th Worcesters in the Moated Grange sector. They were relieved on the 11th, and after another brief period of rest, moved back to Neuve Chapelle and were back in the trenches again on September 16.[20]

This pattern would continue. Relief from the trenches on the 20th, with the battalion transferred to Divisional Reserve at La Fosse. After more training, they were back in the trenches at Neuve Chapelle on September 26. Relieved by the 2/8th Worcesters on October 2, the battalion was back in reserve, training and supplying fatigue parties, until going back into the line again at Neuve Chapelle on October 8. They left the line on the 14th for billets at Croix Barbee, and then back into the line at Neuve Chapelle on the 20th. They came out of the line on the 25th and marched to billets in L'Ecleme on the 27th. On the 27th, one Other Rank would be killed and five wounded in an accident at battal-ion bombing school ("bombing" in the context of Great War British infantry meant throwing hand grenades). This would be a comparatively long period of training and marching. The battalion would leave their billets in L'Ecleme at 8 a.m. on November 1 and begin a long journey to Saint-Pierre Divion, between Thiepval and Beaumont Hamel, on the Somme front. On November 17, after the Battle of the Somme had exhausted itself, A and B Companies of the 2/7th Worcesters would relieve the East Lancashire Regiment in the reserve line of the Hansa trenches near Saint-Pierre Divion, moving into the front line trenches on the 18th, with C and D Companies moving into the support line. C and D Companies would move to the headquarters area the following day to provide a covering party for pioneers working on a new set of trenches. The battalion was relieved on the 21st and was engaged in training and working parties, moving to north of Ovillers, and would move into huts on the 30th.[21]

The 2/7th would be back in the trenches on December 5, this time in Mou-quetfarn, relieving the 2/8th Worcesters. They would be relieved on the 10th, by the 2/7th Royal Warwicks, taking over their huts north of Martinsart. On the 16th they moved off to Hedaville, where they would stay, training and engaging in working parties, moving back to Martinsart on the 22nd (the entry for the 25th notes "Working Parties. Christmas Dinner. Casualties NIL.") until going back to the line at Mouquet in relief of the 2/1st Bucks on the 28th. New Year's Day saw them in the trenches until they were relieved at night by the 2/8th Worcesters, with relief completed by 8:30 p.m. They left Martinsart on the 15th, on the march and arrived in Marcheville on the 19th. Training continued until April 2, when the battalion left Marcheville and marched ten miles into billets at Bussus-Bussuel. From the 14th to the 16th of February the battalion moved by a combination of marching, rail, and road transport to Framerville, where it went into the French sector of the line on the 17th, relieving the French 130th Infantry Regiment, with A and B Companies in the front line and C and D Companies in the support line. The battalion was relieved by the 2/6 Warwicks on February 25 and moved into billets in Harbonnieres. Training continued until March 8th, when the battalion moved to Vauvillers, where A and B Companies went into the trenches and C and D Companies into billets. On the 9th, C and D Companies moved to the front-line trenches at Chaulnes.[22]

This routine would continue, with time in the trenches broken up by periods of travel and training, until the battalion arrived at Poperinghe on August 15 and at Goldfish Camp near Ypres on August 16. On the 17th the battalion moved into the support line trenches at Wieltje, while the attack towards Passchendaele, which had begun on July 31, was grinding on. On that day, the commanding officer's horse was shot out from under him and two Other Ranks were wounded—the War Diary notes the death of the horse before the wounding of the men. The battalion continued to take casualties in the trenches near Ypres. On August 18, three Other Ranks are killed, nine are wounded and one dies of wounds previously received. The 19th would see three more Other Ranks killed, 26 wounded, and one die from wounds suffered on the 18th. The battalion was relieved on the 20th and returned to Goldfish Camp, with three Other Ranks being wounded in the process. On the 22nd the battalion would move to the support trenches at Wieltje, approximately two kilometers northeast of the town of Ypres.[23]

As recorded in the 2/7th War Diary, on August 23, 1917 the battalion relieved the 2/1st Buckinghamshire Battalion in the front-line trenches in the Wieltje sector at Ypres. In the process, nine Other Ranks were wounded, and one Other Rank is recorded as having sustained a self-inflicted wound.[24] On August 24th, one platoon of B Company attacked Aisne House, a German strongpoint in front of the British line. The attack is noted as "unsuccessful." The battalion suffered one Other Rank killed and 11 wounded, with one man dying of wounds.[25] On August 25, at 11: 00 p.m., Second Lieutenant Whale led another attack upon Aisne House, part of a broader attack involving assaults on the Schuler and Gallipoli Farms to the

French soldiers fire machine guns during the second battle of Aisne, 1917.

east.[26] As reported in the 2/7th's War Diary, in the spare language of a military despatch:

> 1 Plat [Platoon] A Coy [Company] under 2d Lt. WHALE took AISNE HOUSE but were driven out. 2 Lt. WHALE 12 OR MISSING. CASUALTIES KILLED OR 3 wounded Lieut. BLACKBURNE GMI[27] & 2/LT HUTCHINSON AN & 9 OR. OR 1 dies from wounds.[28]

Whale was captured during this raid. On a Red Cross card, part of the records which the Red Cross maintained on prisoners of war, it is noted (in French) that Whale had disappeared after an attack on August 25, 1917. His family contact is noted as his brother, "Mr. Wm Whale," address "4, Park Hill Street, Dudley, Worcs. Eng." The card further notes that, on September 19, 1917, Whale arrived at the German P.O.W. camp in Karlsruhe, having been transferred from the camp at Courtrai.[29]

As an aside, between arriving in the trenches in or around July 1916 and his capture on August 25, 1917, James Whale must have received leave to return to England. Officers typically received two weeks' leave roughly once every three months, so Whale probably had three or four periods of leave while his unit was in France. His service record is fragmentary, however, and does not contain any record of his leaves, nor is this information contained in his battalion's War Diary. The proximity of Belgium and France to England made it feasible for officers to easily return home on leave. Paul Fussell noted:

> [W]hat makes experience in the Great War unique and gives it a special freight of irony is the ridiculous proximity of the trenches to home. Just 70 miles from "this stinking world of sticky trickling earth" was the rich plush of London theater seats and the perfume, alcohol, and cigar smoke of the Café Royal. The avenue to these things was familiar and easy: on their two-week leaves from the front, the officers rode the same Channel boats they had known in peacetime, and the presence of the same porters and stewards ("Nice to serve you again, Sir") provided a ghastly pretence of normality. One officer on leave, observed by Arnold Bennett late in 1917, "had breakfasted in the trenches and dined in his club in London."[30]

One could send a hamper from Fortnum & Mason to a soldier at the front. A catalog put out by the London department store for Christmas 1915 included suggestions for boxes to prisoners-of-war ("Customers must be prepared for parcels taking, in exceptional cases, a very long time to arrive. . . . Bread having been found unsatisfactory, the Firm recommend a substantial fruit cake, called 'Scotch Bun,' . . . ").[31] Of course, an officer on leave in London could stop by the store's "Trench Requisites" Department and pick up necessaries to bring back to the front.

Following his repatriation to England, the Army undertook a routine investigation of Whale's conduct which had led to his capture. In his statement dated January 3, 1919, Whale wrote:

> Sir, On the night of August 23rd 1917 at 11: 30 p.m.[32] I was sent with two Platoons to attack a German Strong Point consisting of a concrete emplacement containing machine guns, and a trench immediately behind it manned by enemy machine gun. I reached my first objective the concrete emplacement, detailed an NCO & a section of men to occupy same (as ordered by my C.O.) then went forward to assault my second objective—the trench & M.G. By this time I had only a dozen men with me, the remainder were killed or wounded. There was a very heavy machine gun barrage coming from the enemy front both sides & when we got to within a dozen yards of my second objective I had only two men with me: —my platoon serjt. and my orderly. Telling these to lie low in a shell hole I jumped from shell hole to shell hole trying to find a few more men, stragglers or slightly wounded to make the final assault but whilst looking for my men I wandered right through the German lines & jumped into a hole (an outpost I presume) filled with Germans. I was overpowered, knocked down, disarmed & escorted back by a party of six Germans—to Germany! I am, Sir, your obedient servant, James Whale, L̷ 2/7 Worcester Regt.[33]

On July 22, 1919, the War Office completed its investigation and replied, on a pre-printed form, with Whale's name and Regiment typed in:

> The Secretary of the War Office presents his compliments to Lieutenant J. Whale, The Worcestershire Regiment. and begs to state that he is commanded by the Army Council to inform him that his statement regarding the circumstances of his capture by the enemy having been investigated, the Council considers that no blame attaches to him in the matter.

The investigation was carried out by a Standing Committee of Enquiry composed as follows: —

Major-General L.A.R. PRICE-DAVIES, V.C.[34], C.M.G.[35], D.S.O.[36]
Brigadier-General C.R.J. GRIFFITH, C.B.[37], C.M.G., D.S.O.
Brevet-Lieut.-Col. E.L. CHALLENOR, C.B., C.M.G., D.S.O.[38]

James Whale, himself, wrote a much more colorful description of this incident, and his subsequent internment in a German P.O.W. camp, in a magazine article entitled "Our Life at Holzminden" published in the August 1919 issue of *The Wide World Magazine*. The editor's introduction:

> Of the German prisoner-of-war camps one of the most notorious was that of Holzminden, in Brunswick. It was here the British officers were incarcerated, as many as a thousand being confined at one time. Our Author, who had the misfortune to be interned here, has not only set down his experiences, but in a striking series of drawings somewhat humorously portrayed life and scenes during the captivity.[39]

As "Described and Pictured" by "Our Author," "Lieut. J. Whale":

> An infantry officer expects to be killed, blown up by shell, buried alive, gassed, or at least wounded, but the prospect of becoming a prisoner of war never crosses his mind; yet here I was, a few kilos in front of Ypres, with this worst possible fate upon me.
>
> My platoon had been told off to do a "stunt on a pill-box" at midnight, and we had gone straight into a well-laid trap. It all happened so suddenly that I was stupefied and found it impossible to believe myself cut off from everything British, in the hands of the Huns, to do with me what they would—and yet it was true.
>
> To-morrow I should be reported "missing, believed killed," no longer on the company roll, and No. 2 platoon without an officer. The situation was too horrible. Half an hour ago I had brought fifty men over the top confident and certain of success, and now here I was, a prisoner of war, my job only half done and my men riddled through and through.
>
> Gradually the full horror of my position dawned on me, passed over me like a withering pestilence, and left me dazed, staring dully at the mud around my feet. There were about twenty Huns glaring down at me through the darkness, jabbering away in a horrible language; our "heavies" were still pounding away at their second line, star-shells went up as usual, bullets "pinged" close by my ears, and I was no longer part of the show; it was nothing to do with me, and I was "out."
>
> A great wave of utter hopeless despair swept over me as I realized this was the end of all my hopes; my connection with the war had been snapped and now my interest had gone. Looking back now it is a most remarkable thing to me that al-

THE WIDE WORLD

THE MAGAZINE FOR EVERYBODY

AUGUST 1919

15 CENTS

READ
Flying in
Central Africa
IN THIS NUMBER

though I was quite unconscious of noticing a single thing going on round me—I was so hopelessly "done," I didn't care what happened—I remember every little incident as clearly as if it occurred only a week ago. The jabbering Huns pulling at me from all sides, their goggly eyes gleaming with hate close to mine, their podgy hands feeling all over my body for valuables and their disappointment at finding none; then afterwards the nightmare of the journey back through their lines, the glimpses of German wounded lying in the open groaning unheeded, the haste and terror of the ten guards; every moment of the interminable journey back through mud, gas, and the thousand and one obstacles of a modern battlefield is indelibly stamped on my brain. I remember looking on at the German artillery blazing away, and wondering in a dull, stupid sort of way how many of my men they had killed.

Not until we were five or six kilos behind did my captors stop; if I stumbled in a hole I was kicked from the rear and a bayonet brought perilously near the bottom of my tunic. At length we stopped and I was pushed into an old house containing a crowd of Prussian officers, who handled me as a butcher

Allemagne Nᵒ 31. — Camp d'Holzminden (Brunswick). — Vue générale des baraquements.

German postcard showing POW barracks at Holzminden

handles a piece of pork, grinning the while over their cigars. I
was fearfully exhausted and sank down on to a box, but this so
outraged one of the senior officers that he ordered me to be
pushed outside until I could stand. No prisoner was allowed to
sit in the presence of Prussian officers.[40]

About a month after he was captured, after being interrogated and moved
through several holding facilities, Whale was placed on a train to Holzminden,
a prisoner-of-war camp established for British officers in Brunswick, Lower Saxony, at the site of a former German Army barracks.

Holzminden was a thoroughly bad camp and contained many horrors, notably Neimeyer, the Commandant, but after about three
months of captivity, when my food parcels began to come through
the Red Cross Society, I could see that underneath all the tragedy
there was quite a considerable amount of comedy to be had out of
prison life if one only took the trouble to look for it.[41]

I wonder if anyone back in England had sent Whale a hamper from Fortnum's.

It is not humorous on the face of it, for example, to be suddenly
arrested in the camp by a couple of guards and rushed off to

the dungeons below for no apparent reason, particularly when one is expecting to dine sumptuously in 10 minutes' time on bully beef, rissoles, and Oxo stew; but to the onlookers it was decidedly funny to see the victim, as the sad little procession passed the door of the house where he lived, dart in and rush up to the top floor, transform himself from a flying officer to an old sea-skipper in about two minutes and walk down coolly past the poor bewildered guard, who were puffing and blowing about in their podgy way on the first and second floor, looking for a young "flieger."

On such occasions the Commandant would come in suffering from liver and hate and look round for another victim. Wherever he rushed, however, the crowd would disperse and he would be reduced to making funny little dives among us to try and find out who was laughing so loudly and shouting one of his numerous nicknames. Some poor devil would at length be marched off in triumph by Neimeyer himself amid much cheering from the spectators.[42]

James Whale is mining comedy from tragedy, just as he would later leaven his horror films with comedy.

The article is illustrated with eight drawings by Whale (who would sell some of his drawings after the War), depicting scenes of camp life, such as prisoners huddling around stoves for warmth, preparing for the trickle of shower baths, or playing bridge. Whale "soon . . . found himself devoting his time to the production of plays, for which he could design and paint scenery, act, and participate in the writing of original material. This was, as he later said, his introduction to stagecraft, and it was at Holzminden, in the heart of enemy territory, that the drama began to gain its hold on him."[43] As he describes, along with an illustration:

James Whale titled this POW drawing "Jug."

The British Amateur Dramatic Society was always a source of great pleasure and amusement to me. The "first rehearsals" of any play—particularly a good melodrama—were about the maddest shows I have ever witnessed. To an outsider the sight

Theatricals Behind the Lines & Prison Walls

The drama at the front. Queue of French soldiers waiting for admittance to a "show" behind the lines. The theatre is an old shell-wrecked farm building, and the posters and properties are the work of local talent. Among the amusing notices on the walls is one which reads, "Counterfeit money taken here."

A little tragedy in the great tragedy. Dramatic performances given by Belgian prisoners interned at Amberg, Bavaria. The audience and orchestra, as well as the cast, consisted of allied war prisoners. In view of the amateurish material available, the talent of the actors and the scenery may be counted a very distinct success.

1916 issue of 'The War Illustrated'

of each character straining to get off his lines, shouting at the top of his voice, utterly oblivious of the rest of the cast or the poor devils next door, must have been, to say the least, a trifle "strange." I do not think I have ever been in any room where there was such an awful mess as in the Holzminden British Amateur Dramatic Society. Pots of paint, wigs, flats, and all the properties in true Bohemian confusion, and yet on show nights they jumped together like magic. It was amusing to see a great hefty fellow go into this room half an hour before the show and emerge on time as a charming young thing of eighteen summers and a Clarkson wig.[44]

The arrangements for the productions are described as follows:

On Saturday nights the officers were requested to finish their dinner by six o'clock. Whale and his colleagues would then convert the nondescript room into a space for theater. "The cups and plates were dumped in a convenient corner," said Hugh Dunford, "the tables were pushed up together to one end of the room to form a solid platform, and in an incredibly short period of time the drop scene and the wings were hoisted triumphantly. Then, after two hours' rapt forgetfulness of the surroundings, down came the final curtain, out trooped the audience, and back the tables were pushed into their respective sites. The drill was clockwork."

Photo of a James Whale theatrical production was supplied by Jeannie Barton, granddaughter of A.E.S. Barton pictured on the left dressed as a waiter. Holzminden POW camp in Lower Saxony, Germany.

HOME - JOHN

DRAMATIS - PERSONAE

SAM	(A PROFESSIONAL BLACK-MAILER)	L. R. BLUNN.
PHYLLIS		E. COOKE.
DAPHNE	CHORUS OF THE FRIVOLITY	R. P. COWAN.
WINIFRED	THEATRE	E. S. C. SEN.
SALLY		R CALDICOTT

REV. A. KYLL - JOYE	OF THE ANTI-	BARKER
REV. NOSEY - PARKER	LAUGHTER LEAGUE	H. E. GALER
SHAKESPEARE	. . . . .	HARTLEY
CHARWOMAN	. . . . .	J. WHALE

—— A N D ——

REGINALD JONES (57th LANCERS.)   G. O. Mc ENTEE
(AN ESCAPED P. OF. W.)

LIZZIE (LEADINGLADY OF A LONDON REYUE.)   H. A. YEO

CLAIRE (OF THE FRIVOLITY THEATRE, LONDON) D. G. GOLD

ORCHESTRA.

VIOLINS. Lts. CHURCH, YOUENS,   FLUTE-Serqt.MACICAY
        PURVES   .   CLARINETS - Cpl. BARNES,
VIOLA. CAPT. GRIFFITHS   Pte-RAMPTON
'CELLO. Lt. ELLISON   TROMBONE - LT SQUIRE.

CONTRABASS. Lt. LUSCOMBE. UNDER THE DIRECTION OF Lt.COOMBS

Program for Holzminden POW production of *Home - John* where Whale played a charwoman.

The plays in which Whale participated were extremely popular and he found the enthusiasm of the audience intoxicating. Even camp officials attended the shows, and the increasingly elaborate nature of the productions became something of an obsession. According to Peter Barnsley, it was not unusual for "Company" to send to Cologne for special costumes. "There was nothing that we would less willingly have foregone than our shows," said Dunford, "and the sceneshifters would have done so least of all."[45]

This theatrical experience in the camp gave Whale "a new eye toward a career in the theater. 'I couldn't have followed anything else quite so seriously after that,' he said. 'I sincerely believe that training [in the camp] meant as much to me as anything I ever learned since. The stage presented really the only possible career for me then.'"[46] Thus, Whale's War experiences led, quite literally, to his future career as a theatrical technician, stage actor and director and, later, as a film director.

Whale's other diversion was to play cards with his fellow prisoners:

Bridge was a very popular game in the evening, and after the worries of cooking I used to look forward to a few quiet rubbers with my friends. Occasionally I got them, but very rarely. To get a good game of bridge it is essential to secure comparative quiet, but this, in a room of not less than ten occupants is not an easy matter.[47]

The wagers he made on these games proved to be lucrative for him after the War.

"The news of the Armistice was received in the camp with great excitement; hats were thrown up everywhere and cheer after cheer was raised."[48] Whale and his fellow prisoners would, however, remain in Holzminden for nearly a month after the Armistice, until 9: 15 p.m. on December 8, 1918, when the former prisoners "fell in on the 'square' in four companies and marched out in columns of four."[49] They were taken by special train and then transferred to a Dutch train. "Our feelings as we actually crossed the border into Holland would be difficult to describe."[50] Greeted by cheering crowds (and Admiral Beatty) when they arrived at Hull, they listened as "[a] welcome was read out to us from the King and Queen by the Mayor of Hull from the landing-stage, and then the whole world seemed to be shouting and singing."[51] Upon returning to England, Whale was granted two months' leave, from December 15, 1918 until February 14, 1919.[52] After an additional two months in the Army, he was discharged on April 16, 1919.[53]

After returning home from the War, James Whale raised funds by collecting on notes and IOUs he had obtained in Holzminden by gambling on card games.

Many of the British officers with whom he gambled were from upper-class families and they settled their debts with, as Whale recalled, "cheques written on the back of matchboxes, shaving paper, anything." These chits, worthless in a German prison camp, were quite negotiable at home. After the Armistice and the exchange of prisoners, Whale rushed to cash the make-shift drafts he had squirreled away before any of his comrades could stop payment. He banked the money, sold what sketches he could, and amassed a lovely nest egg of several hundred pounds.[54]

He was able to sell some of his prison-camp drawings to *The Spectator* magazine and used his little nest egg to embark upon a theatrical career.[55] Housing in London being scarce and expensive, Whale found his way to Birmingham, about six miles east of his hometown of Dudley. He enrolled at the Ryland Memorial School and began to volunteer with Barry Jackson's Birmingham Repertory Company. "What he did there, at least at first, is something of a mystery."[56] "Jackson recalled that Whale was a constant backstage visitor, craving employment, until he was finally taken in."[57] Whale would spend most of his time with this troupe with the touring company production of John Drinkwater's *Abraham Lincoln*, designing the sets, working as stage manager, and occasionally playing a small role. "Although occasionally called upon to play Booth himself, Whale's regular role was that of an orderly whose only line was 'A dispatch, sir'. Determined to make an impression, he changed the inflection of the line for every performance."[58]

Whale would finally be added to the payroll of the Birmingham Repertory Company in the summer of 1919, when he entered into rehearsals for the play *The Knight of the Burning Pestle*. "It was directed by the bombastic Nigel Play-

fair, and it marked the beginning of an eight-year association with Playfair that would take Whale from the fringes of the provincial repertory movement to the heart of the West End."[59] Although his part in the play had no lines, Whale was being paid for his work and had thus become a professional actor. Whale's next role would be in a Christmas-time production of Shakespeare's *The Merry Wives of Windsor* at the Gaiety Theatre in Manchester. It was here in 1919 that Whale would meet Ernest Thesiger, who was to become his life-long friend.[60]

Original Birmingham Repertory Theatre

Ernest Frederic Graham Thesiger was born in Chelsea, London, on January 15, 1879. His family background was the complete opposite of James Whale's. Thesiger's father was Sir Edward Pierson Thesiger, K.C.B.,[61] Clerk Assistant to Parliament. His eldest brother was Arthur Lionel Bruce Thesiger, who would become a Circuit Judge; his second brother, Admiral Sir Bertram Sackville Thesiger, became Commander-in-Chief of the East India Station in 1927; and his sister, Sybil Adeline, the youngest of the children, was a member of the Assembly of the Church of England and was invested as a Member of the Order of the British Empire in 1954. His grandfather was Frederic Thesiger, 1st Lord Chelmsford, a barrister who served as Lord Chancellor of England from 1858-1859 and again from 1866-1868. His uncle, Frederic Augustus Thesiger, 2nd Lord Chelmsford, had led British troops to defeat against the Zulus in the Battle of Isandlwana. His first cousins included Frederic John Napier Thesiger, 1st Viscount Chelmsford, the Viceroy and Governor-General of India from 1916-1921, and the explorer and author Wilfred Thesiger.[62] His cousin, Wilfred Gilbert Thesiger, a British diplomat, had been Vice-Consul in Belgrade, the capital of Serbia, from 1901-06, at a time when intrigue was brewing which would eventually lead to the outbreak of the War.

Ernest Thesiger and James Whale on the set of *Bride of Frankenstein*

The hawkish Thesiger immediately took to Whale, whom he later described as "a frail ex-prisoner of war with a faun-like charm." Thesiger boasted of being clairvoyant. "Once I am switched through to a person—that is the only way I can describe the process—he or she cannot hide anything from me."

There was much, the actor discovered, that he and Whale held in common. Thesiger had gone to the Slade, where he studied to become a painter. Both men had been in the war, and both had made their professional stage debuts at the relatively late age of 30. Moreover, Thesiger, though he had married in 1917,[63] was openly homosexual. And so was James Whale.

Thesiger's influence on the younger man was profound. Whale patterned his regal bearing and royalist attitudes on those of Thesiger, and worked to diminish his regional accent as Thesiger, a Cockney,[64] had himself done. "They were both astringent," said Gavin Lambert, who knew both men, "and had similar bearings." Later, Whale would bring Thesiger to Hollywood to appear in two of his most distinguished productions. And, upon his death in 1957, it would be Ernest Thesiger who would write a memorial letter to the *Times* of London.[65]

According to UK gossip press at the time, Doris Zinkeisen was reportedly engaged to James Whale for two years.

Whale would move to Stratford-Upon-Avon in 1920, where he would perform more Shakespeare and begin to acquire knowledge of stage direction.[66] In the fall of 1921 Whale would join Playfair's Liverpool Repertory Theatre, performing in a new series of plays. Whale played the role of The Cannibal King in a production of A.A. Milne's children's review, *Make Believe*. Whale's costume for the role was designed by Doris Clare Zinkeisen, "arguably the most important female of his entire adult life."[67] "Tall, with jet-black hair and light gray eyes, Zinkeisen worked at being exotic."[68] Playfair would abruptly leave Liverpool, taking the play by Arnold Bennett, *Body and Soul*, with him to London.[69] Whale would move between Liverpool and London, acting, and designing.[70] Playfair would take *Body and Soul* to the Euston Palace of Varieties, which he renamed the Regent, "appointing Whale as assistant to Stephen Kerr Thomas, his faithful and long-suffering stage manager."[71]

Whale's natural energy, combined with a sure sense of organization and an unfailing attention to detail, served him well in getting the new theater on its feet. Almost three years after he had made his first tentative appearance on the stage at Birmingham, Whale had finally made it into London, if not quite to the Strand itself.[72]

The Great War and the Golden Age of Hollywood Horror

Elsa Lanchester (in white) at The Cave of Harmony

In 1922 Whale would appear in *Body and Soul*. Around this time, Playfair would present Karel and Josef Čapek's *The Insect Play*, which featured Doris Zinkeisen in the cast. Another of the play's cast members would become significant in James Whale's life. A young actress, artist's model, and dancer, red-haired Elsa Lanchester ran a nightclub in London with Harold Scott, at 107 Charlotte Street, called "The Cave of Harmony."

> It was a lovely firetrap, illuminated only by candlelight. Sometimes we did a midnight one-act play and sometimes we put together a cabaret show. We had a little trio of violin, piano, and drums, and when the dancing stopped, people sat on the floor to watch the show.[73]

Elsa would later, of course, play a role (actually, two roles) in one of Whale's most celebrated motion pictures. Whale was a frequent visitor to "The Cave of Harmony," as Elsa Lanchester recalled after being signed to appear in *Bride of Frankenstein*:

> And I was happy to be working with James, of course. I thought back on the Cave of Harmony days, when he was such a won-

derful tango dancer. And he always danced with Zinkheisen [sic], a very beautiful and famous painter. James and she were engaged to be married, but at some point around the time he was directing the play *Journey's End*, they parted. I don't think James Whale ever got over it. In Hollywood, James always had Zinkheisen's [sic] portrait on the end of his long dining room.[74]

Another member of the cast of *The Insect Play* who would make an appearance later on in James Whale's career was Claude Rains.[75] John Gielgud, also in the cast of *The Insect Play*, stated Whale and Zinkeisen were engaged to be married by March 1923. While Whale was not involved in the play, he "was around it by virtue of his engagement to Zinkeisen and his association with Playfair."[76] Whale and Zinkeisen were considered a couple for nearly two years. Marriage was not uncommon among homosexuals in England at that time, as consensual sexual activity between males was a criminal offense under the law until 1967. Alan Napier had said "As far as my knowledge of James goes, he was completely homosexual. . . But if he thought he and Doris Zinkeisen would make a good business combination, he might have considered marriage."[77] Zinkeisen would go on to marry Captain E. Grahame Johnstone, the managing director of Johnny Walker whisky, but Whale's friends believed "there was something truly singular about their relationship," and that "he really did love her."[78]

Whale would remain with Playfair and in October 1922 would become the stage manager for Playfair's production of John Gay's *Polly* at the Kingsway Theatre in Covent Garden. The show would move to the Savoy, and on June 12, 1923 James Whale would make his debut as a director, at a special Tuesday matinee to benefit the Library Fund of the British Drama League. The program would consist of the main feature, a four-act play entitled *The Man Who Ate the Popomack*, and a one-act play written by Drama League founder Geoffrey Whitworth entitled *Father Noah* ("a mystery of the ark"). Whale was engaged to direct the one-act play, and commissioned Doris Zinkeisen to design the costumes and the set for the hold of the ark.[79] In September he would act as "stage director," assisting the director of the Fellowship of Players production of Shakespeare's *A Winter's Tale*. However, in 1924 Whale's association with Playfair, and his engagement to Doris Zinkeisen, would end. He left London for Stoke-on-Trent, "where he would spend the remainder of the year directing amateur productions."[80]

Whale would join J.B. Fagan's Oxford Players in 1925, where he would assist Fagan working as a scenic designer. "Alan Napier, another of the company's members, said 'Jimmy was hired for the spring semester as scenery director and—he said—assistant director, but he never did any directing, as Fagan did it all.' Napier remembered appreciating Whale's 'dry, sardonic humor' and 'the feeling that this was a very talented man.'"[81] Whale also did quite a bit of acting, with his big break coming in a performance of Anton Chekhov's *The Cherry Orchard* in Oxford. Believed to be unperformable in English, Fagan determined to

Every Evening at 8.15 *o'clock*

The Cherry Orchard

A Comedy in Four Acts

BY

ANTON TCHECHOV

Translated by GEORGE CALDERON

MADAME RANEVSKY, a Landowner	MARY GREY
ANYA, her Daughter	GWENDOLEN EVANS
BARBARA, her Adopted Daughter	VIRGINIA ISHAM
LEONID GAYEF	
Brother of Madame Ranevsky	ALAN NAPIER
LOPAKHIN, a Merchant	FRED O'DONOVAN
PETER TROPHIMOF, a Student	PETER CRESWELL
SIMEONOF-PISHTCHIK, a Landowner	R. S. SMITH
CHARLOTTE, a Governess	JANE ELLIS
EPHIKHODOF, a Clerk	JAMES WHALE
DUNYASHA, a Housemaid	KATHLEEN MOSELEY
FIRS, a Manservant	O. B. CLARENCE
YASHA, a Young Manservant	BYAM SHAW
TRAMP	HERBERT LUGG

Stationmaster, Post Office Official, Guests, Servants, etc.

The Action takes place on Madame Ranevsky's Property

ACT I. A Room that is still called the Nursery

ACT II. In the Open Fields

ACT III. A Sitting Room and a Drawing Room

ACT IV. Same as Act I.

The Play produced by J. B. FAGAN

Assistant Producer...		JAMES WHALE
Stage Manager.........	for	HERBERT LUGG
Asst. Stage Manager	The Oxford Players	VIRGINIA ISHAM

stage it as a comedy. "Whale designed three minimalist sets: a nursery, an open field, and a drawing room," and was cast to play "'the clumsy Ephikhodof,' having been directed by Fagan to a near-perfect slapstick turn. Alan Napier agreed: 'He was absolutely brilliant.'"[82] Nigel Playfair then moved the show to the Lyric Theatre in London, where it opened on May 25, 1925. Whale decided to remain

R. Bruce Crelin

in London rather than return to Oxford. "The success of *The Cherry Orchard* made James Whale more employable as an actor than as a designer or director, a circumstance that was not to his advantage because his range as an actor was so decidedly narrow."[83] After *The Cherry Orchard* closed, Whale was cast in another Chekhov play, *The Seagull*. Unlike *The Cherry Orchard*, *The Seagull* was not a success and closed after 58 performances. Whale would get his second opportunity to direct a benefit performance of *Light O'Love*. This failed to jump-start Whale's directing career, and he would spend the next 18 months with Nigel Playfair.[84] After leaving Playfair again in May 1927 Whale would continue to act, design sets, and occasionally direct.

His career as a director was not very spectacular, although in late 1928 he received a visit while in his dressing room during his appearance acting in *High Treason*. The visitor was Matthew Norgate of the Incorporated Stage Society, who offered Whale a job directing a new play by a playwright who had seen active duty in the trenches, whose day job was as an "outdoor man" for the Sun Insurance Company. As it was to run for only two performances, with its director to be paid only £15 [worth about $1,380 in 2019 dollars, adjusted for inflation][85], Whale was not enthused. Nevertheless, he was persuaded to take the job, with the first performance to take place on Sunday, December 9, 1928 at the intimate Apollo Theatre at the tip of the Strand. The play was entitled *Journey's End*, and the playwright was R.C. Sherriff.[86] It would prove to be the springboard which would propel James Whale into moving to Hollywood and directing films.

1 Curtis, 2.
2 Gatiss, 1.
3 Curtis, 8-10.
4 Curtis, 12.
5 Gatiss, 3 (quoting Alan Napier, interview with Gregory Mank; quoted in *MagicImage Filmbooks Presents Frankenstein*).
6 The Military Service Act would become effective in January 1916, specifying that single men aged 18 to 40 years old were liable to be called up for military service unless they were widowed with children or ministers of a religion—the law was amended in June 1916 to remove the exemption for married men, and the age for conscription was ultimately raised to 51. When the War began, the minimum height for a British soldier was five foot, eight inches tall. By October 11, 1914 this was lowered to five foot five, and after the massive casualties incurred in November, to five foot three. Fussell, 9. "Bantam Battalions" would be raised for men at least five feet in height but under five foot three.
7 National Archives, United Kingdom, Whale, James, Service Record WO374/73337 p. 13.
8 Whale Service Record p. 13.
9 Whale Service Record p. 11.
10 Curtis, 17.
11 Whale Service Record p. 14.
12 The main service records of individual British officers from the Great War were destroyed by enemy bombing during the Second World War. The records which survived are supplementary files kept in alternate locations, so many are fragmentary and incomplete. There are gaps in James Whale's service record, as there are in R.C. Sherriff's and J.B. Priestley's.

13 Gatiss, 4.

14 Fussell, 50.

15 Gatiss, 4.

16 National Archives, United Kingdom, War Diary of the 2/7th Battalion, Worcestershire Regiment, September 1915-January 1918 WO-95-3060-3.

17 War Diary.

18 War Diary.

19 War Diary.

20 War Diary.

21 War Diary.

22 War Diary.

23 War Diary.

24 War Diary.

25 War Diary.

26 War Diary; Curtis, 19.

27 Lieutenant Blackburne had joined the battalion on July 9.

28 War Diary.

29 International Committee of the Red Cross, Whale, James, Red Cross P.O.W. card, https://grandeguerre.icrc.org/en/File/Details/2917172/3/2/.

30 Fussell, 64 (quoting *The Journal of Arnold Bennett* 537 (New York 1933)).

31 Roads to the Great War, https://roadstothegreatwar-ww1.blogspot.com/2014/12/fortnum-mason-provision-front.html.

32 There is a discrepancy in the dates and times. The 2/7th's War Diary records the date of this assault as August 25, 1917 and the time as 11: 00 p.m. The War Diary, which was a contemporaneous record, is likely more accurate than Whale's recollection of events some 18 months after the fact. According to the War Diary, the 2/7th arrived in the trenches on the 23rd and its first assault upon Aisne House, which did not succeed, was on the 24th, and the Diary does not note that Whale participated in this attack.

33 Whale Service Record p. 9.

34 Victoria Cross, Britain's highest award for valor, awarded for gallantry "in the presence of the enemy."

35 Companion of the Most Distinguished Order of St. Michael and St. George, the lowest class of the sixth-most senior order of British chivalry. In the second episode of the second season of the BBC comedy series *Yes, Minister*, entitled "Doing the Honours," which first aired on March 2, 1981, Private Secretary Bernard Woolley (Derek Fowlds), jokingly explains to his boss, political appointee and Minister of the Office of Administrative Affairs (a fictitious Cabinet position), James Hacker (Paul Eddington), what the letters pertaining to the Order mean in the Civil Service. C.M.G. is "call me God," while the next highest class, Knight Commander, or K.C.M.G., means "kindly call me God," while the highest class, Knight Grand Cross, or G.C.M.G., means "God calls me God."

36 Distinguished Service Order, a U.K. military award given for meritorious or distinguished service by officers, usually in combat operations.

37 Companion of the Most Honourable Order of the Bath, the lowest class of the fourth-most senior order of British chivalry, generally awarded to senior military officers and senior civil servants.

38 Whale Service Record p. 8.

39 Whale, J., "Our Life at Holzminden" *The Wide World Magazine* 43: 334 (August 1919).

40 Whale, 334-5.

41 Whale, 335.

42 Whale, 335-6.

43 Curtis, 23.

44 Whale, 338.

45 Curtis, 23

46 Curtis, 24.

47 Whale, 338.

48 Whale, 338.

49 Whale, 339.

50 Whale, 339.

51 Whale, 339.

52 Whale Service Record p. 5.

53 Whale Service Record p. 6.

54 Curtis, 25.

55 Gatiss, 5.

56 Curtis, 25.

57 Gatiss, 5.

58 Gatiss, 5.

59 Curtis, 26.

60 Gatiss, 5.

61 Knight Commander of the Most Honourable Order of the Bath, the second-highest class in Britain's fourth most senior order of chivalry.

62 *See* Dedicated to the Life and Work of Ernest Frederick Graham Thesiger, www.ernestthesiger.org/Ernest_Thesiger/Home.html.

63 Thesiger married Janette Mary Fernie Rankin on May 29, 1917. Despite his open homosexuality, the pair would remain married for nearly 44 years, until his death on January 14, 1961. Janette was the sister of William Bruce Ellis Rankin, whom Thesiger had met while both men were students at the Slade School of Art, and the two would share a relationship until William Rankin's death in 1941.

64 Based upon Thesiger's family background, Some Cockney!

65 Curtis, 28.

66 Gatiss, 6.

67 Curtis, 30.

68 Curtis, 31.

69 Curtis, 29-30.

70 Gatiss, 6.

71 Curtis, 30.

72 Curtis, 30.

73 Lanchester, Elsa, *Elsa Lanchester, Herself* 55 (St. Martin's Press 1983).

74 Lanchester, 133.

75 Riley, Philip J. (ed.), *The Invisible Man* 24–Production Background by Gregory Wm. Mank (Bear Manor Media 2013) (hereinafter "Mank, Production Background, *Invisible Man*").

76 Curtis, 31.

77 Curtis, 32.

78 Curtis, 32-3.

79 Curtis, 34-5.

80 Curtis, 35.

81 Curtis, 36.

82 Curtis, 38.

83 Curtis, 40.

84 Curtis, 41-2.

85 Conversion values for historical pounds into 2019 dollars contained in this book have been taken from the website Nye, Eric W., *Pounds Sterling to Dollars: Historical Conversion of Currency*, https://www.uwyo.edu/numimage/currency.htm.

86 Curtis, 51.

Chapter Five

R.C. Sherriff:
To the End of the Journey and Beyond

Robert Cedric (R.C.) Sherriff was born on June 6, 1896 in Hampton Wick, Middlesex. His father, Herbert "Pips" Hankin Sherriff, was a clerk for the Sun Insurance Company, and his mother was Constance, née Winder. He attended Kingston Grammar School, where he was more interested in sport than studies, having been a member of the rowing, cricket, and hockey teams, and winning several sporting prizes. At the outbreak of the War he was working as a clerk at the same company which employed his father. He had sought a commission in August 1914, but was rejected because his grammar school did not have an Officer Training Corps and was not on the approved list.[1] Although his employers did not wish him to join the Army, he enlisted in the Artists Rifles in November 1915[2] and in January 1916 began training at Hare Hall Camp at Gidea Park, Romford, Essex. According to the "Summary of War Service" contained in his Service Record, he was commissioned a Second Lieutenant in the East Surrey Regiment on September 4, 1916. He arrived in France on September 28, 1916 and joined the 9th Battalion of the East Surreys on October 1.[3] The battalion had suffered badly at the Somme, coming out of the battle with only 10 officers and about 200 Other Ranks, with very few NCOs (a battalion at full-strength numbered about

R.C. Sherriff wearing his East Surrey Regiment uniform

1,000 officers and Other Ranks). Sherriff arrived at the time the unit was receiving new drafts from England, bringing its strength up to 40 officers and about 700 Other Ranks.[4] When he joined the battalion it was in brigade reserve at Estrée-Cauchie (called "Extra-Cushy" by the troops), 10 miles northwest of Arras.[5] Sherriff would serve in C Company, under Captain Hilton, of whom he wrote:

> I never knew whether I really liked Hilton or not—he was a bluff, good natured man; a magnificent soldier who understood and did all in his power to lighten the burden of his men. Yet he had the most relentless sarcasm for people he disliked; he

was quick to note little peculiarities of voice or manner and unmercifully mimic them. But he was the best and easily the most senior Company Commander."[6]

The 9th East Surreys would go into Divisional Reserve at Souchez, near Vimy Ridge, the day after Sherriff joined the unit, where the men would be engaged in laboring on the trenches.[7] On his first night in the front lines, Sherriff would take a tour of Ersatz Crater, a huge hole in no-man's land where the British held one rim and the Germans the other. He would call it "a secluded little hell on earth."[8] His tour would be spent with the battalion exchanging mortar fire with the normally docile Saxon unit opposite them. The British unit which had occupied the line before the 9th East Surreys had been belligerent, and the Saxons were returning the favor. On October 14, the battalion would move to Noeux-les-Mines, in the Hulluch-Loos sector, the site of the disastrous Battle of Loos in 1915.

> One could liken the Loos salient to half a plate, with the enemy looking down into ours from its outer edge. Hulluch on the extreme left, then the shambles of Loos and its Tower Bridge, now reduced to a wreckage of twisted iron girders, and the Loos Crassier shooting out towards the Boche lines, where Hart's and Harrison's craters lay midway in no-man's land. The trenches then curved down across Hill 70, coming to an abrupt turn at the famous Triangle to straighten themselves out toward the Double Crassier—huge mammoths of waste slag and charcoal, which started at the top of Hill 70 to run for some 1000 yards through German and British lines—on the extreme right and neck of the salient.[9]

The 9th East Surreys took over the frontline trenches in the left sub-sector on October 31 and would alternate to brigade support (which meant heavy physical labor for the men) approximately every six days. This routine would continue until February 10, 1917.[10] During this time, Sherriff spent some time working with the engineers, draining trenches, and from January 24 until February 12 was away from the battalion, suffering from neuralgia.[11]

The 9th East Surreys would then move to Lens, and then, in May 1917, would move into the front line in the Ypres Salient, at Hooge.[12] By April, Sherriff was suffering from severe neuralgia and appeared to be on the verge of a mental breakdown.[13] He would receive badly-needed leave, from June 24 to July 4.[14] The battalion would take part in the attack on Passchendaele, which began on July 31, 1917. On August 2, 1917, Sherriff's service record notes tersely that he was "wounded in 3rd Battle of Ypres [Passchendaele], face, hands and leg."[15] Sherriff would describe the incident in more detail:

Soldiers prepare for the 3rd Battle of Ypres. (IWM)

The whole thing became a drawn-out nightmare. There were no tree stumps or ruined buildings ahead to help you keep direction. The shelling had destroyed everything. As far as you could see, it was like an ocean of thick, brown porridge. The wire entanglements had sunk into the mud, and, frequently, when you went in up to your knees, your legs would come out with strands of barbed wire clinging to them, and your hands were torn and bleeding through the struggle to drag them off.

. . . .

Our company commander had made his headquarters under a few sheets of twisted corrugated iron.

"I want you to explore along this trench," he said to me, "and see if you can find B Company [actually "D"] . . . If you can find them, we can link up together and get some sort of order into things."

So I set off with my runner. It was like exploring the mountains of the moon. . . . There were small concrete blockhouses here and there called pillboxes that the Germans built when the swampy ground prevented dugouts.

The Germans were now shelling us with whizbangs . . . We heard the report of it being fired, and we heard the thin whistle of its approach, rising to a shriek. It landed on top of a concrete pillbox that we were passing, barely five yards away . . . The crash was deafening. My runner let out a yell of pain. I didn't yell so far as I know because I was half stunned. I remember putting my hand to the right side of my face and feeling nothing: to my horror I thought the whole side had been blown away.

After the fact, Sherriff realized the top of the concrete pillbox had directed the shrapnel from the shell upwards. However, he had been blasted with a shower of concrete particles from the pillbox.[16] A doctor would take 52 pea-sized fragments of concrete out of him.[17]

He was invalided to England, where he was admitted to hospital on August 3, remaining hospitalized until September 9, 1917.[18] After being released from hospital he was returned to the Depot in Dover and assigned to instruct recruits in musketry.[19] He remained on home service in England, attached to the Third, and then the Twelfth, Battalion of the East Surreys, being promoted to temporary Lieutenant on March 5, 1918 and then to temporary Captain on January 8, 1919, being demobilized on February 26, 1919.[20] He then returned to his pre-war job with Sun Insurance,[21] no longer as a clerk in the office but as an "outdoor man: "

I had to go round seeing clients who didn't answer letters or hadn't filled in forms correctly or were in trouble of various kinds over their insurances. I had to smooth over ruffled people who had made claims that weren't covered by their policies, and trace the ones who had moved and hadn't told us where they had gone to. I also had to keep in touch with our local agents and try to pep up the ones who weren't doing enough business or were slack about sending in the money they had collected.[22]

His territory was the Thames Valley from Putney to Windsor, and for a salary of £6 [about $370 in 2019 dollars, adjusted for inflation] per week, he traveled by tram and bus in town, and on his bicycle in the country, making his rounds.[23] On September 4, 1919 he applied to be considered for appointment to a permanent commission in the Regular Army,[24] but his service record notes "Not selected for appointment to a permanent Commission" on March 15, 1922.[25]

His interest in sport led him to join the Kingston Rowing Club soon after leaving the Army.

Our club-house was on a small island on the Thames: an island that got smaller every year when the winter floods came down and scoured a little more of its banks away. We were always hard up, and in the winter of 1921 we wanted money desperately, for our boats were worn out and could be patched up no longer. How could we raise £100 [about $6,700 in 2019 dollars, adjusted for inflation]—as we must do, if we were to keep going at all? We had a special committee meeting to consider ways and means, but one by one suggestions were turned down. Then somebody said: Why not put on some sort of entertainment? A variety show? We had talent, and sisters and girl friends could be brought in.[26]

The clubhouse was too rickety to support a show, but the property also contained a house with a small theater, equipped with lights, dressing rooms, and a curtain. Since all this equipment was deemed excessive for a mere variety show, the club decided to include a one-act play as the show's finale. As the chairman of the club's entertainment sub-committee, it fell to Sherriff to obtain a suitable play. After visiting an agent specializing in plays for amateur theatrical groups, he obtained a half-dozen. The committee read and rejected them. Sherriff suggested that, rather than put on an existing play which had likely been seen many times elsewhere, why not prepare and present an original play? Despite never having written a play, Sherriff volunteered.[27]

After some difficulties coming up with suitable dialogue, Sherriff wrote a comic one-act play about a group of people sitting in a motor coach, waiting to depart on a tour. Sherriff credited its success to the performances given by two schoolmasters playing a pair of beer-besotted troublemakers. Nevertheless, with the success of this production, the club formed the Adventurers' Dramatic Society, scrapping the variety format and proceeding to put on shows on a regular basis. Their next outing would be three one-act plays; two being established works with a new one by Sherriff. He taught himself by reading as many plays as he could and obtaining a copy of the book *Playmaking,* by William Archer. Sherriff's play, *The Woods of Meadowside,* received favorable press while the two established plays were barely mentioned. In addition to writing the plays, he also took a hand in set design, stage managing, prompting, and even filling in as an actor, if needed. His next venture was more ambitious; a three-act play entitled *Profit and Loss,* which also received glowing notices in the press and "set the pattern for the next three years."[28]

Sherriff continued working, writing, and rowing, with the Adventurers' Dramatic Society putting on one

Sherriff at his rowing club

of his new plays every spring for the next three years. After this time, however, he tired of this approach, and turned the captaincy of the Kingston Rowing Club over to another and, while remaining a member, became less involved with the club's activities. Encouraged by the favorable press received by *Profit and Loss*, he decided to see if any London theatrical agents would be interested in having it produced in a West End theater. Sherriff sent the play to Curtis Brown, the only agent he found in *The Author's Year Book* who didn't require a guinea[29] in order to read a play. The prompt answer was that while they had read the play with interest and pleasure, they felt it unsuitable for the professional theater but would be very interested to read anything else which Sherriff had written. Buoyed by this encouraging response, he sent along a copy of his next play, *Cornlow-in-the-Downs*. This one was passed along to one of the Sunday repertory companies, who had gotten as far as penciling in some of the cast (including Cedric Hardwicke as the leading character). Ultimately, however, the play was returned to him with a note that the company had been unable to find a suitable cast. He sent along two more of his plays to Curtis Brown, but they did not express any interest in them.[30]

Changing his approach somewhat, he pulled out the chapters of a novel he had begun to write several years before.

> The theme was hero worship, and the story began with two boys at school. The elder boy, Dennis Stanhope, was the hero; and Jimmy Raleigh worshipped him from afar. Dennis had everything a boy desired: good looks and charm, supreme ability for games and a gift for leadership that carried the school from strength to strength. Jimmy was an ordinary, plodding boy: he did nothing brilliant in games or work, but his character was modelled and strengthened in the light of his hero.[31]

After leaving school, however, their fortunes reversed, with Raleigh running a successful business and Stanhope drifting aimlessly through life. Raleigh tried to give aid to his former hero, which Stanhope resented. But Sherriff, who was adept at writing dialogue, struggled to flesh out a novel. He simply could not find a way to move the story forward.[32]

As he pondered his ideas, he realized that Stanhope and Raleigh could be characters he knew from the War and could form the basis of a play rather than a novel.

> A Company Headquarters dugout in the front line made a perfect natural setting for the theatre. It was usually one of a chain of dugouts linked together by short tunnels, each with its own way up to the trench by a steep flight of steps. The tunnel to one side would lead into a dugout where some of the officers slept, the opposite one to the quarters of the signalers and runners, and the place where the cook-batman prepared the meals. That made it easy to move the characters in and out as needed.[33]

His familiarity with the characters and the setting would make writing the play come naturally. His original thought for a title was *Waiting*. However, after he finished the play and was in bed reading a book, he "got to a chapter that closed with the words 'It was late in the evening when we came at last to our Journey's End.' The last two words sprang out as the ones I was looking for. Next night I typed them on the front page for the play, and the thing was done."[34]

Journey's End, the seventh play he wrote, would become his best-known. Set entirely in a dugout in a British trench before St. Quentin, on the Somme sector, it begins on the evening of Monday, March 18, 1918. This dugout looks pretty squalid to the casual observer, but it was the Company Headquarters and officers' billet and therefore fairly comfortable, compared with the conditions under which the Other Ranks existed. According to J.B. Priestley: "That dugout we have all seen in productions of *Journey's End* would have looked to me then like a suite in some Grand Hotel. I never did find myself within miles of anything so dry and commodious."[35]

The British High Command knows the Germans are preparing something big. They have an idea where it might happen, and a rough idea of the timing, but do not yet know exactly when an attack will take place. C Company, commanded by Captain Dennis Stanhope, relieves another company in the support-line trench, some 50 yards behind the British front-line trench and about 100 yards from the German lines. Stanhope is a fine officer, a recipient of the Military Cross, whose sense of duty has caused him to refuse leave to which he was entitled. He came straight from school to the front at age 18, and the strain of nearly three years on the Western Front, and a year in command of his company, has frayed his nerves and driven him to drink. Imbibing large quantities of whisky, he is still able to function at a high level (at least most of the time) and would today be considered a "functional alcoholic" suffering from post-traumatic stress disorder. "[H]e's stuck it till his nerves are shattered to bits, and he's called a drunkard."[36] Stanhope's second-in-command is Lieutenant Osborne, who thinks Stanhope is "a long way the best company commander we've got."[37]

Osborne, a schoolmaster before the War (who had once played rugby for England), is level-headed, twice Stanhope's age, and the other officers affectionately call him "Uncle" ["Uncle" was an appellation commonly given to older junior officers, sometimes to those only a few years older than their fellows]. Stanhope relies upon his assistance very much. A bit of comic relief is provided by Private Mason, an officers' servant, known as a "batman," who acts as cook, dealing with the vague Army rations he is given in the best way he can. Dialogue from *Journey's End* illustrates this:

OSBORNE: What are you going to tempt us with tonight, Mason?
MASON: Soup, sir—cutlets—and pineapple.
OSBORNE [*suspiciously*]: Cutlets?
MASON: Well, sir—well, yes, sir—cutlets.
OSBORNE: What sort of cutlets?
MASON: Now, sir, you've got me. I shouldn't like to commit meself too deep, sir.
OSBORNE: Ordinary ration meat?
MASON: Yes, sir. Ordinary ration meat, but a noo shape, sir. Smells like liver, sir, but it 'asn't got that smooth, wet look that liver's got.[38]

• • • •

OSBORNE: What kind of soup is this, Mason?
MASON: It's yellow soup, sir.
OSBOURNE: It's got a very deep yellow flavour.[39]

Mason is dismayed, however, when the unlabeled tin he had been assured contained pineapple chunks proved, upon opening, to contain apricots, a fruit detested by Captain Stanhope:

MASON [*to* OSBORNE]: I've 'ad rather a unpleasant surprise, sir.
OSBORNE: What happened?
MASON: You know that tin o' pineapple chunks I got, sir?
OSBORNE: Yes.
MASON: Well sir, I'm sorry to say its apricots.
OSBORNE: Good heavens! It must have given you a turn.
MASON: I distinctly said 'Pineapple chunks' at the canteen.
OSBORNE: Wasn't there a label on the tin?
MASON: No, sir. I pointed that out to the man. I said was 'e *certain* it was pineapple chunks?
OSBORNE: I suppose he said it was.

MASON: Yes, sir. 'E said a leopard can't change its spots, sir.

OSBORNE: What have leopards to do with pineapple?

MASON: That's just what *I* thought, sir. Made me *think* there was something fishy about it. You see, sir, I know the captain can't stand the sight of apricots. 'E said the next time we 'ad them 'e'd wring my neck.

OSBORNE: Haven't you got anything else?

MASON: There's a pink blancmange I've made, sir. But it ain't anywhere near stiff yet.

OSBORNE: Never mind. We must have the apricots and chance it.

MASON: Only I thought I'd tell you, sir, so as the captain wouldn't blame me.

OSBORNE: All right, Mason.[40]

Then, to add insult to injury, Mason has forgotten the pepper.[41] Other characters are Second Lieutenant Trotter, a rather rotund, jovial fellow, whose hobby back in England was gardening and whose biggest concern is where his next meal is coming from, and Second Lieutenant Hibbert, who claims neuralgia (which Stanhope believes he is faking) so that he will be sent to the rear before the fighting begins.[42]

Stanhope is not pleased when a new Subaltern, James Raleigh, is posted to his Company. Raleigh had, in fact, specifically requested to be assigned to Stanhope's Company, invoking the aid of his uncle, General Raleigh, who is at the base and in charge of detailing officers. Raleigh is a Public-School boy, recently left School, who was at the same School as Stanhope. Raleigh idolized the three-years older boy when they were at School together and Stanhope "was skipper of rugger at Barford, and kept wicket for the eleven. A jolly good bat, too."[43] In another wrinkle, back in England, Stanhope had been involved with Raleigh's sister. Stanhope disdains Raleigh's hero-worship, and fears he will be disillusioned with Stanhope in his current condition, and that Raleigh will write critical things about Stanhope back to his sister in England. Stanhope tells Osborne he will censor Raleigh's letters home, and Osborne strongly objects. When Stanhope opens Raleigh's letter and Osborne

Colin Clive as Stanhope in the British stage play *Journey's End*

The 1929 *The Play Pictorial* features *Journeys End* at the Savoy Theatre, London, 1929. Front cover depicts Colin Clive as Stanhope and Maurice Evans as Raleigh.

reads it, he finds it is full of high praise for Stanhope. At Osborne's urging, Stanhope re-seals the envelope and sends the letter off on its way.

Stanhope relays information which intelligence had received from a German prisoner that the German attack will take place on Thursday, March 21. The Battalion's Colonel informs Stanhope that the Brigadier has decided his company must conduct a "surprise daylight" trench raid across no-man's land, under cover of a smokescreen, to secure a prisoner to find out what German unit is opposing them across the line. Stanhope and the Colonel both agree the idea is absurd and suicidal, but orders are orders and the raid must go forward. Osborne, along with Raleigh, will lead 10 Other Ranks to make the raid. Osborne, with a premonition, gives his personal effects to Stanhope for safe keeping before the raid. Stanhope says "You're coming back, old man. Damn it! what on earth should I do without you?"[44] The raid secures a German prisoner, but Osborne and six of the Other Ranks are killed. The Colonel is more concerned with the capture of the prisoner than the casualties suffered, stating the Brigadier will be very pleased, causing Stanhope to remark icily "How awfully nice–if the Brigadier's pleased."[45]

The climax occurs on the early morning of the 21st, when the Germans mount their Spring Offensive. Heavy shelling rocks the dugout as Mason, the cook, puts down his pots and pans, dons his helmet, picks up his rifle, and goes out of the dugout into the trench. The officers all leave the dugout before dawn to prepare to meet the German attack. In the noise and the chaos, Raleigh has been hit by a shell fragment, which has broken his spine, and he is brought down into the dugout by the Sergeant Major and laid on Osborne's cot. In a scene from *Journey's End*, which would set the pattern for such vignettes to an extent it would become a cliché, Stanhope comforts Raleigh, who does not realize the seriousness of his wounds:

RALEIGH: I say—Dennis –
STANHOPE: Yes, old boy?

RALEIGH: It—it hasn't gone through, has it? It only just hit me?—and knocked me down?

STANHOPE: It's just gone through a bit, Jimmy.

RALEIGH: I won't have to—go on lying here?

STANHOPE: I'm going to have you taken away.

RALEIGH: Away? Where?

STANHOPE: Down to the dressing-station—then hospital –then home. [*He smiles.*] You've got a Blighty one,[46] Jimmy.

RALEIGH: But I—I can't go home just for—for a knock in the back. [*He stirs restlessly.*] I'm certain I'll be better if if I get up. [*He tries to raise himself, and gives a sudden cry.*] Oh—God! It does hurt!

STANHOPE: It's bound to hurt, Jimmy.

RALEIGH: What's—on my legs? Something holding them down—

STANHOPE: It's all right, old chap; it's just the shock—numbed them.

. . . .

RALEIGH: Can you stay for a bit?

STANHOPE: Of course I can.

RALEIGH [*faintly*]: Thanks awfully. [*There is quiet in the dugout for a long time. STANHOPE sits with one hand on RALEIGH'S arm, and RALEIGH lies very still. Presently he speaks again–hardly above a whisper*] Dennis—

STANHOPE: Yes, old boy?

RALEIGH: Could we have a light? It's—it's so frightfully dark and cold.

STANHOPE [*rising*]: Sure! I'll bring a candle and get another blanket.

When Stanhope returns with a blanket, Raleigh gives out a gasp, and is quiet. Stanhope takes Raleigh's hand, and raises it. He lowers the hand, and then goes to sit on a bench, with his back to the dugout wall. A private comes down the dugout steps, and informs Stanhope that Lieutenant Trotter wishes to see him right away. [47] Stanhope slowly rouses himself and leaves the dugout. A shell falls into the doorway, explodes, and the dugout collapses.[48]

The title of Sherriff's autobiography, *No Leading Lady*, comes from comments he received from London's theater managers about the lack of any female characters in *Journey's End*. "('How can I put on a play with no leading lady?' one of them had asked complainingly)."[49] Curiously, his autobiography largely omits things such as his early life or details about his experiences in the War and begins with the opening night of the West End production of *Journey's End*. Oblique references to the War crop up, of course, particularly with respect to the genesis of the play, but details about

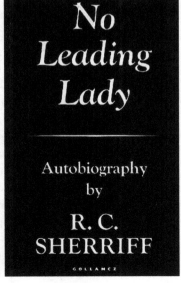

No
Leading
Lady

Autobiography
by

R. C.
SHERRIFF

GOLLANCZ

the War are very sparse and largely confined to the beginning of Chapter 28, when he was writing about the dawn of the Second World War:

> When the first war came I'd just left school and started work in a London office. I'd been a big shot at school: captain of rowing and cricket, and record holder of the long jump in the sports. From that I had become a junior clerk on a high stool, sticking stamps on envelopes, writing "paid" against names in ledgers, filing away old letters and running errands. After that last triumphant term at school it was a demoralising come-down. I hated wearing a high stiff collar and a bowler hat; I hated the journeys on a crowded train; above all I hated the miserable, hopeless monotony of it all. I would look out of the windows at the smoke-grimed, suffocating buildings opposite and think of the river and the playing fields. But there was no escape. I had no qualifications for a better job, and was doomed to sit in that musty office until I was an old worn-out man.
>
> So when the war came it was a merciful, heaven-sent release. I loved the route marches along the country lanes, singing the marching songs with the band ahead of us. I loved the manoeuvres across the downs and guard duty at night, watching the dawn come up behind the trees. It was romantic and exhilarating after those miserable days on an office stool. And when it was all over I went up to the office to show myself off with the three stars of a captain on my shoulders and a gold wound stripe on my sleeve.
>
> There had been bad times in France, but all in all it had been a magnificent and memorable experience, and with my wounds gratuity I bought myself a sculling boat.[50]

His attitude is uncomfortably close to that of Rupert Brooke's "Peace," glad that God "has matched us with His hour." Sherriff had, no doubt, seen unspeakably horrible things while in action, which had produced numerous real, or psychosomatic, bouts of neuralgia. In his autobiography he reduces this to "bad times in France." He, too, is repressing his War experiences, barely mentioning them at all in his autobiography. *Journey's End* itself deals explicitly with the War but is set at the beginning of the German Spring Offensive of 1918, a time when Sherriff was no longer at the front, but was back in England, instructing recruits in musketry, after having been wounded at Passchendaele. Sherriff did not believe *Journey's End* was an anti-war play.

> They [the West End theatre managers] had done their best to get war plays across to the public, and all without exception had

failed. The only thing they hadn't taken account of was that *Journey's End* happened to be the first war play that kept its feet in the Flanders mud. All the previous plays had aimed at higher things: they carried "messages", "sermons against war", symbolic revelations. The public knew enough about war to take all that for granted. What they had never been shown before on the stage was how men really lived in the trenches, how they talked and how they behaved. Old soldiers recognised themselves, or the friends they had served with. Women recognised their sons, their brothers or their husbands, many of whom had not returned. The play made it possible to for them to journey into the trenches and share the lives that their men had led. For all this I could claim no personal credit. I wrote the play in the way it came, and it just happened by chance that the way I wrote it was the way people wanted it.[51]

Sherriff's internalization of his War experiences, then, is more in line with Rupert Brooke's "swimmers into cleanness leaping" than with the disillusionment of Wilfred Owen, Siegfried Sassoon, Robert Graves, or Edmund Blunden.

Although the British public's taste for theater in the early 1920s was for light, uplifting fare, by the end of the decade more serious plays were being accepted. "For the most part, it had taken a decade of virtual avoidance to bring audiences to the point of acceptance [of a realistic play about the War]."[52] However, despite this gradually changing attitude, there was substantial resistance to the play, "a deeply rooted prejudice among theatre managers against plays about the war."[53] As he had with his earlier efforts, Sherriff sent the play off to Curtis Brown. Although believing it to be "a very fine play," there was no one interested in producing it in London.[54] The summer passed, and Sherriff received a telephone call from Curtis Brown. They had sent the

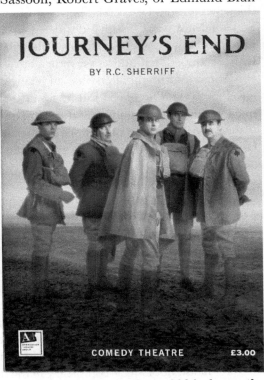

JOURNEY'S END

BY R.C. SHERRIFF

COMEDY THEATRE   £3.00

This program book, from 2004 shows the enduring quality of *Journey's End* on the stage.

play to the Incorporated Stage Society, a theater club. There were several of these clubs, which took over theaters for Sunday evening and Monday matinee performances, when the resident plays in those theaters were not being performed. The theater, of course, had to be completely vacated after the Monday afternoon performance so that it could be rearranged to present its usual play. Geoffrey Dearmer, a member of the Society's committee, wished to meet with Sherriff to discuss *Journey's End*. "The Incorporated Stage Society was a highbrow affair. . . . Their declared policy was to present plays of merit that, while deserving production, had no likely appeal to the general public."[55] Although Dearmer and a few other members of the committee were in favor of having the Society present the play, the majority of the committee was less than enthusiastic about it.

Dearmer, however, thought "*Journey's End* is a wonderful play, and it'll be a sheer tragedy if it isn't produced." The other theater clubs were interested only in plays which might bring in some money, while it appeared *Journey's End* had little chance of commercial success. Dearmer had a bold idea to sway the committee. He told Sherriff to send the play to George Bernard Shaw to read. If Shaw responded favorably to it, the other members of the committee would surely agree to present it. Shaw, though, had a reputation as a man with a massive ego and little time for aspiring playwrights. Making it seem even less likely this scheme would succeed, Shaw was on holiday on the French Riviera. Surely, he would not want his idyll disturbed by an unknown playwright imprecating him to read his play. Nevertheless, Sherriff sent *Journey's End* on to Shaw, along with a stamped, self-addressed return envelope.[56]

About a fortnight later, Sherriff received the play back, in his self-addressed envelope. When he opened it, he found Shaw had carefully removed Sherriff's uncancelled French stamps and returned them, wrapped in a small square of tissue paper, replacing the stamps on the envelope with Swiss stamps. Slipped in between the pages of the play was the following note:

> This play is, properly speaking, a document, not a drama. The war produced several of them. They require a good descriptive reporter, with the knack of dialogue. They are accounts of catastrophes, and sketches of trench life, useful as corrective to the romantic conception of war; and they are usually good of their kind because those who cannot do them well do not do them at all.
>
> They seem to me useless as dramatists' credentials. The best of them cannot prove that the writer could produce a comedy or a tragedy with ordinary materials. Having read this *Journey's End*, and found it as interesting as any other vivid description of a horrible experience, I could give the author a testimonial as a journalist; but I am as completely in the dark as before concerning his qualification for the ordinary professional work of a playwright, which does not admit of burning the house to roast the pig.

As a 'slice of life'—horribly abnormal life—I should say let it be performed by all means, even at the disadvantage of being the newspaper of the day before yesterday. But if I am asked to express my opinion as to whether the author could make his living as a playwright, I can only say that I don't know. I can neither encourage nor discourage him.

G. Bernard Shaw[57]

When Dearmer inquired of Shaw's verdict, Sherriff, deftly taking the statement out of context, replied "Let it be produced by all means." While this was certainly a plus, the committee had evidently changed its collective mind, and the Incorporated Stage Society agreed to put *Journey's End* on as its December production.[58]

The play needed a director. The Stage Society offered it to the leading directors, who either did not have the time to do it or were not interested.

As a last resort they offered it to a young man named James Whale. He was a man-of-all-work in the theatre. He played small parts, designed and painted scenery, and occasionally got a job as stage manager, but had never been in charge of a play in a West End theatre. He told me later that he had never earned beyond £5 [about $460 in 2019 dollars, adjusted for inflation] a week for anything he had done, with occasionally a little extra for designing the scenery. That the Stage Society should offer him the play was a measure of their desperation.[59]

Told he should meet the play's new director, Sherriff found Whale in his dressing room at the Strand Theatre, where he was playing a small part in a play called *High Treason*. Sherriff reports Whale was less than enthusiastic about *Journey's End*, although "he had read it very thoroughly and already knew it backwards." Whale was no doubt aware he was only offered *Journey's End* after it had been turned down by the established

Silent film version (1929) of the play *High Treason*, in which James Whale had a small part. During the play he was offered the directing job of *Journey's End*. Ironically, *High Treason* was written by Noel Pemberton-Billing, an English aviator, inventor, publisher and member of Parliament, a right wing nut who thought homosexuality was infiltrating English society and was linked to German espionage in the context of WWI. He ruined many lives with his homophobic conspiracy theories.

directors, and that he was merely "a stop-gap for the want of anybody else." Whale opined "that certain scenes were too sentimental and would have to be brought down to earth or cut out." Sherriff, desperate to have the play performed in the West End, agreed that Whale could make whatever alterations or amendments to the play that he wished. "He began to thaw when he found out that I wasn't going to argue about the things he wanted to do." Whale told Sherriff "he had been an infantry officer and served in the actual line of trenches where the play was set."[60]

Whale invited Sherriff to come to his flat in Chelsea the next day to look at his design for the play's set.

> I went to his flat in Chelsea and he showed me a beautifully constructed model. I had envisaged little more than a squalid cavern in the ground, but Whale had turned the hand of art to it. By strutting the roof with heavy timbers he gave an impression of vast weight above: an oppressive, claustrophobic atmosphere with a terrifying sense of imprisonment for those who lived in it. Yet with this, through innumerable small details, he had given it a touch of crude romance that was fascinating and exhilarating. Above all it was real. There may never have been a dugout like this one: but any man who had lived in the trenches would say, "This is it: this is what it was like."[61]

Sherriff felt that where an established director would have handed the job of set design to a scene designer, "who would have done a routine job," Whale had applied his own artistry to create "a design for the dugout [which] was in perfect harmony with the production he planned for it."[62]

A 21-year old "obscure young actor" named Laurence Olivier appeared as Stanhope. Sherriff lent him his own Captain's tunic, revolver, holster, and Sam Browne belt to wear on stage ("but the Military Cross ribbon had to be sewn on").[63] The Stage Society had wanted a well-known actor to play the lead, but this did not fit with Whale's vision.

> He was convinced that the keynote of the play was realism, and he couldn't get that if the characters were overshadowed by the names of the actors playing them. He wanted the audience to see a group of soldiers in a dugout rather than an assembly of well-known actors playing the parts of soldiers, and he set out to cast the play regardless of established reputations. He went for actors free from theatrical tricks and produced for the Stage Society a hand of trumps.[64]

George Zucco[65] played "Uncle" Osborne and Maurice Evans played Raleigh.

Program for the first production of Journey's End

Sherriff attended the performance on December 9 and watched most of the play. He left the theater before the final scene, fearing the actor playing the Sergeant Major would drop Maurice Evans as he carried the wounded Raleigh down the dugout steps, and returned in time to see the curtain fall. He thought the audience's reaction rather "tepid;" there was clapping but it "sounded polite and formal," rather than enthusiastic. "It had been perfectly played and beautifully produced, and if it had failed with the audience then the play alone was to blame."[66]

There were no reviews in the press the following day, as the critics would typically attend the Monday afternoon, rather than the Sunday evening, performance. Sherriff attended this performance as well. "Once more the play was beautifully performed." But, once more, Sherriff felt the audience had been unimpressed. As the stagehands broke down James Whale's dugout set, Sherriff feared his play would never again see a major performance. He was sure the critics,

George Zucco appears as Osborne in the play Journey's End

particularly Henry Swaffer of the *Daily Express*, "the most dreaded critic of his day," would savage *Journey's End*:

> If he didn't like a play he would tear it to pieces with a few words from his vitriolic pen, and with his great following of readers there wasn't the ghost of a chance for it when he had done. Maybe he hadn't come: perhaps it would be better if he hadn't. I couldn't imagine him seeing anything in the play: from what I knew of him it wasn't his sort of stuff at all.[67]

Sherriff returned home, spending a restless night dreading the awful notices he felt sure would appear in the next morning's papers. When the morning papers arrived, Sherriff was amazed at the glowing reviews it had received from the critics. The man he most feared, Henry Swaffer, absolutely loved it. Under a headline reading "THE GREATEST OF ALL WAR PLAYS," Swaffer wrote:

> "A new dramatist, R.C. Sherriff, achieved the distinction of compelling to real emotion an audience who were watching a play almost without a plot, with no women in the cast! . . . It was a remarkable achievement. . . *Journey's End* is perhaps the greatest of all war plays. . . This is the English theatre at its best. . . There is no shirking the facts: no concession to fashion. . . It is perfectly acted; each actor cuts a little cameo of stark reality. . . All London should flock to see it. It carries a great lesson—one that is nobly told. . ."[68]

The reviews gave the play the boost it needed.

Maurice Browne had seen the play on December 9 and agreed to produce

First run of *Journey's End*, 1929

it on the London stage.[69] The play would move to the Savoy Theatre on January 21, 1929, with James Whale directing. Olivier had been reluctant to take the role of Stanhope but did so to make an appearance as a dramatic leading man.[70] This worked, as after the first performance of *Journey's End*, Olivier was offered the title role in *Beau Geste*, a new play, which left *Journey's End* without its chief character after its initial two-performance run.[71] The other cast members from the first production were returning, but Whale had only about three weeks to find a new Stanhope.

After auditioning several actors for the role, including Colin Keith-Johnston, who had been a real war hero, having served in both the infantry and the air force, the role would be given to another actor who would work with James Whale again: Colin Clive.[72] After some rough patches in rehearsal, Sherriff suggested the actor take lunch at a nearby pub and have a glass or two of whisky to help steady his nerves. Whale's biographer, James Curtis, called this "a fateful suggestion, one that [Sherriff] later called 'my most useful contribution to the production.' He was right about that in it did move the production of *Journey's End* forward and help push Colin Clive over the psychological barrier that was constricting his work. It also managed, in the space of eight short years, to literally destroy the actor."[73]

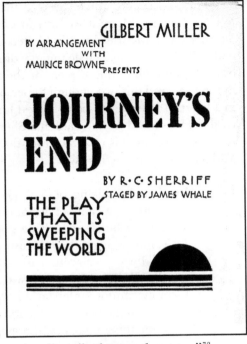

GILBERT MILLER
BY ARRANGEMENT WITH
MAURICE BROWNE PRESENTS

JOURNEY'S END

BY R·C·SHERRIFF
STAGED BY JAMES WHALE

THE PLAY
THAT IS
SWEEPING
THE WORLD

Clive was magnificent in the first performance.[74] On opening night, when the curtain fell at the end of the play, the audience sat in stunned silence, and remained silent as the curtain rose on the main cast. The curtain fell, with the auditorium still in silence, causing Sherriff to fear the entire audience had simply fallen asleep or gotten up and left. Sherriff wrote:

> Was it possible to put the curtain up again? By all the rules of the theatre the curtain was only raised at the end of a play by the clamorous demand of the audience, but not a single one of them had clapped his hands together. Then out of the darkness came a solitary "Bravo!" The curtain rose again, as if to acknowledge the salute of the one remaining member of the audience who hadn't dozed off. This time it was for the small-part actors who by custom took their bow together. The audience began to applaud, slowly, almost reluctantly, like an engine that had stood over-long in the cold. When the curtain rose again upon the actors of the larger parts the applause spread and strengthened until it sounded like a hail-storm on the iron roof of a barn. Maurice Evans, who played Raleigh, George Zucco, and finally Colin Clive took their bows alone, and with each the reception grew more clamorous. Men stood up and cheered: a paper the next morning said, "Even the critics cheered."[75]

The play ran for three weeks at the Savoy, before moving to the Prince of Wales' Theatre, where it would run until July 1930. A deal was done to have another company travel to the United States to present the play on Broadway, with Whale directing. Whale initially did not want to travel to the United States; Sherriff offered him one percent of the author's share of the play's gross profits in the U.S., and this was enough to persuade Whale to make the trip.[76] However, in a letter to Marguerite Lord[77] dated June 16, 1929, written shortly after his arrival in Hollywood, Whale said that Sherriff had never paid him this money, and that, furthermore, his royalties from the stage productions in London and New York had been stopped, as well:

> Incidentally talking of *J.E.* [*Journey's End*], Bob Sherriff has not paid me a cent yet & not only so but I had a most curious letter from him in which he said he should send me a *PRESENT*, much bigger than the usual author's PRESENT which he believed was a cigarette case. All of which made & makes me simply LIVID with fury. How dare he use the word *PRESENT*. I simply cannot understand it, he is such a lamb & *pressed* this Royalty on me because I couldn't get it out of Browne & Miller. . . . Something must have happened to Bob. Somebody has got at him I think & told him about some of my past perhaps!! In the meantime I am very sick about it all. It really almost made me lose faith in humanity. After having done all I did for *J.E.* to think that my widow's mite should be questioned by Browne & Sherriff is really dreadful. Did I tell you that Browne had also cabled to say that pending my return to London he has stopped my Royalties on the Savoy production. I could cry my eyes out. So you see it amounts to this. I am losing from the London show £35 per week plus £40 [approximately $2,800 and $3,200, respectively, in 2019 dollars, adjusted for inflation] per week from the New York production for inflation] per week from the New York production & all because I was a trusting little thing from the mother country. Apart from a bit of fun about it, I really am FURIOUS, so furious I sometimes think I will run away from here, break all my contracts & go & create HELL in London.[78]

Most of the balance of the letter contains a request for assistance in straightening out these financial issues and obtaining payment.

The New York cast (Colin Keith-Johnston (who had been the early favorite for the role in the British production) as Stanhope, Leon Quartermaine as Osborne, and Derek Williams as Raleigh) did six try-out performances in early March 1929 at the Arts Theatre Club in London, which did not go particularly well.[79] Nevertheless, the company departed on schedule. The sets were struck and, along with all the costumes and props, shipped off to New York, where they would be installed, temporarily, in Henry Miller's Theatre on 43rd Street, where the play would be performed—a preview would take place at the Great Neck Playhouse, a converted movie theater on Long Island, so the set had to be shipped there and installed for the performance, before being sent back to Henry Mill-

er's Theatre to be permanently installed. The cast rehearsed in the producer's suite aboard the *Aquitania* as they crossed the Atlantic, as the play would open only a week after the ship docked.[80]

Sherriff traveled to New York with the company, but only remained in the United States for 10 days before returning to England.[81] The play was a considerable hit. While in the U.S., James Whale directed another play for the producer of the Broadway production of *Journey's End*. Rehearsals on the play, *A Hundred Years Old*, began the same day as *Journey's End* opened. The play opened in Albany, New York on April 18, mov-

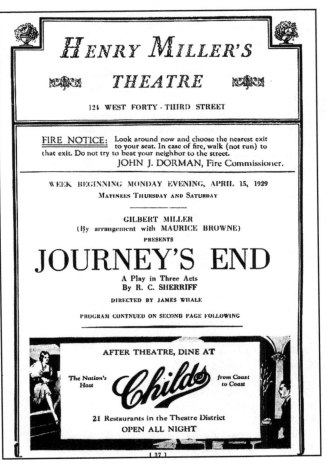

ing to Chicago for 12 weeks, before opening at the Lyceum Theatre on Broadway on October 1, 1929. It was a lackluster show, lasting only 39 performances. Along with *Journey's End* it did, however, cause film producers in Hollywood to take notice of James Whale.[82]

1 Lucas, Michael, *The Journey's End Battalion: The 9th East Surrey in the Great War* Kindle Ed. loc. 1510 (Pen & Sword Books 2012).
2 Lucas, loc. 1511.
3 Lucas, loc. 1507.
4 Lucas, loc. 1491-4.
5 Lucas, loc. 1510.

6 Lucas, loc. 1537 (quoting Sherriff, R.C., *My Diary: Journal of the East Surrey Regiment*, Vol. 1, Nos. 1-4 and Vol. II, Nos 1-2 116 New Series May 1937)).

7 Lucas, loc. 1552 (quoting Sherriff, *My Diary*).

8 Lucas, loc. 1557.

9 Lucas, loc.1587-91 (quoting Hitchcock, F.C., *Stand To: A Diary of the Trenches 1915-18* 200 (London 1937)).

10 Lucas, loc. 1591.

11 Lucas, loc. 1798.

12 Lucas, loc. 2074.

13 Lucas, loc. 1916-1940.

14 Lucas, loc. 2145.

15 National Archives, United Kingdom, Sherriff, Robert Cedric, Service Record WO399/69081 p. 8. This was 23 days before Second Lieutenant James Whale would be captured near Ypres.

16 Lucas, loc. 2224-42.

17 Lucas, loc. 2256.

18 Sherriff Service Record p. 19.

19 Sherriff Service Record p. 8.

20 Sherriff Service Record p. 11.

21 Biographical references are taken from Surrey County Council, Surrey Heritage, www.surreyarchives.org.uk/CalmView/Record.aspx?src=CalmView.Catalog&id=2332&pos=2.

22 Sherriff, R.C., *No Leading Lady* 7-8 (Victor Gollancz Ltd 1968).

23 Sherriff, *No Leading Lady* 8.

24 Sherriff Service Record p. 4.

25 Sherriff Service Record p. 3.

26 Sherriff, *No Leading Lady* 17.

27 Sherriff, *No Leading Lady* 17-18.

28 Sherriff, *No Leading Lady* 25-8.

29 This was the traditional measure of a professional's fee, in the amount of 21 shillings, which equaled one pound, one shilling, and would be the equivalent of approximately $70 in 2019.

30 Sherriff, *No Leading Lady* 30-2.

31 Sherriff, *No Leading Lady* 33-4.

32 Sherriff, *No Leading Lady* 34.

33 Sherriff, *No Leading Lady* 35-6.

34 Sherriff, *No Leading Lady* 39.

35 Priestley, *Margin Released* loc. 1383.

36 Sherriff, R.C., *Journey's End* Kindle Ed. loc. 291 (Penguin Classics Ed. 2000).

37 Sherriff, *Journey's End* loc. 259.

38 Sherriff, *Journey's End* loc. 376.

39 Sherriff, *Journey's End* loc. 686.

40 Sherriff, *Journey's End* loc. 585-609 (emphasis in original).

41 Sherriff, *Journey's End* loc. 686-699.

42 Sherriff had said Hibbert was based upon himself. In letters home to his mother, Sherriff complained of bouts of neuralgia, which appear to have been psychosomatic. Lucas, loc. 1800-5.

43 Sherriff, *Journey's End* loc. 451.

44 Sherriff, *Journey's End* loc. 2202.

45 Sherriff, *Journey's End* loc. 2472.

46 A "Blighty" wound is one which would send a soldier home—to "Blighty," soldier's slang for England.

47 Sherriff, *Journey's End* loc. 3101-68.

48 I was lucky enough to have seen the superb 2007 Broadway revival of *Journey's End*, which starred Hugh Dancy as Stanhope, Boyd Gaines as Osborne (nominated for a Tony Award for Best Performance by a Leading Actor in a Play), Stark Sands as Raleigh, and Jefferson Mays as Mason.

49 Sherriff, *No Leading Lady* 9.
50 Sherriff, *No Leading Lady* 317.
51 Sherriff, *No Leading Lady* 109.
52 Curtis, 52.
53 Sherriff, *No Leading Lady* 42.
54 Sherriff, *No Leading Lady* 40-1.
55 Sherriff, *No Leading Lady* 43.
56 Sherriff, *No Leading Lady* 43-5.
57 Sherriff, *No Leading Lady* 45.
58 Sherriff, *No Leading Lady* 46.
59 Sherriff, *No Leading Lady* 46-7.
60 Sherriff, *No Leading Lady* 47.
61 Sherriff, *No Leading Lady* 47-8.
62 Sherriff, *No Leading Lady* 48.
63 Sherriff, *No Leading Lady* 54.
64 Sherriff, *No Leading Lady* 49-50.
65 Zucco also served in the British Army in WWI and was wounded in the right arm. He would have a prolific film career, including many horror films, both at Universal and for other studios, from the Golden Age through the 1940s, often playing a mad scientist.
66 Sherriff, *No Leading Lady* 55.
67 Sherriff, *No Leading Lady* 58.
68 Sherriff, *No Leading Lady* 61.
69 Curtis, 60-2.
70 Curtis, 55.
71 Curtis, 58.
72 Curtis, 65.
73 Curtis, 67.
74 Curtis, 68-9.
75 Sherriff, *No Leading Lady* 86.
76 Curtis, 72, 74.
77 The editors of the pamphlet containing three of James Whale's letters, written between May 7 and June 16, 1929, state they had been unable to identify this woman, but believed "she probably worked in a co-ordinational capacity at producer Gilbert Miller's Rockefeller Center office."
78 Curtis, James and Pepper, James (eds.), *Arriving in Hollywood: Letters 1929* (Santa Teresa Press 1989) (emphasis in original).
79 Curtis, 72.
80 Curtis, 73.
81 Curtis, 74. It was at this time Carl Laemmle, Sr. offered him the job of writing the screenplay for *All Quiet on the Western Front*, which he turned down.
82 Curtis, 75.

Chapter Six
Jimmy Goes to Hollywood

In 1927, *The Jazz Singer*, starring Al Jolson,[1] was released. It was the first full-length feature film to contain synchronized dialogue. The first spoken words come approximately 17 minutes into the film, when Jolson's character, Jakie Rabinowitz, a/k/a Jack Robin, finishes his first vocal performance, a song entitled "Dirty Hands, Dirty Face," and says, "Wait a minute, wait a minute, you ain't heard nothin' yet!" Although really a silent picture with sound sequences inserted, with Jolson singing several musical numbers and about two minutes of synchronized speech, it heralded the end of the silent picture and the rise of the "talkies."

With the prospect of directing a talking picture version of *Journey's End*, provided he could obtain some experience in film production, while in New York in April 1929 James Whale signed a three-month contract with Paramount Famous Lasky Corporation. He would be paid the princely sum of $500 [about $7,500 in 2019 dollars, adjusted for inflation] per week.[2] "It would renew quarterly and provided for an apprenticeship period during which he would function as an uncredited 'dialogue director' on one or more unspecified productions. He was given a starting date of May 1 and train fare to Los Angeles."[3] He described his arrival in Hollywood in a May 7, 1929 letter to Marguerite Lord:

> Apart from one or two friendly little talks & smoking of innumerable cigarettes & looking at a film now & then, the days just pass by quite uneventfully. The sun rises & goes down, breakfast is eaten & baths are taken but nothing ever seems to happen. I suppose I am soaking it in somewhere. I feel I have been in, on, under & through films for years yet in actual fact I haven't been inside a studio yet. I have been allocated however (that is not the word, but I can't remember, it means put on or shoved or pushed onto or something like that) to a talkie called *Barbary Sheep*, a story of 1907 and the desert by Robert Hitchens. It is most exciting to be on a job but still *NOTHING* happens. . . .
>
> Hollywood is just too marvelous. One feels that the footprints of the Immortals are all here but has a terrible feeling that they are in sand & won't last when civilization comes this way. Everybody is a "star" with the requisite five irregular point☆.
>
> • • • •
>
> I have now taken an "apartment" at the Villa Carlotte, a wonderful Spanish affair on the slopes of the "lovely Beverly Hills." The strangest collection of people live there. Princes of the blood Royal I'm told have the first floor back let. I am on the third floor side. . . . However, the bath is nice & the view charm-

ing when you open the window & lean out & look sideways. I am now going to see a film called "Honk"[4] or something equally British. I know I shall end up burning incense for tea. The mens "costumes" are wonderful. *So* natty & so colourful. Flying open necks, white caps with wisps of curling hair coming out of the sides, check blazers ending up at the left hip by a single silver button or tape. *So* effective! All the men wear numbers of rings on every finger & (so I believe) amber beads inside their cutie blouses. The ladies are all painted in oils & full of ringlets & bits of things hanging from the shoulder.[5]

On June 4 he wrote "I am getting climatized to Hollywood & Talkies a little now but it is still very funny to me. . . . I have not actually started production yet

but I hear vaguely they mean to take up my option. Perhaps when I do a bit of 'Shooting' they will change their mind. . . . I am getting to like Hollywood. It makes me so brown & beautiful."[6]

Whale was originally assigned to a film called *Barbary Sheep*, and when that did not work out, he ended up as a "dialogue expert" on *The Old Lady Shows Her Medals*.[7] Whale mentions this project, briefly, in his letters to Marguerite Lord dated June 4 and 16, 1929, saying in the June 16 letter "I am preparing [it] for a talkie."[8] "Whale's task was simply to rehearse the ac-

The Old Lady Shows Her Medals was originally a play by J.M. Barrie. It was adapted (loosely) by Hollywood as *Seven Days Leave* (1930). The story surrounds WWI soldiers. Although the play ends sadly, the Hollywood version is more focused on music, romance and comedy. The play is still being produced, mostly in the UK, reminding us never to forget the horrors of war.

tors' dialogue with them prior to shooting and give them the benefit of his theatrical skills."[9] After this, he was assigned to serve as the (uncredited) "dialogue director" on a film entitled *The Love Doctor*, which he finished in 15 days, just as the initial three-month period of his contract was to expire, and his "contract with Paramount was unceremoniously permitted to lapse."[10] Although it probably did not appear so to him at the time, this proved a huge break for Whale's career as a film director. Whale decided he liked Los Angeles and would stay in Hollywood. Around this time Whale met David Lewis, who worked in the story department at Paramount.[11] Lewis would later become an executive at Warner Brothers. This meeting would develop into a serious relationship, which would see the two men move into a house together at 788 South Amalfi Drive in Pacific Palisades, in 1937.[12] The men would share the Amalfi Drive home, off and on, until 1954, when Lewis would move out, for good. "Despite the abrupt and hurtful nature of their parting, Whale and Lewis remained very good friends and Lewis was a frequent visitor to the house."[13]

In 1927, filming had started on multi-millionaire Howard Hughes' epic of

Great War aerial combat, *Hell's Angels* (1930). Begun as a silent film, it had a budget of some $2 million [almost $30 million in 2019 dollars, adjusted for inflation] (which would balloon into the neighborhood of $4 million before the picture was finally completed), one of the most expensive films ever made at that time. Hughes had envisioned the film as out-doing Paramount's *Wings* (1927), another epic of First World War dogfighting which had won the first Academy Award for Best Picture in 1929. Production dragged on for so long it became apparent it would not be marketable as a silent film, and Hughes, the producer, decided to re-shoot as much of the film as possible to release it as a fully talking picture. Hughes wanted an English director for the new sound scenes. Hughes had never heard of *Journey's End*, but was impressed with Whale's war record and his successful direction of a war play, so he hired Whale to direct (albeit uncredited) the approximately 60 percent of the film which would have to be re-shot as a sound picture.[14]

Whale's task would be to re-shoot almost the entirety of the film, apart from the flying sequences. Hughes engaged Joseph Moncure March to completely re-write the screenplay, which March found "depressingly bad." March worked on creating a new story which would work with the already completed aerial scenes. Said March:

> Whale gave me the advice and encouragement I needed and let me work it out the way I wanted. I completed a first draft of the script in ten days and, although some revisions and elaborations were subsequently made, the screenplay stayed essentially the way it was from then on. Hughes and Whale liked the result, and I was asked to stay and work with them. . . .[15]

The switch to sound meant that the part of the film's leading lady, Greta Nissen, who had a strong Swedish accent, had to be re-cast. Hughes selected 18-year-old platinum blonde bombshell Jean Harlow (whose given name was Harlean Harlow Carpenter) for the role. She had recently been under contract with the Hal Roach Studio, appearing in three Laurel & Hardy shorts, most spectacularly in the silent short *Double Whoopee* (1929), where bumbling hotel employees Stan & Ollie accidentally catch her dress in the door of a taxi-cab, resulting in her unknowingly entering the hotel lobby in her underclothes. Her final role for Roach was in the Laurel & Hardy silent short *Bacon Grabbers* (1929), where she made a brief appearance at the end as Edgar Kennedy's wife, informing him she had made the final payment on their radio, which the boys had just repossessed (and destroyed in the process). She also makes a fourth "appearance," of sorts, in *Beau Hunks* (1931), but only in a photograph. Ollie is engaged to marry the love of his life, "Jeanie-Weenie," who has "trav-eled all over the world" and is "loved by everyone." He treasures her inscribed photo (a portrait of Harlow). Receipt of a "Dear John" telegram from her prompts Ollie to join the French Foreign Legion, "to forget." Of course, he drags Stan along with him. While settling into the barracks, the boys note that nearly every one of their fellow Legionnaires also has an inscribed photo of Jeanie-Weenie—even the garrison's Colonel (Charles Middleton—of the many roles he played, he is probably best remembered today as the evil "Ming the Merciless," Emperor of the Planet Mongo, in the Universal *Flash Gordon* serials, starring Buster Crabbe in the title role–he would do a second tour of duty in the Foreign Legion in command of Stan & Ollie in *The Flying Deuces* (1939)) has one, framed and hanging on the wall in his office. Clearly, she was indeed "loved by [almost] everyone"!

Although she was beautiful, she wasn't much of an actress.

> Harlow barely had film experience, much less stage experience. "Harlow was quite aware of her deficiencies," said March, "and

a lot of the time it must have seemed like a nightmare to her." Whale took an immediate dislike to the 18-year-old actress, who could not begin to effect a British accent. He made catty comments about her bleached hair, which she insisted was natural [Harlow was a natural blonde, but added peroxide to her hair to achieve the platinum effect that was to become her trademark], and drove her mercilessly. March said, "I had written the character as a beautiful upper-class slut with a talent for fornication, who got tired of her conquests very quickly and left a trail of shattered males in her perfumed wake." Arthur Landau, who was Harlow's agent at the time, remembered Whale describing the character of Helen as a "pig" and Whale clearly directed Harlow to behave like one. As the woman who comes between the two Rutledge brothers before and during the war, she shows little of the allure that would later make her so popular. Whale had no appreciation for her potential as a sex symbol, thinking her common and unskilled. Even a notorious womanizer like Howard Hughes paid her no mind.

"Not only was she inexperienced," March said, "her voice was flat and untrained and she recited her lines with the stilted, wooden quality of a little girl in a grammar school play." In filming her seduction scene with Ben Lyon, Whale encouraged her

to act instinctually, but even that was beyond her. "Tell me," she implored him after a number of takes, "tell me exactly how you want me to do it."

"My dear girl," Whale said, finding her repellant, "I can tell you how to be an actress, but I cannot tell you how to be a woman."

So vehement was Whale's disapproval of Harlow that Hughes stepped in and tried directing her himself. He couldn't get anything out of her either, but it was James Whale's dislike of Jean Harlow that helped shape the character of Helen and, in so doing, set the pattern of crudely appealing women Harlow would play for the rest of her brief life.[16]

Ultimately, however, Harlow's acting improved (somewhat), and her earlier scenes were re-shot, providing passable results.

With his fascination for the very rich, Whale was clearly proud of his association with Howard Hughes. He dropped Hughes' name incessantly and when, at the end of filming, he was rewarded with a $7,000 [approximately $107,000 in 2019 dollars, adjusted for inflation] bonus, Whale promptly bought a new Chrysler with a portion of the money and told friends that Hughes had given him the car as a token of his gratitude for the salvation of *Hell's Angels*.[17]

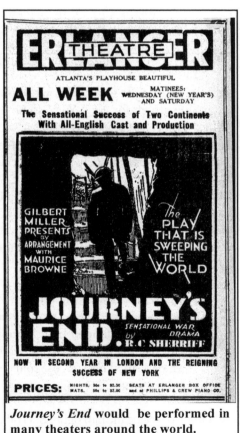

Journey's End would be performed in many theaters around the world.

Before leaving for New York with the cast of the Broadway production of *Journey's End*, R.C. Sherriff was concerned about losing his full-time job with Sun Insurance. He therefore had discussed selling his half-share of the film rights to the play to Maurice Browne for £2,000, provided Browne drew up an agreement to be signed and made payment before Sherriff depart-

TUBBING—BY THE AUTHOR OF "JOURNEY'S END"

Mr. R. C. Sherriff has resumed life at Oxford after returning from Hollywood, and is here seen about to give two of a college crew a bit of tubbing

Newspaper photo featuring R.C. Sherriff

ed. No agreement was put in writing and no payment had been made by the time Sherriff left for New York, so he did not think a firm deal had been made. When *Journey's End* proved to be a smash hit on Broadway, offers for the film rights to the play began pouring in, reaching £16,000 [this was a considerable sum, worth approximately $97,800 at the time, and close to $1.5 million in 2019 dollars, adjusted for inflation]. When Sherriff returned to England, Browne attempted to enforce the "agreement" to buy Sherriff's half-share of the film rights for £2,000. Sherriff protested that his half-share was now worth £8,000. Browne threatened litigation, and in order to avoid an unpleasant situation, Sherriff reluctantly agreed to sell his half-share for £2,000.[18]

> Sherriff, whom [Robert] Douglas described as "a very odd man," lived with his mother for much of his life. Though he was never seen with a woman in a romantic context, neither was he ever thought to be a homosexual. David Lewis, who knew Sherriff through Whale and later worked with him as a producer, described him as "asexual—you couldn't imagine him in bed with anyone."[19]

As a result of selling the film rights, Sherriff was virtually banished from the film project.[20]

As Whale was preparing to direct the new scenes for *Hell's Angels*, plans to make the talking picture version of *Journey's End* were firmed up. Whale was announced to direct the film before he had actually been hired. Maurice Browne held the film rights and wished to keep control of the production. Browne wanted the film to be made in London, with a British cast and company, but the price he wanted for the film rights was too high for any British producer to meet. American producer Morris Gest did a deal with Browne for the film rights for £15,750, but British producers Michael Balcon and Thomas Welsh pooled their resources in an effort to outbid Gest. Gest signed a contract with Browne but failed to keep current with the payments. Browne declared Gest in breach of their contract, and the rights were awarded jointly to Gainsborough Pictures, Ltd. (of which Balcon was the general manager) and a partnership of Thomas Welsh, George Pearson, and T.C. Elder, for a final price of £16,000. There were no suitable facilities at that time to make the sound picture in England.

There was also some urgency to get the production under way, as Universal was soon to begin filming *All Quiet on the Western Front*. Balcon engaged V. Gareth Gundrey to write the screenplay and also wanted him to direct the film. Maurice Browne pressed for Whale to direct, rather than Gundrey. Browne pointed out that Gundrey had never directed a talking film and had no experience, at all, with *Journey's End*, while Whale had both extensive experience with *Journey's End*, having directed the play in London and on Broadway, as well as experience in directing talking pictures, as he was, at that time, still engaged in making *Hell's Angels*. Balcon had done a deal to remake his 1923 silent feature, *Woman to Woman*, as a talkie, in an arrangement with Tiffany-Stahl in Los Angeles. He struck a similar deal for *Journey's End*, with the production to be filmed at the RCA studio in New York City. Grant Cook, executive vice-president of Tiffany-Stahl, had arranged the contract for production of *Journey's End* to be contingent upon the film being directed by James Whale. The Tiffany deal was announced in late June 1929, so at the time he began to film *Hell's Angels*, Whale knew he had been engaged to direct *Journey's End*.[21] Gundry's script, as well, would be found to be unsuitable.

The original plans to film at the RCA studio in New York, using the cast from the Broadway play, had to be scrapped, as Whale was working on *Hell's Angels* in Los Angeles. Since the film was to be produced jointly with Tiffany-Stahl, it would instead be filmed at Tiffany's newly equipped soundstage on Sunset Boulevard in Los Angeles.[22] George Pearson, a member of the consortium which had acquired the film rights, was brought in to supervise the production of *Journey's End*.

> Pearson, at age 54, was one of the leading figures of the British film industry. He started with the Pathé company in 1912, and by 1929 had more than 75 films to his credit as writer, director, or producer—but none of them talkies. And though he was in full partnership with Tommy Welsh and T.C. Elder on the *Journey's End* deal, Pearson had been completely uninvolved in

the negotiations. He was instead in the country, where he had gone to brood over the dismal state of the British film industry and the impending failure of Welsh-Pearson-Elder. When he returned to London, he was asked to leave for the United States with barely a two-day notice.[23]

Pearson would leave England on September 21, 1929, arriving in California on October 3.

Upon arriving in Los Angeles, Pearson met with Grant Cook.

> Pearson found Cook a cordial and friendly man, but met James Whale for dinner at the Roosevelt with a certain amount of trepidation. Whale was set to negotiate his contract and Pearson didn't know quite what to expect. But Whale, as it turned out, was talkative and reasonable, describing the film industry like an old hand and brimming with confidence. He told Pearson he was certain the issues surrounding the script could be solved to everyone's satisfaction and, relieved, Pearson gratefully accompanied him back to the studio, where they auditioned some actors and talked until three in the morning. "Fine impression," wrote Pearson in his diary.
>
> The questions of contracts and scripting occupied most of the week. Knowing he was considered essential to the project, Whale asked for the equivalent of $2,000 [some $29,900 in 2019, adjusted for inflation, or equivalent to an annual salary amounting to more than $1.5 million] a week—a sum not generally commanded by directors with greater standing. Grant Cook, who was used to paying no more than $500 a week for directors, was apoplectic when he learned of Whale's demand; Pearson was similarly astonished. Negotiations extended for three long days, with Pearson acting as the intermediary between Whale, Cook, and the partnership in London.
>
> The contract finally agreed to called for a fee of $20,000 [almost $299,000 in 2019, or about $19,900 per week, adjusted for inflation] for 15 weeks' work, plus $1,333 for each additional week. Whale also had script approval written into his contract, something he unofficially had from the start. For the task of re-writing the script which, as he envisioned it, was nothing more than a sensitive editing of the play, Whale asked for and got Joseph Moncure March, with whom he worked closely on *Hell's Angels*.[24]

March was under contract to Howard Hughes, who did not want to release him. In order to secure March's services for *Journey's End*, Whale had to agree to

Tiffany-Stahl Pictures in Los Angeles, California

perform additional work on *Hell's Angels* beyond the end of his contract on October 31, 1929. Whale agreed to work an additional four days, in exchange for March being released for four days. March was not happy to have to complete a screenplay for a two-hour film in four days, so March agreed to reduce his fee slightly and the deal was extended to five days. Whale's start date for *Journey's End* was pushed back from November 1 to November 7 and March completed the script.[25]

At first, Whale and Pearson would work well together:

March began work at once, with Whale and Pearson contributing their thoughts on the treatment of the play. As Whale told the *Daily Mail*,

> [H]e had waged a successful battle to pilot the play through the maze of Hollywood conventions which were threatening to rob the film of its atmosphere. "There was plenty of tact and firmness needed before we started. Mr. George Pearson, who supervised the production, and I found that Hollywood had quite made up their minds about what the screen version was going to be like—with a love interest, charming English scenery, and the usual war film conventions all thrown in. We held out for our own scenario and our own methods—and were finally given our way amid many dubious head-shakings and general pessimism."[26]

Once the script was completed, the cast began to fall into place.

'[A]lmost every British actor in Hollywood auditioned for a part."[27] "Pearson interviewed actors and shot tests at Tiffany, while Whale directed *Hell's Angels* at Metropolitan. Whale worked a 14-hour day, dining nightly at the Brown Derby with his friend David Lewis."[28] The first roles to be cast were Ian Maclaren as "Uncle" Osborne and Charles Gerrard (a prolific actor whose career

began in silent films in 1916, best known to genre fans for his role as Martin, the attendant in Dr. Seward's sanitarium, in Universal's *Dracula*) as Mason. The next major role to be cast was Raleigh, to be played by Canadian actor David Manners (who would later appear in Universal's *Dracula*, *The Mummy*, and *The Black Cat*). Billy Bevan, formerly a comic with the Mack Sennett Studio, would play Second Lieutenant Trotter. Whale had proposed his friend, David Lewis, to play the neurasthenic Second

Colin Clive as Stanhope (left) and Robert Speaight as Hibbert (right) in the Savoy Theatre production of *Journey's End*, 1929

The Great War and the Golden Age of Hollywood Horror

Lieutenant Hibbert, but Lewis felt his screen "test was terrible. Jimmy always said he liked it, but I never believed him."[29] The role would go to Anthony Bushell. Once again, the last major role to be cast was Stanhope.

Pearson thought Goldwyn's Walter Byron good enough to test but, echoing Maurice Evans' memorable assessment of Colin Keith-Johnston, decided his performance had "no heart—all head and muscle." On Saturday, November 9, Whale tested an American actor, David Gilmore, for the part of Stanhope.

> By Pearson's account, Gilmore moved the entire company to tears. "I have not been so moved since the days of Irving," he wrote. Grant Cook declared himself solidly in favor of Gilmore as Stanhope, but both Whale and Pearson worried about London's reaction to having Stanhope played by an American.
>
> Torn, they decided to shoot another series of tests in which Gilmore affected a clipped British accent. The results were horrendous and the actor was "rejected with regret."[30]

In desperation, Pearson cabled London asking for the loan of Colin Clive, an idea Maurice Browne ruled out as "too dangerous" to the momentum of the play.[31]

The parties arranged a meeting in London with Browne, Grant Cook and the British partners, Michael Balcon and Tommy Welsh. They convinced Browne to release Clive from the play, and assured Browne that Clive would be absent for no more than eight weeks, and the film's producers guaranteed he would return no later than January 13, 1930. "The financial terms were heavy, but truly worth the hazard."[32] Once again, the part of Stanhope would go to Colin Clive (who would play Henry Frankenstein in Whale's *Frankenstein* and *Bride of Frankenstein*). Clive, who was being paid £30 [about $2,300 in 2019 dollars, adjusted for inflation] per week to appear in the London play, would arrive in Los Angeles on December 1 and be paid £500 [almost $38,000] per week for his work on the film.

> Colin Clive has sailed for America to fill the part of Stanhope in the Gainsborough-Welsh-Pearson production of "Journey's End," which is to be made in conjunction with Tiffany Stahl, and work on that picture will now commence. The great advantage of having Colin Clive is, of course, that he gave such a faultless performance in the stage play in the West End of London. The full cast of "Journey's End" will now be as follows :—
>
> Captain Stanhope, Colin Clive (English) ; Lieut. Osborne, Ian MacLaren (English) ; Sec. Lieut. Trotter, Billy Bevan (Australian) ; Sec. Lieut. Raleigh, David Manners (Canadian) ; Sec. Lieut. Hibbert, Anthony Bushell (English) ; and Private Mason, Charles Gerrard (Irish).
>
> James Whale, who directed the stage version of " Journey's End." both here and in America, will be in charge of the picture.

Nevertheless, Sherriff believed Clive's absence caused a break in the play's momentum which never healed:

As 1929 drew near its end it looked as if the play would run through 1930 and on for years and years. "I can't see what there is to stop it," said the box office manager. It was nearly a year old, but the theatre was full every night, and people were booking well into the spring and summer. Up till then the management hadn't put a foot wrong. To make assurance doubly sure they kept it before the public in every way they could. They plastered the London busses with the slogan "All roads lead to Journey's End", and never missed a chance to get some item of news about it into the papers.

Sherriff went to Maurice Browne and implored him not to release Clive to play the part of Stanhope in the film version. He felt Clive's departure would break the momentum which the play had developed. He felt it would be better if an established American star be cast as Stanhope.[33]

The circumstances suggest Sherriff was right about Clive's departure having an adverse effect upon the viability of the London performance. Accustomed to having sold-out houses every night, attendance at the play began to slowly decline. Box office receipts went down, as well. From about £2,000 [about $180,000 in 2019 dollars, adjusted for inflation], they steadily declined over the weeks to £1,807 [about $163,000], £1,776 [about $160,000], £1,707 [about $154,000], to £1,653 [about $149,000].

> The pit and the gallery began to feel the pinch too. The "House Full" boards that had gone out every night for nearly a year went back to their cupboard in the basement, and only came out on Saturday nights.
>
> We all hoped that Clive's return to the cast would put things right again, but the spell was broken: we never got back to crowded audiences. [34]

Clive's return to the play on January 13, 1930 did not stop the decline; the play would see its 500th performance on March 17 and would close on July 6, 1930. "Sherriff had earned £48,000 [approximately $5.1 million in 2019 dollars, adjusted for inflation] in royalties from the worldwide performance rights and the published version, which had sold 175,000 copies."[35]

Once Clive was on board, the remaining cast was completed: Tom Whitely as the Sergeant Major, Robert A'Dair as Captain Hardy, and Jack Pitcairn as the Colonel. "According to Pearson, the first voice tests of Colin Clive using the Photophone system were 'dreadful.' RCA technicians heatedly accused Tiffany of tampering with the equipment. New tests were ordered—it was inconceivable Clive's voice would not record beautifully—and filming was finally allowed to begin on Friday, December 6—one day behind schedule—with Stanhope's arrival in the dugout."[36] Pearson was, at first, impressed with Whale's work:

He [Whale] had a habit of sitting with one foot tucked under him, perfectly still, eyes intent, ears alert for any error in emphasis or inflection. These were really stage rehearsals, unimpeded by camera technique, in order that the players would be word and action perfect when the filming began, and a translation of a play to the screen called for new conventions. The moment arrived after three days of stage rehearsals.

Filming started. Whale was as determined as myself that nothing should go wrong. In that intention we discussed the vital element of camera mobility, and the film's peculiar ability to condense time whereby stage minutes became screen seconds. He was aware of these essentials through his experience with *Hell's Angels*, and so, because of our mutual confidence in each other, all went well. With all the purely technical points agreed, we sat together during filming. When he was satisfied that he had obtained what he wanted by rehearsal, the camera 'take' was made, and during this I retired to the sound booth to check the speech clarity. In this friendly fashion the film was made."[37]

Whale and Pearson would clash over battle trench scenes.

Despite Pearson's recollections, this "friendly fashion" would not continue. Pearson would later question Whale's "camera technique," and Whale would soon begin to resent what he felt was Pearson's interference in his film:

> Pearson's distrust of the sound equipment kept him on the set almost constantly. "I often saw him busying about like a bird dog on this thing and that," said David Manners. "He was very concerned about production costs and at times wailed that this was too costly or that . . ." Filming went smoothly for a few days, until Pearson got a look at the rushes. So crudely had they been staged, he averred, that the first week's footage would have to be scrapped and re-staged.
>
> Defensive and irritable, Whale resisted Pearson's insistence on approving every set-up. After a day's filming under the new arrangement, the quality of the work, in Pearson's estimation, improved markedly and they settled into an uneasy partnership for the remainder of the shoot. Equipment breakdowns plagued the film, putting them three days behind in the first week alone. Pearson quarreled with Whale over composition, with RCA over the sound quality, and with both Tiffany and Balcon over costs. "I have a feeling George was not too happy about producing in California," said Manners, "Cost were ever disturbing him."
>
> Pearson took to lunching with Whale, talking camera theory and the role of dialogue in films vs. stage plays. At first he found Whale receptive, but after so much pontificating about composition and such, Whale grew cool to his advice and eventually tuned him out altogether.
>
> The trench scenes began on December 12, and went well until Pearson began annotating Whale's script with camera angles. "I feel Whale has to be shocked out of his stage ideas," Pearson wrote in his diary, "or we shall have some poor cinema stuff. He is learning at our expense. . . ."
>
> Part of the problem was in Tiffany's selection of Benjamin Kline as the cinematographer. On *Hell's Angels* Whale had enjoyed the counsel of Tony Gaudio, who had directed films himself and would go on to win the Academy Award for his camerawork on *Anthony Adverse*. Kline, by contrast, would spend his career shooting "B" westerns, routine programmers, and Three Stooges shorts. His sense of photographic values did not extend beyond keeping his actors in focus and his set uniformly lighted; Whale would learn nothing from him, nor profit from his expertise.

George Pearson and James Whale with crewmembers on the set of *Journey's End*

As Christmas approached, Whale's resentment of Pearson intensified. Pearson's sense of picturization was based solely on silent principles, while his understanding of montage was influenced by the work of Russian masters Pudovkin and Eisenstein (though his films didn't reflect it). Whale, on the other hand, was trained for the talkies and knew from his work on *Hell's Angels* and *The Love Doctor* that dialogue decided the cut, not story nor characterization. *Journey's End* was a filmed stage play that would have to reflect sound theatrical values if its translation to the screen was to be successful. On Christmas Eve, Pearson took Whale to lunch and gave him a copy of *Pudovkin on Film Technique*, which is likely the only book on film theory Whale ever read.[38]

Pearson's intransigence would continue. With only four days left before Clive had to return to England, Pearson watched the rushes with March and David Lewis and found them "not good at all." "He gave Whale his notes the next morning, but with just three days left, Whale told him there was nothing to be done."[39] There was simply no time to re-shoot Clive's scenes in three days. "Pearson stormed off the stage and did not return until December 30, the day Clive's scenes were completed."[40]

Billy Bevan's scenes as Trotter were completed the same day as Clive's. David Manners and Ian Maclaren finished their scenes on December 31. "[T]he last day in the studio came on January 3, when the dugout was summarily destroyed in a shell blast and the ghostly image of a single candle flame was momentarily left flickering in its wake."[41]

Five days of exteriors remained, but there were delays due to rain and the film didn't actually wrap until January 22—almost three weeks behind schedule—when the company shot until two in the morning on the same patch of land in Culver City where the massive gates of King Kong's Skull Island would soon rise and where, in 1939, the facade of Tara would be built for *Gone With the Wind*.

During the storms, Whale and Pearson cut the film they had already shot. In the close confines of the cutting room, the two men got considerably on each other's nerves. Whale found Pearson's fussiness and impatience grating, while Pearson objected to Whale's constant talk of money and the jobs he would get. With the cost of *Journey's End* creeping toward $300,000 [about $4.6 million in 2019 dollars, adjusted for inflation] and the 15-week term of Whale's contract nearly up, Grant Cook asked him to forego the weekly payments contractually due him to finish the picture, a proposal Whale regarded with horror. He refused, prompting Cook to plead his case through Pearson, who had grown to resent the slow pace at which the editing was proceeding. "Whale is really useless at the mechanical side of things," he groused in his diary. "I wish he wouldn't be so money grubbing."

When Whale held his ground on the question of salary, Cook suggested to George Pearson they fire him and finish cutting the picture themselves. Pearson resisted, secretly worried Cook would cut the film too severely for its American release. He agreed only to "hurry Whale along," but no amount of hurrying would finish the film by February. *Journey's End* was not ready for preview until March 13, 1930, when it was successfully shown to a capacity audience at the California Theater in San Bernardino, some 50 miles east of Los Angeles.

Pearson departed for England the next day, leaving Whale to bask in the glory of *Journey's End* by himself.[42]

"WELL, WHAT DO YOU WANT?"

A TIFFANY PRODUCTION
In conjunction with
GAINSBOROUGH —— PICTURES, Ltd.
and WELSH·PEARSON·ELDER, Ltd.
Continuity by Joseph Moncure March

TIFFANY presents
"JOURNEY'S END"
WITH
COLIN CLIVE
by special permission of Maurice Browne, Ltd.

FROM THE PLAY BY R.C. SHERRIFF — Produced
by arrangement with Maurice Browne
Directed by
JAMES WHALE
CAST: Ian MacLaren · Anthony Bushell · David Manners
Charles Gerrard · Thomas Whitely · Billy Bevan

Original lobby card #3 from _Journey's End_

The film followed the stage play fairly closely. However, Whale did move the camera outside the dugout for an opening sequence showing the soldiers, under shellfire, moving up through a rear area, into a ruined village and through a communications trench on their way to the line. Eleven additional scenes took place either out in the trench or in no-man's land, most notably the daylight raid in which Osborne and six Other Ranks are killed, and the German attack on the morning of March 21. These scenes are not, of course, shown or described in detail in the play, which has its action confined entirely within the dugout. Watching the daylight trench raid scene in the film, one wonders how much the action and the staging were influenced by Whale's experiences having led the "stunt on a pill-box," which resulted in his capture at Wieltje near Ypres, on August 25, 1917.

> _Journey's End_ remains a considerable achievement for a first-time film director [first-time as a _credited_ film director, that is—Whale had already directed approximately sixty percent of _Hell's Angels_]. Whale managed to open out the action of the stage play without compromising the tightness of the original script. His approach is restrained and a little too careful, particularly his

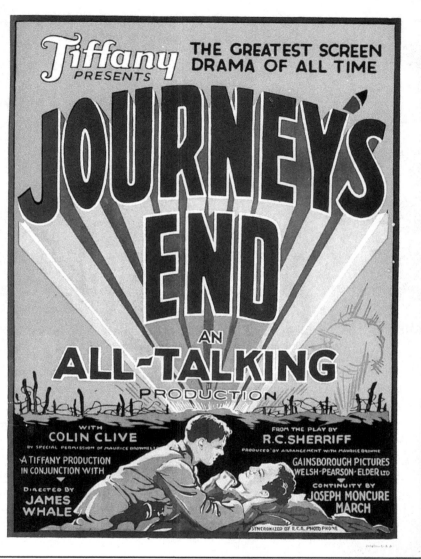

Original window card for *Journey's End*

preservation of the proscenium arch, but his camerawork is fluid and interesting. The battle scenes, which are the chief cinematic invention of the piece, are vivid and different. It is clear
that Whale was excited by the possibilities of new film techniques and determined to master the medium quickly.

Several of Whale's favourite film conventions are established in *Journey's End*, particularly his device of introducing a

character in darkness, moving into light, and building up their mystique via descriptive dialogue. The heroic Stanhope, after all the fulsome praise of his men ("The finest officer in the battalion"), wanders into the dugout with his only thought for whisky.[43]

Following the successful preview in San Bernardino, Whale would travel to New York and attend the film's premiere on April 8 at the Gaiety Theater, less than a half-mile from Henry Miller's Theatre, where the play was still running.[44] The film was a smash hit.

> James Whale, who staged the original London and New York productions of "Journey's End," will arrive today on the Olympic to supervise final rehearsals of the company which will reopen the play on Monday at Henry Miller's Theatre. The Ile de France today will bring Danielle Bregis, who will be prima donna of Connolly and Swanstrom's production of "Princess Charming," scheduled to begin rehearsals on Aug. 11.

NY Times, Broadway Notes 7/29/1930

Whale's careful, almost pedantic filming of the play had much the same impact on its opening night audience as had the stage version before it. George Gorbard of the *New York World* reported "a seemingly stunned audience remained seated and inarticulate for a full minute after the picture had been completed and the lights had been turned up." Gorbard went on to call *Journey's End* "undoubtedly the greatest picture of the year."

The critical praise in New York centered on two principal elements of the film: Colin Clive's astounding performance as Captain Stanhope, meticulously preserved on film and seen for the first time in the United States, and Whale's own careful direction. "It bears the stamp of all-around perfection," said the New York *Evening Post*, "and James Whale has unquestionably placed himself along with the foremost screen directors."

The second night at the Gaiety was bought out by an entire division of New York troops, and the audience included General John J. Pershing, who had commanded the American expeditionary forces in Europe in 1917-18. Whale lingered in Manhattan just long enough to absorb the critical adoration of the daily papers; the magazine notices, equally enthusiastic, would trickle in for weeks.[45]

The film went into general release on April 15, 1930 and a review appeared in *Variety* the next day.

"No crystal gazing required to forecast a big measure of success for this picture," wrote the unnamed reviewer, "because so many elements enter into the situation to insure its future. Intrinsic power of the story alone would be sufficient. On top of that, the production had the enormous advantage of the well-advertised success of the play and thoroughly capable translation to the screen. . . ."[46]

Whale traveled to England for the London premiere at the Tivoli Theatre on April 14, arriving at Paddington Station just 24 hours prior to the event.

> The next afternoon, he gave an interview to the theatrical correspondent of the *Daily Mail* in which he defended the rigid theatricality of the film and its fidelity to the play. "The triumph which has greeted our flouting of the accepted conventions has been so decided that it has left us gasping a little," he said. "There was plenty of tact and firmness needed before we started."
>
> The London notices rivaled the American reviews, with British critics obviously proud of the fact that a talkie with such widespread appeal could legitimately said to have been "British made." R.C. Sherriff noted with satisfaction that March's careful pruning of the text followed the stage play "in all the important details." James Agate, the play's most fervent admirer, went so far as to declare that the film was actually better than the play "if only for the reason that it is more real," showing war, via Whale's external battle scenes, "as the essentially foul, beastly thing that it is in reality."
>
> *Variety's* London correspondent filed a review that ran in New York on April 30: "If one regards this as a British film," he wrote, "it is hardly too much to say that it comes near to, if it is not actually, the best that has ever been done. It is a pity it was not made here; but it is a still greater pity that it could not have been made here. For it is foolish to delude ourselves that so much sheer technical excellence as this film has from first foot to last could have been obtained in a British studio"
>
> Overnight, Whale found himself at the very pinnacle of the British film industry with the most critically honored film of the season. The success of *Journey's End* would have allowed him to work comfortably in any aspect of the industry, but he expressed little interest in directing films in the United Kingdom. The obvious limitations of an English career held little appeal for him alongside the money and prestige he now saw in Hollywood. *The Film Daily*, published in New York, named Whale one of the best directors of 1929-30, based on a nationwide poll of over 300 journalists. On the strength of just one film, he found

himself ranked alongside King Vidor, Clarence Brown, Frank Lloyd, and Ernst Lubitsch.

Michael Balcon's wise determination to beat *All Quiet on the Western Front* into release paid off handsomely. In just two months, *All Quiet* was out as well, and Lewis Milestone's cinematic masterpiece rolled over the cheaper, more constricted and theatrical *Journey's End* like a celluloid steamroller.[47]

Unfortunately, the film has not been officially released on either DVD or Blu-Ray, although there are DVD bootlegs floating around which have been burned from either an old VHS tape or a television broadcast. This is a shame, as the film truly merits a restoration and a first-class Blu-Ray release. I am frankly surprised that no one had produced such a disc to coincide with the 100th anniversary of either "Operation Michael" or the Armistice.

Shortly after the release of *Journey's End*, Whale had hired an agent named S. George Ullman, whose claim to fame had been representing the late Rudolph Valentino. Ullman gave bad advice (as relayed by David Lewis, Ullman told Whale "to get out of Hollywood so he could deal"). Ullman didn't "deal," and his advice effectively prevented Whale from immediately capitalizing on the success of *Journey's End*, "and the release of *All Quiet* pretty much wiped *Journey's End* from the industry's collective memory."[48] R.C. Sherriff had written another play, *Badger's Green*. Completely different than *Journey's End*, it was based upon a play Sherriff had "written when the twilight had fallen over the Adventurers' Dramatic Society" of the Kingston Rowing Club, "about a country village that became the target for a development company, and the project split a previously happy community into two hostile camps."[49] Sherriff called the village Badger's Green, and that became the name of the play. James Whale was in England following the British premiere of *Journey's End*, read Sherriff's new play and liked it. Both men wanted to do something to set themselves apart from *Journey's End* and war plays, and a story about a pastoral English country village would do the trick. *Badger's Green* would move into the Prince of Wales' Theatre after *Journey's End* closed. James Whale would direct. "The rehearsals were a joy" and "The first

HAIL 'JOURNEY'S END' FILM.

London Spectators Expect It to Set New Record for Engagement.

Wireless to THE NEW YORK TIMES.

LONDON, April 14.—With the stage production of "Journey's End" about to be withdrawn on May 24, after a run of more than 600 performances, the screen version of R. C. Sherriff's play was seen for the first time at the Tivoli Theatre tonight.

The film reviewer of The London Times tomorrow will say that while it represents "a careful transference from the stage to the screen, the film has not the vitality of the play, an indefinable shadow of remoteness hanging always between the spectator and his illusion." He has the highest praise for the acting, direction and mechanics of the picture, however.

The film was enthusiastically received. The virtually unanimous opinion was that it was likely to establish a new record for a film engagement here.

night was a glittering occasion, and everybody looked happy, chattering away, laughing, greeting friends."[50] On the second night, the bottom fell out. Unlike the glowing notices heaped upon *Journey's End*, however, the critics savaged *Badger's Green*, with Hannan Swaffer's verdict "SHERRIFF TRIES AGAIN AND FAILS."[51] Not only was the play a flop–many believed it was due to Whale's direction and his inability to play up the comic aspects, and his arrogant handling of the actors.[52]

Whale, with two more shows to direct for Gilbert Miller, returned to New York. With six weeks to fill at Henry Miller's Theatre, Gilbert Miller decided to do a revival of *Journey's End*, which Whale would direct, made up of cast members from various touring companies. The play was received with little enthusiasm. Whale's next project was to direct a pair of one-act plays by the Hungarian playwright Ferenc Molnar for Miller, *The Violet* and *One, Two, Three!* "Whale lavished most of his attention on *One Two, Three!* (which required a cast of 24) and designed a spectacular art deco set to go with it." Reviews were good for Ruth Gordon's performance in *The Violet*, but not very good for the rest of the program, which closed after a month.[53]

Howard Hughes had held *Hell's Angels* from release until 1930, but its arrival on screen did not do much for Whale's career either. The film had been:

> [H]eld from release too long to impress anyone with its crude three-camera technique. All the attention and praise focused on the combat footage Hughes himself had directed in 1927, and the talking passages directed by Whale were greeted with yawns from audiences and hoots from critics who found the dialogue stilted and the staging wooden. "With his four million dollars," wrote critic and playwright Robert Emmet Sherwood, "Mr. Hughes acquired about five cents' worth of plot, approximately thirty-eight cents' worth of acting, and a huge amount of dialogue, the total value of which may be estimated by the following specimen. Boy: 'What do you think of my uniform?' Girl: 'Oh, it's ripping!' Boy: (nervously) 'Where?'"[54]

"Whale didn't want to remain at Tiffany. He disliked Phil Goldstone, who had replaced John M. Stahl as production chief, and quarreled with Grant Cook over money." [Cook refused to pay Whale the $1,333 (approximately $20,500 in 2019 dollars, adjusted for inflation) he was owed per week for the six additional weeks he had spent working on *Journey's End*.][55] Unfortunately, Ullman's flawed strategy gave Whale little option but to try to bear up and work with Goldstone. However, production at Tiffany was winding down, and James Whale didn't really have very much to do there.

Whale would meet with Carl Jr. at Universal in February 1931.[56] The men discussed adapting Robert Emmet Sherwood's play *Waterloo Bridge* for the screen;

Whale had prepared for the meeting by reading the play. Laemmle Jr., "who was known to be a sucker for foreign directors," was impressed by Whale, and on March 14, 1931 Whale would sign a contract with Universal for a year's employment with an option at six months, and Universal announced Whale would direct *Waterloo Bridge*.[57] Playwright Benn Levy, who had adapted *The Man With Red Hair* for the stage, was brought in to adapt Sherwood's play for the screen.[58]

Waterloo Bridge (1931) is a romantic melodrama set in wartime London. Myra Deauville (Mae Clarke, who would play Henry Frankenstein's fiancée, Elizabeth, in *Frankenstein*) is an American working as a chorus girl on the London stage. The show she is working in closes. Unable to find employment in another show, or elsewhere, she turns to prostitution to support herself. She heads to one of her favorite spots, Waterloo Bridge, just in time for a Zeppelin raid. Roy

Things end badly for Kent Douglass, Doris Lloyd and Mae Clarke on *Waterloo Bridge*.

WATERLOO BRIDGE

Cronin (Douglass Montgomery, as Kent Douglass), a 19-year-old American who is a Private in the Canadian Army, newly arrived in London on leave, meets Myra on the bridge and they take shelter together. They end up in Myra's flat, where they chat, smoke cigarettes, and eat some fish and chips. Myra tells Roy she is a chorus girl—Roy does not realize she is a prostitute.

Of course, Roy and Myra fall in love, but theirs is a doomed romance. While Myra had run away from home as a teenager to escape her abusive, alcoholic parents, Roy is from a very well-to-do background. His stepfather, Major Wetherby (Frederick Kerr, who would play Henry's father, Baron Frankenstein, in *Frankenstein*; the Major is the same doddering old, hard-of-hearing fool as the Baron—indeed, they are pretty much the same character), of the Royal Army Medical Corps,[59] has a big house in the country. Roy wants to introduce Myra to his family. She is reluctant, so Roy takes her on a "drive" in the country and just happens to end up at the Major's house, where they also meet Roy's mother, Mary (Enid Bennett), and his sister, Janet (Bette Davis). Their doomed romance ends, tragically, on Waterloo Bridge with another Zeppelin raid. Mae Clarke would recall shooting this final scene:

> "I remember it—a night scene on the back lot of Universal. The feeling of that scene was so overpowering! Everyone felt a reality over pretense. By that time, we had all learned to take advantage of every second Mr. Whale could give us—because his finger and his mind were in every single facet of the production. You'd ask, 'Where is Mr. Whale?' 'Oh, he's up on the boom crane tower, creating the bomber effect.' (He wanted to see Myra from the bomber's point of view.) You'd ask, 'Where's Mr. Whale now?' 'Oh, he's in checking the sound.' He knew just where he wanted the shadows . . . everything. It was HIS picture: a James Whale Production!"[60]

"[W]here *Journey's End* betrayed the careful work of a novice, *Waterloo Bridge* would represent an assured advancement in style that would lead to a string of 20 distinctive features over the next decade."[61] The reception was lukewarm when the film premiered in Los Angeles on September 3, 1931, but it did much better in the east, booking solid earnings as both a commercial and artistic success.[62] Despite having some 500 feet trimmed by the British Board of Film Censors, removing all reference to Myra as a prostitute, the film was a hit in Britain, as well, despite the cuts causing Whale to have been "horrified."[63] As a result of the success of *Waterloo Bridge*, Whale would enter into a five-year contract with Universal.[64]

Unfortunately, *Waterloo Bridge* would soon disappear from view to the extent it was long regarded as a "lost film." It was a "Pre-Code" film. In 1930, the Motion Picture Producers and Distributors of America ("MPPDA") promulgated its "Code to Maintain Social and Community Values." The man in charge of interpreting the Code was the President of the MPPDA, Will H. Hays; the Code became known as the "Hays Code" and the organization interpreting it as the "Hays Office." The Code was enacted to counter the scandals which had wracked Hollywood in the 1920s and was designed to ensure that only wholesome entertainment could be shown on the screen, in order to prevent "lowering the moral standards of those who see it." At first, compliance with the Code was voluntary and there was no mechanism in place to enforce it. On June 13, 1934, the Code was amended to create the Production Code Administration ("PCA"), empowered to interpret and enforce the Code. Compliance with the Code then became mandatory, and after July 1, 1934 no motion picture could be released without receiving a certificate of approval from the PCA. At that point, it became impossible to secure PCA approval for *Waterloo Bridge* without

Whale's *Impatient Maiden* would also become a victim of the Hays Office. Studio still featuring LewAyres and Mae Clarke

making significant cuts, so the film could not be re-released and was considered valueless. The release of MGM's sanitized remake in 1940 ensured continuing obscurity for Whale's film.[65] The film is available today in the Warner Archives Collection DVD box set of Pre-Code films entitled "Forbidden Hollywood Collection Volume 1," which also includes *Red-Headed Woman* (1932), starring Jean Harlow, and *Baby Face* (1933), starring Barbara Stanwyck.

1 Jolson was, at the time, the most popular singer in the United States, and still holds the record as one of the, if not the, biggest draws in the history of Broadway.

2 Gatiss, 43.

3 Curtis, 75-6.

4 In an endnote, the editors of the pamphlet say this is "Probably *Honky Tonk*, an early talkie that starred Sophie Tucker in her motion picture debut. Directed by Lloyd Bacon, this Warner Brothers release opened in New York on June 4, 1929."

5 Curtis & Pepper, *Whale Letters* (emphasis in original).

6 Curtis & Pepper, *Whale Letters*.

7 Curtis, 78.

8 Curtis & Pepper, *Whale Letters*.

9 Gatiss, 43.

10 Curtis, 81.

11 Curtis, 81.

12 Gatiss, 104.

13 Gatiss, 162.

14 Curtis, 84-6.

15 Gatiss, 45 (quoting March, Joseph Moncure, *Look*, letter, New York, March 1954).

16 Curtis, 89.

17 Curtis, 90.

18 Sherriff, *No Leading Lady* 162-8.

19 Curtis, 108.

20 Curtis, 91.

21 Curtis, 92.

22 Curtis, 91-4.

23 Curtis, 93.

24 Curtis, 94.

25 Curtis, 95.

26 Gatiss, 47.

27 Curtis, 95.

28 Curtis, 95.

29 Curtis, 97.

30 Curtis, 97.

31 Curtis, 96.

32 Curtis, 98.

33 This is a curious opinion regarding the use of a "name" actor known to Americans in the film.

Sherriff had previously lauded Whale's decision to go for the realism of unknown actors in the play as opposed to well-known performers. This attitude betrays something of economic self-interest on Sherriff's part. No doubt he had an author's pride in seeing his play have an extended run, but he had sold the film rights for £2,000, and thus had no further financial interest in the film, no matter whether it was a smash hit or an obscure flop. He was, however, receiving royalties from performances of the play. The decision to use Clive in the film was certainly a boon to posterity, as his performance was preserved on film and available to be seen long after the original play had closed, and the original principals had died.

34 Sherriff, *No Leading Lady* 190-1 (emphasis in original).
35 Gatiss, 51.
36 Curtis, 98.
37 Gatiss, 49-50 (quoting Pearson, George, *Flashback* (London Allen & Unwin 1957)).
38 Curtis, 99-100.
39 Curtis, 101-2.
40 Curtis, 102.
41 Curtis, 102.
42 Curtis, 102-3.
43 Gatiss, 51.
44 Curtis, 103.
45 Curtis, 103-4.
46 Curtis, 104.
47 Curtis, 104-5.
48 Curtis, 114-15.
49 Sherriff, *No Leading Lady* 195.
50 Sherriff, *No Leading Lady* 198-9.
51 Sherriff, *No Leading Lady* 201.
52 Curtis, 107-8.
53 Curtis, 110.
54 Curtis, 115.
55 Curtis, 114-15.
56 Curtis, 114.
57 Curtis, 116.
58 Curtis, 117.
59 Known by the acronym "R.A.M.C.," the propensity for a wounded soldier's personal belongings often to disappear somewhere between battlefield and hospital caused the troops to refer to this organization as "Rob All My Comrades."
60 Mank, Production Background, *Frankenstein* 27 (emphasis in original).
61 Curtis, 105.
62 Curtis, 125-6.
63 Curtis, 126.
64 Curtis, 126.
65 Curtis, 126.

Chapter Seven
In Which Frankenstein Makes a Monster

With the success of *Dracula*, Universal had decided to make "another horror film." As was the case with *Dracula*, which was not based directly upon Bram Stoker's book, but rather upon a stage play which was loosely based upon the source novel, so also was the case with *Frankenstein*. It was during a 1930 revival of Peggy Webling's play, *Frankenstein*, at the Little Theatre in London, starring Henry Hallat as Frankenstein and Hamilton Deane as the Monster, that the Christian names of the characters from the novel, Victor Frankenstein and Henry Clerval, would be swapped—this swap would be carried over in Universal's *Frankenstein*, with Victor Frankenstein becoming Henry and Henry Clerval becoming Victor Moritz.[1] Universal obtained the film rights to Peggy Webling's play, which was itself only loosely based upon Mary Wollstonecraft Shelley's novel (which was in the public domain), from Webling and John Balderston.[2] Universal paid $20,000 [about $337,000 in 2019 dollars, adjusted for inflation], plus one percent of the world gross[3] for the rights.[4] Universal chose 30-year old Frenchman Robert Florey to direct its new horror star, Bela Lugosi.[5] Florey would prepare a five-page synopsis:

[H]is major inspirations being the Germanic Cinema and the Grand Guignol of Paris. The adaptation reduced Mary Shelley's sly, insidious Monster to a grunting, rampaging monstrosity. Schayer [Richard Schayer, scenario editor at Universal] approved it and Florey began collaboration on a final script with his friend Garrett Fort, who had worked on the shooting script of DRACULA. Florey was responsible for the crude touch of a criminal brain being placed in the Monster. A happier contribution was the climax in the old windmill, an inspiration Florey received after looking out his apartment window on Ivar Street in Hollywood and seeing the windmill trademark of the Van de Kamp Bakery.[6]

Curiously, at the same time Florey and Fort were to begin working on their script, as part of the deal by which it had acquired the rights to the Webling play, Universal engaged John L. Balderston to adapt it into a screenplay.[7] Schayer gave Florey the go-ahead to proceed with a full screenplay, but the deal with Balderston had made him nervous. Florey demanded that Universal sign a contract with him which promised he would both write and direct *Frankenstein*. "The studio slyly complied by devising a contract which promised Florey he would indeed write and direct—and young Florey signed it, overlooking the fact that nowhere did the document specify that the film was to be *Frankenstein*."[8] Florey then proceeded with the screenplay.

FILM NOTES

UNIVERSAL'S most interesting announcement of the week is that "Frankenstein," the old thriller by Mary Wollstonecraft Shelley, wife of the poet, may come to the screen in a version by that company. Negotiations for the dramatic rights to "Frankenstein" have been concluded between Universal, Peggy Webbling, who made the first version, and John Balderston and Hamilton Deane, authors of the version now being played in England.

Hamilton Deane is now appearing in "Frankenstein" in London. The book has been published in practically every language since it first appeared in 1817, and has been the inspiration for numerous writers and composers.

Perhaps the greatest surprise in Florey's original, however, are the personalities of the protagonists. Frankenstein is simply a smug, bullying, mad doctor, with little personality and no sympathy for his creation; the first time we see Monster and Monster-Maker together after the laboratory creation sequence, Frankenstein is torturing his creature with a whip and a hot poker! As for the Creature, he is simply a howling, hellish demon, totally devoid of the profound sympathy which later made Karloff's monster movie mythology.[9]

Lugosi was unenthusiastic about playing a character with no dialogue. As Florey later said in an interview with Gregory Mank: "Lugosi kept exclaiming 'Enough is enough!,' that he was not going to be a grunting, babbling idiot for anybody and that any tall extra could be the Monster. 'I was a star in my country and will not be a scarecrow over here!'"[10]

Florey shot two test reels with Lugosi as the Monster, striding around the sets of Castle Dracula, menacing Edward Van Sloan. Jack Pierce created the make-up, and with Karl Freund at the camera [Gifford is incorrect here—the cinematographer on the *Frankenstein* test was Paul Ivano] it may come as no surprise that the Monster looked like the Golem. Lugosi wore a broad wig and had a polished, clay-like skin. Said Van Sloan, "He looked like something out of *Babes in Toyland!*"[11]

Florey would dispute the description of the Monster's makeup:

> Over the decades Florey insisted that the makeup worn by Lugosi in the test was "identical" to the makeup later made world famous by Boris Karloff. He added that he had suggested the neck bolts himself, and that after Pierce applied them, Lugosi angrily yanked them off.[12]

There are conflicting stories of how the test went:

> The test was finally completed, despite all the problems, and ran for twenty minutes. It was hastened to a screening-room for Junior Laemmle's approval. Here, history provides us with conflicting accounts. Florey and Ivano [Paul Ivano, a friend of Florey's who had acted as cinematographer on the test[13]] both insisted that the top-brass reaction was excellent and that all the principal directors on the lot wanted to make *Frankenstein* as a result. The more familiar account states that Junior burst out laughing at Lugosi's appearance and stalked from the room leaving a somewhat shell-shocked Florey in his wake. Then, Lugosi roared "Ivano! My close-up was *magnificent!*" and gave the cameraman a box of dollar cigars before leaving in turn. Ivano gave the cigars to the hapless Florey, who must have guessed by now that things weren't going his way.[14]

Unfortunately, no film of the test has survived. Gregory Mank relates an interesting story of a magazine advertisement which purported to offer a copy of the test for sale:

> In the December 1969 issue of *Film Fan Monthly*, a former agent of Lugosi, who earned notoriety by selling copies of the actor's personal effects after his death, placed this advertisement:
> "BELA LUGOSI buffs: For sale: Screen test that Bela Lugosi made for the original *Frankenstein*. 35 mm sound, running time 21 minutes; same scene is shown twice with change in lighting, etc. Between scenes camera was left running and Carl Laemmle, James Whale, Colin Clive, and Lugosi can be seen and heard discussing the test and wardrobe Lugosi was wearing. Film can be examined and screened BEFORE purchase is made. Price:

Universal advance publicity for *Frankenstein* starring Bela Lugosi

$4,000.00 [almost $28,000 in 2019 dollars, adjusted for inflation]...."

This offer was obviously a fraud; it was, of course, Florey (not Whale) who directed Lugosi's test, and Clive was still in England at the time. The author knows of one individual who made an appointment to see this test reel; he was stood up.

In all probability, there is no surviving copy of the famous test reel. Considering its inferior reputation, the test was probably destroyed by the studio at the first opportunity.[15]

Paul Ivano's detailed recollections about the test are quoted extensively by Gregory Mank; Ivano had supposedly kept some of the footage in his garage, but it "had succumbed to nitrate disintegration."[16]

Robert Florey, who collaborated in preparing the screen situations for "Frankenstein" and is just finishing directing "Murders in the Rue Morgue," has been assigned to a third weird thriller at Universal City. He is to direct the filming of H. G. Wells' "The Invisible Man." Florey formerly made pictures in France. He is a Frenchman.

"[*Waterloo Bridge*] had so impressed Carl Laemmle, Jr., that he offered Whale the pick of any project to which the studio owned the rights. Out of 30-odd properties, Whale chose *Frankenstein*, but only because nothing else interested him."[17] This resulted in Florey being removed from the project.[18] Florey consulted his contract, only to find it did not specify that the film he would write and direct would be *Frankenstein*.

Still, Florey did not surrender immediately. He hoped an appeal to Bela Lugosi to join him in storming Junior's office might help; after all, Lugosi was a star with influence. However, Lugosi, while sympathetic to Florey, was never thrilled by Florey's script or the idea of playing a mute idiot, and was totally repulsed by Jack Pierce's ladles of makeup. Indeed, he had serious second thoughts about doing *Frankenstein* at all.[19]

Frankenstein would go to James Whale, while Florey would go off to write and direct, and Lugosi to star in, *Murders in the Rue Morgue*. "Florey soothed himself with the thought that at least he would have a major writing credit with *Frankenstein*, but this, too, was not to be; Whale removed Florey's name from the credits. Florey would protest, and this time Universal took his side, but too late to amend the domestic prints; Florey's name would appear only on foreign prints of the film."[20]

Said James Whale: "'I thought it would be amusing to try and make what everybody knows is a physical impossibility seem believable.'"[21] "At least, he reasoned, it wasn't another war picture."[22] Certainly not a war picture, but I would submit Whale's choice of *Frankenstein*, out of some 30 properties, reflected Whale's desire to explore, in an oblique fashion, themes which had arisen from his experiences in the War. As David J. Skal has written: "The *Frankenstein* pictures continued to be a cultural dumping ground for the processed images of men blown to pieces, and the shell-shocked fantasy obsession of fitting them back together again."[23]

On July 11, 1931, while still at work on *Waterloo Bridge* and before Francis Edward Faragoh had been brought in to work on the screenplay, Whale se-

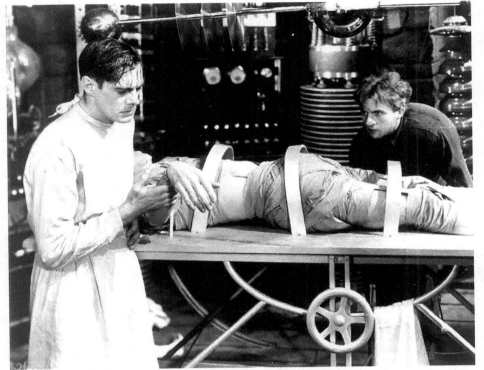

Frankenstein echoes the aftermath of a WWI fantasy of being able to put a man back together. Colin Clive and Dwight Frye check their creation.

lected the first "three members of the cast: Dwight Frye, Edward Van Sloan, and 72-year-old Frederick Kerr, whom Whale had asked to play the old Baron. 'Frederick Kerr is an asset to any picture,' he later said, 'and I wanted him because he is conventionally well-bred enough to not interfere with the personal liberty of any son over 18 years old.'"[24] While Whale may have thought highly of Kerr, his performance as the hard-of-hearing, doddering old Baron is one of the weakest points in the film. His conversation with, and put-downs of, the obsequious Burgomaster (Lionel Belmore), is probably his finest hour; his subsequent buffoonery much less so.

Whale's propensity to see the humor in the horror, something he absorbed from the War, would be much more successful in his casting of Dwight Frye. Frye had had a promising career on Broadway as a leading man, garnering rave reviews for his performance as Melvin Tuttle in *A Man's Man* as well as for subsequent roles.[25] On August 1, 1928, Frye, then 29 years old, would marry Laura May Bullivant. They would remain married until Frye's death at age 44 on November 7, 1943. When the couple returned from their honeymoon, Dwight, Laura, and Dwight's mother, Ella, would open a tea room in Manhattan, at 44 West 69th Street, near Central Park. "The Tea Room attracted a theatrical clientele, as well as many stockbrokers."[26] With the stock market crash in 1929,

Frye would give up the Tea Room and he and Laura would move to Hollywood, where Dwight would seek stardom in the movies.[27] He would snag several film roles, and in 1930 would be cast as Renfield, upright solicitor transformed into fly-eating lunatic in the thrall of the vampire, in Universal's *Dracula*. His performance was brilliant, but it was a double-edged sword. His role in *Frankenstein* would be as Fritz, Frankenstein's hunchbacked laboratory assistant, whose eccentric scuttling, sock-pulling, and muttering would be a high point of the film. The Broadway leading man with his scrapbook full of glowing reviews would, unfortunately, soon find himself typecast playing lunatics, half-wits, freaks, and bit parts.

Edward Van Sloan would be cast as Henry Frankenstein's old mentor from the University, Professor Waldman. He had played a similar character in *Dracula*, Dr. Van Helsing, a role he would reprise in *Dracula's Daughter* (with his "Van" mysteriously turning into "Von"). He would also play a similar character in *The Mummy*, Professor Muller. There is, however, an essential difference between Professor Waldman, on the one hand, and Van (or Von) Helsing and Muller on the other. Professor Waldman is a stolid, old-line, conservative professor of medicine, who was deeply suspicious of and skeptical about the lines of research which Henry Frankenstein was pursuing ("Herr Frankenstein was interested only in *human* life."). Van (or Von) Helsing and Muller are also stolid, no-nonsense fellows, but they differ in a very significant way from Dr. Waldman. Van (or Von) Helsing is a physician, but also an expert on the occult and vampires, who firmly believes in things that science cannot explain, and identified Dracula as a vampire. Professor Muller is an archeologist, but also an expert in mystic ancient Egyptian rites as set forth in the Book of the Dead, who pegs Ardath Bey as the re-animated mummy, Im-ho-tep. One cannot imagine Dr. Waldman believing in the occult, vampires, or re-animated ancient Egyptian mummies. In one of Whale's later films we will meet Henry's other mentor at University, who could not be more different from Dr. Waldman.

Meanwhile, following Florey's removal and Whale's assignment to *Frankenstein*, work continued on the screenplay.

> Whale's revamping of *Frankenstein* began. Having read Florey's script, he perused Balderston's adaptation (which included such episodes as the Monster beholding sunlight for the first time and accidentally drowning a young girl). The director screened such German fantasies as *The Cabinet of Dr. Caligari* (1920, with Conrad Veidt as the corpse-like somnambulist Cesare), *Der Golem* (1920, which also contained a fateful meeting between the giant monster and a little girl), and Fritz Lang's *Metropolis* (1926, with its awesome electrical laboratory), as well as MGM's *The Magician* (1926, with its tower laboratory and evil dwarf assistant). He discussed these ingredients with contract writers Garrett

Fort (who had worked on the script of *Dracula* and had written the dialogue for Florey's treatment) and Francis Edwards [sic] Faragoh. As a new script evolved, containing Whale's favorite material from Florey's script, Balderston's adaptation, the silent films and his script conferences, the director turned his thoughts to casting.[28]

The revised script would make the Monster a sympathetic character. "Pity for the Frankenstein Monster was not a new idea, but it had been so obscured by Balderston's adaptation of the Webling play—and in the screenplay Florey and Fort had derived from it—that it seemed new."[29] Pity is, of course, a theme straight from British reminiscences of the Great War. The parts of Dr. Waldman, Fritz, and the old Baron Frankenstein had already been cast. Of the main characters, Henry Frankenstein, his fiancée, Elizabeth, and his friend, Victor Moritz, remained. And, of course, the Monster.

Universal wanted Leslie Howard to star in the film as Henry Frankenstein. Whale "demanded" the part go to Colin Clive.[30]

Colin Clive, member of the original stage company of "Journey's End," and the English actor who made a name for himself in Tiffany's talkie version of the film, may return to Hollywood.

James Whale, who directed the stage and screen productions of the play, is at Universal, preparing to direct "Frankenstein," and wants Clive to play the role of the doctor. Universal has cabled him an offer to London, where he is starring on the stage.

Whale vetoed Leslie Howard. He remembered how cinemagoers wept at the anguish of the cadaverous, alcoholic, demon-ridden Captain Stanhope. It was a heartbreaking performance by Whale's young discovery, Colin Clive, and the only choice for the role of Frankenstein.[31]

Clive accepted Whale's offer and departed Southampton for New York aboard the *Aquitania* on August 8, 1931. "Colin Clive arrives in New York Friday afternoon, August 14. Awaiting him is a special delivery parcel from James Whale, with this letter: "

"I am sending you herewith copy of the script *Frankenstein*.

"It is a grand part and I think will fit you as well as Stanhope. I think the cast will be old Frederick Kerr as your father, Baron Frankenstein; John Boles as Victor, Bela Lugosi or Boris Karloff as the Monster, Dwight Frye as the Dwarf, Van Sloan as Dr. Waldman, and I am making a test of Mae Clarke as Elizabeth. Although it is largely an English cast, I do not want too much English accent about it, so in studying the part please keep this in mind. Of course, I do not want an American accent, but it is well to talk to as many Americans as you can to get that looseness, instead of what Americans think of as an English tightness, in speech. Do not let this worry you, it is merely a note."[32]

Whale selected this "haunted, highly strung actor who had played the tortured Captain Stanhope in the stage and film versions of *Journey's End*. He realized that Clive's nerve-racked intensity was also the perfect quality for Henry Frankenstein—a man on the edge if there ever was."[33] Whale had said he wanted Clive for the role "because he had exactly the right kind of tenacity to go through with anything, together with the kind of romantic quality which makes strong men leave civilization to shoot big game. . . ."[34] David Manners, who had played Raleigh to Clive's Stanhope in the film version of *Journey's End*, had this to say to Gregory Mank about his co-star:

> "To me, his face was a tragic mask, I know he was a tormented man. There seemed to be a split in his personality: one side that was soft, kind, and gentle; the other, a man who took to alcohol to hide from the world his true nature. . . .
>
> "Today he would find help. Every one of us wanted to help then, but when he was on the bottle, which was most of the time, he put on the mask of a person who repelled help and jeered at his own softness. . . .
>
> "He was a fantastically sensitive actor—and as with many great actors, this sensitivity bred addiction to drugs or alcohol in order to cope with the very insensitive world around them."[35]

On screen, Clive would portray obsessed, haunted Frankenstein in precisely the manner Whale had envisioned. Later Clive would say:

> I think *Frankenstein* has an intense dramatic quality that continues throughout the play and culminates when I, in the title role, am killed by the Monster that I have created. This is a rather unusual ending for a talking picture, as the producers generally prefer that the play end happily with the hero and heroine clasped in each other's arms.[36]

Much to Clive's chagrin, a last-minute revision would save Henry, who would be similarly reprieved in a later film, as well.

"'For Elizabeth, Henry's fiancée, I asked for Mae Clarke because of her intelligence, fervor and sincere belief that FRANKENSTEIN would claim the public's interest,' said Whale." Ms. Clarke had starred in Whale's first Universal picture, *Waterloo Bridge*. Mae Clarke had her doubts:

Edward Van Sloan and Colin Clive in *Frankenstein*

> When we had our first rehearsal meeting, I said, 'Really? British
> Lady Elizabeth?' Mr. Whale said, 'I think so. We don't have to
> go in for the broad 'A'—just a word here and there for flavoring.'
> I worried about the English accent, but finally Mr. Whale said,
> "When you speak—remember to cross your 't's."[37]

Whale would alter the script to enhance the part, adding Elizabeth into the meeting
with Dr. Waldman and into the creation scene. "The idea of Frankenstein's fiancée
being present at the creation of a man delighted Whale's quirky taste."[38]

Whale cast John Boles, "solid, handsome leading man then alternating
between roles as singing baritones in such fare as 1930's CAPTAIN OF THE
GUARDS and KING OF JAZZ and romantic melodramas such as 1931's
SEED,"[39] as Victor Moritz, friend of Henry Frankenstein and unrequited
lover of Elizabeth. "A U.S. spy in Germany, Bulgaria, and Turkey during World
War I, the pleasant, 35-year old Texas born actor was a fine foil to Clive."[40]

But who would play the Monster? Although Whale's letter to Clive men-
tioned that the part would go to either Bela Lugosi or Boris Karloff, at this point,
Lugosi was pretty firmly off the project and on his way to play Dr. Mirakle in
Florey's *Murders in the Rue Morgue*. In the summer of 1931, Boris Karloff, the

Englishman with the Russian name, who had been a journeyman actor in Hollywood, picking up whatever work he could, saw his career beginning to advance.

Indeed, since beginning his life as William Henry Pratt in Dulwich, England on November 23, 1887, Karloff had survived his exile by an unloving family, the agony of near-starvation, the wrath of rent-seeking landladies, the Saskatchewan tornado of 1912, the indignation of western America's most woebegone gypsy-like stock companies, and the heartache of at least three broken marriages. Arriving in Canada in 1909, a black sheep, due to his love of theatre, in a family of British diplomats, he labored as a farmer and a lumberjack before making his stock debut with the Jean Russell/Ray Brandon Players of Kamloops, British Columbia, as old Hoffman the banker in Molnar's *The Devil*. . . He had won the job by lying about his experience. "When the curtain went up I was getting thirty dollars a week," remembered Karloff. "When it descended, I was down to fifteen!". . . .

The stage finally delivered Karloff to Hollywood. He soon found his "type" when as a French Canadian trapper villain in *The Deadlier Sex*, 1920, he tried to rape Blanche Sweet. However, fortune proved elusive and only then in 1931, after about 80 movie roles, some California stage work and a spell as a truck driver, was the skinny, bowlegged Karloff enjoying some notice. In Columbia's *The Criminal Code*, he won praise as the murderous jailbird Gallaway, a role he had created in the West

Coast stage company; in RKO's *Young Donovan's Kid*, he twitched as dope peddler Cokey Joe, out to hook little Jackie Cooper; and in the classic newspaper melodrama *Five Star Final*, just completed at Warners, he was an obscene joy as fake preacher/real pervert, T. Vernon Isopod, leering at the fishnet hosiery of blonde floozie Ona Munson and inspiring Edward G. Robinson to snarl, "You're the most blasphemous thing I've ever seen—It's a miracle you've not been struck dead!" Then playing a gangster in *Graft* at Universal, Karloff (whose weekly salary had risen to $350 per week) [about

Edward G. Robinson and Boris Karloff in a studio shot for *Five Star Final*

HOLLYWOOD, Cal., Sept. 8.—Sir Philip Sidney's description of "Frankenstein" was: "A tale which holdeth children from play and old men from the chimney corner." I don't think I can improve on that. It points to a new mood in motion picture making when such stories as this, and "Dr. Jekyll and Mr. Hyde" are chosen in a year when production executives are singularly careful as to investments and exploitation managers are solicitous to secure something which will fit in with the public fancy.

Perhaps the public fancy is ready for novelty; and the gruesome is the most truly novel thing the talking picture can give. Mary Wollenstonecraft Shelley has penned a tale which for horrors, rivals anything Edgar Allen Poe ever thought of.

James Whale, that British director who has given motion pictures two notable successes — "Journey's End" and "Waterloo Bridge," is translating the weird Shelley story into Gelatine. And he has brought Colin Clive to Hollywood—for the second time—to play the role of the young doctor whose ghoulish experiments are the motif of the tragedy.

"Queer family, those Shelleys, while the husband was writing about skylarks the wife was creating this tale of monsters," said Colin Clive amiably as he dropped into a chair during a brief interval from work.

"Naturally I like everything that is different and this is a distinct variation from the part of Stanhope and from the sort of thing I attempted this winter in New York. The theme of the story—a young scientist who creates a human being and informs it with life—fits in with some of the most recent scientific experiments of the day. That he brings to life a monster who understands nothing but murder—a fiend whose compulsion is to kill—makes the weird story one of the most gripping and compelling things ever filmed."

Boris Karloff, a Russian actor who has electrified local producers with his brilliant portrayal of Dr. Isopod in "Five Star Final," will play the part of the monster. The make-up—which, like that of Mr. Hyde, is being kept secret—takes two hours to accomplish. In transit from his dressing room to the stage Karloff wears a sort of cage over his head with thick veiling which conceals him from the studio staff as well as casual passersby. The arms are concealed beneath a large smock. During the course of the picture, the hands and arms must turn from black to livid white—a make-up mystery which will rival anything Lon Chaney ever attempted, and which will not be revealed until the entire picture is completed and released.

Karloff, who is Russian, speaks the most perfect English one could wish for. His voice, a mellow, exquisite baritone, will be heard to excellent advantage. It is one of the fine ironies of Hollywood that up to this actor's appearance in "The Big House," he was allowed to work for $10 a day in the extra ranks—none of the so-called keen eyes of the industry or the supposedly keen ears of the casting directors, catching the prize that lay hidden in their midst. It remains for the youngest producer in Hollywood, Carl Laemmle jr., to discover the value of this actor and put him under contract to Universal.

Mae Clarke will play the role of Elizabeth, Frankenstein's sweetheart in the unnatural tragedy. Her work in Hollywood has been notably good—as the banjo-voiced girl in "The Front Page" she won the acclaim of critics, and as the lovable unfortunate of "Waterloo Bridge" she cemented that acclaim.

Colin Clive—half British, half French—has English reserve and modesty coupled with Gallic charm. He comes to Hollywood only to play a part and then back to the stage again. This time he may be kept at Universal for some time. The studio is even now casting about for a role which will suit this versatile and magnetic actor, when "Frankenstein" is finished.

"Frankenstein" is one of the most direct departures from sex gelatine—a product which has been regarded as the most profitable of all ventures for some time now—which Hollywood has ever made. It is based on sincere effort and true values. Garrett Fort worked on the screen adaptation. James Whale is considered one of the truly inspired directors of this locale. No finer cast could possibly be assembled. No more hair-rising story could be imagined. The trend of the times is toward the unearthly, the ghoulish, the weird, the fourth-dimensional. "Frankenstein" achieves all of these things. Truly motion pictures are making some radical departures for 1932.

. . . . .

Error-filled syndicated movie column from 9/9/31 raises eyebrows today!

R. Bruce Crelin

$5,900 in 2019 dollars, adjusted for inflation—certainly not a bad salary, particularly in Depression-era America] was working so steadily that his fourth (possibly fifth) wife Dorothy had forsaken her school librarian job. They could even desert the "shack" (Dorothy's word) they shared atop Laurel Canyon, where they had gaily entertained on those Prohibition evenings by brewing green beer in the bathtub.[41]

The story of how Karloff was cast is a familiar one.

The inability to find a suitable actor [for the part of the Monster] was now causing Whale some concern, a fact he reflected to David Lewis. "Jimmy was absolutely bewildered," Lewis said, "although I didn't realize they needed a monster as badly as they did until he told me one day." Then, during the filming of his latest assignment, *Graft*, Boris Karloff entered the Universal commissary. "I was having lunch," Karloff explained, "and James Whale sent either the first assistant or maybe it was his secretary over to me, and asked me to join him for a cup of coffee after lunch, which I did. He asked me if I would make a test for him tomorrow. 'What for?' I asked. 'For a damned awful monster!' he said. Of course, I was delighted, because it meant another job if I was able to land it. Actually, that's all it meant to me. At the same time I felt rather hurt, because at the time I had on a very good straight make-up and my best suit—and he wanted me to test for a monster!"[42]

Whale's biographer James Curtis disputes the dates, noting *Graft* was in production from June 22 through July 12, 1931, at a time when Whale was still working on *Waterloo Bridge* and was likely not involved in seeking out cast members

for *Frankenstein*.[43] This would seem to agree with Whale's letter to Clive in mid-August 1931, in which he stated that both Bela Lugosi and Boris Karloff were under consideration for the part of the Monster. Be that as it may, the commissary story is satisfying even if it may not be entirely accurate. An alternate, and perhaps more factually plausible, if less emotionally satisfying, story is that David Lewis had seen Karloff's performance on stage in Martin Flavin's play, *The Criminal Code*, in May 1930 at the Belasco Theater in Los Angeles. Since Karloff had appeared in a number of films which were in theaters at the time Whale told Lewis about his search for an actor to play the Monster, it is quite possible Lewis saw Karloff in one of these films, and remembering his performance in *The Criminal Code*, mentioned Karloff's name to Whale. Indeed, this is the story that Lewis would tell.[44]

Nevertheless, James Whale was fascinated by Karloff's appearance.

> "Boris Karloff's face fascinated me. I made drawings of his head, added sharp bony ridges where I imagined the skull might have joined. His physique was weaker than I could wish, but that queer, penetrating personality of his, I felt, was more important than his shape, which could be easily altered."[45]

This alteration would not be so easy. Karloff would be sent to Universal's makeup empresario, Jack P. Pierce, to work up a look for the Monster. Whale passed his drawings to Pierce, asking "him to concoct a functional makeup, something that would give the monster an unearthly appearance but allow a full range of facial expressions."[46] Pierce would move slowly in creating his concept.

> Pierce's stalling tactic was, Karloff believed, instrumental in getting him the role. "I was just a freelance actor, but he [Pierce] was on the inside of the studio and he knew the importance of the film and the part. Because of his own position in the studio, he was able to forestall the test until he felt we were quite ready to do it. In fact he stalled it off for about three weeks. If I had asked for that I would have been thrown out on my ear, but in his position he was able to do it."[47]

In 1939, Pierce would tell the *New York Times* how he created the Monster's makeup:

I made him the way text books said he should look. I didn't depend on imagination. In 1931, before I did a bit of designing, I spent three months of research in anatomy, surgery, medicine, criminal history, criminology, ancient and modern burial customs, and electrodynamics.

My anatomical studies taught me that there are six ways a surgeon can cut the skull in order to take out or put in a brain. I figured that Frankenstein, who was a scientist but no practicing surgeon, would take the simplest surgical way. He would cut the top of the skull off straight across like a potlid, hinge it, pop the brain in and then clamp it on tight. That is the reason I decided to make the Monster's head square and flat like a shoebox and dig that big scar across his forehead with the metal clamps holding it together.[48]

. . . .

Karloff himself made one significant contribution to the makeup. "Finally, when we were in the last stages my eyes seemed too normal and alive for a thing that had only just been put together and born, so to speak." So Pierce put mortician's wax on the lids, veiling the eyes. With cheesecloth he simulated "pores" in the skin; with cotton strips soaked in collodion he produced "veins" and with a black beauty mark he accented Karloff's cadaverous face, (a touch Karloff further accentuated by removing a dental bridge).

. . . .

Junior Laemmle was amazed. Awed by the makeup, the producer also noted what Pierce had so wisely allowed: Karloff's gaunt, sensitive face was free for the play of emotion. The Laemmles approved Karloff's casting for a natural reason rath-

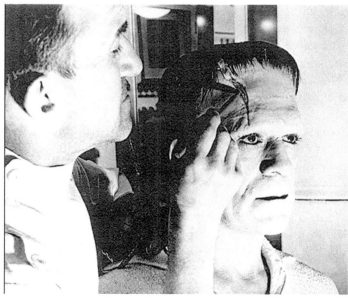

Jack Pierce works on Karloff's hand makeup for *Frankenstein*.

er than a cosmetic one: "Karloff's eyes mirrored the suffering we needed."[49]

With casting complete, and the Monster's makeup in place, *Frankenstein* went before the cameras on August 24, 1931, with a 30-day shooting schedule and a $262,000 [about $4.4 million in 2019 dollars, adjusted for inflation] budget.[50]

Shooting began with the opening scene in the cemetery.[51] Karloff's first appearance as the Monster would come on the tenth day of shooting.[52] He would face a grueling ordeal in bringing his "dear old Monster" to artificial life. "It took from four to six hours a day to make me up," said Karloff. "I felt like an Egyptian mummy as Jack ladled the layers of makeup on me."[53] The cast had to be on set at 9: 00 a.m., so Karloff had to begin the process of being transformed into the Monster at 4: 00. Said Karloff:

> To fill out the Monster costume I had to wear a double quilted suit beneath it. We shot in mid-summer. After an hour's work I'd be sopping wet. I'd have to change into a spare undersuit often still damp from the previous round. So I felt, most of the time, as if I were wearing a clammy shroud. No doubt it added to the realism![54]

The heat of the studio lights would cause the mortician's wax on his eyelids to crumble and melt, falling into his eyes and causing great pain.[55] Karloff would take his lunch alone, in his studio bungalow, stripping off completely to cool down. "Outside, stars and starlets strolled by on their way to the commissary, mercifully unaware that inside the bungalow lurked a naked Monster."[56] One incident with Boris in costume would provoke action from Carl Sr.:

This appears more a studio stunt than a leisurely walk for Karloff and Pierce.

One morning, very early in production, Karloff would take a little walk to escape the soundstage heat. As the laconic Pierce later validated, a pretty young studio secretary came around a corner. Karloff looked down and smiled. The secretary looked up and fainted. Word of her prostration reached Uncle Carl who quickly dashed off one of his personal mandates: "Some of our nice little secretaries are pregnant, and they might be frightened if they saw him!" Hence, Universal habitués beheld the sight of Karloff, a blue veil covering his head, strolling hand in hand with Pierce as the sympathetic make-up genius guided the player to and from the set. The actor was forbidden to leave the soundstage except for his bungalow lunch and two guards (probably Laemmle relatives) took up posts outside the stage door to safeguard against visitors and presumably an escape attempt by Boris. News of this intrigue became a popular topic around Hollywood, *Variety* noting it as the "kind of secrecy that makes publicity".[57]

"[S]ome of Karloff's worst agony" would come at the end of the shooting day, when his makeup was removed. "For one and a half to two hours each night, burning oils, severe acids ('plus a great deal of bad language!' added Karloff) stripped the makeup from the actor's face." His 15 to 16-hour days violated the Academy of Motion Picture Arts & Sciences' directive that an actor not work for more than 12 hours, unless given an expanded rest period on the following day. Karloff appealed to the Academy, and as a result his reporting time was moved from 4: 00 a.m. to 5: 30, Pierce streamlined the makeup process, and Karloff's day would end a bit earlier. Karloff was a staunch advocate for actors' rights, and was a founding member of the Screen Actors Guild in 1933.[58]

Karloff, however, was not at first impressed with his performance as the Monster. "One evening after viewing the rushes, the disheartened Karloff turned to Edward Van Sloan, and commented mournfully that *Frankenstein* would 'ruin my career.' 'Not so, Boris, not so,' smiled Van Sloan. 'You're MADE!'"[59] Karloff himself would not see the finished film until around Christmas, 1931, when he and his wife, Dorothy, were visiting one of Dorothy's friends, and they all decided to go to the theater and see the film. As Karloff told the story:

> Suddenly, out of the eerie darkness and gloom, there swept on the screen, about eight sizes larger than life itself, the chilling, horrendous figure of me as the Monster!
>
> And, just as suddenly, there crashed out over the general stillness the stage whisper of my wife's friend. Covering her eyes, gripping my wife by the shoulder, she screamed:
>
> "Dot, how can you live with that *creature*?"[60]

The film would make Karloff, after spending some two decades as a struggling actor, into an "overnight success." Karloff would later say, "'The part was what we call a 'natural'. Any actor who played it was destined for success.' Modest Boris, for not one of the actors who followed in his eighteen-pound boots achieved his stature."[61]

Mae Clarke was actually frightened of Karloff's Monster in makeup and costume. "[O]ne of the most famous moments comes when the black-clad Monster sneaks into the chamber of the bride and scares her into hysterics. The hysterics almost became genuine."

> Mae Clarke: "When we rehearsed it, I said, 'Boris, what are we going to do about this? . . . when we play it, and I have all my motors running and turn and see you, I'll fall to the floor! I won't make it to the bed!' Boris said, 'Mae, I'll tell you what I'll do. When you turn

around, my one arm is up-camera; focus on the little finger—I'll be wiggling it—and you'll know it's Boris in makeup.' So I looked at Boris' little finger and I was alright—JUST!"[62]

This "Boudoir Scene" is one of the most effective in the film and would also be one which raised the objections of the British censor.[63]

One incident would occur during filming which was not a credit to James Whale. In a scene near the end of the film, the Monster has knocked Henry Frankenstein unconscious and carries him up a hill.

Following supper, Karloff was required back on the soundstage to film Frankenstein's confrontation with his creation. Frankenstein is struck down and the Monster carries him up a hill towards the old windmill. It was this scene that proved, for Karloff, to be the most physically demanding of the entire shoot. Although filmed in long shot where stand-ins or, in Clive's case, a dummy could easily have been used, Whale insisted on no substitutes.[64] Karloff would carry Clive up the hill. The scene was repeated over a dozen times before Whale was content. Karloff's daughter, Sara Jane, recalled: "The most difficult part of the shoot was my father carrying Colin Clive up that hill time and time and time again until they got it right. Ultimately, he ended up having three back surgeries. He really suffered the rest of his life, physically, because of . . . the physical difficulties in shooting that film."[65]

"Whale's sadism even spread to his friend Clive. Seeking 'realism,' Whale demanded that Clive and Karloff tussle so long and so hard at the climax that Clive finally dislocated an arm."[66]

Shooting wrapped on October 3, 1931, five days behind schedule and almost $30,000 [about $500,000 in 2019 dollars, adjusted for inflation] over budget.[67]

> James Whale gave Karloff the greatest entrance an actor could hope for. From the grave-robbing prologue, all is literally build-up until the man-made man lies, bandaged and shrouded, waiting for life. Fervid Frankenstein, student of chemical galvanism and electro-biology, has stitched together a body from pieces hacked from coffin and gibbet. In his skull lies a brain stolen from medical university by his hunchbacked assistant. Little does Henry know that Fritz dropped the chosen brain and brought an abnormal one instead."[68]

Frankenstein had an audience for his efforts to bring his creation to life. Elizabeth, Victor Moritz, and Professor Waldman have arrived at the watchtower laboratory in the teeth of a raging storm, just as Henry was ready to complete

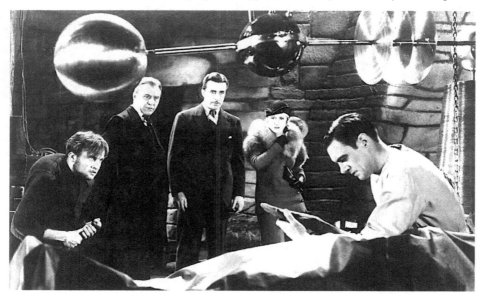

Frankenstein has an audience as he works on his patchwork Creature. Pictured left to right: Dwight Frye, Edward van Sloan, John Boles, Mae Clarke, Colin Clive

his experiment. He addresses the witnesses: "One man crazy![69] Three very sane spectators."

> "Think of it Fritz. The brain of a dead man waiting to live again—in a body I made with my own hands!" Henry has gone beyond the ultraviolet to discover "the great ray which first brought life into the world". At the height of the storm he raises his man through the roof of the tower laboratory, bathing him with lightning. The table is lowered; one hand raises slowly: "It's alive! It's alive." Fadeout.[70]

In an ironic twist, things would not go the way Henry planned. The Monster would kill Fritz, who sadistically and continually tormented him with burning torches and a whip. Frankenstein and Waldman resolve to destroy the Monster. They sedate him, and Waldman prepares to dissect, noting that the sedatives he had been administering to keep the Monster unconscious are becoming less and less effective. As Waldman prepares his surgical instruments, the Monster stirs. Grabbing Waldman by the back of the neck, the Monster kills him and escapes into the forest.

The film climaxes as Frankenstein leads a mob of villagers, bearing torches, to seek out and destroy the Monster. The Monster confronts Frankenstein and carries him to the old windmill. The Monster flings Frankenstein from the top of the structure, where, draping over one of the sails of the mill as he falls, he plummets to his apparent death. The mob sets the mill on fire. As the mob of villagers

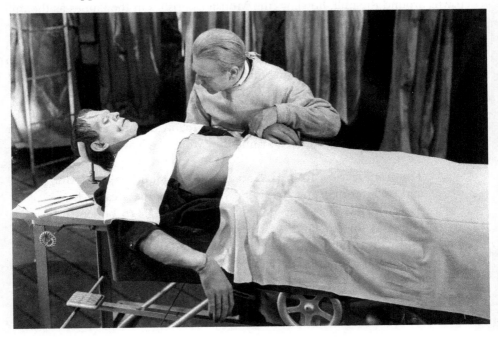

Did Whale's POW release influence the torch-wielding villagers and the windmill finale?

crowds around the mill, howling, the Monster perishes in the flames as the mill collapses. Professor Poole relates the collapse of the burning mill as reflecting "the catastrophic entombment of Raleigh" at the end of *Journey's End* [of course, Raleigh was already dead at that point], and "of bodies being buried beneath the carnage of trenches, the living and the dead sealed beneath the collapse of thousands of pounds of dirt[71] and concrete from shells and sap mines."[72] The scene of the cheering villagers surrounding the mill as it burns is reminiscent of Whale's description of the reaction he and his fellow prisoners had, nearly four weeks after the Armistice, upon learning they would be leaving Holzminden:

> The coming away from Holzminden was even more wonderful and exciting than the Armistice. To all of us the idea of freedom was too gloriously delicious for anything. To be leaving Hunland for England was intoxicating, and everybody went wild with delight. Tables, chairs, old clothing, and everything we couldn't bring home were dragged outside into the "apell platz" for a fire. We *must* have a bonfire! A match was put to a little pile and in less than ten minutes a huge fire was crackling merrily. The idea grew and streams of officers were soon feed-

ing the flames. The Huns, who were expecting to get all these articles as perquisites, were furious and tried to put it out with hose pipes. But the hose was quickly cut and the fire piled up and up. The people from the town thought the camp was on fire and came and stared through the railings. A weird sight we must have looked dancing and leaping about like wild Indians.[73]

As we will see later on, the scene at the burning mill will be repeated in the sequel.

A central theme, and irony, of *Frankenstein* is that a creator cannot control his creation, and indeed cannot even anticipate the consequences which might result from his actions—the classic ironic dichotomy between "expectation" and "actuality." Henry Frankenstein wants to discover the origins of life; he has found "the great ray which first brought life into the world," and uses that discovery to bestow life upon a manufactured body he stitched together, which had never before lived. He is successful, but his creation soon goes off beyond his control, in ways in which Frankenstein could not have anticipated. This parallels the origins of the Great War. Governments, supposedly in control of their own affairs, allowed a series of circumstances which transformed a minor incident in the Balkans into a major disaster that engulfed most of the world in a horrible war which would last for more than four years (despite the opinions expressed on all sides that it "would be over by Christmas"). While Frankenstein's Monster was responsible for a handful of deaths, the circumstances created by the governments of Europe resulted in millions of needless deaths.

The novel also shares this theme, but as a work from the early 19th Century it is not concerned with the details of how Victor Frankenstein constructed his creature or endowed it with life. Shelley is primarily concerned with morality and philosophy, not with science or technology, and simply writes that Frankenstein "succeeded in discovering the cause of the generation of life; nay, more, I became myself capable of bestowing animation upon lifeless matter."[74] There is no elaborate "creation" scene in the novel—Frankenstein simply "collected the instruments of life around me, that I might infuse a spark of being into the lifeless thing that lay at my

WAR'S TOTAL CASUALTIES ARE 26,000,000 MEN, LONDON PAPER SAYS

LONDON, Nov. 11.

THE Express estimates the casualties of European nations during the war as follows:

Germany—6,900,000.
Austria—4,500,000.
France—4,000,000.
Britain—2,900,000.
Turkey—750,000.
Belgium—350,000.
Roumania—200,000.
Bulgaria—200,000.

New York Evening World, 11/11/18

THE GREATER
DICKINSON
Thursday - Friday - Saturday

LAST TIMES TONITE
CLAUDETTE COLBERT
in
"SECRETS OF A SECRETARY"

At Last -- Kansas Can See This Picture

Watch his eyes!
He lives - he
breathes - he
walks - he sees
What is he
man or monster?

See

FRANKENSTEIN
THE THRILLER OF THE YEAR!

NEXT WEEK THE WEEK OF GOOD PICTURES

Mon.-Tues.-Wed.	News Years Eve	THUR.-FRI.-SAT.
Paul Lucas	"MIDNIGHT FROLIC"	JACKIE COOPER
Sidney Fox	"COMPROMISED"	ROBERT COOGAN
in	Free Noisemakers	in
Strictly	For All	"SOOKY"
"Dishonorable"	Reserve Your Seats Now	

feet."[75] In contrast, the film devotes considerable attention to the gathering of the materials to construct the Monster, and the technological marvels in Frankenstein's laboratory which he uses to animate his creation. Indeed, the scene in Frankenstein's laboratory where he instills life into the Monster, with the help of Kenneth Strickfaden's marvelous electric gizmos, places science and technology at the center of the film. Interestingly, in 1928, James Whale had acted in a play entitled *After Death*, in which he played a corpse brought back to life by electricity.[76]

In doing this, *Frankenstein* also casts doubt upon the idea of society's continuing, positive progress and the benefits of science and technology. "Progress" had been ingrained in the European psyche for at least a century. The idea that scientific discoveries are two-edged swords, which can be used for good or ill, was a constant of the "atomic monster" science fiction films of the 1950s, but this concept, as well, can trace its origins back to the irony and disillusionment of the War:

> But the Great War was more ironic than any before or since. It was a hideous embarrassment to the prevailing Meliorist myth which had dominated the public consciousness for a century. It reversed the Idea of Progress. The day after the British entered the war Henry James wrote a friend:
>
>> The plunge of civilization into this abyss of blood and darkness . . . is a thing that so gives away the whole long age during which we have supposed the world to be, with whatever abatement, gradually bettering, that to have to take it all now for what the treacherous years were all the while really making for and *meaning* is too tragic for any words.

James's essential point was rendered in rowdier terms by a much smaller writer, Philip Gibbs, as he remembered the popularity during the war of what today would be called Black Humor. "The more revolting it was," he says, "the more . . . [people] shouted with laughter":

It was . . . the laughter of mortals at the trick which had been played on them by an ironical fate. They had been taught to believe that the whole object of life was to reach out to beauty and love, and that mankind, in its progress to perfection, had killed the beast instinct, cruelty, blood-lust, the primitive, savage law of survival by tooth and claw and club and ax. All poetry, all art, all religion had preached this gospel and this promise.

Now that ideal was broken like a china vase dashed to the ground. The contrast between That and This was devastating. . . . The wartime humor of the soul roared with mirth at the sight of all that dignity and elegance despoiled.[77]

"But I think the First War cut deeper and played more tricks with time because it *was* first, because it was bloodier, because it came out of a blue that nobody saw after 1914. . . . After that your mind could not escape from the idea of a world that ended in 1914 and another one that began about 1919, with a wilderness of smoke and fury, outside sensible time, lying between them."[78] "Out of that world of summer, 1914, marched a unique generation. It believed in Progress and Art and in no way doubted the benignity even of technology. The word *machine* was not yet invariably coupled with the word *gun*."[79] The themes of "progress" as an illusion and science and technology run amok can be traced directly to the War.

James Whale, 1931

R. Bruce Crelin

203

Another aspect is the Monster as an essentially innocent, pitiable being, driven to rage and violence due to the circumstances of his creation and the actions of others. Florey had "developed a script in which the monster emerged as a pure brute, devoid of even the half-articulate pathos that Balderston and Webling had given it."[80] This was rejected and the skeleton of Florey's script was re-written by Garrett Fort and Francis Faragoh into a shooting script for James Whale, which added a deep note of pathos to the Monster.[81] The Monster is

a creature to be pitied. He, of course, had no say in his creation. When he is first revealed, he is a simple being. Frankenstein opens a skylight, showing the Monster sunlight for the first time, and the Monster reaches up to try to touch the light. Echoing a line Clive addressed to Raleigh in *Journey's End*, Frankenstein tells the monster to "sit down," and the Monster complies.

Karloff was extremely upset about the drowning of the child Maria.

Despite the plot device of the Monster having been given a "criminal brain," the Monster does not really exhibit criminal behavior. He kills Fritz, Frankenstein's hunchbacked assistant, but only for self-protection, after being continually provoked and driven into a mad frenzy by Fritz constantly tormenting him with burning torches and a whip. Similarly, he kills Dr. Waldman, but only as Waldman is preparing to dissect, and destroy, him. He does not intend to kill the little girl, Maria (Marilyn Harris). After playing a game with her, floating flowers in the lake, when the flowers are gone, he tries to float the girl, and is saddened when she drowns. Indeed, during shooting, Karloff objected to the scene, saying the Monster need not kill little Maria at all. Said Karloff:

> Well, that was the only time I didn't like Jimmy Whale's direction. . . . My conception of the scene was that [the Monster] would look up at the little girl in bewilderment, and *in his mind*, she would become a flower. Without moving, he would pick her up gently and put her into the water exactly as he had done to the flowers— and, to his horror, she would sink. Well, Jimmy made me pick her up and do THAT (motioning violently) over my head which became a brutal and deliberate act. . . . The whole pathos of the scene, to my mind, should have been, and that's the way it was written—completely innocent and unaware.[82]

The crew agreed, but Whale demanded the drowning. "'You see,' says Whale, 'it's all part of the *ritual*.'"[83] One wonders what sort of "ritual" Whale was referring to—could it have had to do with the War's unreasoning destruction of innocents, an outcome which was largely not envisioned or intended when the War started, an act which shocked and saddened the Monster as well as the audience.

As such, the Monster can be seen as a metaphor for the innocents who went to war, either willingly as volunteers, ignorant of the true circumstances they would meet at the front, or unwillingly as conscripts, who were commanded to fight and to kill, and underwent, at the very least stress, terror, fear, and privation, and

Countries allowed young teens to fight in the war.

at the worst, devastating wounds or death. He has been cobbled together out of spare parts, in much the same way as the New Army had been cobbled together from civilian volunteers, and later on, when men were involuntarily conscripted and sent to fight. Whale would further develop this idea of the Monster as an embodiment of the suffering of many, in the film's sequel.

Frankenstein had its first public showing in a preview on October 29, 1931 at the Granada Theatre in Santa Barbara, California.

> Its effect was instantaneous. "Up came the first shot in the graveyard and you could hear the whole audience gasp," Lewis explained. As the screening continued, the reaction grew. "The film has been imitated so much that today those scenes don't bother people," he said. "But in 1931, this was awfully strong stuff. As it progressed, people got up, walked out, came back in, walked out again. It was an alarming thing." When the film ended there was no applause, only shocked silence. According to *Film Weekly* the manager of the Granada Theatre was, "aroused at 2 a.m. by his house telephone and a man's voice which said, 'I saw *Frankenstein* at your place and can't sleep—and I have no intention that you should either!'"
>
> The preview cards were not kind. "Story is about a man destroyed by his own creation. Look out this doesn't happen to Universal," one viewer wrote. "Junior was scared to death," Lewis recalled. "He said, 'Jesus, God, we've got to do something! This thing's a disaster!' He thought no one was going to come to see it."[84]

No thriller ever made can touch it . . . this tale of
a monster who looked like a man . . . conceived in madness . . . built with love!

A UNIVERSAL PICTURE with
COLIN CLIVE ~ MAE CLARKE
JOHN BOLES ~ Boris KARLOFF
Frederic Kerr • Edward Van Sloan • Dwight Frye
Adapted by John L. Balderston from the play by Peggy Webling
From the strange story by Mary Wollstonecraft Shelley
Directed by JAMES WHALE
Produced by Carl Laemmle, Jr.

Pounds with Drama!
Burns with Passion!
Startles with Thrills!
Shocks with Surprise!

"FRANKENSTEIN"
THE MAN WHO MADE A MONSTER

— More amazing than "The PHANTOM"
— More fascinating than "DRACULA"

Changes were made. They had to be made quickly, as the film was scheduled to play the entire RKO circuit of 175 screens beginning November 21.

Henry would survive the fall from the burning mill. Mae Clark was brought in, but Colin Clive had already left the United States. The new scenes were shot on November 3. "Frederick Kerr returned as the Baron to toast 'a son to the House of Frankenstein.'[85] Behind him, through a doorway, could be seen Henry, lying in his sickbed, being nursed by Elizabeth. An unidentified actor took Clive's role in the scene."[86] "They shortened a scene by a river where the Monster floats flowers with his first friend, a little girl, then tries to float her; he is saddened when she sinks. The abrupt cut made things worse, adding awful implication when the child next appears, dead and draggled in the arms of her father."[87] "Laemmle Senior, reportedly, also wanted the entire lake scene cut. Whale resisted."[88] A prologue was added, with Edward Van Sloan, out of character and at his most avuncular, stepping out from behind a curtain and breaking the fourth wall by addressing the audience directly, with a polite warning:

> How do you do. Mr. Carl Laemmle feels it would be a little unkind to present this picture without just a word of friendly warning. We are about to unfold the story of Frankenstein, a man of science, who sought to create a man after his own image without reckoning upon God. It is one of the strangest tales ever told. It deals with the two great mysteries of creation: life and death. I think it will thrill you. It may even shock you. It might even horrify you. So, if any of you do not care to subject your nerves to such a strain, now's your chance to. . . Well, we've warned you!

The Great War and the Golden Age of Hollywood Horror

The film was a smashing success at the box office and a critical triumph. *Frankenstein* would earn more than $1 million [Approximately $18.7 million in 2019 dollars, adjusted for inflation] in its first domestic release. One of the biggest moneymakers in Universal's history, it was named as number 7 on the *New York Times'* list of the 10-best films of 1931, and was played at the very first Venice Film Festival in 1932 (despite having been banned in Italy).[89]

Frankenstein was a Pre-Code film, and thus not subject to mandatory censorship, although on Friday, November 13, 1931 it "was reviewed and awarded its MPPDA seal," being "passed uncut."[90]

> Many misconceptions have taken root about the extent of *Frankenstein* censorship in the United States. Most of the notable excisions—the drowning of the little girl, Colin Clive's line "I know what it feels like to be God," etc., were demanded cut by the MPPDA only after the film's proposed rerelease in 1937. The six states with censor boards, of course, could, and would, snip as they pleased—Kansas was particularly bad. But in censor-lite California, the film seems to have been shown intact—Clive's "God" line, for instance, was quoted in a San Francisco review. And the drowning scene was apparently still in place when Universal submitted the film to the MPPDA for reissue clearance; the industry censors made their formal objection to it on June 9, 1937. (The scene, found largely intact at the British Film Institute, was finally restored to a videodisc version of *Frankenstein* released by MCA in the 1980s, but still lacks close-ups of the child sinking, etc.—details the English censors marked for excision.)[91]

The film can now be seen in near pristine condition on Blu-Ray.

1 Mank, Gregory William, *It's Alive: The Classic Cinema Saga of Frankenstein* 13 (A.S. Barnes & Company, Inc. 1981).
2 Rigby, 97.
3 This would lead to litigation in the future, as Balderston, and Webling's estate, would contend the one percent applied not only to *Frankenstein*, but also to *all* the subsequent Universal films which featured Frankenstein's Monster. The matter was ultimately settled.
4 Mank, Production Background, *Frankenstein* 22.
5 Gifford, 83.
6 Mank, Production Background, *Frankenstein* 22.
7 Mank, Production Background, *Frankenstein* 22.
8 Mank, *It's Alive* 13.
9 Mank, Production Background, *Frankenstein* 23.
10 Mank, Production Background, *Frankenstein* 25.
11 Gifford, 83-6.
12 Mank, Production Background, *Frankenstein* 25.
13 Mank, Production Background, *Frankenstein* 24.
14 Gatiss, 70-1 (emphasis in original).

15 Mank, *It's Alive* 15, note *.

16 Mank, Production Background, *Frankenstein* 25.

17 Skal, *The Monster Show* 129.

18 Rigby, 97. Florey would later direct Lugosi in *Murders in the Rue Morgue*.

19 Mank, *It's Alive* 17.

20 Mank, Production Background, *Frankenstein* 27.

21 Gifford, 86.

22 Skal, *The Monster Show* 129.

23 Skal, *The Monster Show* 186.

24 Curtis, 135.

25 Mank, Gregory William, Coughlin, James T., and Frye, Dwight D., *Dwight Frye's Last Laugh: An Authorized Biography* 61-7 (Luminary Press 1997).

26 Mank, et al, *Dwight Frye* 77-80.

27 Mank, et al, *Dwight Frye* 87-92.

28 Mank, *It's Alive* 17-18.

29 Curtis, 133.

30 Mank, Gregory William, *Bela Lugosi and Boris Karloff: The Expanded Story of a Haunting Collaboration* 74 (McFarland & Company, Inc. 2009).

31 Mank, Production Background, *Frankenstein* 30.

32 Mank, Gregory William, *"One Man Crazy!" The Life and Death of Colin Clive, Hollywood's Dr. Frankenstein* 109 (Midnight Marquee Press, Inc. 2018).

33 Skal, *The Monster Show* 129.

34 Mank, *Lugosi & Karloff* 74.

35 Mank, *It's Alive* 22.

36 Mank, *It's Alive* 22 (quoting "Clive of Frankenstein," *The New York Times*, November 15, 1931, p. 6x).

37 Mank, Production Background, *Frankenstein* 31.

38 Mank, Production Background, *Frankenstein* 31.

39 Mank, Production Background, *Frankenstein* 31.

40 Mank, Production Background, *Frankenstein* 31.

41 Mank, Production Background, *Frankenstein* 29-30.

42 Jacobs, Stephen, *Boris Karloff: More Than a Monster* 91 (Tomahawk Press 2011).

43 Curtis, 136.

44 Curtis, 137-8.

45 Gifford, 86.

46 Curtis, 138.

47 Jacobs, 93 (quoting Gifford, Denis, *Karloff: The Man, The Monster, The Movies* (Curtis Books 1973)).

48 My Uncle Ed was an anatomy professor at Yale University Medical School, and his son, my cousin Bob, was a *bona fide* "Monster Kid" back in the mid-1960s. I wish I had asked Uncle Ed, back then, if Pierce's anatomical musings were really scientifically accurate.

49 Mank, Production Background, *Frankenstein* 32-4.

50 Mank, Production Background, *Frankenstein* 34.

51 Mank, Production Background, *Frankenstein* 34.

52 Curtis, 142.

53 Mank, Production Background, *Frankenstein* 34.

54 Mank, Production Background, *Frankenstein* 34.

55 Mank, Production Background, *Frankenstein* 34.

56 Mank, Production Background, *Frankenstein* 35.

57 Mank, Production Background, *Frankenstein* 35.

58 Mank, Production Background, *Frankenstein* 35-6.

59 Mank, Production Background, *Frankenstein* 40.

60 Mank, *It's Alive* 37.

61 Gifford, 89.

62 Mank, Production Background, *Frankenstein* 39.

63 Gifford, 89.

64 This is indeed curious. In this scene, a dummy could have easily been used to substitute for Clive, and the difference would not have been apparent to the audience. Contrast this with the scene where the Monster flings Frankenstein from the top of the mill—a dummy had to be used for that one, of course—but the flaccid, flopping dummy used for that scene looks painfully obvious.

65 Jacobs, 100-01 (quoting Karloff, Sara Jane, "The Frankenstein Files," *Frankenstein* DVD (Universal Home Video 1999)).

66 Mank, Production Background, *Frankenstein* 40.

67 Mank, Production Background, *Frankenstein* 40.

68 Gifford, 89.

69 This line would become the title of Gregory William Mank's biography of Colin Clive: *"One Man Crazy!" The Life and Death of Colin Clive* (Midnight Marquee Press, Inc. 2018).

70 Gifford, 89.

71 In one of many thousands of such incidents which must have occurred during the War, on March 7, 1918, 19 soldiers in the American 165th Infantry Regiment were killed when they were buried alive and trapped in a dugout in the Rouge Bouquet wood, which had collapsed during an intense German artillery barrage. New Jersey poet Joyce Kilmer, who was a sergeant in the 165th, wrote a poem about the incident, entitled "Rouge Bouquet." Kilmer was killed in action at age 31 on July 30, 1918. The 165th was formerly the 69th New York Infantry—a National Guard unit whose designation was changed when it was called into Federal service for the War—all Guard units called into Federal service in 1917 were re-designated with numbers in the "100s." President Kennedy would later return the unit's designation as the 69th to it. The Rouge Bouquet incident is depicted in the film *The Fighting 69th* (1940), starring James Cagney as the fictitious Private Jerry Plunkett, along with actors playing actual historical characters: Pat O'Brien as the 165th's Chaplain, Father Francis P. Duffy, who has a statue in his honor at Duffy Square in Manhattan; George Brent as the 165th's commanding officer, William "Wild Bill" Donovan, a recipient of the Medal of Honor in the War and the head of the Office of Strategic Services, the predecessor of the CIA, during World War II; and Jeffrey Lynn as Joyce Kilmer.

72 Poole, loc. 4055-60.

73 Whale, J., "Our Life at Holzminden" 339 (emphasis in original). I am grateful to Christopher Bram, author of *Father of Frankenstein*, for pointing out the similarity to me.

74 Shelley, Mary W., *Frankenstein* 45-6 (Barnes & Noble Books 1993).

75 Shelley, 51.

76 Gatiss, 18.

77 Fussell, 8 (quoting *The Letters of Henry James*, ed. Percy Lubbock (2 vols., New York, 1920), II, 314 (emphasis in original), and Gibbs, *Now it Can be Told* 131).

78 Priestley, *Margin Released* loc. 1197-1202 (emphasis in original).

79 Fussell, 24 (emphasis in original).

80 Skal, *The Monster Show* 128.

81 Skal, *The Monster Show* 129.

82 Gatiss, 79 (emphasis in original) (quoting Parry, Mike and Nadler, Harry, *Castle of Frankenstein*, 9, 1966).

83 Mank, *Lugosi & Karloff* 85 (emphasis in original).

84 Jacobs, 102-3.

85 Which, as Denis Gifford points out, is "a prophetic phrase foretelling two sequels unborn." Gifford, 89.

86 Jacobs, 103.

87 Gifford, 89.

88 Jacobs, 103.

89 Mank, Production Background, *Frankenstein* 41.

90 Jacobs, 103.

91 Skal, *The Monster Show* 137.

Chapter Eight
J.B. Priestley and the Benighted:
An Old, Dark House

John Boynton (J.B.) Priestley, christened "John" but always known as "Jack," was born on September 13, 1894 in Bradford, in the West Riding of Yorkshire.[1] At age 16 he had to make a choice: either "to leave school that summer or . . . to stay there to work for a university scholarship."[2] He chose to leave school "to become a very junior clerk" with a firm that exported "wool tops"—wool that had been washed and combed and was ready to be spun into yarn—"Helm and Company, Swan Arcade, Bradford."[3] Priestley did not think much of his value to his employer, however, and could not understand why he had not been sacked prior to his decision, in the late summer of 1914, to join the Army.[4] Unlike the other two principal subjects of this book, Priestley entered the Army as a Private and saw action initially as an Other Rank, a Lance Corporal, and not as a commissioned officer.

He enlisted on September 7, 1914,[5] "a few days" before he turned 20 years old.[6] "So early in September I joined, like a chump, the infantry–to be precise, the Duke of Wellington's West Riding Regiment, known in some circles as 'The Havercake Lads', in others as 'The Dirty Duke's'."[7] The report of his physical examination in his enlistment papers records him as five feet, eight and a quarter inches tall, weight 131 pounds, with a "fresh" complexion, blue eyes and dark brown hair, his religious denomination noted under "Other Protestants" as "Theosophists."[8] He reported to the regimental depot at Halifax, and after a

J.B. Priestley

week or two commuting back and forth from home to the barracks by early morning tram (what an ironic simulacrum of commuting to a civilian job), "left with a thousand others, by train at four in the morning, for a tented camp at Frensham in Surrey. There I found myself in Number 8 Platoon, B Company, 10th Duke of Wellington's, 69th Brigade, 23rd Division."[9] The men in his outfit "were almost all West Riding men. In my company there were a few suburban junior clerks and the like, of my sort, with whom I soon made friends. And the closer of these, whose names I still remember, were all killed, even before the Somme battles in 1916."[10]

Priestley and his companions were volunteers: "New Army men," members of "Kitchener's Army."

It is not true, as some young critics of the First War British high command have suggested, that Kitchener's Army consisted of brave but half-trained amateurs, so much pitiful cannon fodder. In the earlier divisions like ours, the troops had months and months of severe intensive training. Our average programme was 10 hours a day, and nobody grumbled more than the old regulars, who had never been compelled before to do so much for so long. It was only in musketry that we were far behind the Regular Army, simply because we had to wait for months for the rifles we would eventually use.[11]

Priestley found life under the bell-tents at this camp to have been particularly wretched, and the unit moved, first to Victorian brick barracks at Aldershot and then, at the end of February 1915, to billets in private homes in Folkestone.[12] His unit then moved to Maidstone, where Priestley was promoted to Lance-Corporal on April 7, 1915[13] and put in charge of billeting.[14] Then, in August 1915, "very late and dark one night," he sailed for France.[15]

British front line at Bois Grenier, near Armentieres. August 1915

Upon arrival in France, his unit moved toward the front and, luckily, was "initiated by degrees" into the trenches:

> We relieved the long-service Regulars of the 8th Division in what was then a quiet sector, Bois Grenier—Laventie—Fleurbaix, where in many places the two front lines were wide apart, so that we had listening posts out in no-man's land. I spent two or three hours alone in one of these, I think on my second or third night in the line, staring so hard at black nothing that it stopped being black or nothing and began to crawl with greyish shapes; I would then shut my eyes for a few moments, and when I opened them again the shapes had vanished.[16]

Priestley would spend his 21st birthday in the front-line trenches.[17]

The noise of the War, Priestley said, was what chiefly broke down a man's nerves.

> Now the First War, with its massed artillery, was the noisiest of all time; the sound hit you harder and harder as the months

passed; some things you got used to—sniping and machine gun
fire if you were not entangled in the open and a sitting duck,
hand bombs and rifle grenades if you had sandbags and room
to dodge—but as time went on the vast cannonading, drum-
ming hell into your ears, no matter whether it was their guns or
yours, began to wear you down, making you feel that flesh and
blood had no place in this factory of destruction.[18]

Scheduled to be part of the disastrous Battle of Loos, on September 25,
1915, Priestley was spared when an assault launched on his unit's right failed
to gain ground, so his unit was not ordered to attack.[19] He described an "Edgar
Allan Poe setting" where his company held a support trench which ran through
a French civilian cemetery, "with great crosses and monuments of marble and
granite all round us, unbelievable at night when the darkness was split by the
white glare of Véry lights and the shadows were gigantically grotesque, though
often we had not time to notice them, having to duck down as machine-gun
bullets ricocheted off the funeral stones."[20]

Priestley was wounded in the hand and sent to a hospital, and then a convalescent camp, in France, before returning to the front.[21] In March 1916 his entire
division was pulled out of the line in order to move south to relieve a French
division.[22]

Outside any plan of campaign, without any battle being fought,
any honours being won, we went through the mincer. It was
not long before our own B Company, with a nominal fighting
strength of 270, had been reduced to a grim and weary 70. Two
hundred men had gone somehow and somewhere with nothing
to show for it.[23]

One particularly brutal and effective German weapon was the *Minenwerfer*, or "mine thrower." They were mortars which came in three varieties. The
"Schwerer," or "heavy," used mostly for siege work against large fortifications,
which fired a 250 millimeter shell weighing 210 pounds; the "Mittlerer," or
"mid-sized," which fired a 170 millimeter shell weighing 110 pounds, and the
"Leichter," or "light," which came in two varieties; one fired a 91.5 millimeter
shell weighing about 8.5 pounds, while the other fired a 75.8 millimeter shell
weighing about 10 pounds. All these weapons fired their shells on a high, arcing
trajectory, designed to fall into an enemy trench. "Up and then down came those
monstrous canisters of high explosive, making hell's own din when they landed,
blasting or burying us. If there was any infantryman who was not afraid of these
things, who was not made uneasy by any rumours they would shortly be arriving,
I never met him."[24] One morning, on March 24, 1916, Priestley was sorting out
the breakfast rations for his platoon in a small dugout in the side of the trench,

Austro-Hungarians with a heavy 22.5 cm Austrian *Minenwerfer*.

something he regularly did, in that same place, when a *Minenwerfer* shell landed in the trench, two or three yards away from where he was standing.

> I had done it many times before, hardly ever to anybody's compete satisfaction, but on this morning I suspect that it saved my life. After the explosion when everything had caved in, nobody was certain I was there, but several fellows knew the platoon rations were in there somewhere: that stuff would have to be dug out. There I was, then, deciding on each section's share, when I heard a rushing sound, and I knew what it meant and knew, though everything had gone into slow motion, I had no hope of getting away before the thing arrived. . . . All I knew at the time was that the world blew up.[25]

Priestley was dug out from under the cave-in and, lucky not to have been blown to bits but with injuries significant enough to be "Blighty," was shipped back to England to convalesce, ending up, on June 18, 1916, at "the military hospital at North Evington, a suburb of Leicester."[26]

From the hospital:

> [B]efore the summer was over, I was sent to convalesce to a country house in Rutland. It was an unbelievable move. After

all, the hospital was like the one I had known at Le Tréport; it was, so to speak, only a clean white extension of the war world I had lived in for the past year; it might almost have been an immense hygienic dugout. The country house in Rutland was in another world, outside the war, but it was not at all the one I had known before I enlisted. It belonged to light comedy and those trifling novels, not without charm and an appealing absurdity, that were one of the literary fashions before 1914. Even Rutland itself was as near to being an imaginary county as the map of England would allow.[27]

"In autumn rain I left Rutland and its cast of unlikely characters, its summer day's dream, to report to the depot at Halifax, wedged firmly in reality. From there I was dispatched for further treatment to a convalescent camp at Ripon," which he described as "a bad camp."[28] Shortly thereafter he was moved "to a larger and better convalescent camp just outside Alnwick in Northumberland," which he described as "exile in some cosier Siberia." He did not require further medical treatment but was not yet deemed fit to return to service. At this time, he applied for a commission as an officer.[29]

"We were now well into 1917, the only full year of the war I was never near the front, never out of England."[30] After being passed as fit, he was "temporarily attached to the Third Battalion on Tyneside, waiting to be sent as a cadet to an O.T.C."[31] Assigned to the 16th Officer Cadet Battalion at Kinmel Park Camp in North Wales,[32] he was then commissioned a Second Lieutenant in the Devon Regiment. This resulted in his being discharged from the West Riding Regiment on January 29, 1918, having been commissioned,[33] and posted to Devonport, where he remained until the summer of 1918.[34] Three years after he had first gone to France he returned there, along with "a little batch of us subalterns," aboard "a fantastic American ship" as "the only British aboard among thousands of American troops, new, raw and hearty, with nothing in their mode of

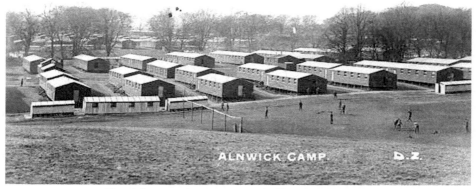

Alnwick convalescent camp in Northumberland

address to distinguish their rank."[35] Two of the new subalterns he had crossed to France with, "the two I knew best, friends I made at Devonport, were killed within a few days."[36] In a September attack, he got lost on the field but still managed to capture a frightened young German, pointing him "in what I hoped was the direction of the British and not the German Army."[37] With his "head going round, too short of breath to move any further, I took a rest in a shellhole, where I was found by a couple of stretcher bearers. So much for my last glimpse of action in the Great War."[38] His service record notes this as a "Gas Shell wound" incurred on September 18, 1918.[39]

From the hospital he went to the Medical Board Base Depot at Rouen, awaiting a fitness determination by a medical board.[40] Classed as B2, "unfit for active service but fit for something," he was sent for duty at the Labour Corps Depot.[41] Two or three days after the Armistice, he was sent for duty at a prisoner of war camp near Calais.[42]

> Though the fighting was over, conditions were no easier, perhaps rather more chaotic, so that problems of transport, rationing, supplies, medical services, were no joke, especially with such an odd mixture involving seven to eight hundred men. This was easily the most responsible job that had come my way in the Army, and it lasted for a couple of weeks or so and I enjoyed every moment of it, planning and working hard with several decent and conscientious senior noncoms."[43]

"One morning in the early spring of 1919 in some town, strangely chosen, in the Midlands—and I have forgotten both the date and the place—I came blinking out at last into the civilian daylight."[44] He was "released from actual military duty" and his commission as a temporary Second Lieutenant was released on March 16, 1919.[45]

Priestley's experiences in the War made him highly critical of the British Army High Command and the manner in which the War was prosecuted:

> (The British Army never saw itself as a citizens' army. It behaved as if a small gentlemanly officer class still had to make soldiers out of under-gardeners' runaway sons and slum lads known to the police. These fellows had to be kept up to scratch. Let 'em get slack, they'd soon be a rabble again. So where the Germans and the French would hold a bad front line with the minimum of men, allowing the majority to get some rest, the British command would pack men into rotten trenches, start something to keep up their morale, pile up casualties and drive the survivors to despair. This was done not to win a battle, not even to gain a few yards of ground, but simply because it was

supposed to be the thing to do. All the armies in that idiot war shoveled divisions into attacks, often as bone-headed as ours were, just as if healthy young men had begun to seem hateful in the sight of Europe, but the British command specialised in throwing men away for nothing. The tradition of an officer class, defying both imagination and common sense, killed most of my friends as surely as if those cavalry generals had come out of their châteaux with polo mallets and beaten their brains out. Call this class prejudice if you like, so long as you remember, as I hope I made plain in an earlier chapter, that I went into that war without any such prejudice, free of any class feeling. No doubt I came out of it with a chip on my shoulder; a big, heavy chip, probably some friend's thigh-bone.)[46]

Despite this assessment, Priestley was able to see some comedy amidst the tragedy and horror:

Unlike most of my contemporaries who wrote so well about the war, I was deeply divided between the tragedy and comedy of it. I was as much aware as they were, and as other people born later can never be, of its tragic aspect. I felt, as indeed I still feel today and must go on feeling until I die, the open wound, never to be healed, of my generation's fate, the best sorted out and then slaughtered, not by hard necessity but mainly by huge murderous public folly. On the other hand, military life itself, the whole Army "carry on", as we used to say, observed closely, seemed to me essentially comic, the most expensive farce ever contrived. To a man of my temperament it was almost slapstick, so much gigantically solemn, dressed-up, bemedaled custard pie work, but with tragedy, death, the deep unhealing wound, there in the middle of it.[47]

James Whale was, of course, well-known for leavening his horror with humor, said to be a means of breaking the audience's tension so that laughs would come where the director wanted them, rather than at inopportune moments. Whale's seeing the humor in the horror was likely also a result of his experiences in the War, and his being "deeply divided between the tragedy and the comedy of it."

Priestley's 1927 novel, *Benighted*, would form the basis for Whale's 1932 film, *The Old Dark House* (the book was published in the United States under this title). Priestley was not enthused about the prospect of his novel being adapted for the screen, "believing that the queer inmates of that house would shrivel under the spotlights."[48] However, he relented, selling the film rights to Universal on January 6, 1932 for $12,500 [almost $234,000 in 2019 dollars, adjusted for inflation]. "According to David Lewis, they were bought specifically for James Whale."[49]

Karloff's next film was to be *The Old Dark House*, an adaptation of J.B. Priestley's novel, to be directed by James Whale. It is believed the picture had its origins in the latter half of 1931 when, during a trip to England, Carl Laemmle Sr. met James Whale's old acquaintance—the playwright Benn W. Levy. Having been impressed by Levy's work on the script for *Waterloo Bridge*, Laemmle invited him to Universal to write the screen adaptation of *The Invisible Man*. Levy left for America on the *S.S. Bremen*. He arrived in New York on 25 October 1931 and made his way to Universal City. Unfortunately, Laemmle had neglected to tell anyone at the studio of Levy's appointment. He was therefore loaned to Paramount where he was put to work writing the screenplay for *The Devil and the Deep* (1932). When the script was completed Levy returned to Universal to work on *The Old Dark House* and completed the screenplay in early March 1932.[50]

Sardonic humor underlies the entire film. "Whale was an admirer of Paul Leni's 1927 silent picture *The Cat and the Canary* with its mix of comedy and horror, and wanted to direct a picture in a similar vein."[51] Apart from transforming Sir Roderick Femm (Elspeth (billed as John) Dudgeon) from the eldest brother of the other Femms into their 102-year-old father, the first three-quarters of the film follows the plot of the book quite closely. It is only after the appearance of Saul Femm (Brember Wills) that the film departs radically from the book, ending upon a much happier note than the book did. Additional dialogue for the film was penned by R.C. Sherriff. Filming began on April 18, 1932.[52]

> Two Boris Karloff productions went into the hands of the adapters last week at the Universal plant. Benn W. Levy, author of "The Devil Passes" and "Mrs. Moonlight," is in charge of "The Old Dark House," a novel by J. B. Priestley. With this assignment "The Old Dark House" takes on a more or less British hue. Mr. Levy is an Englishman, and so is Mr. Priestley, and so is James Whale, who will direct the film. Mr. Karloff also hails from the other side of the pond.
>
> The second of Mr. Karloff's productions is "The Invisible Man," one of H. G. Wells's stories. Garrett Fort is handling the work of adaptation. Mr. Fort, by the way, adapted "Frankenstein" and "Dracula." Robert Florey, having completed "Murders in the Rue Morgue," will direct "The Invisible Man," which is about a scientist whose ability to disappear into thin air causes some unusual complications.

Shooting was broken twice daily by a ritual of tea breaks. "The first morning at 11 o'clock the commissary sent over a lot of trays of tea and, I guess, crumpets," [Gloria] Stuart explained. "I was never asked to observe them, or have them—and the whole English contingent, with the exception of Melvyn Douglas and me [presumably Raymond Massey, as a Canadian and hence a citizen of the British Commonwealth, was included in these tea breaks on that basis], were asked to have tea. So they had elevenses that morning and Melvyn and I sat off by ourselves and the British contingent sat by themselves with James. And then later in the afternoon at 4 o'clock the commissary sent over more tea and they had fourses—and Melvyn and I sat by ourselves and talked . . . and this went on every single day and we were never, never, never asked to have tea with the rest of the actors."

• • • •

Although the majority of Thesiger's dialogue was lifted from Priestley's book, the Whale/Thesiger collaboration provided the picture with its wittier moments. "He and James seemed to enjoy reading," said Stuart. "I remember several times Thesiger saying 'How does it sound this way?' or 'Would you like it this way?' Or James saying 'I think, Ernest, that you should give a little more emphasis here.'" It was an amiable partnership as Stuart observed. "I would say the two of them enjoyed each other very, very much during the entire film," she said. [53]

Whale did not, however, have a particularly good relationship with Boris Karloff. Karloff did not appreciate the way Whale, as described in the chapter on *Frankenstein*, had rather sadistically forced him to carry Colin Clive repeatedly up a hill, to the extent it exacerbated a back injury which would plague Karloff for the rest of his life. Whale, on the other hand, resented how Karloff's popularity arising from *Frankenstein* had seemingly eclipsed his own:

Boris Karloff, meanwhile, remained relatively in the background. To Whale's chagrin he had received most of the credit for *Frankenstein's* success. As a result Whale believed the picture's reception had changed the star, as he told his friend Curtis Harrington. "He said Karloff was very amusing and amused," explained Harrington. "He didn't take himself too seriously. Then when he suddenly became a big star because of *Frankenstein* and became the king of horror films, he began to take himself very seriously."

Despite his attitude towards Karloff, Whale's irritation did not reveal itself on set. "I understand that Boris and James were not great friends at that point," said Stuart. "I didn't know that. I was not aware of it and I don't think that anyone in the cast was aware of it. I think maybe Karloff was aware of it. I think that James gave him his due. I think that James wanted him in every scene that he was written into and larger than life, and giving a great performance. I never had the feeling that there

was any difficulty at all between James and any of the cast. I heard later that Karloff and he were not friendly but it was not apparent at all and I was on the set almost every day." Unlike Whale, Stuart had nothing but admiration for her co-star. "Boris was so gentle, so soft spoken, such a gentleman," she said. "Never raised his voice, was as charming and considerate an actor as you could possible work with. He was the antithesis of this 'Morgan' person."[54]

The dread in the book, and also the film, comes right out of the irony of the Great War. "This dread comes not from any human agency, but from the sense that the universe itself is not a rational thing, and that humanity's place within it is not an exalted one."[55] This echoes Philip Gibbs' observation, as quoted by Paul Fussell as set forth in the previous chapter on *Frankenstein*, of the Black Humor so popular during the War; "the laughter of mortals at the trick which had been played on them by an ironical fate." The book, in ways not possible for a film, delves into the minds of the characters, but the same ironic sensibility, at the hands of Whale's expert direction, also underlies the film. Curiously, however, despite Whale's War experiences (or perhaps because of them), the War looms much larger in the novel than it does in the film, although many ironic sensibilities remain. Whale, himself, rarely spoke of his experiences in the trenches.

> When Whale talked firsthand of his time as a captive—which he did more frequently than of his experiences in battle—the stories concerned the time he put to good and productive use in the camp at Holzminden—gambling, painting, and producing amateur theatrics—and not of any particularly harrowing experiences he faced at the time of his capture.[56]

Further regarding Whale's reticence to discuss his War experiences, Professor Poole writes:

> We unfortunately have really nothing from the director himself regarding how the war shaped his vision of horror. Whale never spoke openly about the relationship of his experience of the war to his horror films, but this should surprise exactly no one. He seldom spoke about the war at all. Whale never gave interviews about his experiences on the western front or as a prisoner of war even in relation to his three major World War I films. Moreover, the concept of a director's "vision" for a film had little meaning in the 1930s. This would be particularly true at a studio such as Universal, whose chief executive viewed filmmaking as something akin to Henry Ford's assembly line.
>
> There's little reason to argue over what Whale's monster films are "really" about, given his silence on the matter.[57]

I must disagree with Professor Poole on two of his conclusions. It is certainly true that during the era of the "Studio System" in Hollywood directors were tightly constrained by management and largely lacked the opportunity to impose their own "visions" upon their films. However, during Universal's Golden Age, when the Laemmles owned the studio, Carl Jr. gave James Whale a remarkable degree of freedom to construct his films exactly as he wished. Indeed, few directors in Hollywood during the 1930s had as much freedom as James Whale did at Universal. As Carl Jr.'s favorite director, this was pretty much the way in which Whale was treated at all times when Universal was under the control of the Laemmles. By the time of *Bride of Frankenstein*, Whale would have complete creative control over all aspects of the film.

As for analyzing what Whale's horror films are "about" in the context of his War experiences, the fact Whale did not explicitly discuss "how the war shaped his vison of horror" does not preclude analysis of the subject. One may nevertheless examine the history of Whale's involvement in the War, and what he actually did write about his experiences, and, in light of the literary themes which came out of the War, apply them in analyzing his films. Of course, no such analysis can be akin to reading Whale's mind. But even if Whale had spoken or written about his War experiences, "the memoir is a kind of fiction, differing from the 'first novel' (conventionally an account of crucial youthful experience told in the first person) only by continuous implicit attestations of veracity or appeals to documented historical fact."[58] Regarding *The Old Dark House*, perhaps, even in 1932, Whale's own background rendered him not ready to address the full extent of Penderel's War experiences, as detailed in the book, in the film, but rather to deal with them more obliquely.

Motorist Philip Waverton (Raymond Massey), his wife, Margaret (Gloria Stuart), and their friend, Roger Penderel (Melvyn Douglas—the role was originally envisioned for Colin Clive, but he was committed to filming *Lily Christine* in England)[59], are driving through a remote part of Wales in a torrential thunderstorm—the rain is coming down, in an oft-repeated line, "in buckets." Raymond Massey, born in Toronto, Ontario, Canada on August 30, 1896, was a veteran of the War, as well. He enlisted in the Canadian Army at the outbreak of the War, serving on the Western Front as a First Lieutenant in the Royal Canadi-

an Regiment of Artillery. He was wounded in Belgium, near Zillebeke, in 1916 and invalided to Canada. He also served as a Major in the Canadian Army in the Second World War and was wounded again and invalided out of the Army in 1943. He became an American citizen in 1944.

The travelers have been stranded when the road is washed out by a flood. They find themselves stopped near the Femm family's titular Old Dark House. Standing outside in the pouring rain, they pound aggressively at the front door, only to have it opened by a large, brutish, unpleasant-looking man, with only the left side of his scarred face visible through the partially opened door. We later learn this man is the Femm's butler, Morgan (Boris Karloff; "a brute"

Raymond Massey of the Royal Canadian Army

Ernest Thesiger

and a drunkard—described by Priestley as "A huge lump of a man . . . a shapeless man with a full black beard and matted hair over a low forehead."[60]). Opening the door a bit farther, disclosing his entire, and none too pleasant, face, he grunts something unintelligible ("Even Welsh ought not to sound like that," says Penderel), and closes the door, only to return shortly and roughly motion the travelers inside. There they meet the scion of the family, Horace Femm, described by Priestley as "A man so thin, with so little flesh and so much shining bone... he was almost a skeleton. . . ."[61] Brilliantly portrayed by James Whale's old friend, Ernest Thesiger, "at his most nostrilled,"[62] he introduces himself to the stranded travelers: "My name is Femm. Horace Femm." He pronounces "Femm" as though it has two syllables. Thesiger had also seen combat on the Western Front in the British Army. Like Priestley, he was an Other Rank; unlike Priestley he did not seek a commission. Ernest Thesiger had enlisted in the British Army at age 35 on September 1, 1914, a few days before J.B. Priestley had enlisted. In his memoirs, *Practically True*, Thesiger describes his enlistment:

> I thought a kilt would suit me, so I applied at the London Scottish Headquarters, but my Scottish accent, assumed for the occasion, was apparently not convincing, and I was referred to another London regiment. Getting into a taxi, I consulted the list of recruiting stations and found myself in a queue outside the Headquarters of the Queen Victoria Rifles in Davies Street. I came away a few hours later a private in His Majesty's Army.[63]

He was assigned to the 1/9th (Territorial) Battalion (County of London) of the London Regiment, known as Queen Victoria's Rifles, with the rank of "Rifleman" (Private), Service Number 2546. Two months after he enlisted, in November 1914, he arrived overseas. Unlike Priestley, who had joined a "New Army" unit, Thesiger had joined a Territorial battalion and did not receive "months and months of severe intensive training" prior to being shipped out, and his time at the front would be short. In late December, some four months after he had enlisted, he found himself arriving at the front in Belgium. He

The Great War and the Golden Age of Hollywood Horror

described his arrival, which occurred on New Year's Eve, 1914, and the irony which happened the next day:

> Arriving in the reserve trenches on the 31st of December, we found that all the dug-outs were knee-deep in water, so we set to work to dig others—but it was like digging on the seashore, each shovelful of earth we took out was replaced by a bucketful of water. Luckily there was a deserted and partially ruined barn on a line with our trenches, and we were sent there to rest, after receiving strict injunctions not to make any noise or show any light. Making a deep nest in the straw that nearly filled the barn, I slept until daybreak. I was sharing my breakfast and the remains of my Christmas chocolate with my neighbour when we heard a noise like that of an approaching express train, and a shell exploded on the roof, ripping off all the tiles which fell with a clatter on to those who were sleeping in that half of the barn. As our habitation seemed none too healthy, we began to make arrangements for a speedy move, but a sergeant at the door ordered us to stay where we were. Then again came that ominous rushing noise, and I crouched into my bed of straw knowing that death was coming towards us. There followed a deafening crash and then darkness.[64]

On the morning of New Year's Day, January 1, 1915, less than two months after his arrival across the Channel, following the "deafening crash" described above, he was wounded. David J. Skal refers to *Practically True*:

> One winter day, Thesiger recalled in his memoirs, his battalion was hiding in a half-ruined barn in France.[65] While in the midst of sharing breakfast and the remains of his Christmas chocolate with his neighbor, a shell crashed through the roof of the structure. "There is a scene in *L'Aiglon*," Thesiger wrote, "where the ghosts of Wagram are heard calling out, 'My leg!' 'My arm!' My head!' and that is the scene to which I awoke. All around me my friends were groaning and telling the world of the wounds they had received." Thesiger realized that he was not dead, but was not sure that he could move.

> > Then my eyes fell upon my hands. They were covered with blood and swollen to the size of plum-puddings. My fingers were hanging in the oddest way, and I guessed most of them to be broken. I managed to stagger to my feet,

wondering as I did so whether my breakfast companion had escaped before the explosion. I could not see him, but he had left his two boots behind, and knowing that next to his rifle a soldier values his boots, I decided to take them to him. But how? I couldn't use my hands. Perhaps, I thought, I could lift them with my teeth. Still rather shaky on my legs, I stooped down carefully and then saw that in each boot a few inches of leg still remained. That was all there was of him with whom a few moments before I had been eating chocolate.[66]

Thesiger described the follow-up in *Practically True*:

Without looking round—I had seen enough—I made my way out of that charnel-house, leaving the bodies of twelve of my friends behind, while thirty others had been wounded. An officer outside told me to find my way to the dressing-station, and holding my hands above my head for fear that if I stumbled they would get more damaged, I walked back to a farm where I could get bandaged up. I looked at my hands from time to time to assure myself that all my fingers were still there—I could feel nothing—but was convinced that I would never be able to use them again. At the dressing-station a liberal application of iodine effectually did away with the numbness that had so far come to my rescue, and I fainted with the pain. Forty-eight hours afterwards I was in hospital at Le Treport, and three weeks later in England.[67]

The wounds to his hands would be sufficient to end the War for him. As recorded in his pension file: "Shell wound. Rt. Hand. Fracture of phalanges of metacarpal bones. Originated 1-1-15 in Belgium. Hand is now stiff & disabled. Two operations for removal of fragments." [68] He was discharged on May 21, 1915, as "no longer physically fit for active service."[69] He had been in the Army slightly less than nine months. He was awarded a pension of 20 shillings (one Pound Sterling [about $104 in 2019 dollars, adjusted for inflation; a 1915 shilling being worth approximately $5.15 in 2019 dollars]—the base pay for a Private serving at the front in 1914 was one shilling per day) per month, for a period of one year, and would receive a 1914 Service Star with Mark of Distinction, the British War Medal, the Allied Victory Medal, and the Silver War Badge in 1920.

Horace gives the travelers a somewhat lukewarm greeting. He picks up a bunch of flowers, which he says his sister, Rebecca (Eva Moore), was on the

Gloria Stuart and Eva Moore in a studio publicity photo

point of arranging, and tosses them nonchalantly into the fire. He explains that Morgan is dumb, unable to speak. The travelers ask for shelter, when Rebecca, who "is a little deaf," arrives, coming down the stairs and telling the little group they can't stay. The travelers explain the road is washed out behind them, and probably ahead as well, and that the raging storm and floods threaten to bring down the whole side of the mountain upon which the house sits, and the house as well. Horace reluctantly agrees to let them stay, and Rebecca cries "No beds! They can't have beds!" Mrs. Waverton goes to Rebecca's room to change out of her wet clothes, and Rebecca accompanies her. As Margaret is changing, Rebecca regales her with tales of family history, telling her how the Femms' sister, Rachel, had died in the very bed in the room, in prolonged agony, month after month, having suffered a spinal injury in a riding accident. She tells of the wild parties which her father, "a wicked, blasphemous old man," her brothers, and Rachel had had, filling the house with "Laughter and sin. Laughter and sin." She tells Margaret: "You're wicked, too. Young and handsome, silly, and wicked. You think of nothing but your long, straight legs and your white body, and how to please your man. You revel in the joys of fleshly love, don't you?"

Eva Moore, who was, at age 62, the oldest member of the cast, played her character wonderfully as a deaf, hideous, religiously fanatical harridan. She had been "an actress of legendary beauty in the 1890s who had played leading parts with most of the great actor managers of her day."[70] This makes her speech, when Mrs. Waverton is changing into her low-cut, slinky dress, even more poignant. As she fingers the material of Margaret's dress, she says "That's fine stuff, but it'll rot." Then, pointing to Margaret's chest, she says "That's finer stuff still, but it'll rot too, in time." Gloria Stuart, so young and beautiful in this film, at age 86 would play the 101-year old Rose Dawson Calvert in James Cameron's *Titanic* (1997). Ms. Stuart would die on September 26, 2010, at age 100. Stuart, herself, wondered why Whale insisted her character change into this slinky dress:

> What Mrs. Waverton changes into goes unspecified in the book, but in the film, Whale gave Gloria Stuart the most unlikely of dresses. "James had me change into a Jean-Harlow-style, bi-as-cut, pale pink velvet gown with spaghetti straps and earrings and pearls," she remembered. "And I said, 'Why me, James? Nobody else is changing. Why am I changing?' He said, 'Because Boris is going to chase you up and down the corridors, up and down the stairs, and I want you to appear as a white flame.' So, all right, I put on the dress and Boris chased me up and down the corridors, and I was a white flame. It was strictly a matter of camera and style—there was no legitimate reason for me being in that dress. Lilian Bond didn't have to change, and she came in very wet. But Karloff didn't chase her."[71]

The "white flame" business was apparently foreshadowing the appearance of Saul Femm towards the end of the film.

Horace, giving a sniff to the top of the bottle, asks Penderel to join him in a drink: "It's only gin, you know. Only gin. I like gin." Horace gives Penderel

Although the war is over, Penderel (Melvyn Douglas) isn't out of danger.

a toast, "to illusion," which he fears he will not appreciate, "being young." Penderel replies, "Illusion? Ha. On the contrary, I am precisely the right age for that toast, Mr. Femm." Horace replies "I presume you are one of the gentlemen slightly, shall we say, battered by the war." Penderel agrees, saying "Correct Mr. Femm. War generation slightly soiled, a study in the bittersweet, the man with a twisted smile." The party then sits down to a roast beef dinner, during which we hear Thesiger get an incredible amount of mileage out of the oft-repeated line, "Have a Potato." The lights flicker during dinner—Mrs. Waverton assumes it is due to the storm. Horace replies: "On the contrary. We make our own electric light here. And we are not very good at it. Pray don't be alarmed if they go out altogether." During dinner there comes a loud knocking at the front door. Two other stranded travelers, Sir William Porterhouse (Charles Laughton, in his first

Charles Laughton of the Huntingdonshire Cyclist Battalion

Hollywood role), a self-made wealthy Yorkshire industrialist, and his female companion and erstwhile chorus girl, Gladys DuCane (Lilian Bond), whose surname, we soon discover, is actually Perkins, seek shelter from the storm.[72] They join in the meal, with Sir William providing an impromptu rendition of the first few lyrics of "The Roast Beef of Old England."

Like J.B. Priestley, Charles Laughton was also born in Yorkshire, in the North Riding town of Scarborough, on July 1, 1899, where his parents were the proprietors of the Pavilion Hotel. He enlisted in the Army in 1917, most probably shortly after his 18th birthday, and served initially as a Private, Service No. 48603, with D Company of the 2/1st Huntingdonshire Cyclist Battalion, a bicycle infantry Territorial unit formed for home defense on February 27, 1914, before the outbreak of the War. This unit did not leave Britain during the War, spending most of its time on coastal defense in Lincolnshire. He was subsequently transferred to the 7th (Service) Battalion of the Northamptonshire Regiment, a New Army unit which had gone overseas in September 1915 as part of the 73rd Brigade, in the 24th Division. Laughton was part of a draft of men sent to the 7th Northamptonshires from the 2/1st Huntingdonshire Cyclist Battalion on August 9, 1918. Laughton was gassed near the end of the War—most probably on September 6, 1918 in the Lens sector, in France, north of Arras, as the entry for this date in the 7th Northamptonshire's War Diary[73] contains the only mention of gas casualties during the period Laughton was with the unit: "A few slight gas casualties. Probably over 2000 shells fell in vicinity."[74]

During a conversation among the five stranded travelers and Mr. Femm, Penderel asks Gladys what her intuition says about him. She replies, "I think he doesn't quite fit into these times;" the current state of the world making him into "a kind of fish out of water." Penderel says "You see, I've not much sympathy with fish out of water although I happen to be one myself. My trouble is I don't think enough things are worthwhile. Now, Sir William here would put tremendous energy into anything to make even a few pounds. Now I don't think it's worth it." Porterhouse thinks this is a rebuke aimed at him (for all his wealth, Sir William is rather an insecure fellow, much as Laughton evidently was in real life), but Penderel assures him it was not intended that way. Penderel is simply unable to find a place for himself in the post-war world. Of course, Penderel and Perkins fall in love.

The idea of being unable to fit back into civilian life, along with the idea the War took all the best while leaving the less deserving behind, and coupled with the guilt of having survived when others died, color Penderel's personality. The book is more explicit. Philip Waverton, two years older than Penderel, is also revealed as a veteran, although "[u]nlike him, Penderel didn't seem to have escaped from the War yet, and every night with him was still the night before one moved up to the line."[75] Penderel refers to himself as "one of the ugly ducklings of the War generation, the sort that will never become swans."[76]

> I went into the War when I was 17, ran away from home to do it, enlisting as a Tommy and telling them I was 19. I'm not going to talk about the War. You know all about that. It killed my father, who died from over-work. It killed my elder brother, Jim, who was blown to pieces up at Passchendaele. He was the best fellow in the world, and I idolized him. It was always fellows like him, the salt of the earth, who got done in, whether they were British or French or German or American. People wonder what's the matter with the world these days. They forget that all the best fellows, the men who'd have been in their prime now, who'd have been giving us a lead in everything, are dead. If you could bring 'em all back, fellows like Jim, hundreds and hundreds of thousands of 'em, you'd soon see the difference they'd make in the place. But they're dead, and a lot of other people, very different sort of people, are alive and kicking. . . . Well, I saw all this, took an honours course in it, you might say, for it was the only education I got after the fifth form. Then towards the end of the War I fell in love. I was convalescent in a country house and it was spring.[77] She was staying there, and every time

we went out walking every little gust of wind snowed down blossom on us. . . . I'd never seen a place so thick with apple blossom and cherry blossom. And she'd be waiting down there. We became engaged. . . . The world was all made over again and I'd only got to see the War through to find it all waiting for me. I thought about nothing else, went back to France, went through the dust and gas of the last push in the summer and autumn of 'eighteen, thinking about nothing else. Then just after the Armistice I got a letter. It was all a mistake; we weren't really suited, too young to know then; she'd found someone else; we'd always be friends. All very reasonable, no doubt, but you see I'd been thinking about nothing else. I got out of the Army, went home and saw her once, and gave it up.[78]

"Well, the good fellows were nearly all gone, love was off, and the world was in a filthy muddle, but there was still work."[79] This idea of the War having killed off the best and deprived society of the future contributions of those who had needlessly died, leaving behind the unworthy, is a common theme in the literary remembrances of the War. As Priestley wrote: his "generation's fate, the best sorted out and then slaughtered, not by hard necessity but mainly by huge murderous public folly."[80] One example, quoted in Chapter 2, is Wilfred Owen's poem, "Strange Meeting", in which a dead German soldier expresses a similar sentiment:

"Strange friend," I said, "here is no cause to mourn."
"None," said that other, "save the undone years.
The hopelessness. Whatever hope is yours,
Was my life also; . . . .

For of my glee might many men have laughed,
And of my weeping something had been left,
Which must die now. . . ."

Another is Robert Graves' "The Last Post: "

"God if it's *this* for me next time in France . . .
O spare the phantom bugle as I lie
Dead in the gas and smoke and roar of guns,
Dead in a row with the other broken ones,
Lying so stiff and still under the sky,
Jolly young Fusiliers, too good to die."

"For a War Memorial," by G.K. Chesterton:

The hucksters haggle in the mart
The cars and carts go by;
Senates and schools go droning on;
For dead things cannot die.

. . . .

Still to the last of crumbling time
Upon this stone be read
How many men of England died
To prove they were not dead.

And poor, mad Ivor Gurney's "To His Love: "

He's gone, and all our plans
  Are useless indeed.
We'll walk no more on Cotswold
  Where sheep feed
  Quietly and take no heed.

Casualty figures can be toted up, but it is impossible to quantify what contributions the dead may have made to humanity had they lived, or what personal or private relationships may have been enriched by their presence.

Morgan lets Saul, kept locked in an upstairs room by the other Femms, loose. The first glimpse we get of Saul is a quivering hand on the banister as he descends the staircase. The character of Saul is another major change from the book. In the novel, Saul is a large, nasty brute of a man, much like Morgan. In contrast, in the film Saul is a small man, appearing at first timid and almost as a frightened child, when he begs Penderel for protection. He claims his family keeps him imprisoned unjustly, and that Morgan beats him. Whale, in a quick cutaway shot to Saul's face after Penderel turns away, gives us a sharp reveal of Saul's true nature. He is an insane pyromaniac who knows "things about flame that nobody else in the world knows." He knows "flames are really knives. They're cold, my friend, sharp and cold as snow. They burn like ice."

Two damaged souls find love—Lillian Bond and Melvyn Douglas give viewers a happy ending.

Meeting Gladys Perkins gives Penderel, both in the film and the book (in the book her real name is Gladys Hoskiss), a new resolve and a new lease on life, and makes the ending of the film, "in the cold light of day," much more optimistic than the ending of the novel. The original ending of the film was ambiguous regarding Penderel's fate (in the book, he dies in a struggle with Saul Femm), but after previews Whale called back his actors and added a few additional lines by Melvyn Douglas and Lillian Bond to create a happy ending for the couple. Since the author of the screenplay, Benn Levy, had already returned to England when these additional lines were shot, it is likely they were written by R.C. Sherriff, who had been present during much of the filming.[81]

Unfortunately, *The Old Dark House* was savaged in the trade papers:

> When *The Old Dark House* was previewed in early July, the *Hollywood Filmograph* published a blisteringly negative review, perhaps a lingering aftershock to the widespread outrage accorded the earlier release of [Tod Browning's] *Freaks*. "Evidently James Whale has a flair for pictures of this character," wrote Arthur Forde, "but he 'shot his bolt' with *Frankenstein*. In fact, all studios better lay off such productions." *Variety* followed the lead of the *Filmograph* in condemning the film, calling it "a somewhat inane

picture" and completely ignoring the contributions of Ernest Thesiger and Eva Moore.[82]

Although the reviews in the trade papers had been a disaster, those in the

New York newspapers were generally favorable. "Business for *The Old Dark House* began well, but was soon influenced by poor word-of-mouth."[83] Unlike *Frankenstein*, the film was a disappointment at the box office. This may have been due to Whale's failure to have made better use of Boris Karloff, leaving the actor "to lurch wordlessly about, padded and brooding, employing the occasional hand gesture but otherwise keeping to the background. Whale's approach was artistically valid but commercially irresponsible; as successful as *The Old Dark House* is on many levels, it fails miserably as a showcase for the talents of Boris Karloff."[84]

Regarded as a classic today, it failed to appeal to audiences in 1932. Like *Waterloo Bridge*, *The Old Dark House* also became a "lost film." It was awarded a reissue certificate by the PCA after a few cuts and went into general re-release in 1939. As with *Waterloo Bridge*, another remake would drive the film into the shadows.[85] Universal's rights to the story lapsed in 1957 and returned to the Priestley literary estate, so the film was not included in the "Shock Theater" television package, in which a number of old Universal horror films were syndicated for television in October 1957. Columbia acquired the rights to *Benighted* from the Priestly

Cast and crew, including Lilian Bond, Melvyn Douglas, Gloria Stuart and behind them James Whale, pose on the set.

estate, and *The Old Dark House* (1963), a joint production of Columbia Pictures and Hammer Films, directed by William Castle, was released. The 1963 film is a disaster; a quite unfunny horror "comedy" starring Tom Poston, Robert Morley, and Janette Scott, and having almost nothing to do with either Priestley's novel or Whale's film. Whale's film disappeared from view and was believed to have been lost, until the efforts of Curtis Harrington led to the discovery of the original nitrate negative in Universal's vaults in 1968. The first reel was too deteriorated to allow a print to be made. Luckily, there was a lavender protection print of the first reel available, so new 35mm prints of the film were struck. This story is detailed in "Curtis Harrington Saves THE OLD DARK HOUSE," which appears as an extra alongside a stunning restoration of the film on the excellent Cohen Media Group Blu-Ray released in October 2017.

1 Hanson, loc. 146.
2 Priestley, *Margin Released* loc. 47.
3 Priestley, *Margin Released* loc. 192.
4 Priestley, *Margin Released* loc. 229.
5 National Archives, United Kingdom, Priestley, John Boynton, Service Record WO339/105913 p.15.

6 Priestley, *Margin Released* loc. 833.

7 Priestley, *Margin Released* loc. 1161.

8 Priestly Service Record p. 18.

9 Priestley, *Margin Released* loc. 1219.

10 Priestley, *Margin Released* loc. 1227.

11 Priestley, *Margin Released* loc. 1232.

12 Priestley, *Margin Released* loc. 1256.

13 Priestley Service Record p. 16.

14 Priestley, *Margin Released* loc. 1303.

15 Priestley, *Margin Released* loc. 1341.

16 Priestley, *Margin Released* loc. 1350.

17 Priestley, *Margin Released* loc. 1195.

18 Priestley, *Margin Released* loc. 1359.

19 Priestley, *Margin Released* loc. 1374.

20 Priestley, *Margin Released* loc. 1397.

21 Priestley, *Margin Released* loc. 1416.

22 Priestley, *Margin Released* loc. 1426.

23 Priestley, *Margin Released* loc. 1454.

24 Priestley, *Margin Released* loc. 1469.

25 Priestley, *Margin Released* loc. 1478.

26 Priestley, *Margin Released* loc. 1487.

27 Priestley, *Margin Released* loc. 1514.

28 Priestley, *Margin Released* loc. 1590.

29 Priestley, *Margin Released* loc. 1608.

30 Priestley, *Margin Released* loc. 1627.

31 Priestley, *Margin Released* loc. 1636.

32 Priestley, *Margin Released* loc. 1651.

33 Priestley Service Record p. 24.

34 Priestley, *Margin Released* loc. 1665-71.

35 Priestley, *Margin Released* loc. 1688.

36 Priestley, *Margin Released* loc. 1697.

37 Priestley, *Margin Released* loc.1702.

38 Priestley, *Margin Released* loc. 1707.

39 Priestley Service Record p. 11.

40 Priestley, *Margin Released* loc. 1712.

41 Priestley, *Margin Released* loc. 1717.

42 Priestley, *Margin Released* loc. 1745.

43 Priestley, *Margin Released* loc. 1769.

44 Priestley, *Margin Released* loc. 1897.

45 Priestley Service Record p. 6.

46 Priestley, *Margin Released* loc. 1844.

47 Priestley, *Margin Released* loc. 1884.

48 Priestley, *Margin Released* loc. 2436.

49 Jacobs, 112.

50 Jacobs, 112.

51 Jacobs, 112.

52 Jacobs, 114.

53 Jacobs, 114-15.

54 Jacobs, 115-16 (emphasis in original).

55 Priestley, J.B., *Benighted* Intro. by Orrin Grey to Kindle Ed. loc. 87 (Valancourt Books 2013).

56 Curtis, 20-1.

57 Poole, loc. 4107-11.

58 Fussell, 310.

59 Jacobs, 113.

60 Priestley, *Benighted* loc. 305.

61 Priestley, *Benighted* loc. 380.

62 Gifford, 97.

63 Thesiger, Ernest, *Practically True* (W. Heinemann 1927),
quoted at www.ernestthesiger.org/Ernest_Thesiger/Military_Service.html

64 Thesiger, quoted at www.ernestthesiger.org/Ernest_Thesiger/Military_Service.html

65 In Belgium, actually, according to Thesiger's military pension records.

66 Skal, *The Monster Show* 185-6.

67 Thesiger, quoted at www.ernestthesiger.org/Ernest_Thesiger/Military_Service.html

68 Fold3.com, Thesiger, Ernest, Pension File p. 7
https: //www.fold3.com/browse/250/huJpt80fQ41jvpIn1H9wPiTQSj8Qsbd-ZvpNUNp5i

69 Thesiger Pension File p. 2.

70 Curtis, 174.

71 Curtis, 177-8.

72 Priestley had said "the five persons who visit the house are intended for real persons, but the inmates . . . are only various forms of post-war pessimism pretending to be people." Curtis, 173, n. *.

73 The entry for October 9, 1918 contains a particularly nasty passage, about an effort to reconnoiter a sugar factory and then attack the Germans in the village of Cagnoncles:

> -Order of attack: D Coy (Capt. Pearson MC)—Left Front;= B Coy (Capt. B. Wright MC)—Right Front; C Coy (2/Lieut W. W. Boal) Left Support; A Coy (Capt Williamson MC)—Support. Having taken the high ground on his, Capt Pearson went personally with a strong patrol to reconnoitre the village and failed to return. 2/Lieut Boal, whilst moving forward with Support Company, was mortally wounded by a shell. 2/Lieut Cutting and 2/Lieut Clements were both killed whilst leading their men forward. 2/Lieut Cook and 2/Lieut Osborn were wounded. The village, being too strongly held chiefly with machine guns, which were continuously sweeping the ridge and slope leading to the village, it was decided to dig in and wait for artillery to give the necessary support. Battalion scouts, who had been operating in front during the day, were sent forward to get in touch with Canadians on the left. This was done. Information received that 2/Lieut Boal had died of wounds. Casualties: 4 Officers killed, 2 officers wounded, 85 OR's killed and wounded.

At this time, the War would continue for only 33 more days. My great-uncle, my paternal grandmother's brother, served with the American Army in the 327th Infantry Regiment, part of the 82nd Infantry Division, and was killed in action by enemy shellfire in the Argonne Forest on October 10, 1918.

74 *See* the *Charles Laughton Pages* of the *Hunts Cyclist* website,
www.huntscycles.co.uk/C%20L%201%20Home%20Page.htm, which contains a detailed account of Laughton's wartime service.

75 Priestley, *Benighted* loc. 229.

76 Priestley, *Benighted* loc. 1187.

77 Much like the time Priestley had spent convalescent at the idyllic country house in Rutland.

78 Priestley, *Benighted* loc. 1152-63.

79 Priestley, *Benighted* loc. 1168.

80 Priestley, *Margin Released* loc. 1884.

81 Curtis, 182, n. *.

82 Curtis, 182.

83 Curtis, 183.

84 Curtis, 179.

85 Curtis, 183.

Chapter Nine
In Which R.C. Sherriff Pens an Invisible Man

In 1929, two years before the book would be published in the United States, Universal had acquired the film rights to *The Road Back*, a novel by Erich Maria Remarque and the sequel to his *All Quiet on the Western Front.*[1] James Whale was to direct. The project languished. In 1932, R.C. Sherriff wrote a screenplay for *The Road Back*, which James Whale proclaimed to be "magnificent."[2] *The Road Back* would not be made until 1937 and, as more fully described in the Epilogue, much to Whale's displeasure, he was pulled from the film, which was then heavily edited with new, slapstick scenes added in order to appease the Nazi government in Germany. Sherriff would soon make a significant contribution to Universal's Golden Age of Horror. James Whale's next Universal Horror would

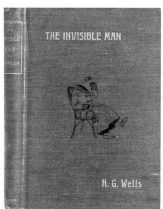

be an adaptation of H.G. Wells' novel *The Invisible Man*. The picture would, however, go through a long and convoluted development process before Whale would finally be installed to direct, and a suitable screenplay produced.

On September 22, 1931, Universal bought the film rights to *The Invisible Man* for $10,000 [approximately $168,000 in 2019 dollars, adjusted for inflation]; the contract gave Wells script approval. On December 29, Universal announced plans to make *The Invisible Man*, starring Boris Karloff, with production to start as soon as Karloff, on loan to Paramount, had finished work on *The Miracle Man*. The studio envisioned James Whale to direct. Whale, however, even at this time, was reluctant to be pegged as a "horror director." Whale was not interested, and spent his time preparing to make *The Road Back*. Karloff came back to Universal, but *The Invisible Man* did not start production. At this point, in late January 1932, Universal had its star pegged for the role, but had no screenplay and no director.[3] Universal then assigned the film to Robert Florey, who collaborated with Garrett Fort, with whom Florey had worked on his version of *Frankenstein*, on a screenplay.[4] The script was based upon Philip Wylie's novel, *The Murderer Invisible*, and featured an invisible octopus, invisible rats, and blowing up Grand Central Station.[5] Carl Jr., already unhappy with Florey's *Murders in the Rue Morgue*, rejected this screenplay and, a week later, Florey was gone from Universal.[6]

John L. Balderston, who had worked on the screenplays for *Dracula* and *Frankenstein*, wrote an eight-page treatment and three complete screenplays: one dated May 9 based upon the Garrett Fort version, one dated May 21, entirely of his own devising, and another dated June 6, a collaboration with Cyril Gardner, now installed as the director of *The Invisible Man*.[7] John Huston and Universal scenario editor Richard Schayer also took cracks at treatments—"the latter an unwieldy courtroom drama in which the hero renders his lab assistant invisible and is then forced to stand trial for his 'murder.'"[8] "Any work that gets as far as Wells is summarily rejected."[9] In November 1932 *The Road Back* was shelved, Whale was reassigned to *The Invisible Man*, and Preston Sturges was engaged to write the screenplay:

> Sturges, the celebrated author of *Strictly Dishonorable*, turned *The Invisible Man* into an elaborate revenge scenario incorporating aspects of the *Frankenstein* legend. Dr. Sarkov, a Russian chemistry professor who lost his family at the hands of the Bolsheviks, devises a way to make the maniacal Boris Karloff invisible. Sarkov uses him to murder the Soviet official responsible for the crime, but loses control of his creation. The Invisible Man initiates a reign of terror, culminating in an attempt to kill both Sarkov and his fiance [sic] before he himself is destroyed.

When Sturges turned in his screenplay Universal fired him.[10]

At this point, James Whale, himself, took a shot at drafting a treatment. It is reproduced as an appendix to the Gatiss biography. The treatment, dated January 3, 1932 and noted as starring Boris Karloff, "is high Gothic—a wildly baroque tale that might have become Universal's most bizarre and truly disturbing horror show."[11] Whale's scenario is indeed bizarre, containing an element of Lon Chaney's unmasking in *The Phantom of the Opera*. "An important personage lies dying in a magnificent bedchamber," attended by priests, doctors, and relatives. A servant makes his way into the room. The doctors and hangers-on attempt to exclude him, but the dying man bids him come forward. The servant says he knows of a man, a great healer, who could cure the old man's affliction and save his life. The servant says this mysterious figure is known as "the invisible man." The old man asks the servant to fetch the mysterious stranger. The servant specifies that he must have a coach and a driver to take him to the secret place where this stranger abides, and that the servant will return with him. The coachman drives the servant to a spot where he instructs him to stop and remain where he is.

Boris Karloff, who will be seen next in J. B. Priestley's "The Old Dark House," is scheduled to don some more of his celebrated make-up for "The Invisible Man." This H. G. Wells story will enter production at the Universal studios around the first week in October, by which time Mr. Karloff will have finished his present assignment in "The Mask of Fu Manchu." An interesting feature of "The Invisible Man" production is that E. A. Dupont, producer of the old film "Variety," will be the director. Some time ago Carl Laemmle brought Mr. Dupont over for Universal, but he returned to the Continent following a disagreement over his first picture. Since then he has been directing pictures in Germany and Great Britain.

James Whale in 1932

The servant passes "through weird gates past shadowy trees" to "a queer black churchyard, with gleaming crosses, and grim ghostly monuments." The servant arrives at a family vault, enters, and knocks upon "a monument, somewhat like an upturned sarcophagus, tall and grim, an exquisitely carved angel's head with spreading wings at the top." His knock is answered by the stranger's voice, who then emerges from the tomb, his face "wrapped entirely in bandages, rather like a mummy," wearing "a pair of heavy dark glasses." The servant tells the stranger that his master is dying, that it is a matter of life and death, and that the stranger must come with him at once. The stranger invites the servant down beneath the ground, into the tomb, to a chamber whose walls "are lined with coffins, resting on marble slabs." Hearing what a great man the servant's master is, the stranger agrees to help, disappearing into another room and emerging with a hat, stick, and a small bag.

The scene then changes back to the bedchamber of the sick man. The people inside hear a carriage approach. The servant enters the room and relays the invisible man's instructions—everyone but the patient must leave the room, and the patient must be blindfolded.

> The stranger is now brought in to the house by the servant. His entrance is full of mystery and we avoid shots of his face. The CAMERA being either behind, or at such an angle it accentuates the weirdness of the mysterious figure. They cross the hall, mount the great staircase, stand for a moment outside the bedroom. The stranger asks if his instructions are carried out, and they enter.

Shots of the stranger's hands are seen as he examines the patient, prepares a draught of medicine, and gives it to the patient, whose labored breathing becomes calm and regular as he drifts off into a peaceful sleep. With the stranger's back to the camera, someone who has been concealed in the room (perhaps the patient's daughter), "rushes forward dramatically, and tearing off the stranger's cloak and hat, demands to know who he is."

> It is child's play to watch a tense moment here, as the gruesome face savagely turns upon her and looks into the CAMERA. [This is, of course, reminiscent of the Lon Chaney unmasking sequence in *The Phantom of the Opera*.]
>
> In a weirdly tender scene the girl might here discover her lover, who had mysteriously disappeared, because of a horrible disfigurement to his face during scientific experiments for the good of the poor sick. [Not unlike the wounded in the War, many of whom returned home with grievous, disfiguring injuries.] After a heartbreaking scene she enters the most exclusive order of nuns in a convent, and banishes herself from the world.

The stranger then returns to his subterranean lair. "His hands clasped in religious fervour, he prays: "

> OH THOU WHO ART INVISIBLE
> and to whom nothing is unseen
> who carest for the sick and fatherless,
> who created the earth and all that is upon
> it, to whom there is no mystery in man or
> beast: THOU who gavest and takest away, hear
> the prayer of thy servant, and remove from
> the eyes of mortal man the harmful sight of
> this frightful face, that I may be allowed
> to do thy will unseen.

He then discovers the means to make himself invisible and does so, with the help of the servant. The room he had entered previously is revealed to be his laboratory. In making himself invisible, however, his desire to help and cure others has been transformed into a desire to kill.

> His first victim is the poor, crazed servant and we FADE OUT on the delightful spectacle of his being slowly strangled to death by invisible hands. As a crowning piece of horror and before the death rattle of the victim announces his demise, the stranger's horrible face, which now has the added terror of a murderous

mind, becomes visible in the victim's last fleeting moment from this beautiful world. Having been suspended in the air the victim falls dead on the floor, with a face of frozen horror. The corpse receives a violent kick from an invisible foot, and our CAMERA panning down, traces footsteps of naked feet, treading in blood, to the door. [A strikingly gory scene, but one wonders where the blood came from, as the victim was strangled to death.] Coming up to the door handle we hear a squeak, and the door opens on its own accord, almost immediately, however, closing to the accompaniment of soft laughter, dying away as the invisible man FADES OUT in to the lovely night.

If this is too mild [!!!] the corpse could be lifted by invisible hands, dragged swiftly out, and flung either on to a grave in the churchyard, or into a still farther recess in case we wish to pile future corpses into a funeral pyre. [!!!!!]

After "[a] short series of diabolical murders is planned and executed," the invisible fiend decides to murder the girl, in church, as she is about to take her final vows as a nun. Whale describes the religious panoply of priests, nuns, and white-clad novices, while a seemingly floating knife, accompanied by the sounds of naked footfalls, makes its way stealthily through the church. "We cut several times during the ceremony to this playful knife, somewhat in the nature of the hand on the bannisters in *The Dark House*. . . ." Just as the girl is about to receive her sacrament, the knife plunges down, killing her. However, the invisible man, overcome by remorse, turns the knife on himself, plunging it into his own heart.

> Who, as his life's blood ebbs swiftly away, becomes gradually visible, revealing for an instant, a face so fantastically horrible that even we who are used to such dishes, close our eyes, as the sound of a dull flopping thud forces the sickening news through our other senses, that the lovers are united at last!
> Finis[12]

Pretty strong stuff there from Mr. Whale!

Whale's treatment—rendered in the overripe prose of a non-writer—was structurally flawed but imaginative in its individual scenes. It was given to Gouverneur Morris in November 1932, and by Christmas Morris had fashioned a screenplay from it. Junior Laemmle was pleased enough to have the script submitted to the MPPDA (as a "preliminary," he cautioned) and James Wingate said it seemed to be satisfactory from the standpoint of the Code "with the exception of scattered instances of mild profanity." His approval meant nothing, however, when H.G. Wells rejected the material.[13]

James Whale, disappointed by Wells' rejection, again abandoned *The Invisible Man*.[14]

The game of "musical directors" would now continue, with German émigré E.A Dupont, recently signed to Universal by Junior Laemmle, appointed as *The Invisible Man*'s

E. A. Dupont Leaves for Hollywood
E. A. Dupont, German director of "Variety" and other films, left New York for Hollywood yesterday to make pictures for Universal. The first will be "The Invisible Man," adapted from the novel by H. G. Wells, with Boris Karloff in the leading rôle.

new director. Novelist John Weld, who had also just joined Universal, was tasked with drafting yet another screenplay.[15] Weld decided to go back to the source, and obtained a copy of Wells' novel from the local library (Universal didn't have one, and Preston Sturges had been told to ignore the book when he was writing his screenplay, "as it stank."[16]), and wrote a treatment which largely followed the novel, removing the Wylie novel as a source and abandoning the previous efforts.[17] Not surprisingly, Wells approved this treatment, which was actually based upon his book.[18]

Whale and Sherriff discussing a sequel to *All Quiet on the Western Front*, called *The Road Back* (1937).

But now, E.A. Dupont was out, and, for the third time, James Whale was brought back in as the director. On February 3, 1933, Universal announced that R.C. Sherriff, likely brought in at Whale's urging, had been engaged to write the screenplay for *The Invisible Man*.[19] At the time, Sherriff was ensconced at New College, Oxford, rowing for the crew team and reading for a degree in history in preparation for a new career as a schoolmaster. Offered about £5,000 [about $616,000 in 2019 dollars, adjusted for inflation] for the job, Sherriff was still undecided, but a misunderstanding with a reporter resulting in a newspaper story appearing which said he had been engaged to write the screenplay, all but made his decision for him.[20] "I went down to the post office and sent a cable off to Whale. 'Delighted to write script for *Invisible Man*. Coming as quickly as I can.'"[21]

Meanwhile, on February 13, 1933, a headline in *The Hollywood Reporter* announced, "Universal Studios Closed for Six Weeks," with only a skeleton crew and 15 writers remaining on the payroll. The same issue announced that James Whale, whose contract ran for 40 of 52 weeks of the year, would be taking his 12-week layoff at the same time, and when he came back would direct *The Invisible Man*.[22] Boris Karloff was in Britain, having been loaned out to Gaumont-British Studios to make *The Ghoul*, and wanted to stay to make two more pictures, but Universal demanded he be back in Hollywood by May in order to begin work on *The Invisible Man*.[23]

With his mother in tow, Sherriff sailed from England, arriving in New York.

> The journey across America was unforgettable. . . . As [the train] crept majestically out of Grand Central Station in New York, we had first a long evening running beside the Hudson river, with the paddle steamers going by, lit up like fireflies in the dark; a day of green fields and grazing cattle; a night on the prairie, looking out across the desolate country to small solitary lights in the distance and wondering what those lonely people were doing and thinking in their boundless solitude; a dawn when we woke to find ourselves in the desert, with the cacti growing as tall as trees. One morning the engine began to labour in its climb into the mountains. We heard it panting and groaning and felt the train going slower and slower, until finally it stopped to take on another engine. For a while we ran more easily, but began labouring again as the way got steeper; until we halted again to take on a third engine to push us from behind. It was night when we reached the summit. When we stopped for the spare engines to be taken off we walked up and down outside, looking up at the wondrous spangle of stars through the crystal clear air above the desert mountains.
>
> On the last day there was a long and gentle descent with the engine holding the train back instead of pulling it. Gradually

we left the barren desert country and began to see small areas of grass and maize kept green by the endless drawing of water from deep wells. By afternoon we saw the first orange groves, and that evening we reached Los Angeles, feeling like children at the end of an unexpected but memorable holiday. [24]

Universal put Sherriff and his mother up in a suite on the top floor of the Château Elysée, and James Whale, bearing a bottle of whisky (a boon during Prohibition), popped in for a visit while Sherriff and his mother were unpacking.[25]

Sherriff visited the studio and Whale took him to meet Laemmle Senior; "Uncle Carl: "

He was friendly and affable, but didn't have much to say and didn't ask me any questions. He took it for granted that an English writer was a creature from another world who didn't talk his language, and being a shrewd, sensible little man, he couldn't see the point of wasting time trying to make contact.

"Take him round to meet Junior," he said to Whale.

Junior Laemmle was a young edition of his father who had recently come from college to be productions manager of the studio. It was a family business, and that's what made it friendly and intimate. Junior, with good schooling and his years at college, brought to the studio the things his father hadn't got. He mightn't have been so shrewd and tough, but he was equipped to make easy contact with everybody who came to work there. He was genuine and sincere and likable. "This *Invisible Man* story," he said, "we reckon it's fine stuff for the screen, but we haven't hit on the right approach. Jimmy Whale's got a hunch that you're the feller to do it, and if you go to the story department they'll give you everything we've had done."[26]

Sherriff visited the story department, where he was shown "a pile of scripts, a dozen or more, about a foot high." Told they'd all had "good stuff in 'em," none "quite hit the bull's eye," Sherriff accepted the pile as it was pushed across the table to him. Sherriff had intended to bring a copy of Wells' novel with him but had forgotten to pack it in his bag. Knowing it would take some time to wade through all the earlier versions of the screenplay, Sherriff thought it would be useful to refer to the book.

ALTHOUGH two English studios have offered Universal to keep Boris Karloff busy in Blighty until the late Summer, Carl Laemmle Jr. has cabled Mr. Karloff to return to Hollywood as soon as he finishes "The Ghoul," now being filmed in London by British-Gaumont. Mr. Karloff left England for America in 1909 and this is his first return since he became a stage and screen actor. Upon his return in Universal City he will be featured in "The Invisible Man," which R. C. Sherriff is now adapting from the novel by H. G. Wells.

"Have you got a copy of the book?" I asked.

The story editor looked at me in puzzled surprise. "What book?" he enquired. It seemed that he had forgotten that all those scripts he was giving me had originally begun with a little novel by H.G. Wells.

I explained that a copy of the original story would be useful to refresh my memory, but he waved my suggestion aside.

"We *did* have a copy, he said, "but I guess one of them writers forgot to send it back. I haven't seen it for a long while, but it didn't have anything in it except the big idea of a feller who takes something that makes him go invisible. Everything worth using in that old book has gone into these scripts, and a great deal more besides, because these chaps are swell writers and they worked up a lot of stuff that Mr. H.G. Wells never thought of." His telephone was ringing again and he wanted to get rid of me. "We've fixed you up in a nice little office round the corner," he said. "There's a secretary waiting, and one of my boys'll take all this stuff along for you." He led me to the door and gave me a hearty slap on the shoulder. "If you give us a job like that *Journey's End* of yours, then we won't have another thing to worry about!"[27]

Just as John Weld had previously done, Sherriff went off in search of a copy of Wells' book. While Weld was able to locate a copy of the then out-of-print book in the library, Sherriff had to resort to a shopping trip in Los Angeles. After visiting a number of book shops, to no avail, he ultimately found a copy in a "musty old box" at an open stall in a market in the Chinese quarter of town.[28]

Sherriff and his mother moved from the Château Elysée to Santa Monica, where they "found an old timber-framed hotel on the palisades overlooking the Pacific." Ensconced in a bungalow in the garden of this hotel, Sherriff began to work in earnest upon the screenplay for *The Invisible Man*. As well, his fame as the author of *Journey's End* earned him invitations to gala Hollywood dinner parties, dining with such luminaries as Charlie Chaplin, Ronald Colman, Boris Karloff, and Norma Shearer.

In the meantime, on May 8, 1933, *The Hollywood Reporter* ran a story that

Boris Karloff, whose loan-out to Gaumont-British had been cancelled, had left London on the 6th to return to Hollywood and commence work on *The Invisible Man*. Then, on May 13 *The Hollywood Reporter* drops a bombshell: Universal has offered *The Invisible Man* to William Powell. Karloff would arrive back in Hollywood on May 16, to find that his part had been offered to Powell (Powell would turn it down), but the paper reported that Boris Karloff was "definitely out" of the project.[29]

Sherriff had crafted a script which held closely to Wells' story. He turned his manuscript over to his secretary to be typed up.[30]

> When she had got it all typed out my secretary said it was too long. In the way they set them out at the studio a script played to an average of a page a minute, and there were ten pages too many.
>
> This was a shock, because there wasn't a scene in it that I hadn't already cut to the bone.
>
> "But you don't have to worry," she said. "The story department has had a lot of experience in cutting scripts down. If you leave it to them they'll soon get ten pages out of it."
>
> But I didn't want that to happen at any price, because I was reasonably sure they'd go at it with a carving knife and slice out big chunks anyhow and anywhere, mutilating scenes vital to the story. The only thing was to start afresh and write the screenplay all over again. It was an exhausting job, but good practice in dramatic economy, and I soon began to find lines of twenty words that could be spoken just as effectively in ten.
>
> I sweated over it for a week, working most of the nights, for time was running short. But it came out all right in the end. When my secretary typed out the new version it was down to a hundred pages, so I gave the whole thing a final polish and sent it round to the story editor.
>
> What would happen next I didn't know.[31]

On June 1, when Sherriff's screenplay was almost completed, Boris Karloff's option under his contract with Universal came up. Karloff had earlier foregone a contractual raise from $750 to $1,000 [about $14,750 and $19,700, respectively, in 2019 dollars, adjusted for inflation] per week in exchange for Universal's promise that his weekly salary would be raised to $1,250 [about $24,600 in 2019 dollars, adjusted for inflation] when his contract came up for renewal. Universal reneged on its promise, and "Karloff walked," to be later wooed back into the fold.[32] The bottom line was that Karloff was now definitely out of *The Invisible Man*.

Sherriff was worried Universal would notice his screenplay was too closely based upon Wells' novel and felt that he had done nothing but transcribe the book into a screenplay.

> My main anxiety was that the studio might by now have come across their long-lost copy of the original novel. If they had, and compared it with my script, they'd probably say to each

June 15, 1933

Mr. Harry Zehner
Universal Studio
Universal City, California

Dear Mr. Zehner:

We have read the script of THE INVISIBLE MAN.
Although it seems to be in agreement with the Code - with
the exception of a few details - we feel that because of
its unusual theme, we should like to reserve our final decision both in regard to Code and censorship until we have
seen the picture. At the present time, the following items
should be given some further consideration.

The following instances of profanity should be
removed:

Scene B-7:   Flora: "Ford God's sake..."
Scene B-12: The Stranger: "My God..."
Scene B-21: Villager: "God...."
Scene B-24: The Gaunt Man: "....damn"
Scene B-33: Man: "God..."
Scene D-9:   Invisible man: '....by God.."
Scene E-49: Kemp: "...For God's sake.."
Scene E-79: Flora: "Thank God.."

With further reference to the Code, as well as
official censorship, we believe that it would be advisable
to remove the portion of the line in scene E-6 in which the
Invisible Man says, "...The food is visible inside me until
it is digested", since this conjures up some rather unpleasant
details, and is likely to prove offensive.

With reference to official censorship, we assume you
will handle the various murders in such a way as to keep them
from being either so brutal or gruesome as to cause them to be
eliminated.

With all good wishes,

Sincerely yours,

James Wingate

JBMF

Correspondence from Motion Picture Production Office re: *The Invisible Man* **script**

other, "This guy's pulled a fast one on us. He's copied the whole damn thing out of the book—just like Wells wrote it. He hasn't thought up anything of his own, and all the good money we've paid him has gone down the drain."

When a week had gone by without a word, I began to fear the worst. I needn't have worried, because the silence was merely due to their having copies made for handing round to all concerned, and the first word came from Whale, who drove down one evening to see me at Santa Monica.[33]

Whale adored Sherriff's screenplay, but Sherriff feared his enthusiasm for it was simply a ploy to get *The Invisible Man* project moving again. "The studio just told him to forget about *The Invisible Man* and make a sequel to *Frankenstein* next."

Whale assured Sherriff that his enthusiasm for his screenplay was not to avoid the *Frankenstein* sequel, but was rather due to his genuine admiration of the material. Junior Laemmle had a copy of Sherriff's screenplay but had not yet read it. Whale maneuvered Carl Jr. into reading the screenplay. He absolutely loved it.[34]

> For one thing I was devoutly thankful. It was clear that their long-lost copy of the original Wells novel had not turned up. Nobody even mentioned it, and with such acclaim ringing in my ears it would have been professional suicide to tell them that the whole screenplay, from start to finish, had come straight from Wells and not from me. Hollywood was young, ambitious, basking in the glory of breaking into untilled golden land. If they bought an old book like *The Invisible Man* it was only because it had in it a germ that they could fertilise and make grow into something far beyond the imagination of its creator, and that's why I knew how disastrous it would be to tell them what I had done. When they asked what had inspired me to write such a wonderful script I told them that it was all due to them for giving me a free hand, and that I was very happy to have given them something in return.
>
> Before lunch was over everything was settled. The sequel to *Frankenstein* was put on the shelf and Whale was to begin *The Invisible Man* as soon as he was ready. The publicity manager went back to his office to announce it to the press, and the others went back to their offices convinced that they had a money-spinner in their hands.[35]

Sherriff was too modest. While his screenplay did follow the form and spirit of the novel very closely, he would add a few new wrinkles of his own:

> Hearkening back to Whale's treatment and the subsequent screenplay by Governeur [sic] Morris, Sherriff decided to add "something in the chemical mixture which the man used to make himself invisible that accidentally and unfortunately turns him into a homicidal maniac." Having known Wells since the early days of *Journey's End*, Sherriff went and explained the problem to him. "He agreed with me entirely that an invisible lunatic would make people sit up in the cinema more quickly than a sane man," said Sherriff, "but he countered with a suggestion more profound than mine. He suggested that the condition of invisibility itself should be the factor which drives the man insane. Obviously, it was a better idea from an artistic point of view, but I did not think it practical for the screen. It

would take too long to show the gradual process of developing insanity, and as the man was invisible beneath his face bandages, we should not have his features to help us show his gradual deterioration."[36]

Sherriff's solution was to invent a drug, called "monocaine."

Sherriff would leave Hollywood for England, to return to Oxford, after his work on *The Invisible Man* had been completed. Before he left, however, Universal agreed that, when his studies were over, Universal would "have first option on his services to write three screenplays, to be paid in English money at £6,000 [almost $740,000 in 2019 dollars, adjusted for inflation] a time." Even better for Sherriff, the agreement specified that he need not return to Hollywood but could perform his work at home.[37]

Whale cast the film himself.[38] With Boris Karloff now out of the picture, Whale considered Colin Clive for the title role. Clive, anxious to return to England after he finished a picture he was doing with Lionel Barrymore for MGM, passed on the role.[39] Whale then recalled an actor he knew from *The Insect Play*, who had played a different role in each of the play's three acts.[40] The actor's name was Claude Rains. The role of The Invisible Man presented unique challenges for an actor. When he is visible, he is fully clothed, wearing gloves and dark glasses, with his head covered in bandages. His face will not be revealed to the audience until the end of the film, when it appears in a brief shot following his death. Rains had to act primarily with his voice and, to a lesser extent, in pantomime when his character is clothed. Rains' unique, husky voice is the primary means by which Griffin's character is conveyed to the audience. The singular timbre of Rains' voice was due to his having been gassed in the War.

Claude Rains of the London Regiment

Voice, of course, was an important consideration in casting the part, and at some point Whale was inspired to think of Claude Rains for the role. Whale had known Rains (who had never appeared in a film) since the days of *The Insect Play*, when Whale was engaged to Doris Zinkeisen and everyone in their circle seemed to be working for Nigel Playfair. Rains was already working in New York when Whale arrived there in 1929, appearing at the Martin Beck Theater under a three-year contract with the Theatre Guild.

Whale thought Rains' soothing voice would make a wonderful counterpoint to the violent nature of the Invisible Man, and he quickly became obsessed with the idea of casting Rains in the part. Exactly when this occurred is uncertain, but according to David Lewis, Rains was Whale's choice "from the very start." It is likely Whale encountered a good deal of resistance from Junior Laemmle over the idea because Rains had no name recognition outside of London and New York. But as their starting date grew nearer, Rains became more a necessity than an option, and Whale managed to cinch the deal with a screen test.[41]

Rains, whose full name was William Claude Rains, was born on November 10, 1889 into a poor family in London, in working-class Clapham, south of the Thames—"the wrong side." His mother had borne 10 children—only three survived infancy.[42] He also served in the British Army on the Western Front. He enlisted in the 1/14th Battalion (County of London), London Regiment (London Scottish) as a Private in 1915.[43]

Rains chose to join the London Scottish Regiment, in part because of its theatrical uniform and its self-bestowed, bloodthirsty sobriquet "The Ladies From Hell."

"I saw this solider in his magnificent kilt," Rains recalled. The regiment's kilt was fashioned from the homespun cloth known as Hodden Grey—tartans had been rejected to avoid favoring one clan over another. Besides, the regiment's first commander, Lord Elcho, observed, "A soldier is a man hunter. As a deer stalker chooses the least visible of colors, so ought a soldier to be clad."

"I wanted to look just like that," Rains said. "It was the actor in me." He often told the story of how he followed the kilted soldier on the street right into an enlistment office.[44]

His efforts were more successful than Ernest Thesiger's, who had tried to bluff his way into the London Scottish using an assumed accent, ending up in another battalion of the Regiment, the 1/9th (Territorial) Battalion (County of London), London Regiment (Queen Victoria's Rifles) instead (although being a member of "The Ladies From Hell" would certainly have suited Ernest). In the

Battle of Vimy, 1917

spring of 1916, having already attained the rank of Lieutenant, Rains arrived with his unit at Vimy Ridge, just north of Arras.[45] He was gassed at Vimy Ridge in 1917, resulting in 90 percent blindness in his right eye (something he would go to great pains to conceal throughout his life) and injuries to his vocal cords, which would render him mute for a time and ultimately result in his characteristic husky voice.[46]

"After being hospitalized on the French Coast near St. Cecile, he was invalided to Bagthorpe Military Hospital, a converted workhouse in Nottingham."[47] On May 10, 1917 he was transferred to the Bedfordshire Regiment,[48] most likely to its 11th Battalion, comprised of men either over-age or rendered unfit for duty overseas, who would perform home defense duties in dispersed locations. Men who recovered sufficiently were sent back overseas. Rains would remain in England for the duration of the War. He would be discharged from the Army in 1919 with the temporary rank of Captain.[49] Like R.C. Sherriff, Rains applied for a regular commission after the War, but he abandoned his application and returned to his prewar career in the theater.[50]

The Invisible Man began shooting late in June of 1933.[51] When he signed on to play the role, however, the five-foot-six-inches tall Rains had no idea his face would not be seen throughout the film, except in a brief shot at the end, after his character had died. Rains would relate the following to a reporter:

> "For five years, five years, mind you, I was prating to the The-
> atre Guild about my 'artistic integrity.' I was so cock-a-hoop
> about it. My 'artistic integrity.' Then the first day at the studio

James brought over some bandages. I asked him about them, and he said, Oh yes, I was to be bandaged during most of the picture. And there I had been fighting with the Theatre Guild about my 'artistic integrity.' Oh, it served me right!"

Rains laughs about it in later years, but in the summer of 1933, *The Invisible Man* is no laughing matter for the actor, who has learned only after his arrival in Hollywood that his face will not be seen.

"Not my eyes!" laments Rains, proud of his piercing features. "Not even *just my eyes!*"[52]

Further indignities will follow. He is taken to a laboratory, where "men in white coats" make a cast of his body, nail him into it, and then smear plaster over his head, sticking straws up his nose so he could breathe. "He battles not only claustrophobia and his own bantam temperament, but also memories of his hospitalization during the war."[53]

Special effects were, of course, key to the film's success, and the effects in the film hold up surprisingly well even today. John P. Fulton was in charge of special effects. Some effects, such as furniture moving, doors and drawers opening and closing, and the like, were done with fine wire, not visible to the camera. "For example, in the scene where the Invisible Man rides a bicycle through the village, wires from a 'boom' or 'dolly' actually perform the action."[54]

Little did Claude Rains know what Jack Pierce had in store for him on *The Invisible Man*

For the unforgettable shot where Rains, in ghoulishly good humor, unwraps his bandaged head to reveal to the villagers—nothing!—Rains' own head is hidden below his collar, the bandages actually wrapped around a thin wire frame invisible on the screen.[55]

Most of the scenes where Griffin is shown with his clothes visible and the rest of him not, had to be shot using a laborious multiple printing process. Gregory Mank quotes an interview with Fulton, published in the September 1934 issue of *American Cinematographer* magazine:

The wire technique could not be used, for the clothes would look empty, and would hardly move naturally. So we had recourse to multiple printing—with variations. Most of these scenes involved other, normal characters, so we photographed those scenes in the normal manner, but without any trace of the Invisible Man. All of the action, of course, had to be very carefully timed, as in any sort of double exposure work. . . .

Then the special process work began. We used a completely black set—walled and floored with black velvet, so to be as nearly non-reflective as possible. Our actor was garbed from head to foot in black velvet tights, with black gloves, and a black headpiece rather like a diver's helmet. Over this, he wore whatever clothes might be required. This gave us a picture of the unsupported clothes moving around on a dead black field. From this negative, we made a print, and a duplicate negative which we intensified to serve as mattes for printing. Then, with an ordinary printer, we proceeded to make our composite: first we printed from the positive of the background and the normal action, using the intensified, negative matte to mask off the area where our Invisible Man's clothing was to move. Then we printed again, using the positive matte to shield the already printed area, and printing in the moving clothes from the 'trick' negative. The printing operation made our duplicate, composite negative to be used in printing the final masterprints of the picture.[56]

These techniques, however, after the preliminary work described above, having his body casted and his head plastered, were also pretty tough on Claude Rains.

> Yet the Special Effects magic takes a terrible toll on the star. In his black velvet tights, gloves, and black helmet with air hoses attached, Rains evokes some horrid deep-sea diver mutant; he's able only to hear clearly the rush of his own air supply as Fulton tries desperately to shout to him through a megaphone; he must be perfectly precise in his movements, under merciless lights on a hot soundstage in summer heat. A tendency to place accidentally his black-gloved hand over a part of his visible costume results in as many as 20 agonizing "takes."
>
> At least once—due to the heat, a faulty air hose, exhaustion, or all of these—Rains faints on the set.
>
> Still, the actor endures, sometimes relieved by a double. And, perhaps as a wry comment on the outrageousness of this whole mad business, Rains still wears his homburg hat between scenes—now cocked atop his diving helmet.[57]

There is still controversy surrounding the final scene when, as life leaves his body, Jack Griffin slowly becomes visible again, as the indentation in the pillow (a plaster pillow and a blanket made of papier-mâché) becomes first a skeleton, then adding blood vessels and muscle, and finally Claude Rains' face as that of the dead Griffin. Some say a dummy was used throughout, while others say Rains himself appears in the final shot—Rains' daughter, Jessica Rains, "firmly believes it's her father in the flesh in the fade-out."[58]

The opening scenes of *The Invisible Man* follow the novel's plot fairly closely. Whale and Sherriff veered off from Wells' story when it came to the Invisible Man's actions after he had rendered himself invisible. A mysterious traveler, his head swathed in bandages, has hiked through a blizzard to the Lion's Head Inn in the village of Iping.

The secret which Universal studios jealously guarded within the impenetrable walls of a forbidden sound stage for months will be revealed on the screen of the Ritz Theater next Friday and Saturday when H. G. Wells' startling "The Invisible Man" opens its long awaited engagement there.

Filmed in the utmost secrecy with "No Visitors" signs attached to locked doors, "The Invisible Man" during its production created more intriguing conjectures than any photoplay made in Hollywood in years. Until the film's recent release, only a select group of 20 people actually knew the amazing manner in which this spectacular motion picture was made, and they were under oath not to tell.

Writers, photographers, executives, were strictly barred as the cameras ground on the strangest character ever to be created by Hollywood, an unseen star! Naturally, of all places Hollywood possesses, the most easily accelerated curiosity, and rumors of every color were racing about the city of make-believe while "The Invisible Man" accomplished his spine-tingling career.

Whale, meanwhile, has a grand time directing *The Invisible Man*. Indeed, having been an actor in London, appearing in such plays as 1928's *A Man With Red Hair* (with Charles Laughton as

James Whale, Arthur Edeson, Forrester Harvey and Claude Rains

the title role sadist, and Whale as his lunatic son), he likely wishes he could play the Invisible One himself. The director delights in the snowy night opening at the Lion's Head Inn, with its host of eccentrics the director bases on his own "Black Country" youth in Dudley, England: a derby-sporting hambone playing a player piano; a gaggle of old women drinking by the staircase; the dart-throwing villagers. He works as smoothly as ever with his cinematographer Arthur Edeson, cameraman of *All Quiet on the Western Front* and Whale's *Waterloo Bridge*, *Frankenstein*, *The Impatient Maiden* and *The Old Dark House*. Director and cinematographer treat Rains to a deluxe entrance, with three quick, increasing close-ups—just as Karloff had received in *Frankenstein*.[59]

The Invisible Man rents a room from the frenetic landlady, Mrs. Jenny Hall (Una O'Connor) and her laconic husband, Herbert (Forrester Harvey). Setting up an array of chemical apparatus in his room, he demands privacy and struggles to find the "way back."

Jack Griffin (Claude Rains) is a chemist in the employ of Dr. Cranley (Henry Travers). Griffin and his colleague, Kemp (William Harrigan) are assisting

Cranley in his work, which involves methods of preserving food. Harrigan, who played the cowardly Kemp, was also a veteran of the Great War. He served in the American, and not the British, Army. A Captain, he led one of the units which helped relieve the famous "Lost Battalion;"[60] nine companies of the 77th Infantry Division under the command of Major Charles Whittlesey, which had been cut off and surrounded by the Germans in the Argonne Forest on October 2, 1918, remaining surrounded for nearly a week before being relieved by other American units.

But Griffin, who is in love with Cranley's daughter, Flora (Gloria Stuart—her exclusion from the tea breaks during the filming of *The Old Dark House* presumably did not indicate any animosity towards her on the part of James Whale), has, with Cranley's consent, been working on his own mysterious project in secret in his spare time. Griffin disappears (as it turns out, quite literally). Although he had burned all his papers, Cranley and Kemp find an unburned scrap of paper which indicates Griffin's work had involved a drug called monocaine. The English literature describes the drug's bleaching properties—it had been used to bleach cloth, but its use was abandoned because it destroyed the fibers of the fabric. An obscure German reference also mentions that the drug induces madness. Kemp opines that Griffin would have never touched anything with madness in it, but Cranley responds that Griffin may not have known that fact, as it was mentioned only in the obscure German source which Cranley had

Rains and Whale take a tea break during filming

R. Bruce Crelin

once stumbled upon, purely by accident. Griffin had, indeed, experimented with monocaine.

It had made him invisible and was now beginning to drive him mad. "The drug seemed to light up my brain. Suddenly I realized the power I held, the power to rule, to make the world grovel at my feet." He reveals his plans to Kemp: he will gain power by embarking upon a reign of terror, murdering people great and small. "Even the moon is frightened of me, frightened to death! The whole world is frightened to death!" He begins by killing a police inspector and then derailing a train. The timid Kemp betrays Griffin to the police. In retaliation, Griffin kills him, riding with Kemp is his car as he attempts to flee. Revealing himself to Kemp at the hour he had appointed to kill him, Griffin traps Kemp in his car and propels it towards a cliff, where it crashes and burns.

> Universal had also picked up a recent Philip Wylie novel called *The Murderer Invisible*, which may have fed into Sherriff's script via the transformation of Griffin into a murderous megalomaniac. Though delighted with the finished film, Wells' only complaint related to this possibly Wylie-derived detail; hardly surprising, given Wells' disgust at Wylie's recent adaptation of *The Island of Dr. Moreau*. Observing that "instead of an invisible man we now have an invisible lunatic," Wells called it "a liberty

H. G. Wells, S. F. Ditcham and James Whale at Universal's INVISIBLE MAN luncheon

H. G. WELLS ON UNIVERSAL'S "THE INVISIBLE MAN"

A TRIUMPH OF TRICK PHOTOGRAPHY

Famous Author's Tribute

he could not condone." Whale's unruffled response was that "in the minds of rational people only a lunatic would want to make himself invisible anyway."[61]

Wells' objections could not have been all that strenuous, however; his contract with Universal gave him final approval over the script,[62] he had nixed a number of prior screenplays, and he was "effusive in his praise" of the finished film at a trade reception, along with Whale and Sherriff, prior to the film's British premiere:

> "Hollywood used to buy what they called the 'film rights' to a story, . . . and then kick the author out of the studios and guard the door with a dog. I have sent the following telegram to Carl Laemmle through Mr. Durham, managing director of Universal Pictures, Limited: CONGRATULATIONS ON 'THE INVISIBLE MAN' WHICH CONSIDER FILMED FLAW-LESSLY CARRYING OUT MY STORY FAITHFULLY."[63]

R. Bruce Crelin

This detail of Griffin's insanity may not, however, have been due to Wylie.[64] Sherriff had certainly seen the numerous prior drafts of the screenplay, but *No Leading Lady* does not mention him as having relied upon the Wylie book, or any elements of it which had found their way into any of those earlier efforts. Indeed, the John Weld screenplay, the last prior version drafted before Sherriff was brought on board, had eschewed the Wylie novel and the other treatments, and had been based directly upon Wells' novel. Sherriff's fears, as expressed in *No Leading Lady*, had been that Universal might discover how closely his screenplay followed the Wells novel. Rather, the elements in the Sherriff screenplay reflect themes from the Great War. Indeed, according to Curtis, Sherriff had run the insanity idea past Wells and received his full approval. Furthermore, Sherriff had confirmed that monocaine had "accidentally and unfortunately" led to insanity.

Griffin meddling with a drug which he did not fully understand, leading to unintended consequences, insanity, murder, and eventually his own destruction, reflects the ironic themes of the Great War. The film does not explain Griffin's motivations for his research into invisibility, but it was surely not so that he could go mad, commit murder at will, and attempt to rule the world. Indeed, the screenplay makes clear in Dr. Cranley's remarks that the link between monocaine and madness is described only in a single, obscure German reference, with which Griffin was most likely unfamiliar. The English references, said Cranley, describe only the drug's bleaching properties, and this is what likely inspired Griffin to attempt using the drug to create invisibility. He presumably had some practical, or even noble, purpose behind his research, but whatever that may have been, it was quickly supplanted by the madness brought on by the drug. Even if, as Whale had opined, "only a lunatic would want to make himself invisible anyway," Griffin's homicidal megalomania did not commence until after he had become invisible and the monocaine had begun to affect his mind.

The clear implication in Sherriff's screenplay, made explicit by his comments as related by Curtis, as depicted in the film under Whale's direction, is that Griffin had no idea of any link between monocaine and madness at the time he began his research. Griffin's subsequent madness was an entirely unknown and unanticipated consequence of his experiments. As had happened with Henry Frankenstein and his creation, Jack Griffin's experiments with monocaine take him into an unintended direction, leading to deaths of innocents (in Griffin's case, many more deaths, including, ultimately, his own, than had been caused by the Monster in *Frankenstein*). This is another version of the theme of the Great War as signaling the end to the century old Meliorist myth of Progress, as well as obliterating the ideas of the benignity of science and technology. But it is not limited only to outcomes caused by science, but also to any human activities undertaken without a full understanding or anticipation of their likely conse-

quences. Again, we see a misguided effort, undertaken in blind ignorance of its eventual potential outcome, lead to horrific results. This encapsulates the themes surrounding the beginnings of the Great War. Jack Griffin, of course, has his head wrapped in bandages and wears his dark glasses in order to conceal his invisibility. However, the bandages also evoke dressings worn by those who suffered grievous wounds in the War. Many survived with horrible, disfiguring facial wounds. Some wore dark glasses due to blindness caused by gas, shell fragments, or bullets. As previously mentioned, Claude Rains had suffered 90% blindness in his right eye caused by poison gas, an injury which he managed to successfully conceal throughout his life. The landlady of the Red Lion, Jenny Hall, despite her histrionics, does not even hesitate to rent a room to a man who arrives at the Inn with his head covered in bandages, even though it is winter and out of season, necessitating the room being prepared for a guest. This suggests sympathy for those wounded warriors who returned from the War bearing significant battle scars.

Once again, Whale injects humor into the film and, once again, some of it works, and some of it doesn't. Una O'Connor's screeching histrionics as Jenny Hall, the landlady of the Lion's Head Inn, are simply grating on the nerves and tend to detract from, rather than add to, enjoyment of the film. (However, whatever a viewer may think about Una O'Connor's performances in James Whale's films, she was one of Whale's favorite actresses. Her performances gave exactly

Losing his grip on reality, Griffin skips down the road singing.

what James Whale wanted.) Other touches, however, work well. The phlegmatic Constable Jaffers' (E.E. Clive) remarks when Griffin begins to strip off his bandages and his clothing ("'E's invisible, that's wot's the matter with 'im!") and after Griffin strips down to only his shirt ("'Ow can I 'andcuff a bloomin' shirt!") work very well, as does the scene of Griffin, having just stolen them by stripping them from a policeman, skipping down a lane as a pair of disembodied trousers, singing "Here we come gathering nuts in May!"

1 Curtis, 168-9.
2 Curtis, 188.
3 Mank, Production Background, *Invisible Man* 14-15.
4 Curtis, 197.
5 Mank, Production Background, *Invisible Man* 16.
6 Curtis, 197.
7 Curtis, 197.
8 Curtis, 197.
9 Mank, Production Background, *Invisible Man* 17.
10 Curtis, 197-8.
11 Mank, Production Background, *Invisible Man* 18.
12 Gatiss, Appendix.
13 Curtis, 198.
14 Mank, Production Background, *Invisible Man* 19
15 Curtis, 199.
16 Curtis, 199.
17 Mank, Production Background, *Invisible Man* 22.

R. Bruce Crelin

French 1951 reissue poster for *The Invisible Man*

The Great War and the Golden Age of Hollywood Horror

18 Curtis, 199.

19 Mank, *Invisible Man* 22.

20 Sherriff, *No Leading Lady* 241-4.

21 Sherriff, *No Leading Lady* 247.

22 Mank, Production Background, *Invisible Man* 22.

23 Mank, Production Background, *Invisible Man* 22.

24 Sherriff, *No Leading Lady* 250.

25 Sherriff, *No Leading Lady* 251-2.

26 Sherriff, *No Leading Lady* 253-4.

27 Sherriff, *No Leading Lady* 255 (emphasis in original).

28 Sherriff, *No Leading Lady* 261-2.

29 Mank, Production Background, *Invisible Man* 22-3.

30 Sherriff, *No Leading Lady* 264-7.

31 Sherriff, *No Leading Lady* 267-8.

32 Mank, Production Background, *Invisible Man* 23-4.

33 Sherriff, *No Leading Lady* 268.

34 Sherriff, *No Leading Lady* 268-72.

35 Sherriff, *No Leading Lady* 272.

36 Curtis, 200.

37 Sherriff, *No Leading Lady* 272-76.

38 Mank, Production Background, *Invisible Man* 24-34.

39 Curtis, 201-2.

40 Mank, Production Background, *Invisible Man* 34.

41 Curtis, 202.

42 Skal, David J., with Rains, Jessica, *Claude Rains: An Actor's Voice* Kindle ed. loc. 85-91 (University of Kentucky Press 2008).

43 Fold3.com, Rains, William C. British Army World War I Medal Rolls Index Cards, 1914-1920 https://www.fold3.com/image/250/325441532.

44 Skal, *Claude Rains* loc. 428-33.

45 Skal, *Claude Rains* loc. 449.

46 Mank, *Invisible Man* 26.

47 Skal, *Claude Rains* loc. 449.

48 Rains, British Army World War I Medal Rolls Index Cards, 1914-1920.

49 Skal, *Claude Rains* loc. 452-6.

50 Skal, *Claude Rains* loc. 478-85.

51 Mank, Production Background, *Invisible Man* 24.

52 Mank, Production Background, *Invisible Man* 37 (emphasis in original).

53 Mank, Production Background, *Invisible Man* 37.

54 Mank, Production Background, *Invisible Man* 39.

55 Mank, Production Background, *Invisible Man*, 39-40.

56 Mank, Production Background, *Invisible Man* 40-41.

57 Mank, Production Background, *Invisible Man* 41-2.

58 Mank, Production Background, *Invisible Man* 42.

59 Mank, Production Background, *Invisible Man* 38.

60 Mank, Production Background, *Invisible Man* 29.

61 Rigby, 141 (quoting a reprint in *The AFI Catalog of Motion Pictures Produced in the United States: Feature Films 1931-40*, Berkeley and Los Angeles 1993).

62 Curtis, 196.

63 Curtis, 221 (emphasis in original).

64 James Curtis opines that Universal had purchased the rights to the Wylie book not to use in its own production, but to keep it out of the hands of competitors. Curtis, 199 n. *.

Chapter Ten
In Which Frankenstein Builds a Bride

The fourth, and final, of Whale's Golden Age Universal Horrors, and the one regarded by many as not only his best, but also as the best horror film from that era—some say the best gothic horror film ever made—was *Bride of Frankenstein*. Universal had considered a sequel to *Frankenstein* even before the film had

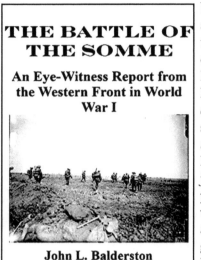

THE BATTLE OF THE SOMME

An Eye-Witness Report from the Western Front in World War I

John L. Balderston

Balderston was a newspaper war correspondent during WWI

been released. The project had gone through a series of different iterations, with different treatments done by a variety of writers (including a seven-page treatment by Robert Florey, who had originally been assigned to helm *Frankenstein*, entitled *The New Adventures of Frankenstein—The Monster Lives!*; this was summarily rejected, and when his *Murders in the Rue Morgue* flopped at the box office and his treatment for *The Invisible Man* was rejected, Florey was dropped from Universal's payroll).[1] Whale set John L. Balderston to work on the screenplay, now entitled *The Return of Frankenstein*, but felt that the writer was going stale, so Whale asked R.C. Sherriff to have a go—his draft was not suitable, either.[2] "William Hurlbut fashioned the story that was filmed almost completely from scratch, save for some scenes based upon an earlier treatment by Tom Reed."[3] Both Hurlbut and Balderston received credit as authors of the screenplay.

Although Carl Jr. was the nominal producer, James Whale had complete control of all aspects of the film.

> Studio policy during *The Bride of Frankenstein* [sic] was to give Whale whatever he wanted—in terms of script, casting, and production support. "He had complete control from beginning to end," said Ted Kent [the film's editor]. "I don't believe he could have worked any other way." Junior Laemmle, who would take the producer's credit on *Bride*, was in Europe when the film entered production and did not return until it was nearing completion. "He left Jimmy alone," said Jack Latham, who worked on the film. "I don't remember him ever coming down to the set." Whale effectively functioned as his own producer on *Bride*; the control he maintained is arguably the only way he could have achieved such a perverse— and captivating—mix of comedy and horror.[4]

Hold your breath!—the Bride of Frankenstein is coming!?!

SHIVERS and shakes! Gurgles and shrieks! Frankenstein!

Not so many years ago we had a confab with a chain advertising head. "Keep that monster face out of the ads," he ordered. "Cut it out of the trailer. Wipe it off the theatre front. It'll drive away business!" "But pul-eeze, Mister," we pleaded, "that face will pull. That face will stop them in their tracks and send them scooting into the theatre." "Nonsense," he bristled. "Let us try just once," we begged. "All right, just once" he compromised.

Once was enough. "Frankenstein" is now show history. Smacko, socko, loco went the house records from border to border and coast to coast. The monster made the nation's hair stand on end. It was a face that made a fortune for the picture business!

And here's mighty grand news for showmen—the face that made a fortune is going to make another fortune for you. The monster is coming back! And he's calling for a bride! *And he GETS his bride!* A new Frankenstein wave of hysteria will engulf the land. Faces will pale and knees will wobble and hearts will stop beating when the mighty Karloff sweeps on your screen and says, "Come on folks, meet the bride!"

They're only shooting "Frankenstein" now; but NOW is the moment for you to start advertising for that SECOND fortune! NOW is the time to let the gossip columnists know that they searched far and wide for a woman who would DARE to play the role of the bride of the monster.

Tease "The Bride of Frankenstein" in your lobby, in your newspapers and even on your screen with advance production notes. The millions who made box-office history for "Frankenstein" are eagerly waiting to meet the bride!

Give the monster the works!

JOE WEIL

R. Bruce Crelin

Whale, pictured with Ernest Thesiger, insisted *Bride* be made on his own terms.

Whale certainly left his indelible mark on the film. His annual salary at Universal in 1935 was $105,000 [almost $2 million in 2019 dollars, adjusted for inflation].[5]

> Whale always took his films seriously, but *The Bride of Frankenstein* [sic] was made with a deliberate sense of amusement. "I think he had great fun with it," said his friend Jack Latham. "He was very amused by Boris and Ernest Thesiger and their characters; they amused him very much."[6]

"Novelist Christopher Bram describes *Bride* as a comedy about death."[7]

> If Whale had to make a sequel, he insisted it would be entirely on his own terms. From its inception, the film was intended as a pitch-black comedy. He told Sherriff that he considered he had milked the original idea dry, therefore the only solution was to take an entirely different approach. Rather than the stark realism of the original, Whale wanted a fantasy of epic proportions and a great deal more of the macabre humour in which he so liked to indulge.

. . . .

Whale's problem would be to satisfy those eager for genuine horror, while at the same time getting away with as much tongue-in-cheek campery as he could. He confessed to David Lewis that he was approaching the whole endeavour as a "hoot" but, even though he was now secure as Universal's "Ace" director, he would have to walk a very narrow margin between comedy and terror in order not to alienate both his audience and Junior Laemmle.[8]

"Pitch-black comedy" is also a legacy of the War, as Paul Fussell quoted Philip Gibbs: "'The more revolting it was,' he says, 'the more . . . [people] shouted with laughter.'"[9] Bruce G. Hallenbeck, on the other hand, included *The Old Dark House* in his book, *Comedy-Horror Films*, but did not include *Bride of Frankenstein*.[10] There was significant disagreement about the tone of the film:

> Junior Laemmle was worried about the humor of the picture and upset that Whale had not played up more horror, as Junior had requested, then ordered, then begged him to do. John Balderston, meanwhile, bitterly resented the horror flourishes Whale had given to the satire Balderston had written, and disowned the film![11]

It just goes to show—you can't please everyone! My personal belief is that, with a few exceptions, the comic elements enhance the film.

Whale cast the film with many actors from his previous films, plus a few new additions. One of the new faces was the gorgeous 17-year-old Valerie Hobson, who would take over the role of Elizabeth, Henry Frankenstein's bride (indeed, one could say *she* is actually the "Bride of Frankenstein"). Mae Clarke, who had played Elizabeth in *Frankenstein*, was in poor health after having been injured in an automobile accident in 1933. Hobson, whose father was a Captain in the Royal Navy, was born in Ireland on April 14, 1917. She had, by 1935, become "Universal's top heroine of melodrama,"

E.E. Clive and Karloff add some comedy

R. Bruce Crelin

267

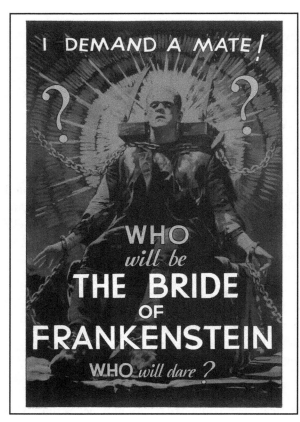

I DEMAND A MATE!

? ?

WHO
will be
THE BRIDE
OF
FRANKENSTEIN
WHO *will dare* ?

having appeared in *The Man Who Reclaimed His Head* (1934), *The Mystery of Edwin Drood* (1935), *Life Returns* (1935), and *Rendezvous at Midnight* (1935).[12] Ms. Hobson, a Universal contract player, would receive $200 [approximately $3,700 in 2019 dollars, adjusted for inflation] per week for her estimated four-week stint on the film.[13]

Another new face was English-born Elsa Lanchester, wife of Charles Laughton. Whale would cast Ms. Lanchester in a dual role. In a prelude, she would play Mary Wollstonecraft Shelley, the author of the novel, *Frankenstein*. She would also appear as the Monster's Mate, credited in the opening and closing credits with only a "?".

In a publicity ploy reminiscent of David O. Selznick's heralded 1939 quest for the perfect Scarlett O'Hara, Universal began "leaking" the names of possible choices for the Monster's Mate. Would it be Arletta Duncan, a shapely brunette who was glimpsed as one of Mae Clarke's bridesmaids in *Frankenstein* and was dispatched to Karloff's farm for a picnic and publicity shots? Would it be Phyllis Brooks, a willowy blonde destined to become a cult favorite, recently praised by William Saroyan as ". . . the strange beautiful super-real girl of motion picture art itself. . . ?" Would it be Brigitte Helm, who had played the saintly Maria and her sinuously evil, robotrix twin in Lang's *Metropolis*?

If the vanity of any of these ladies bristled at being considered for the part of a Female Monster, it would not have helped to learn that they were all merely victims of the studio's quest for bogus publicity. For, despite the publicized screen tests (which the studio considered worth their cost in publicity), James Whale knew from the film's inception exactly whom he

wished to cast not only as the Monster's Mate, but also as Mary Shelley in the Prologue as well.[14]

Whale had decided upon Ms. Lanchester from the start.[15] "Her name was suggested for the Bride in Balderston's script of 9 June 1934. In the script of 23 June, Lanchester is listed against both roles of Mary Shelley and the Bride."[16] She would receive $1,250 [approximately $23,400 in 2019 dollars, adjusted for inflation] per week for an estimated two weeks of work.[17]

In the opening scenes, I played Mary Wollstonecraft Shelley, dressed extremely elegantly, sweeter than sugar. I am delicately embroidering while sitting on a satin divan beside a crackling fire, as an electrical storm rages outside the window. My husband,[18] Percy Bysshe Shelley, and his constant companion, Lord Byron, are arguing with me about the propriety of writing a gothic horror piece that is so sacrilegious—*Frankenstein*.

MARY SHELLEY (shuddering): "Lightning alarms me."

LORD BYRON (laughing): "Astonishing creature! You, my dear young lady, frightened of thunder?—when you have written a tale that froze my blood! How difficult to believe that that lovely brow conceived a monster created from the corpses of rifled graves!"

MARY SHELLEY: "And why shouldn't I write of monsters? My purpose was to write a moral lesson!"

In the prologue, Mary Shelley's dress was the most fairy-like creation that I have ever seen before or since in a film. It had a low neck, tiny puffed sleeves, and a bodice that continued in a long line to the floor and onto a train about seven feet long. The entire white net dress was embroidered with iridescent sequins—butterflies, stars, and moons. It took seventeen Mexican ladies twelve weeks to make it. The dress traveled around the country and appeared in the foyers of all the big openings of *The Bride of Frankenstein* [sic].

It was James Whale's idea that, later in the film, Dr. Frankenstein's second creation, the strange and macabre female monster, should be played by the same actress. Quite a contrast to the sweet and dainty Mary Shelley. We shot the prologue first, and it took only two or three days. Then I worked another week or ten days as the Monster's Bride.[19]

The magnificent dress would invite the attention of the Hays Office, as it displayed too much of Ms. Lanchester's décolletage. "The shots early in the picture," wrote Breen [Joseph I. Breen, the PCA censor], "in which the breasts of the character of Mrs. Shelley are exposed and accentuated, constitute a code violation." The opening scene was trimmed, and some close-ups of Ms. Lanchester removed, some cuts due to the censor and some due to Whale's own decision to shorten the prologue.[20]

Elsa Lanchester's magnificent dress would go on tour!

Her part in *Bride of Frankenstein* would prove to be of enduring popularity.

I suppose the quickest way you can shut me up nowadays [1983 when her autobiography was published] is to ask me about *The Bride of Frankenstein* [sic]. To this day, nine out of ten photo-

Douglas Walton, Gavin Gordon and Elsa, whose "dress" shocked the censors.

graphs I get in the mail for autographing are of the Bride. I'm grateful for *The Bride of Frankenstein* [sic], of course—it became a kind of trademark for me, in the same way that Captain Bligh and Henry the Eighth were for Charles.

· · · ·

The Bride is one of the few films that has followed me all the time. It keeps popping up on television several times a year, especially at Halloween. Nowadays there seems to be a kind of underground cult around it—the face of the Bride is even featured on a New York disco. I'm not unhappy that it happened. It's sometimes pleasant to have very young kids in markets or in the street recognize you as the Bride of Frankenstein. Because, changed as I have, obviously, I apparently haven't turned into a type that looks like everybody else. And I'm flattered that I'm recognizable in a part I played in the 1930s.[21]

While the makeup was iconic, it was her performance, much in the same way as Karloff had done with the Monster, that truly made the character.

Australian actor O.P. Heggie, "A specialist in benign old men,"[22] was brought in, at $1,500 [Approximately $28,000 in 2019 dollars, adjusted for inflation] per week for one week's work, to play the blind hermit who befriends the Monster and teaches him a few simple words.[23] "Whale's insistence to cast the actor, however, caused a lapse in production. On 19 February, with nothing but Heggie's scenes left to shoot, production temporarily shut down. It resumed ten days later when the actor became available."[24]

The remainder of the main cast had all appeared in Whale's earlier films. Una O'Connor, who had played frenetic landlady Jenny Hall in *The Invisible Man*, was cast as Minnie, a screeching Frankenstein family servant who had somehow managed to have gone unseen in the first film. She signed on for five weeks at $850 [approximately $16,000 in 2019 dollars, adjusted for inflation] per week.[25] Valerie Hobson recalled her in an April 1989 interview with Gregory William Mank:

> She was a busy little Irish body, terribly busy; as she played in the film, so she was really in life. She used to do a great deal of knitting—always crocheting, or knitting away. Tiny little ankles, and little chicken legs. She was rightly in much demand those days.[26]

Whale would remain in contact with Ms. O'Connor for the rest of his life, leaving her a specific bequest of $10,000 [approximately $94,000 in 2019 dollars, adjusted for inflation] in his will.[27]

Whale had originally wanted his star of *The Invisible Man*, Claude Rains, to play the part of Dr. Septimus Pretorius, but Rains was unavailable.[28] Whale then cast his old friend, Ernest Thesiger, who had brilliantly portrayed Horace Femm in *The Old Dark House*, at $1,000 [approximately $18,700 in 2019 dollars, adjusted for inflation] per week for three weeks' work.[29] Dr. Pretorius, another of Henry's former mentors from his University days, had been "booted" from the University for "knowing too much." This mentor is the polar opposite of Henry's other old mentor at University who we met in *Frankenstein*, Professor Waldman. Indeed, one could see Waldman as among the prime movers involved in "booting" Dr. Pretorius from the faculty! Unlike Waldman, Pretorius would not only accept the idea of the existence of vampires and re-animated mummies, but if he ever met either one, he would most probably share a glass of gin and a cigar with it. Said Valerie Hobson of Thesiger:

> Yes, he was a duck! A darling duck of a person. He was a terribly sweet man—he really had a kind and gentle heart. (I don't think he had a very strong 'male' approach to things!) He was one of the very first people to make 'almost camp' fun. He did

it as a serious thing, you know—oooh, the sort of arched eyebrow and arched nostril, and everything else, but in fact it *was* what we would call nowadays 'camp'. He was really sweet and terribly funny.

. . . .

Certainly, with his wonderful pointed eyebrows, he looked like a devil—I don't think I ever saw Ernest looking like anything else but! He had an amusing face, an amusing twinkle. He had a pointed nose and pointed eyebrows, and you felt that if he were going to dance, he would have pointed feet!"[30]

Thesiger gave such a brilliant, definitive performance as Pretorius that it is difficult to imagine anyone else in the role, even an actor as magnificent as Claude Rains.

The other principal cast members had appeared in *Frankenstein*. Dwight Frye, who had played Frankenstein's assistant, the hunchbacked Fritz, returned, at $500 [approximately $9,300 in 2019 dollars, adjusted for inflation] per week for three weeks, to play a similar role, Karl. Originally a larger part, in which his character was involved in a subplot concerning him murdering his Aunt and Uncle Glutz in order to steal their money, and blaming the murders on the Monster, the entire subplot was deleted.[31] Karl would assist Dr. Pretorius in his grave-robbing efforts, as well as procure a new heart ("it was a very fresh one") when the one previously on hand proved to be unsuitable. According to Denis Gifford, the original script called for Karl to murder Elizabeth and remove her heart, so that Henry Frankenstein's bride would become part of the Monster's Mate: the Bride of Frankenstein literally becoming a part of the Bride of the Frankenstein Monster.[32] Others have said, however, that this was never a part of any drafts of the screenplay. In the film, Karl murders a girl carrying a basket down the street to obtain the heart ("It was a—police case").

Colin Clive would return to reprise his role as Henry Frankenstein. "Clive's health, however, had deteriorated since the first *Frankenstein*. By now he was an acute alcoholic having originally started drinking to abate his nerves prior to appearing on stage in *Journey's End*. His condition would contribute to his premature death by tuberculosis on 25 June 1937, aged only 37."[33]

Valerie Hobson . . . also had a sense of Clive's instability. "I realized he was inclined to be a hysterical actor," she said, "but what is more, I think Jimmy Whale held him in reserve, because

Valerie Hobson and Colin Clive

it was precisely that hysterical quality in Colin that he needed."
According to Hobson, Clive created a perceptible tension on
the set. "People had to watch him like a hawk to see that he
shouldn't drink," she said, "and that made one a little bit nervous. I remember that he had a dresser who stuck very close to
him, and maybe he was a paid dresser who made quite sure he
didn't have a nip."[34]

"Clive's whole performance was built on hysteria and was—by necessity—a
more limited and less shaded performance than the one he delivered in *Frankenstein*."[35] Valerie Hobson said:

Colin Clive was a strange, quiet, buttoned-up, saturnine
sort of man. He reminds me of a very early James Mason
(I played in one of James' first films); they had the same sort
of quality. At least James Mason was a fighter, who gave the
impression of being able to unravel his own emotional problems. But Colin Clive . . . he had a sort of hounded, rather
naïve quality, like a man who couldn't fight back—whatever
his problems were.[36]

R. Bruce Crelin

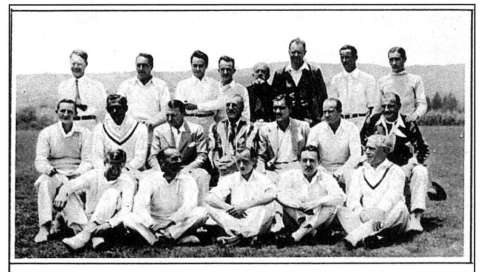

HOLLYWOOD CRICKETERS: BORIS KARLOFF, CLIVE BROOK, C. AUBREY SMITH, RONALD COLMAN, H. B. WARNER, DESMOND ROBERTS, CLAUDE KING, MURRAY KINNELL, AND R.C.SHERRIFF, AUTHOR OF "JOURNEY'S END," AND OTHER WELL-KNOWN ACTORS.

Newspaper article on the Hollywood Cricket Club

Clive's alcoholism and accompanying ill-health actually added to the character of Henry in the film.

> Charisma has deserted Henry Frankenstein. No longer the attractive, zealous dreamer of the original film, the Monster Maker (as played by the dissipating Clive) is a living wound, a shrill neurotic, too painfully tormented by the creation and abandonment of his Monster to be truly sympathetic. As Clive glares at the heavens while the Bride receives his electrical miracle of Life, his cadaverous face is haunting and grotesque, leering with the agony of an addict hooked on blasphemy.[37]

Clive's performance meshes perfectly with the atmosphere of the film.

Of course, the most significant returning performer from *Frankenstein* was Boris Karloff, now billed simply as "Karloff," having another go at the role of the Monster, the role which had made him a horror star. Karloff would be paid $2,500 [Approximately $47,000 in 2019 dollars, adjusted for inflation] per week for five weeks of shooting.[38] Said Valerie Hobson in her interview with Gregory Mank:

> Well, I remember that the very first time I saw Boris Karloff, he was in full gear as the Monster! I had been warned what he

was going to look like, and I thought he was absolutely extraordinary; I hadn't realized his boots were so built up, and he'd be
so *huge*. I was totally amazed! And then to hear a very gentle,
English voice coming out of that awful makeup—and with a
pronounced lisp! Boris was a very gentle man. . . Very kindly
and of a sweet disposition, and (one of the most precious things
to me as a young girl in America)—he was so *English*. There was
a little coterie of about eight Englishmen, of which Boris was
a pillar; C. Aubrey Smith was alive in those days, and he and
Boris and the others used to play Cricket, and get together, and
they made a little English club of themselves.[39]

She credited "Boris' kind eyes" as being the key to his ability to evoke sympathy for the Monster through the makeup—"Most monsters have frightening
eyes, but Boris, even in makeup, had very loving, sad eyes."[40] There would be one
rather large bone of contention between Karloff and Whale, brought about by
the Monster's dialogue in the film. The Monster, of course, had been extremely
articulate in Shelley's novel, going so far as quoting Milton. Karloff, however,
objected to having the Monster speak. He felt "it weakened his weirdness."[41]

His great charm and humor won Karloff, again, the admiration
of the entire company—except, as before, from James Whale.
The very conscientious star had implored the very headstrong
director to scrap the Monster's dialogue:

The speech . . . stupid! My argument was that
if the Monster had any impact or charm, it was
because he was inarticulate . . . this great, lum-
bering, inarticulate creature. . . .

Whale cavalierly ignored Karloff's concern. Elsa
Lanchester believes the reason was as much one of arrogance
as of conception:

That was a thing in which James Whale was
rather nasty. He was very derogatory about Boris Karloff; he'd say, "Oh, he was a *truck driver*."
Maybe in the early days, he had to do some
hard work, but Boris Karloff was a well-educat-
ed, very gentle, nice man.

Egomania was the villain here. Whale still bristled that it
was Karloff who had won the lion's share of attention for *Fran-*

kenstein. Some days on the set of the sequel, Whale even seemed to be competing with Karloff for the attention of the ever-vigilant publicity photographers. The director struck comic poses with the iron Monster stand-in (built due to the impracticality of making a live double), posed elegantly with cheroot in hand, and feyly daubed "muck" on Karloff's costume. It was all a sad conceit of the *nouveau riche* Whale, who had conveniently forgotten that his own father had been an iron laborer.[42]

Cinematographer John Mescall and Whale ham it up for publicity shots.

Of course, James Whale would prevail over his star's objections. The Monster would speak, and "Karloff, despite his objections, managed to pull it off. He created a cavernous voice for the Monster, one in accord with the original conception. . . ."[43]

Bride of Frankenstein went into production on January 2, 1935, under the working title *The Return of Frankenstein.*[44] The film had a 36-day shooting schedule and a $293,750 [approximately $5.5 million in 2019 dollars, adjusted for inflation] budget (about $30,000 [around $560,000] more than the budget on *Frankenstein*).[45] "Whale seemed slightly wary of young Valerie Hobson, unsure of her mettle and amused by her innocence."[46] His manner of introducing her to her co-star, Colin Clive, was, one may say, unique:

> The first time I ever saw Colin Clive, I was dressed in a flimsy nightgown, and had to climb into bed with him. And I was introduced to him as I arrived in the bed! Jimmy Whale:
>
> > "Mr. Clive, this is Miss Hobson. Now, let's get on with the scene!" So James Whale must have had a sense of humor, because that was a bit farfetched even for Hollywood![47]

James Whale's "farfetched" sensibilities led him to take an extraordinary interest in the lingerie worn by the actresses. He insisted Valerie Hobson not wear anything under her satin bridal gown. Said Ms. Hobson in her interview with Gregory Mank:

729-P.76

GWM: "Whale was known to be fastidious as a director, even masterminding the costumes. Was the incredible bridal gown you wore in the opening his concept?"

VH: "Yes—I'm afraid I thought it was a horrid dress! It was extremely thick, brocaded satin (I don't happen to like satin)—terribly heavy, with weights all around the bottom, so it wouldn't hang out into a fur bridal train. I was sort of wobbling around in it, and I thought it made me look like an elephant! And I wasn't allowed to wear any underclothes. It was Jimmy Whale's

idea, you know—'You mustn't wear any underclothes.' A lot of nonsense, but that was his idea. So heavy, I could barely stagger around in it. It really was very odd."[48]

Whale demanded that Anne Darling, who played the shepherdess who falls into the water and is saved by the Monster, wear black lacy panties (even though her underwear would never be visible onscreen). Whale had her lift her skirt and found her to be wearing white panties. He immediately sent to wardrobe for a lacy black pair. "Meanwhile, the irrepressible Elsa Lanchester, aware of Whale's lingerie fetish on *Bride of Frankenstein*, responded in her usual eccentric way. As the vainglorious Bride, she'd pull up her shroud between takes and 'flash' the company, revealing that the 'Bride' herself was a no-lingerie gal—and a natural redhead."[49]

Jack P. Pierce, Universal makeup artist, had modified the Monster's makeup somewhat. The Monster's hair was singed, and scars were added to his face to reflect his ordeal in the burning mill at the end of *Frankenstein*. Pierce created a rubber headpiece that was less time-consuming to apply than the cotton and collodion application which he had used for *Frankenstein*.[50] Nevertheless, Karloff still had to undergo five hours of makeup and costuming in order to be ready to shoot. Said Karloff:

"The watery opening scene of the sequel, THE BRIDE OF FRANKENSTEIN [sic], was filmed with me wearing a rubber suit under my costume to ward off chill. But air got into the suit. When I was launched into the pond, my legs flew up in the air, and I floated there like some obscene water lily while I, and everyone else, hooted with laughter. They finally fished me out with a boat-hook and deflated me."

The "obscene water lily" failed to mention that, shortly after the shooting stopped, he fell into the pond and dislocated a hip. While Junior Laemmle and Whale despaired about a possible production shutdown, Karloff visited the studio doctor, had the hip strapped and bandaged—and returned to work![51]

His injury necessitated even more preparation time for Karloff. He would awaken at 4:30 a.m. and undergo an infra-red treatment on his hip. After a quick breakfast of toast and coffee, he would leave for the studio at 5: 20 a.m., arriving at 6 a.m. to have his face massaged, soothed, and oiled in preparation for the application of his makeup. At 7 a.m. Pierce would begin to apply the makeup, and by 12: 30 p.m., after a brief rest, Karloff would be ready to don his costume.[52] He would suffer another injury later on in the filming, when he fell over a box in the crypt scene, wrenching his back and tearing several ligaments.[53]

Colin Clive would also suffer an injury on the set, falling and tearing ligaments in his knee. As a result, for most of the film he was either shot in close-up while standing on crutches or sitting down. "On-set the accident was generally attributed to the actor's now acute drinking problem fueled, perhaps by his unhappy home life."[54]

Whale collaborated with Jack P. Pierce, Universal's makeup artist, in creating the concept for the Bride. Said film editor Ted Kent: "I know the Bride's make-up was Whale's conception," he said. "He was very clever with his pencil and I saw several sketches he made showing details such as how her hair should look."[55] In her autobiography, Ms. Lanchester detailed her experiences in being made up as the Monster's Mate:

> Apart from the discomfort of the monster makeup and all the hissing and screaming I had to do, I enjoyed working on the film. I admired Whale's directing and the waiting-for-something-to-happen atmosphere he was able to create around us. He and Jack Pierce, the makeup man, knew exactly what they wanted, so I didn't have to do many makeup tests. They had Queen Nefertiti in mind for the form and structure of the Bride's head.
>
> I spent long hours in the makeup room. Jack Pierce, of course, was the creator of the first Frankenstein makeup, and so he was elevated even further in his own heaven when a Bride was to be born. He had his own *sanctum sanctorum*, and as you entered (you did not go in; you entered) *he* said good morning

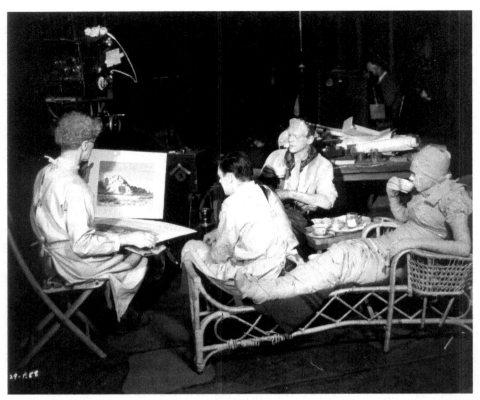

Studio publicity photo shows Ernest Thesiger, Colin Clive, Boris Karloff and Elsa Lanchester having afternoon tea.

first. If I spoke first, he glared and slightly showed his upper teeth. He would be dressed in a full hospital doctor's operating outfit. At five in the morning, this made me dislike him intensely. Then, for three or four hours, the Lord would do his creative work, with never a word spoken as he built up the scars with spirit gum, pink putty, red paint, and so on. Nowadays, you can buy stick-on scars for a few cents at a joke shop. But Jack Pierce fancied himself The Maker of Monsters—meting out wrath and intolerance by the bucketful.

I've often been asked how my hair was made to stand on end. Well, from the top of my head they made four tiny, tight braids. On these was anchored a wired horsehair cage about five inches high. Then my own hair was brushed over this structure, and two white hair pieces—one for the right temple and the other from the left cheekbone—were brushed over the top.[56]

"He took so long to make Karloff up and so long to make me up, we'd only have an hour or two together."[57]

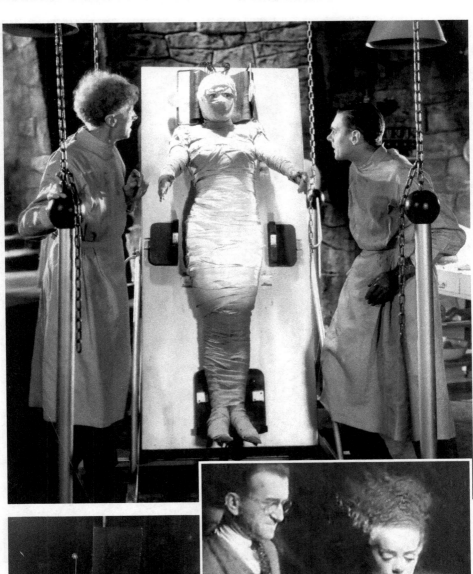

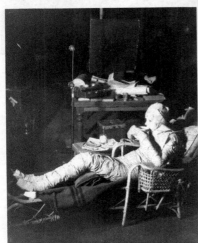

Above: Jack Pierce closely supervises Elsa applying her lipstick for this magazine photo.
Left: A bandaged Elsa enjoys her tea break.

"The challenge for Whale in the climactic creation scene was to improve upon the original."[58]

For the climactic creation sequence, the studio had again leased Kenneth Strickfaden's laboratory equipment. They had the pieces transported from storage in their creator's garage to the Universal lot. The paraphernalia was then enhanced by additions from the studio technicians. "The special effects and electrical departments made up numerous meaningless gadgets, switches, and indicators," recalled Ted Kent, "and Mr. Whale chose the most interesting."[59]

Karl is on the roof with Ludwig, the other lab assistant, as they lower the "cosmic diffuser" and send down the wires. Henry joins his assistants on the roof to supervise the launching of the kites skyward to capture the lightning to infuse life into the Monster's Mate. In much the same way as his Fritz, Dwight Frye's Karl would meet his fate at the hands of the Monster. As Karl brandishes a torch to try to get the Monster to leave the roof, the Monster flings Karl over the parapet of the tower to his screaming death. "When the sequence was ready for production, Whale departed liberally from the script, allowing the scene to build its own momentum with a minimum of dialogue."[60] The film would wrap on March 7, 1935, 10 days behind schedule and $100,000 [approximately $1.9 million in 2019 dollars, adjusted for inflation] over budget.[61] Universal would earn a tidy profit of just under $1 million [approximately $18.5 million] on the film.[62]

One interesting component of *Bride of Frankenstein*, which sets it apart from the earlier Universal Horrors, is its music score. The early Universal Horrors, *Dracula* and *Frankenstein*, had no musical scores at all, merely musical themes played over the opening and closing credits. *Bride of Frankenstein* has "one of the first Hollywood scores to use a symphony orchestra to impressionistic effect."[63]

> James Whale would personally choose the composer. Whale had met Franz Waxman, recently arrived in California, at a party at the home of the German actress/screenwriter Ms. Salka Viertal. Having admired Waxman's score for the picture *Liliom* Whale approached the composer and told him about his film. "Nothing will be resolved in the picture," Whale explained, "except the end destruction scene. Will you write an unresolved score for it?"[64]

Bride of Frankenstein would have a full orchestral score, with different musical themes:

> Waxman accepted the challenge—he would happily have scored a Charlie Chan picture had an offer been tendered—and produced what is probably still to this day the greatest score ever written for a horror movie. Three distinctive themes, representing the Monster, the Bride, and Thesiger's Pretorius, weave leitmotifs throughout the film. The score is alternately romantic, exciting, and horrifying as it builds to a clamorous creation scene in which the rhythmic thumping of a kettledrum suggests the newly beating heart of the Bride. At Whale's suggestion, Waxman ended the score with "a big dissonant chord," as if the powerful explosion of the laboratory had rocked the very foundations of the theater. Whale clearly wanted the destruction of the Monster and his mate to be definite and irrevocable,[65] lest

This 1993 soundtrack was the first release for Waxman's *Bride* score.

he might be pressured into making yet another sequel. (He blew up Henry and Elizabeth for good measure.) "With the lightning and thunder of the heavens for accompaniment," the script concluded, "the structure that was the laboratory collapses into a burning heap, the cloud of smoke and dust disperses a little and settles down over the scene, and the thunders of a jealous and triumphant Jehovah roll for positively the FINAL FADE OUT."[66]

"The 'Female Monster' theme (which has reminded many viewers of Rogers' and Hammerstein's 'Bali Hai' of their 1949 Broadway musical SOUTH PACIFIC) climaxes with the explosion of the tower laboratory, in a finale a la Wagner's GOTTERDAMMERUNG."[67] "The recording of the score, played by a reduced 22-piece orchestra and conducted by Mischa Bakaleinikoff, was made in a single nine-hour session attended by Waxman and Whale. The success of Waxman's score, which would later be adapted and used in the serials *Flash Gordon*, *Buck Rogers* and others, ensured the composer's appointment as the studio's music director."[68]

Bride of Frankenstein opens with an exterior shot of a château, smoke rising from the chimney, while a violent thunderstorm rages. Whale was fond of opening his horror films with raging storms, doing so with three of his four Universal Horrors. Both *Bride* and *The Old Dark House* open with thunder, lightning, and heavy rain, while *The Invisible Man* opens with a blizzard. In both *Frankenstein* and *Bride*, Frankenstein harnesses the lightning from violent thunderstorms in order to provide the force to endow his creations with life. The scene shifts to the interior of the Swiss château, where a servant (Una O'Connor) walks three Borzoi across the foreground. Mary Wollstonecraft Shelley, her "husband," Percy Bysshe Shelley (Douglas Walton), and George Gordon, Lord Byron (Gavin Gordon), are relaxing in front of a fire while the storm rages outside. Says Lord Byron:

> How beautifully dramatic—the cruelest, savage exhibition of nature—at her worst without—and we three, we elegant three, within. I should like to think that an irate Jehovah was pointing those arrows of lightning directly at my head—the unbowed head of George Gordon, Lord Byron—England's greatest sinner!

The discussion turns to Mary's story of *Frankenstein*. "The air itself is filled with monsters." A flashback sequence summarizes the events of the first film. She reveals that the Monster had not, in fact, been destroyed by the fire at the mill. . . .

The film then picks up just where *Frankenstein* had ended. As the mill blazes away, and finally collapses, the villagers are dancing around it and hollering. This scene is again reminiscent of James Whale's description of the prisoners at the end of their confinement at Holzminden. Henry is brought back to the castle. The Monster has been saved by falling through the floor of the burning windmill into the water of a pond beneath the structure. He now commits his first intentional, unprovoked murder; that of Little Maria's father, Hans[69] (Reginald Barlow), followed swiftly by his second, of Hans' wife (Mary Gordon—a prolific actress with many screen appearances, both credited and uncredited; she played Mrs. Hudson, Sherlock Holmes' landlady, in ten of the Holmes films starring Basil Rathbone and Nigel Bruce), as a silent owl looks on. (Although his rage at this time is almost understandable, having just been nearly burned to death by a mob of villagers who had danced and cheered at his predicament.) He then provokes horrific screeches from Minnie, who had lingered behind after the mill fire and now runs back to the Frankenstein castle. As in *The Invisible Man*, Ms. O'Connor's performance here is mostly grating rather than amusing. After Henry's presumed

Minnie (Una O'Connor) meets a thoroughly pissed-off Monster.

dead body is brought back to the castle, it is again revealed that he was not killed when the Monster flung him from the top of the mill at the end of *Frankenstein*.

A loud knocking at the front door heralds the arrival of Dr. Pretorius one night while Frankenstein is in bed, talking with Elizabeth. Minnie answers the door and shows Pretorius in—"there's no sich name" mutters Minnie as she leads him up the staircase. Introducing him to Henry and Elizabeth, she says "he's a very queer-looking old gentleman, sir," who has come "on a secret grave matter." This is, I think, Ms. O'Connor's best performance in the film, far better than her screeching and caterwauling. Elizabeth leaves. Dr. Pretorius invites Henry to his lodgings, where he proposes the two men pool their knowledge and create a female being, combining Frankenstein's technique with Pretorius' discovery of growing creatures "like cultures—from seed," as nature does. Pretorius will create an artificial brain using his technique, while Frankenstein will use his knowledge to stitch together a body. Pretorius toasts the new partnership with gin (sharing a love of gin with Horace Femm, Pretorius says it is his "only weakness"): "To a new world of Gods and Monsters!" Pretorius has, however, failed to produce full-sized beings, succeeding only in producing homunculi, which he keeps in little glass jars inside a coffin-shaped case. He displays his miniature people to Frankenstein: a queen, a king (an inside joke, modeled after Henry VIII in Alexander Korda's *The Private Life of Henry VIII* (1933), in which Elsa Lanchester's husband, Charles Laughton, portrayed the title character, winning a Best Actor Oscar, and Lanchester herself played Anne of Cleves, the fourth, and least favorite, of Henry's wives, who at least had the good fortune to leave the Royal Presence with her head still on her shoulders), an archbishop, a ballerina (who will only dance to Mendelsohn's "Spring Song"), a suave, Mephistophelian character whom Pretorius believes resembles himself ("or do I flatter myself?"), and a mermaid ("an experiment with seaweed"). An additional figure is a boffo baby, described in the shooting script as "already as big as the Queen and looking as if it might develop into a Boris Karloff. It is pulling a flower to pieces," played by 10-year-old little person Billy Barty. Pretorius thinks he "will grow into something worth watching." Although the scenes with the baby were cut from the film, "some shots of it can still be glimpsed in the final picture."[70]

Meanwhile, the Monster has been roaming the countryside. He frightens a young girl herding sheep (Anne Darling). She falls into a stream and the Monster rescues her. Nevertheless, his appearance terrifies her, and she screams. Two hunters, Robert A'Dair[71] and Jack Curtis, hear her screams and shoot the Monster, injuring his arm. He is captured, bound and tied to a pole. In this scene, the Monster is securely bound, and tied to a pole, his arms above his head. He is raised up prior to being dumped into a cart, and for an instant is seen writhing against the ropes as the upright pole pauses before it is dropped. In a caption under a still of this scene, Gifford points out "Whale mocked the crucifixion."[72] This has been the standard interpretation, repeated often, as for example in Gatiss' 1995 biography of Whale: "[Whale] took the opportunity here to subversively mock Christianity through Pretorious's quips and the Monster's treatment at the hands of the villagers."[73] David Skal refers to "the direct comparison of the Frankenstein monster to Christ" and "the film's omnipresent cruciform imagery" as "mak[ing] a statement more 'blasphemous' than anything Breen [the PCA censor] ordered cut."[74] Whale certainly displays a propensity for insult-

ing organized religion: Pretorius' derisive comments about "Bible stories," the Monster overturning the statue of a Bishop in the cemetery; and where wedding bells ring out on the score as the "Bride of Frankenstein" is revealed, is certainly a mockery of the wedding ceremony. But the crucifixion imagery, and the comparison of the Monster to Christ, in the film are something else altogether. They have nothing whatever to do with a mockery of organized religion and everything to do with Great War imagery.

The crucifixion has a prominent part in Great War mythology, which, in light of Whale's background, most surely underlies the Monster's "crucifixion" scene, the other crucifixion imagery, and the portrayal of the Monster as a Christ-like figure.

> Another well-known rumor imputing unique vileness to the Germans is that of the Crucified Canadian. The usual version relates that the Germans captured a Canadian soldier and in full view of his mates exhibited him in the open spread-eagled on a cross, his hands and feet pierced by bayonets. He is said to have died slowly. Maple Copse, near Sanctuary Wood in the Ypres sector, was a favorite setting. The victim was not always a Canadian. Ian Hay, who places the incident as early as spring, 1915, maintains that the victim was British, that he was wounded when captured, and that he was crucified on a tree by German cavalrymen, who then "stood round him till he died."
>
> The Crucified Canadian is an especially interesting fiction both because of its original context in the insistent visual realities of the front and because of its special symbolic suggestiveness. The image of crucifixion was always accessible at the front because of the numerous real physical calvaries visible at French and Belgian crossroads, many of them named Crucifix Corner. One of the most familiar terrain features on the Somme was called Crucifix Valley after a large metal calvary that once stood there. Perhaps the best-known calvary was the large wooden one standing in the town cemetery at Ypres. It was famous—and to some, miraculous—because a dud shell had lodged between the wood of the cross and the figure of Christ (it stayed there until 1969, when the excessively weathered crucifix was replaced).[75]

"Roadside calvaries were not likely to go unnoticed by British passersby, not least because there was nothing like them on the Protestant rural roads at home."[76]

> But another reason the image of crucifixion came naturally to soldiers was that behind the lines almost daily they could see some Other Ranks undergoing "Field Punishment No. 1" for

minor infractions. This consisted of being strapped or tied spread-eagled to some immobile object: a favorite was the huge spoke wheel of a General Service Wagon. Max Plowman once inquires, "Wouldn't the army do well to avoid punishments which remind men of the Crucifixion?"

Reminded of the Crucifixion all the time by the ubiquitous foreign calvaries and by the spectacle of uniformed miscreants immobilized and shamed with their arms extended, the troops readily embraced the image as quintessentially symbolic of their own suffering and "sacrifice." Forty years after the war Graves recalls the one-time popularity of George Moore's *The Brook Kerith* (1916), and observes:

Crossroads calvary

It is in wartime that books about Jesus have most appeal, and *The Brook Kerith* first appeared 40 years ago during the Battle of the Somme, when Christ was being invoked alike by the Germans and the Allies for victory. . . . This paradox made most of the English soldiers serving in the purgatorial trenches lose all respect for organized Pauline religion, though still feeling a sympathetic reverence for Jesus as our fellow-sufferer. Cross-road Calvaries emphasized this relationship.

The sacrificial theme, in which each soldier becomes a type of the crucified Christ, is at the heart of countless Great War poems like Robert Nichols' "Battery Moving Up to a New Position from Rest Camp: Dawn," in which the men passing a church congregation at Mass silently solicit their intercessory prayers:

> Entreat you for such hearts as break
> With the premonitory ache
> Of bodies whose feet, hands, and side
> Must soon be torn, pierced, crucified.[77]

Perhaps the most striking example is Siegfried Sassoon's "The Redeemer," in which an officer, watching one of his men carrying a load of boards in a muddy trench, not only sees a *resemblance* to Christ carrying the Cross, but says the soldier actually *is* Christ at Golgotha:

> He faced me, reeling in his weariness,
> Shouldering his load of planks, so hard to bear.
> I say that He was Christ. . . .
> Then the flame sank, and all grew black as pitch,
> While we began to struggle along the ditch,
> And someone flung his burden in the muck,
> Mumbling, "O Christ Almighty, now I'm stuck!"

Wilfred Owen draws the same equation between his soldiers and the Christ who approaches His Crucifixion. In a letter to Osbert Sitwell written in early July, 1918, he speaks of training new troops in England:

> For 14 hours yesterday I was at work—teaching Christ to lift his cross by numbers, and how to adjust his crown; and not to imagine he thirst until after the last halt. I attended his Supper to see that there were no complaints; and inspected

his feet that they should be worthy of the nails. I see to it that he is dumb, and stands at attention before his accusers. With a piece of silver I buy him every day, and with maps I make him familiar with the topography of Golgotha.

(Better prose, by the way, is hardly to be found in the war, except perhaps from the hand of Blunden.) The idea of sacrifice urged some imaginations—Owen's among them—to homoeroticize the Christ-soldier analogy. Leonard Green, in his short story "In Hospital" (1920), depicts a handsome boy dying of wounds. "His blood poured out in sacrifice," says Green, "made possible the hazardous success of the more fortunate. He was the pattern of all suffering, He was Christ. . . . He was my God, and I worshipped him."[78]

Isaac Rosenberg, in "Dead Man's Dump," writes of "plunging limbers," "Racketed with their rusty freight, Stuck out like many crowns of thorns." "All this considered, the rumor of the Crucified Canadian seems to assume an origin and a locus, as well as a meaning. He is 'the pattern of all suffering.' His suffering could be conceived to represent the sacrifice of all. . . ."[79]

Similarly, the "crucifixion" scene in *Bride of Frankenstein*, in light of this significant Great War mythic symbolism, represents not a mocking of the crucifixion, but a reference to the Monster as a metaphor for "the pattern of all suffering," a Christ-like figure, himself, representing "the sacrifice of all," not in the specific sense of redemption, resurrection, or any "organized Pauline religion," but rather as the metaphor established in the Great War as symbolizing the suffering of all involved in the War. Rather than "mocking the crucifixion," the scene is a metaphor straight from the mythology of the Great War.

There is another scene which suggests the Monster as a Christ-like figure in the context of Great War imagery. When the Monster appears, frightening the shepherdess and causing her to fall into the water, he disrupts the classic pastoral image of sheep, placidly and peacefully grazing, tended by a watchful shepherd. His efforts in rescuing the girl only increase her panic and distress, and the scene's pastoral nature is completely overcome when the hunters shoot the Monster, wounding him in the shoulder. The pastoral image comes into the War in two ways.

First, "the irony of the original . . . the change from felicity to despair, pastoral to anti-pastoral"[80] as embodied by the change from the idyllic summer of 1914 to the hor-

rors of the trenches. This is precisely what happens in this scene—the Monster's appearance frightens the shepherdess and disrupts the pastoral scene. The Monster rescues, and tries to comfort the girl, thereby attempting to restore the pastoral, but the girl's fright continues to disrupt the tranquility. Finally. the hunters' gunshots obliterate it and complete the transformation from pastoral to anti-pastoral.

Next, with the idea of the officer, particularly company-grade officers (Lieutenants and Captains), as a "shepherd" with his soldiers as his "flock." Edmund Blunden ends his memoir, *Undertones of War*, with this sentence: "No destined anguish lifted its snaky head to poison a harmless young shepherd in a soldier's coat."[81] In the Christian liturgy, Christ is both the "Shepherd" who tends his "Flock:" his Apostles, Disciples, and, ultimately, all those who are members of his Church, and is also the "Lamb." Keeping the focus on Great Britain, in the Church of England, Jesus Christ is the "Lamb of God [in the Roman Catholic Tridentine Mass, the 'Agnus Dei'] Who Takes Away the Sins of the World." By his suffering and death, Christ has taken on the sins of all mankind, redeeming them and making salvation possible. The soldiers of the War have been likened to lambs needlessly slaughtered. Unlike Christ, however, the suffering and the death of the soldiers did not bring redemption or salvation to anyone, but only led to even more suffering and death. The Monster can also be seen as a metaphor for those soldiers who had suffered and died in the War. Like the soldiers, the Monster kills, but also like the soldiers he suffers and, as many soldiers did, ultimately dies.

After his "crucifixion," the Monster is taken to the village and chained onto a huge chair in a dungeon. He manages to rip the chains loose from their fasten-

ings and escape, knocking down the guards in the process. In a scene shot later and added on to mask some continuity gaps caused by elimination of some scenes, the Monster is roaming through the woods. He encounters a Gypsy family[82] cooking dinner over an open fire and burns himself when he tries to steal a chicken which had been roasting on a spit. In pain from the burns, he runs off back into the woods, where he hears the strains of "Ave Maria" being played on a violin. He follows the music to the hut of a blind hermit. In another pastoral moment, the hermit welcomes the Monster, believing

him to be simply a man who has been afflicted with muteness.

Crucifixion imagery appears again in this scene. After the hermit has befriended the Monster and the Monster appeared to have achieved a sort of salvation, or at least a sanctuary, a crucifix mounted on the wall of the hut remains briefly visible, suffused in an ethereal glow, after the scene has faded out. According to the commentary by Scott MacQueen on the "Legacy" Blu-Ray of *Bride*,

this glow was done on his own by the film's editor, Ted Kent, and "Whale didn't much care for it but let it stay." This is unlikely, considering the care Whale took with respect to the smallest detail of every aspect of the film. It is hard to believe this bit would have been left in the final release prints had Whale truly objected to it. Indeed, Kent himself had said Whale "had complete control from beginning to end" over the film.[83] Kent would also edit many of Whale's later films. I must here also disagree with Mark Gatiss, who sees this scene, and the glowing crucifix at its end, as "gently mock[ing] the blind man and his religion for discovering the answer to his prayers in the shape of a seven-foot-tall, murdering monster."[84] The Monster has, indeed, committed murder, but the interlude with the hermit shows that, despite his "criminal brain," the Monster is not simply a wanton killer, but will respond in kind to gentle and compassionate treatment. This image, instead, both further enforces the idea of the Monster as a secular metaphor for Christ's sufferings, the "pattern for all suffering," just as the soldiers of the Great War were seen as a similar metaphor. As was the scene with the shepherdess, the Monster's interlude with the hermit represents the pastoral.

The hermit befriends the Monster, gives him bread and wine (and a cigar!), and teaches him a few rudimentary words: "friend," "fire," "wood," "drink," "bread," "good," "bad."[85] Their idyll is interrupted when two hunters (John Carradine and Nat Clifford) who have lost their way in the wood arrive seeking directions—they tell the protesting hermit that his guest is Frankenstein's Monster—says Carradine: "This is the fiend that's been murdering half the countryside! Good heavens man, can't you see?!" Of course, the blind hermit cannot see. Says Clifford: "Frankenstein made him out of dead bodies." In the ensuing chaos the hermit's hut catches fire and burns. The Monster, again badly treated by the humans, disappears back into the wood. The interval with the hermit shows quite emphatically that the Monster was not irredeemably evil, and that given kindness and understanding he would respond positively. Once again, it is two hunters who break in on the idyllic scene, abruptly changing pastoral to anti-pastoral, chasing the Monster away from his place of sanctuary, and destroying the hermit's home in the process. Only then does the Monster revert to his violent ways, which are not inherent but instead are brought on by his rejection and physical abuse by most human beings.

The Monster, fleeing from the villagers who have chased him from the burning hut, enters a cemetery. He overturns the statue of a bishop, which reveals the entrance to an underground crypt. This scene also involves crucifixion imagery, but not as forcefully as Whale had originally wanted. In the version of the screenplay that was to be shot, the Monster encountered a crucifix in the churchyard and attempted to rescue the figure of Christ from the cross. Joseph I. Breen objected to the scene.

> Whale tried to reason with Breen: "Although this scene, including the figure of Christ on the cross, as I explained to Mr. Shurlock, was meant to be one of supreme sympathy on the part of the Monster, as he tries to rescue what he thinks is a man being persecuted as he was himself some time ago in the wood, if you still find this objectionable I could easily change it to the figure of death. . . ."
>
> Breen did indeed find it objectionable, and the shot was scotched. The image of Christ, however, was still carefully placed within the frame, making the implication of the scene clear when the action is not.[86]

The crucifix not only remains in the shot but is highlighted; appearing as lit by a single beam of light piercing through the clouds. The scene as originally written, with the Monster attempting to rescue what he believes to be a man being

persecuted, further fits the image of Christ as "the pattern of all suffering" as reflected in Great War imagery.

Pretorius, seeking raw materials for the female creation, has arrived at the crypt around the same time the Monster has. Pretorius has brought two grave robbers, Karl and Rudy (Neil Fitzgerald), into the crypt to steal the bones of a teenage girl. The henchmen leave, and Karl remarks "If it's much more like this, what'cha say, pal, we give ourselves up and let 'em hang us!" Rudy replies, "That goes for me, too," and Karl adds "This is no life for a murderer!" Pretorius remains behind to eat his picnic dinner and drink a bottle of wine. The Monster, who had sought refuge in the crypt from the pursuit which followed his ousting from the hermit's hut, stumbles upon Pretorius, who is smoking an after-dinner cigar. "Smoke—friend?" queries the Monster, to which Pretorius replies: "Yes, I hope so! Have a cigar—they're my only weakness." The Monster intones: "I love dead. Hate living." Using the Monster as leverage (with a reprise of the "sit down" line from *Frankenstein*, only this time it's the Monster speaking to Frankenstein), and having him kidnap Elizabeth as a hostage to ensure Henry's compliance, Pretorius forces Frankenstein to cooperate in creating the "Bride." The Bride rejects the Monster. Of course, things do not end well, thanks to the infamous "lever." As the scene was originally shot, everyone—Henry Frankenstein, Elizabeth, Pretorius, the Monster, and the Monster's Mate, would die in the explosion.

Only days before the picture opened Whale decided to make one final amendment. To Colin Clive's displeasure [Clive had been happy seeing Henry Frankenstein killed, believing it to be punishment for his impiety][87] the director decided the ending should be changed so that Henry and Elizabeth survive the climactic explosion. Karloff, Hobson, and a disgruntled Clive were recalled to shoot additional footage. The complex and expensive set-up had ruled out a reshoot of the explosion so in the release print Clive can still be seen inside as the watchtower collapses.[88]

In the revised ending, the Monster motions to Henry and Elizabeth—"Yes—go! You live! Go!" He then turns to Pretorius and the Bride and says "You stay! We belong dead." As the Bride hisses like an angry swan, a tear rolls down the Monster's cheek as he pulls down the dreaded "lever," blowing Dr. Frankenstein's laboratory, and everyone and everything in it, "to atoms." Henry embraces Elizabeth and they watch from a distance as the laboratory building collapses. The various cuts made, both at the behest of the PCA and due to Whale's desire to tighten the picture, brought the running time down from 90 minutes to 75.[89]

Bride of Frankenstein shares the Great War themes of the repudiation of the ideas of progress and of the benignity of science and technology with *Franken-*

stein and *The Invisible Man*. Indeed, in this case, the evil Dr. Pretorius forces Frankenstein to comply with his plans by using Frankenstein's own creation against him. As in *Frankenstein*, the Monster remains an example of corrupted innocence, but now the corruption is complete. In *Frankenstein*, the Monster killed deliberately only in situations where his actions could, at least to some extent, be justified. He killed his tormentor, Fritz, and the man who was about to destroy him, Dr. Waldman. He also drowned little Maria, but purely by accident. In *Bride*, he is wantonly committing murder right from the get-go, including of those who had done nothing to him, such as Maria's parents, a young girl, Frieda, and Herr and Frau Neumann. Nevertheless, his act in saving the shepherdess from drowning and his interlude with the hermit show that, if given respect and affection, he is no irredeemable killer. Instead, he faces hostility from virtually all of humanity, rejected by his creator, and rejected even by his artificial "Bride," and this hostility breeds the Monster's rage and, ultimately, his destruction.

1 Curtis, 234.
2 Curtis, 235-6.
3 Skal, *The Monster Show* 184.
4 Curtis, 237.
5 Mank, *It's Alive* 50.
6 Curtis, 238.

7 Poole, loc. 4293.

8 Gatiss, 110-11.

9 Fussell, 8.

10 Hallenbeck, Bruce G., *Comedy-Horror Films; A Chronological History, 1914-2008* (McFarland & Company, Inc. 2009).

11 Riley, Philip J. (ed.), *MagicImage Filmbooks Presents: The Bride of Frankenstein* 34—Production Background by Gregory Wm. Mank (MagicImage Filmbooks 1989) (hereinafter "Mank, Production Background, *BOF*.").

12 Riley, Philip J. (ed.), *MagicImage Filmbooks Presents: The Bride of Frankenstein* 21—Introduction, interview of Valerie Hobson by Gregory Wm. Mank (MagicImage Filmbooks 1989) (hereinafter "Mank, Hobson Interview, *BOF*.")

13 Mank, Production Background, *BOF* 28.

14 Mank, *It's Alive* 53-4.

15 Mank, Production Background, *BOF* 29.

16 Jacobs, 168.

17 Mank, Production Background, *BOF* 29.

18 A concession to the PCA. Historically speaking, in June 1816 at the time of the Lake Geneva interlude, Mary and Percy were not married, and Shelley was still married to his then-pregnant wife, Harriet. Mary and Shelley married in December 1816, shortly after the heavily pregnant Harriet had drowned herself in the Serpentine in Hyde Park in London.

19 Lanchester, 133-4 (emphasis in original).

20 Jacobs, 174.

21 Lanchester, 133, 136-7.

22 Curtis, 248.

23 Mank, Production Background, *BOF* 28.

24 Jacobs, 168.

25 Mank, Production Background, *BOF* 28.

26 Mank, Hobson Interview, *BOF* 23.

27 Curtis, 388.

28 Jacobs, 166.

29 Mank, Production Background, *BOF* 28.

30 Mank, Hobson Interview, *BOF* 23 (emphasis in original).

31 Jacobs, 175.

32 Gifford, 115.

33 Jacobs, 166.

34 Curtis, 240.

35 Curtis, 240.

36 Mank, Hobson Interview, *BOF* 22.

37 Mank, *It's Alive* 63.

38 Mank, Production Background, *BOF* 27.

39 Mank, Hobson Interview, *BOF* 21 (emphasis in original).

40 Mank, Hobson Interview, *BOF* 21.

41 Gifford, 124.

42 Mank, *It's Alive* 57-8 (emphasis in original).

43 Mank, *It's Alive* 58.

44 Mank, Production Background, *BOF* 30.

45 Mank, Production Background, *BOF* 27.

46 Curtis, 241.

47 Mank, Hobson Interview, *BOF* 22.

48 Mank, Hobson Interview, *BOF* 22.

49 Mank, *Lugosi & Karloff* 218.

50 Jacobs, 169.

51 Mank, Production Background, *BOF* 30.
52 Mank, Production Background, *BOF* 30.
53 Jacobs, 172.
54 Jacobs, 170.
55 Jacobs, 173.
56 Lanchester, 134-6 (emphasis in original).
57 Mank, *It's Alive* 59.
58 Curtis, 245.
59 Jacobs, 173.
60 Curtis, 245.
61 Mank, Production Background, *BOF* 34.
62 Rigby, 151.
63 Mank, Production Background, *BOF* 33.
64 Jacobs, 165-6.
65 The destruction, at least of the Monster, would hardly be "definite and irrevocable." He would appear in five more "serious" Universal sequels (and be played by Boris Karloff one more time, in *Son of Frankenstein* (1938)), and one Abbott & Costello comedy. The call of the box office is powerful revivification.
66 Curtis, 245-6.
67 Mank, Production Background, *BOF* 33-4.
68 Jacobs, 166.
69 In *Frankenstein*, Maria's father, then named Ludwig, was played by Michael Mark.
70 Jacobs, 175.
71 A'Dair had played Captain Hardy in *Journey's End* (1930), the officer whose company is being relieved in the trenches at the beginning of the film.
72 Gifford, 104-5.
73 Gatiss, 118.
74 Skal, *The Monster Show* 189.
75 Fussell, 117-18.
76 Fussell, 118.
77 Fussell, 118-19. *The Brook Kerith* is a novel which postulates Jesus was a mere mortal man who did not die on the cross, but was removed from the tomb while still barely alive by Joseph of Arimathea, who hid Jesus until his health recovered, and that the entire Christian religion is a fiction concocted by Saint Paul. In the novel, Jesus then joins a religious brotherhood living in a mountain fastness above the Brook Kerith and works as a shepherd.
78 Fussell, 119-20.
79 Fussell, 120.
80 Fussell, 24.
81 Blunden, 167.
82 The old gypsy woman who wants her "pepper and salt" is played by Elspeth Dudgeon, who, billed as "John," had played 102-year old Sir Roderick Femm in *The Old Dark House*.
83 Curtis, 237.
84 Gatiss, 118.
85 This scene is burlesqued brilliantly in *Young Frankenstein*, with Gene Hackman playing the hermit and Peter Boyle the Monster.
86 Curtis, 247. Instead, the Monster overturns the statue of the bishop, while the crucifix remains in shot for the entire time.
87 Mank, Production Background, *BOF* 27.
88 Jacobs, 175.
89 Jacobs, 174.

Epilogue

Ernest Thesiger's successful career would continue long after *Bride of Franken-stein*, and he would be busy acting on the stage and screen until shortly before his death. He would appear in more than 40 films following his appearance in *Bride of Frankenstein*. Notable films include *Scrooge* (1951), a film version of Charles Dickens' *A Christmas Carol* starring Alastair Sim in the title role, playing the part of the undertaker. He appears in the "Ghost of Christmas Past" segment as attending at Jacob Marley's (Michael Hordern) death, and then again in the "Ghost of Christmas Yet to Come" segment, having purloined Scrooge's watch, fob, seal, pencil case, sleeve buttons, and brooch from the dead man's lodgings and sold them to Old Joe (Miles Malleson). He also appeared in *The Man in the White Suit* (1951) as Sir John Kierlaw, the

Karloff and Thesiger in *The Ghoul*

leader of a group of industrialists who try to suppress a fabric invented by Sidney Stratton (Alec Guinness) which never gets dirty or wears out. He would play the Emperor Tiberius in *The Robe* (1953) and Jamie Lloyd in *Psycho* (1960). His last film role was as Stefano in *The Roman Spring of Mrs. Stone* (1961). He also appeared extensively on the stage in Britain and on Broadway, including as Jaques in the longest-running Broadway production of Shakespeare's *As You Like It*, alongside Katharine Hepburn's Rosalind. Thesiger was an expert at petit point embroidery (his sobriquet was "The Stitchin' Bitch" and he would often stitch away on set when not needed before the cameras).

"After his hands were severely wounded in France during WWI, he spearheaded the creation of the Disabled Soldiers' Embroidery Industry, which provided work at home by which bedridden and shell-shocked veterans could supplement their pensions."[1] He wrote a book

on the subject, *Adventures in Embroidery*, published in 1941. He was awarded the honor of Commander of the Order of the British Empire (CBE) in 1960. He would make his final stage appearance in *The Last Joke*, with John Gielgud and Ralph Richardson, only a week before his death. He died in his sleep from natural causes in Kensington on January 14, 1961, the day before his eighty-second birthday. His body is buried in Brompton Cemetery in London.

J.B. Priestley had a brilliant career as an author, playwright, broadcaster, literary critic, social commentator, and peace activist. He wrote some 43 plays between 1931 and 1974. Some, known as his "Time Plays," used the concept of split time, where the play begins again after a random comment by a character and continues without the random comment having taken place, altering the course of the action. He was fascinated by the concept of alternate and parallel time. Many of his plays were performed on television, and he wrote a number of television scripts as well. He produced one film, *Last Holiday* (1950), starring Alec Guinness, Beatrice Campbell, and Kay Walsh, for which he also wrote the screenplay. He was the author of some 32 works of fiction between 1927 and 1976, and more than 60 works of non-fiction between 1918 and 1977. During

the Second World War he broadcast a series of "Postscripts" for the BBC; short talks which followed the Sunday evening news, intended to raise civilian morale, in 1940 and 1941. He was known as "The Voice of the Common People." The programs were ended when the government thought he had become too critical of its policies. He ran for Parliament as an Independent in the 1945 General Election

J.B. Priestley's radio show *Postcripts*

but lost. Never a member of the Labour Party, his views were generally considered to be leftist. He was a co-founder of the socialist Commonwealth Party in 1942. However, unlike other leftists at the time, he did not support Josef Stalin of the Soviet Union, and wrote an essay criticizing George Bernard Shaw's support for the Soviet dictator. Priestley disliked dictators, regardless of their professed political stripes. He was a United Kingdom delegate to the United Nations Educational, Scientific, and Cultural Organization ("UNESCO") in 1946-7, and a founder of the Campaign for Nuclear Disarmament in 1958. He rejected the offer of both a knighthood and a peerage but accepted the Order of Merit (OM) as a personal gift from the

Queen, without political connotations. He died of pneumonia at age 89 on August 14, 1984, and his body was cremated. His ashes are interred at an unrecorded and undisclosed spot in the cemetery of the parish church in Hubberholme in the Yorkshire Dales.

R.C. Sherriff continued to have a successful career as a screenwriter, both in Hollywood and in Britain, as well as a playwright, novelist, and television writer. After the success of *Journey's End*, Sherriff had bought a house in the country called Rosebriars for £6,500 [about $696,000 in 2019 dollars, adjusted for inflation], where he and his mother would live. Sherriff was devoted to his mother and they lived together until she died. Following the failure of *Badger's Green*, however, his fortunes changed, and he feared a shortfall in his income would not allow him to keep the house. With a solid year of income before the day of reckoning would come, he decided to attend Oxford, obtain a degree in history, and become a schoolmaster. This was something he had wanted to do when younger but could not afford. He was accepted at New College, where he enrolled as a special student and joined the crew team. However, the offer to write the screenplay for *The Invisible Man* came along, and he decided to return to Hollywood, leaving Oxford behind.[2] He would return to Oxford following his work on *The Invisible Man*, but his health would prevent him from winning his rowing blue, and when it became evident he would not qualify for an honours degree, he left Oxford, notifying Universal he was now ready to return to work.[3]

Above: R.C. Sherriff
Below: His Academy Nomination

After his work on the Universal Horrors he would write a number of screenplays for successful films. *Goodbye, Mr. Chips* (1939), filmed in England and starring Robert Donat and Greer Garson, would earn him an Oscar nomination for best adapted screenplay. He would follow this with screenplays for *The Four Feathers* (1939),

Lady Hamilton (1941), *This Above All* (1942), *Odd Man Out* (1945), *Quartet* (1948), *No Highway* (1950), *The Dam Busters* (1955), and *The Night My Number Came Up* (1955). Although his later plays would never meet with the success he had achieved with *Journey's End*, after the Second World War a number of his plays would be well-received, including *Miss Mabel* and *Home at Seven*. Sherriff had spent time working at an archeological site, the ruins of a Roman villa at Angmering. Ten years after the dig, he was inspired to write a play, *The Long Sunset*, in which he imagined what life had been like for the family who had inhabited that villa in Roman Britain.

R.C.SHERRIFF
King John's Treasure

The play did not appeal to the commercial producers in the West End, so he approached the BBC about putting it on as a radio play. The BBC agreed, and the broadcast, on BBC Home Service radio on April 23, 1955, was a great success. "I found out later that, besides myself, about five million other people had also listened to it, enough to have filled a West End theatre every night for 15 years." This led to *The Long Sunset* being staged by the Birmingham Repertory Theatre and then moving to the Mermaid Theatre in London. The Cambridge examiners chose the play for their modern English examinations, leading to bus-loads of students attending the play for a five-week stretch.[4]

The film companies had begun to cool off when I was doing nothing but assignments for the screen, but when I began to have successes in the theatre they came after me again and offered me the best they had. I wrote the screenplay for *The Dam Busters*, which hit the bull's eye and took me on to the top of the world with the film studios; and from then on, in those golden years, I could write anything I wanted to. I rang the changes to keep from getting in a rut. First a stage play; then a novel; after that a screenplay; then something new for television. Always something different; a boys' adventure story called *King John's Treasure*, a play about the East End called *The Telescope*, and a thriller for television called *Cards with Uncle Tom*.[5]

His last published work, an historical novel entitled *The Siege of Swayne Castle*, a tale of medieval combat and intrigue, was published in 1973. R.C. Sherriff died at age 79 on November 13, 1975 in Kingston Hospital, Kingston Upon Thames. His ashes are interred at St. Wilfred's Chapel in Church Norton, West Sussex.

James Whale's career did not fare well at his old studio once the New Universal took control from the Laemmles in 1936. Whale had been Carl Jr.'s favorite director, and he had given Whale pretty much a free hand in presiding over his pictures. This would most emphatically not continue under the new regime. The cost of his lavish production of *Show Boat* (1936) had helped push the Laemmles over the financial brink at Universal. Whale's companion, David Lewis, then an ex-

Paul Robeson and James Whale on the set of *Showboat*

ecutive at MGM, was to produce a film version of James Hilton's novel, *Goodbye Mr. Chips*, to be made in England, with Charles Laughton starring and R.C. Sherriff writing the screenplay. Lewis wanted Whale to direct and it was all but arranged until the New Universal executives shot the deal down, not wishing to lose one of their only two top directors. The New Universal then entered into a contract with Whale to pay him $75,000 [Almost $1.4 million in 2019 dol-

lars, adjusted for inflation] to direct a film version of Eric Maria Remarque's novel *The Road Back*, his sequel to *All Quiet on the Western Front*.[6]

The Road Back (1937) was to be Whale's masterpiece, and by all accounts it would have been. R.C. Sherriff wrote a brilliant adaptation of the novel. But then, studio interference and ugly international politics would intervene. At first, the studio seemed happy with Whale's performance. "A week into filming, on 8 February, Murphy [the New Universal's Production Manager, Martin Murphy] refers to Whale as a 'conscientious worker'. Only a week later, however, on the 15th, he comments on Whale's 'physical and mental condition' as giving concern and the company as working 'very hard.'"[7] As production went on, the film

fell behind schedule and costs mounted, leading to even more dissatisfaction from New Universal's management.

The story had a strong anti-war theme, involving German soldiers returning home after the War, and the difficulties they faced integrating back into a peacetime society which had also been disrupted by the War; its ending referred explicitly to the re-emergence of German militarism under the Nazis. By 1933, Adolf Hitler had consolidated his control over the German government, which became a Nazi dictatorship. Remarque himself had fled Germany upon the rise of the Nazis. The Nazi government in Germany felt *The Road Back* cast Germans and Germany in an unfair light, which did not conform to Nazi ideology. The Nazi government applied pressure on the New Universal, attempting to shut down production of the film. These efforts did not succeed. Whale finished the picture in late April 1937, some 20 days behind schedule and with a budget approaching $1 million. Now, New Universal's management would cave to the Nazis. Cuts were demanded, and new, slapstick comic scenes, utterly alien to the spirit of the film, were to be added. Whale refused to make the cuts or add the new scenes. A new director was brought in to finish the picture and shoot the new, comic scenes, in order to placate the Nazis. Whale was devastated, but there was nothing he could do. What was said to have been a brilliant film was ruined. "Tragically, only the butchered print survives today."[8] While this was true in 1995, when Mark Gatiss' book was published, this is no longer the case. In 2016, through the efforts of The Library of Congress, in cooperation with NBCUniversal and The Film Foundation, a restored version as close as possible to Whale's original vision, running 100 minutes, was produced. The restored "long version" of *The Road Back* premiered at the Museum of Modern Art in Manhattan on June 10, 2016.[9] Ironically, despite the cuts and the addition of the slapstick scenes, the Nazis would ban the film in Germany anyway.

Next, James Whale would direct *The Great Garrick* (1937) for Warner Brothers, a screwball comedy starring James Brian Aherne as a celebrated 18th Century actor. He would direct three other films away from Universal: *Port of Seven*

Seas (1938), a melodrama starring Wallace Beery and Maureen O'Sullivan for MGM, *The Man in the Iron Mask* (1939), a swashbuckler based upon the Alexandre Dumas novel starring Louis Hayward and Joan Bennett, distributed by United Artists, and *They Dare Not Love* (1941), a romantic drama starring George Brent and Martha Scott, for Columbia. His last three films for the New Universal were *Sinners in Paradise* (1938), *Wives Under Suspicion* (1938), and *Green Hell* (1940). *Green Hell*, a jungle adventure starring Douglas Fairbanks, Jr., Joan Bennett, and John Howard, with George Sanders, Alan Hale, and Vincent Price, was hugely expensive (mostly due to the gigantic Incan Temple set, later used to improve the production values of *The Mummy's Hand* (1940)) as well as a box-office and critical flop, and would later appear on many "worst films" lists. Although Whale

had likely already reached the end of his rope at Universal, this film made it abundantly clear that his career at the studio was at an end.

James Whale was essentially retired from the film business after 1941. Despite the end of his film career, Whale had made a great deal of money from his efforts and managed his funds wisely. "'Jimmy was enormously proud of being so rich,' said Alan Napier. "When I visited his beautiful home, it was as if he was saying 'My dear boy, you've come to the right place.'"[10] When the United States entered the Second World War, many in Hollywood volunteered their services to support the war effort, and many famous directors would make training films for the U.S. Army. James Whale volunteered, and over six weeks in 1942 directed *Personnel Placement in the Army: The Army A.G.O. Form 20 Card* (1942). Unfortunately, no copy of the film survives.[11] Whale would turn down a number of offers to direct films, until he agreed to take on the last film he would helm; a short based upon a play by William Saroyan, entitled *Hello Out There* (1949), with Marjorie Steele, Harry Morgan, and Lee Patrick. The film was never released, but was shown in 1989, on the occasion of Whale's 100th birthday, along with some of Whale's other work, at the San Sebastian International Film Festival in Spain.[12] Whale would also direct a few plays on the stage

James Whale appears to be in *Green Hell* in this photo from the set.

James Whale at home c. 1934

through 1952. In retirement, Whale traveled and would spend his time painting in the studio which he had built at his Amalfi Drive home. Whale often hosted parties. He enjoyed the companionship of handsome young men and went through a period of hosting "risqué" pool parties at his home.

In the spring of 1956, James Whale suffered a stroke. He would suffer additional strokes, more debilitating than the first one, in the months to come. He apparently made a good recovery and went back to live in his Amalfi Drive home. On May 29, 1957, James Whale failed to answer his housekeeper's intercom call for lunch. When she went to look for him, she found him, fully dressed, at the bottom of his swimming pool. Speculation was that he had suffered a heart attack and had fallen in (an autopsy proved this not to have been the case), had accidentally fallen in, or even that foul play had been involved (he had an abrasion on his forehead, evidently caused by his head striking the bottom of the pool). His death was ultimately ruled as accidental. Whale had left an envelope, inscribed on the front with "TO ALL I LOVE." The envelope contained a note. Mystery would surround James Whale's death for many years. Due to the stigma attached to suicide at that time, this note was suppressed and would not be made public until more than 25 years after Whale's death.[13] On the front of the note was written:

To ALL I LOVE,

Do not grieve for me. My nerves are all shot and for the last year I have been in agony day and night—except when I sleep with sleeping pills—and any peace I have by day is when I am drugged by pills.

I have led a wonderful life but it is over and my nerves get worse and I am afraid they will have to take me away. So please forgive me, all those I love and may God forgive me too, but I cannot bear the agony and it [is] best for everyone this way.

The future is just old age and illness and pain. Goodbye to all and thank you for your love. I must have peace and this is the only way.

Jimmy

On the reverse side he wrote:

p.s.

Do not let my family come—my last wish is to be cremated so nobody will grieve over my grave. No one is to blame—I have wonderful friends and they do all they can for me, but my heart is in my mouth all the time and I have no peace. I cannot keep still and the future would be worse. My financial affairs are all in order and I hope will help my loved ones to forget a little. It will be a great a shock, but I pray they will be given strength to come through and be happy for my release from this constant fear. I've tried very hard all I know for a year and it gets worse inside, so please take comfort in knowing I will not suffer any more.

J.[14]

In a last wry, ironic gesture, James Whale had left a book on his bedside table. Its title: *Don't Go Near the Water*.[15] James Whale's body was cremated, according to his wish. However, his ashes were not scattered, but "were placed in a niche in the Columbarium of Memory at Forest Lawn Memorial Park in Glendale."[16] "Tragically, Whale took his own life just months before the television release of *Frankenstein* and *The Invisible Man* put his work in front of millions of new viewers."[17] He would never know the critical reappraisal and acclaim which his work would receive.

> James Whale's quest to reinvent himself succeeded far better than he could ever have dreamed: The "Would-Be Gentleman" became a true gentleman: respected, loved by those who truly knew him and, after all these years, rightly acknowledged as a superb filmmaker.
>
> Just before Whale died, he wrote a letter to his old friend John Rowe, expressing his joy at his brother's discovery of family documents relating to 17th-century members of the Whale clan. They had been, it appeared, considerable landowners and "gentlemen". "I cannot help a feeling of comfort in my old age", wrote James Whale, "that I was born right."[18]

*   *   *

Universal's Golden Age of Horror began a dozen years after the Armistice, and ended eight years later, some 20 years after the cessation of hostilities.

James Whale, who directed four of the most notable films from this Age, saw combat in the British infantry on the Western Front as a Second Lieutenant and spent some 16 months in a German prisoner-of-war camp. The War left a profound impression on everyone who saw combat. James Whale found his inspiration for a theatrical career while a prisoner of war, and the effect of his War experiences can be seen in his Golden Age films; *Frankenstein*, *The Old Dark House*, *The Invisible Man* and *Bride of Frankenstein*.

In collaboration with R.C. Sherriff, who had also seen combat as a Second Lieutenant in the British Army on the Western Front, Whale would achieve his first notable success as a director. Directing *Journey's End* on stage, both in London and on Broadway, led to his entry into the film industry in Hollywood and his job di-

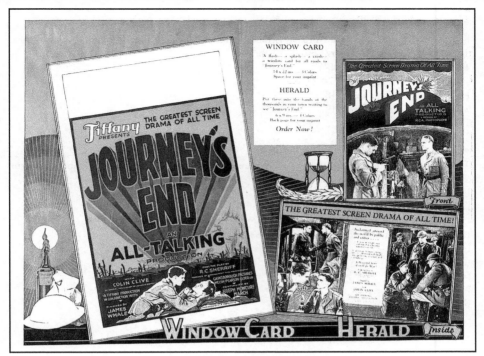

***Journey's End* pressbook back cover**

recting the film version of *Journey's End*. The success of *Journey's End* led to him signing a director's contract with Universal. This, in turn, led to *Waterloo Bridge*; its success led to Whale being offered the pick of his next project and to his selection of *Frankenstein* as that project. I believe his War experiences were, at least in part, behind his decision to choose *Frankenstein* as his next subject at Universal, and carried over to influence the film, as well as his three subsequent Universal Horrors. Sherriff would also write additional dialogue for *The Old Dark House*, the screenplay for *The Invisible Man*, and would work on the adaptation of *Bride of Frankenstein*.

J.B. Priestley, who wrote *Benighted*, the novel upon which *The Old Dark House* was based, also served in combat in the British Army on the Western Front, first as an Other Rank and later as a Second Lieutenant. Great War themes are pervasive in the novel, and are reflected in the film, as well.

Ernest Thesiger, who appeared in both *The Old Dark House* and *Bride of Frankenstein*, served as a Private soldier and was wounded in Belgium on New Year's Day, 1915. Claude Rains, the star of *The Invisible Man*, also served in the British Army on the Western Front and was gassed at Vimy Ridge.

From the outdoor sets originally built for Universal's *All Quiet on the Western Front* which were used for the European villages in virtually every Universal horror film from the Golden Age through the 1940s, to the War's use as a plot element in *The Black Cat*, to its influence on James Whale's Universal Horrors with the assistance of R.C. Sherriff and J.B. Priestley, the Great War had a significant impact upon Universal's Golden Age Horrors.

R. Bruce Crelin

1 Dedicated to the Life and Work of Ernest Frederick Graham Thesiger, http: //www.ernest-thesiger.org/Ernest_Thesiger/Embroidery.html.
2 Sherriff, *No Leading Lady* 208-47.
3 Sherriff, *No Leading Lady* 277-82.
4 Sherriff, No *Leading Lady* 348.
5 Sherriff, No *Leading Lady* 349.
6 Gatiss, 128-9.
7 Gatiss, 131.
8 Gatiss, 132-3.
9 Museum of Modern Art, https: //www.moma.org/calendar/events/2082#happening-occur-rences.\.
10 Curtis, 347.
11 Curtis, 348.
12 Curtis, 368.
13 Mank, Production Background, *Frankenstein* 26.
14 Curtis, 380-5.
15 Gatiss, 168.
16 Curtis, 387.
17 Curtis, 388.
18 Gatiss, 171.

Bibliography

Berg, Louis (May 12, 1946). "Farewell to Monsters" (PDF). The Los Angeles Times p. F12. Archived from the original (PDF) on September 20, 2009. Retrieved April 6, 2019.

Blunden, Edmund, *Undertones of War* (Folio Society 1989).

Bram, Christopher, *Father of Frankenstein* (E.P. Dutton 1995).

Charles Laughton Section of the Hunts Cyclist Website, www.huntscycles.co.uk/C%20L%201%20Home%20Page.html.

Clark, Christopher, *The Sleepwalkers: How Europe Went to War in 1914* (HarperCollins 2013).

Curtis, James, *James Whale: A New World of Gods and Monsters* (University of Minnesota Press 1998).

Curtis, James and Pepper, James (eds.), *Arriving in Hollywood: Letters 1929* (Santa Teresa Press 1989).

Dedicated to the Life and Work of Ernest Frederick Graham Thesiger, https://www.ernestthesiger.org/Ernest_Thesiger/Embroidery.html.

Dedicated to the Life and Work of Ernest Frederick Graham Thesiger, http://www.ernestthesiger.org/Ernest_Thesiger/Home.html.

Dedicated to the Life and Work of Ernest Frederick Graham Thesiger, http://www.ernestthesiger.org/Ernest_Thesiger/Military_Service.html.

Fold3.com, Rains, William C., British Army World War I Medal Rolls Index Cards, 1914-1920 https://www.fold3.com/image/250/325441532.

Fold3.com, Thesiger, Ernest, Pension File https://www.fold3.com/browse/250/huJpt80fQ41jvpIn1H9wPiTj8Qsbd-ZvpNUNp5i.

Foley, Robert T. and McCartney, Helen (eds.), *The Somme: An Eyewitness History* (Folio Society 2006).

Fussell, Paul, *The Great War and Modern Memory* (Oxford University Press 1975).

Gatiss, Mark, *James Whale: A Biography or The Would-be Gentleman* (Cassell 1995).

Gibbs, Philip, *Now It Can Be Told* (New York 1920).

Gifford, Denis, *A Pictorial History of Horror Movies* (Hamlyn 1973).

Gilbert, Martin, *The First World War: A Complete History* (Henry Holt 1994).

Graves, Robert, *Goodbye to All That* (Folio Society 1981).

Hallenbeck, Bruce G., *Comedy-Horror Films; A Chronological History, 1914-2008* (McFarland & Company, Inc. 2009).

Hanson, Neil and Priestley, T. (eds.), *Priestley's Wars* (Great Northern Books 2008).

Harington, General Sir Charles, *Plumer of Messines* (John Murray 1935).

Hemingway, Ernest, *The Sun Also Rises* (The Easton Press 1990).

International Committee of the Red Cross, Whale, James, Red Cross P.O.W. card, https://grandeguerre.icrc.org/en/File/Details/2917172/3/2/.

Jacobs, Stephen, *Boris Karloff: More Than a Monster* (Tomahawk Press 2011).

Lanchester, Elsa, *Elsa Lanchester, Herself* (St. Martin's Press 1983).

Lucas, Michael, *The Journey's End Battalion: The 9th East Surrey in the Great War* (Pen & Sword Books 2012).

MacMillan, Margaret, *The War That Ended Peace: The Road to 1914* (Random House 2013).

Mank, Gregory William, *Bela Lugosi and Boris Karloff: The Expanded Story of a Haunting Collaboration* (McFarland & Company, Inc. 2009).

Mank, Gregory William, *It's Alive: The Classic Cinema Saga of Frankenstein* (A.S. Barnes & Company, Inc. 1981).

Mank, Gregory William, *"One Man Crazy!" The Life and Death of Colin Clive, Hollywood's Dr. Frankenstein* (Midnight Marquee Press, Inc. 2018).

Mank, Gregory William, Coughlin, James T., and Frye, Dwight D., *Dwight Frye's Last Laugh: An Authorized Biography* (Luminary Press 1997).

Museum of Modern Art, https://www.moma.org/calendar/events/2082#happening-occurrences.\.

National Archives, United Kingdom, Priestley, John Boynton, Service Record WO339/105913 (33 pages).

National Archives, United Kingdom, Sherriff, Robert Cedric, Service Record WO399/69081 (37 pages).

National Archives, United Kingdom, War Diary of the 2/7th Battalion, Worcestershire Regiment, September 1915-January 1918 WO-95-3060-3 (116 pages).

National Archives, United Kingdom, Whale, James, Service Record WO374/73337 (18 pages).

Nye, Eric W., *Pounds Sterling to Dollars: Historical Conversion of Currency*, https://www.uwyo.edu/numimage/currency.htm.

Osborn, Jennifer (ed.); Milano, Roy (photo captions), *Monsters: A Celebration of the Classics from Universal Studios* (Del Ray Books, imprint of Random House, Inc. 2006).

Owen, Wilfred, *Poems* (Chatto & Windus, 1920).

Poole, W. Scott, *Wasteland: The Great War and the Origins of Modern Horror* (Counterpoint 2018).

Powell, Geoffrey, *Plumer: The Soldiers' General* (Pen & Sword Books Ltd. 1990).

Priestley, J.B., *Benighted* (Valancourt Books 2013).

Priestley, J.B., *Margin Released: A Writer's Reminiscences and Reflections* (W. Heinemann 1962).

Rigby, Jonathan, *American Gothic* (Signum Books 2017).

Riley, Philip J. (ed.), *MagicImage Filmbooks Presents Frankenstein* (MagicImage Filmbooks 1989).

Riley, Philip J. (ed.), *MagicImage Filmbooks Presents The Bride of Frankenstein* (MagicImage Filmbooks 1989).

Riley, Philip J. (ed.), *The Invisible Man* (Bear Manor Media 2013).

Roads to the Great War, https://roadstothegreatwar-ww1.blogspot.com/2014/12/fortnum-mason-provision-front.html.

Sassoon, Siegfried, *Sherston's Progress* (Folio Society 1993).

Shelley, Mary W., *Frankenstein* (Barnes & Noble Books 1993).

Sherriff, R.C., *Journey's End* (Penguin Classics Ed. 2000).

Sherriff, R.C., *No Leading Lady* (Victor Gollancz Ltd 1968).

Skal, David J., *Hollywood Gothic* (W.W. Norton & Company 1990).

Skal, David J., *Something in the Blood: The Untold Story of Bram Stoker, the Man Who Made Dracula* (Liveright Publishing Corp. 2016).

Skal, David J., *The Monster Show: A Cultural History of Horror* (W.W. Norton & Company 1993).

Skal, David J., with Rains, Jessica, *Claude Rains: An Actor's Voice* (University of Kentucky Press 2008).

Surrey County Council, Surrey Heritage,
    www.surreyarchives.org.uk/CalmView/Record.aspx?src=CalmView.Catalog&id=2332&pos=2.
Taylor, A.J.P., *The First World War* (Perigee Books 1980).
Thesiger, Ernest, *Practically True* (W. Heinemann 1927).
Tuchman, Barbara, *The Guns of August* (The Easton Press 1987).
U.S. Inflation Calculator, https://www.usinflationcalculator.com.
Weintraub, Stanley, *Silent Night: The Story of the World War I Christmas Truce* (The Free Press 2001).
Whale, J., "Our Life at Holzminden" *The Wide World Magazine* 43: 334 (August 1919).

Author Bio

Photo credit: Kathy Cacicedo; kc.photographer.director@gmail.com

R. Bruce Crelin was born in Paterson, New Jersey, birthplace of Lou Costello, on August 26, 1959, 23 days before Veronica Carlson's 15th birthday. After his family made several moves, he ended up, at age four, in a town in northeastern New Jersey called Wayne, where he grew up and lived until he went to college.

As a young child he was too afraid to watch horror movies, although he did dress up as devils and ghosts for Halloween. His cousin Bobby, however, was a true monster kid, who initiated him into the world of Universal horror. The first horror movie he remembers having seen was the Castle Films digest of *The Creature Walks Among Us*, projected and narrated by his Uncle Ed, Bobby's father. He saw *Beneath the Planet of the Apes* at age 10 at a drive-in theater in northern New Jersey, with his parents and his little sister, Kim.

He teamed up with his then best friend, Tim, reading Denis Gifford's *A Pictorial History of Horror Movies*. In those pre-home video days (not even Beta or VHS existed yet!), he and Tim scanned the T.V. listings each week, watching *Kaiju* films on "The 4:30 Movie" and staying up late on Friday and Saturday nights to watch Universals and Hammers. Inspired by Gifford, he and Tim checked out Blackhawk Films Super 8 prints of *Nosferatu*, *The Phantom of the Opera*, *The Hunchback of Notre Dame*, and other silent classics from the town library. As a seventh grade English project, along with Tim and several other buddies, he helped make an 8mm version of Joseph Payne Brennan's short story, "Slime" – Bruce played Henry Hossing, a hobo who gets eaten by the Slime. He and Tim then each obtained Super 8 cameras and embarked on a career making science fiction, horror and comedy films. He remembers seeing *Tales From the Crypt* in the cinema at around age 13.

Still a monster fan, if no longer a Monster Kid, he lives in northwestern New Jersey with his wife, Allison, their Boston Terrier, Brie, their Border Terrier, Chubby, their cat, Lewis, and his extensive collection of Blu-Rays, DVDs, and books, while pretending to be a responsible member of society. His lifelong ambition is to play Elisha Cook, Jr.'s role as Sam, the morgue attendant, if anyone ever decides to do a remake of *Blacula*.

Visit www.midmar.com
for all the Midnight Marquee Press titles